T0341039

Combating Inequality

Economic inequality has recently gained considerable academic attention. However, two important aspects of inequality have not been discussed systematically: its multidimensional nature and the question of what can be done to reverse it. This book offers insights from scholars representing the Global Labour University, which operates in Brazil, Germany, India, South Africa and the USA. They analyse the various drivers of inequality, assess policy responses and discuss counter-strategies.

The main findings of this book are that rising levels of inequality cannot be addressed only with the standard policy responses, namely education, financialised forms of social policy and 'green growth'. In addition, the way markets currently function needs to be corrected.

The chapters in this volume focus on specific fields of contemporary capitalism where important drivers of inequality are located, for example the labour market, the financial system, the tax system, multi-national corporations and gender relations. Other chapters discuss in detail where political opportunities for change lie. They critically assess existing countermeasures, the idea of a 'green economy' and its implications for inequality, and existing campaigns by trade unions and new social movements against inequality. In line with the global nature of the problem, this book contains case studies on countries both from the Global North and South with considerable economic and political weight.

This book provides academics, political practitioners and civil society activists with a range of ideas on how to drive back inequality. It will be of interest to those who study political economy, development economy, labour economics and the politics of labour.

Alexander Gallas is an Assistant Professor in the Department of Politics at the University of Kassel, Germany.

Hansjörg Herr is Professor for Supranational Integration at the Berlin School of Economics and Law, Germany.

Frank Hoffer is a Senior Researcher at the Bureau for Workers' Activities at the ILO and the international coordinator of the Global Labour University, Switzerland.

Christoph Scherrer is Professor for Political Science and Director of the International Centre for Development and Decent Work, University of Kassel, Germany.

Combating Inequality

The Global North and South

**Edited by Alexander Gallas,
Hansjörg Herr, Frank Hoffer
and Christoph Scherrer**

LONDON AND NEW YORK

Mitbestimmung · Forschung · Stipendien

First published 2016
by Routledge
2 Park Square, Milton Park, Abingdon, Oxon OX14 4RN

and by Routledge
711 Third Avenue, New York, NY 10017

Routledge is an imprint of the Taylor & Francis Group, an informa business

British Library Cataloguing in Publication Data
A catalogue record for this book is available from the British Library

Library of Congress Cataloging-in-Publication Data
Combating inequality : the Global North and South / edited by Alexander Gallas, Hansjörg Herr, Frank Hoffer and Christoph Scherrer.
  1. Income distribution—Developing countries.   2. Equality—Developing countries.
3. Poverty—Developing countries.   4. Economic development—Developing countries.
5. Developing countries—Economic policy.   I. Gallas, Alexander, editor.
  HC59.72.I5C66 2016
  339.2—dc23
                                                                    2015024819

ISBN: 978-1-138-91685-2 (hbk)
ISBN: 978-1-315-68934-0 (ebk)

Typeset in Times New Roman
by Graphicraft Limited, Hong Kong

Contents

Figures

Tables

Contributors

Mark Anner is an Associate Professor of Labour and Employment Relations, and Political Science at Penn State University. He directs the Center for Global Workers' Rights and Penn State's MPS Program in Labour and Global Workers' Rights, which is a part of the Global Labour University network.

Akua O. Britwum is a Senior Research Fellow and Head of the Centre for Gender Research, Advocacy and Documentation, University of Cape Coast, Ghana. She is also a Senior Research Associate, Faculty of Humanities, University of Johannesburg. Her research covers the economics of violence against women, gender and leadership in trade unions, and informal economy workers organising.

Daniel Detzer obtained a bachelor's degree in Economics and a master's degree in International Economics. He works as a FESSUD Research Fellow at the Department of Business and Economics of the Berlin School of Economics and Law. His current and past research fields include banking and financial systems, financial crises, financial regulation, macroeconomics and European imbalances.

Trevor Evans is Professor of Monetary Theory, Monetary Policy and International Monetary Relations at the Berlin School of Economics and Law. He previously worked at the Coordinadora Regional de Investigaciones Económicas y Sociales in Managua, Nicaragua. He has published widely on monetary and financial developments in the United States, Europe and Central America.

Alexander Gallas, lead editor of the present volume, is an Assistant Professor in the Department of Politics at the University of Kassel, Germany. His research interests include strikes and industrial action, labour relations in Europe, class theory and state theory. He is Editor of the *Global Labour Journal* and has written a monograph entitled *The Thatcherite Offensive: A Neo-Poulantzasian Analysis*.

Jayati Ghosh is Professor of Economics at Jawaharlal Nehru University, New Delhi. She has authored or edited ten books and more than 160 scholarly articles, and writes several columns in newspapers and online blogs. She is Executive Secretary of the International Development Economics Associates (www.networkideas.org), a global network of heterodox economists.

Sarah Godar studied Economics and Sociology at the University of Potsdam, Germany. She graduated with a master's in International Economics from the Berlin School of Economics and Law. Her research interests include macroeconomics, fiscal policy and income distribution.

Tandiwe Gross works as a Programme Coordinator for the Global Labour University. Prior to that she worked as a consultant for the Bureau for Workers' Activities at the ILO as well as for various trade union and NGO networks. Her research interests include labour rights in global supply chains, corporate accountability and organising in the informal economy.

Eckhard Hein is Professor of Economics at the Berlin School of Economics and Law, member of the Coordination Committee of the Research Network 'Macroeconomics and Macroeconomic Policies' (FMM) and managing co-editor of the *European Journal of Economics and Economic Policies: Intervention*. His research focuses on money, financial systems, distribution and growth, and post-Keynesian macroeconomics.

Christoph Hermann is a Lecturer in the Department of Sociology and a Visiting Researcher at the Institute for Research on Employment and Labour, UC Berkeley. His publications include *Capitalism and the Political Economy of Work Time*, which was published in 2014.

Hansjörg Herr is Professor for Supranational Integration at the Berlin School of Economics and Law. His research interests include post-Keynesian macroeconomics, European integration and development economics. He has published in all these fields (for example the monograph *Decent Capitalism: A Blueprint for Reforming our Economies*, with Sebastian Dullien und Christian Kellermann).

Frank Hoffer is a Senior Researcher at the Bureau for Workers' Activities at the ILO and the international coordinator of the Global Labour University. He worked formerly with the German Trade Union Federation, the German Foreign Service and the Centre for Social Policy at the University of Bremen, Germany. He holds a PhD in Economics from the University of Bremen.

Jakir Hossain is an Associate Professor at the Institute of Bangladesh Studies, University of Rajshahi, and Chairman at the Development Synergy Institute, Dhaka, Bangladesh. He has written articles and policy papers on labour rights, decent work, social dialogue, the multilateral trading regime, poverty and injustice, skill formation and learning, and education and development.

Pierre Laliberté is a Senior Advisor at the Bureau for Workers' Activities at the ILO and the Editor of the *International Journal for Labour Research*. Formerly with the Canadian Labour Congress, the Quebec Federation of Labour and the United Steelworkers of America, he holds a PhD in Economics from the University of Massachusetts at Amherst.

Lena Lavinas is Professor of Welfare Economics at the Institute of Economics at the Federal University of Rio de Janeiro, Senior Researcher at the Brazilian

National Research Council (CNPQ), and Research Fellow at desiguALdes.net (Freie Universität Berlin). Most of her research focuses on social policies, poverty issues and inequality.

Birgit Mahnkopf is Professor for European Social Politics at the Berlin School of Economics and Law. Her research focuses on the economic, political and social consequences of globalisation, on the political economy of European integration and on various aspects of socio-ecological transformation. She has published 12 books and more than 130 articles in books and journals.

Marcelo Manzano is an Assistant Professor of Brazilian economy at Facamp, Campinas, Brazil. He obtained an MA in Social and Labour Economics from the State University of Campinas (Unicamp) and works on the following topics: labour relations in Brazil, vocational education and training systems, the development of the Brazilian economy and public policy analysis.

Christopher Morris is an undergraduate and majors in Politics and Philosophy. He is a volunteer member of Ntinga Ntaba ka Ndoda, an organisation run by the people of Keiskammahoek South – a network of rural villages in the Eastern Cape Province of South Africa. He has a keen interest in the building of social movements and organisations of working and rural people.

Christoph Paetz obtained a master's degree in International Economics from the Berlin School of Economics and Law. He is currently working on his PhD thesis about rule-based fiscal policy as a participant in the doctoral programme of the Macroeconomic Policy Institute (IMK) at the Hans Böckler Foundation, Düsseldorf, Germany. His research interests include fiscal policy, European economic policy and macroeconomics.

Thomas I. Palley is an economist living in Washington, DC. He is Senior Economic Policy Adviser to the AFL-CIO. His two most recent books are *Financialization: The Economics of Finance Capital Domination* and *From Financial Crisis to Stagnation: The Destruction of Shared Prosperity and the Role of Economics*. He holds a master's in International Relations and a PhD in Economics, both from Yale University.

Bea Ruoff is a Research Fellow and has a master's in International Economics from Berlin School of Economics and Law. She is engaged in labour market and trade union research and teaches Economics at the Berlin School of Economics and Law.

Carlos Salas holds a PhD in Economics. He is Assistant Professor at the Institute of Economics at the State University of Campinas, Brazil. His research interests include Latin American labour markets, informality, wages, precarious jobs and gender segregation.

Anselmo Santos is Professor at the Institute of Economics at the State University of Campinas, Brazil (Unicamp). He holds a PhD in Economics from

Unicamp and is also Researcher and Director of the Labour Economics and Trade Unionism Study Center (CESIT) at Unicamp.

Christoph Scherrer is Professor for Political Science and Director of the International Centre for Development and Decent Work, University of Kassel, Germany. He has recently published the edited volume (together with Bob Jessop and Brigitte Young) *Financial Cultures and Crisis Dynamics*.

Timm B. Schützhofer holds a degree in Political Science and a master's in Global Political Economy. His research interests include decent work in development contexts as well as fiscal policies in natural resources-dependent countries. He is working on a PhD thesis at the Department of Politics, University of Kassel, Germany, and holds a scholarship from the Rosa Luxemburg Foundation, Berlin.

Heike Solga is Director of the research unit Skill Formation and Labor Markets at the WZB Berlin Social Science Center and full Professor of Sociology at the Freie Universität Berlin, Germany. Her research interests include education, labour markets and life course research.

Achim Truger is a Professor of Economics, particularly Macroeconomics and Economic Policy, at the Berlin School of Economics and Law as well as a Senior Research Fellow at the Macroeconomic Policy Institute (IMK) at the Hans Böckler Foundation, Düsseldorf, Germany. His research interests include applied macroeconomics, fiscal policy, public finance and tax policy.

Edward Webster is Professor Emeritus in the Society, Work and Development Institute (SWOP) at the University of Witwatersrand, Johannesburg and director of the Chris Hani Institute, Johannesburg. His research interests lie in the world of work and the changing nature of labour. He is currently completing a manuscript for a book entitled *Labour after Globalization: Old and New Sources of Workers' Power.*

Michelle Williams is Associate Professor in Sociology at the University of the Witwatersrand, Johannesburg, and Chairperson of the Global Labour University Programme, also at Witwatersrand. Her publications include *The Roots of Participatory Democracy: Democratic Communists in South Africa and Kerala, India* and the edited volume *Marxisms in the Twenty-first Century* (with Vishwas Satgar).

1 Introduction

Alexander Gallas[1]

The inequality impasse

Economic inequality has gone mainstream. The list of critics of the increasing disparities in wealth and income in many countries around the globe is long; it reads like a *Who's Who* in politics, business and civil society. Among those who have voiced concerns are Nobel Prize-winning economists like Paul Krugman, Robert Shiller and Joseph Stiglitz; business magnates such as Warren Buffett and Bill Gates; religious leaders, for example the Archbishop of Canterbury, Desmond Tutu and Pope Francis; and a significant number of political heavy-weights, among them Hillary Clinton, Barack Obama, Vladimir Putin, Dilma Rousseff, Xi Jinping and Jacob Zuma. Furthermore, international institutions like the Organisation for Economic Co-operation and Development (OECD) (2015) and the International Monetary Fund (IMF) (Ostry et al., 2014) as well as the rating agency Standard & Poor's (2014) have recently published studies critical of rising economic inequality, while Thomas Piketty's book *Capital in the Twenty-First Century* (2014) has been a huge success among book-buyers and has received broad coverage in the news media (cf. Kaufmann and Stützle, 2015: 17ff.).

Some of the illustrious names listed may only be paying lip-service to an agenda aimed at curbing inequality for reasons of self-promotion or political tactics, and not because they are making a serious commitment to tackling the issue. And quite a few of them have been proponents of free-market agendas, which have contributed significantly to driving up inequality.[2] But the fact that they feel the need to comment at all is indicative of the attention the issue has been receiving lately. The recent debates differ markedly from those during the heyday of neoliberalism, when inequality was often presented as a lamentable but unavoidable side effect of economic growth that people simply had to get used to.[3] It appears that there is a considerable number of forces in politics, civil society and academia agreeing that part of the broader economic crisis charac-terising our day and age is an 'inequality crisis' (Gallas, 2014). According to its critics, economic inequality is detrimental to economic growth,[4] undermines social cohesion[5] and threatens democracy (Gallas et al., 2014).

However, this shift in perceptions has so far failed, on the whole, to translate into groundbreaking material change. Quite the contrary: in most parts of the world, the levels of economic inequality are consolidating at a very high level – or are continuing to rise. At the same time, there are very few examples of successful government interventions tackling the issue. In fact, it appears difficult in some countries to mobilise people behind an agenda for change.[6] In the UK, Ed Miliband, a critic of inequality, lost the general election of May 2015 against David Cameron, who had embarked on the deepest public spending cuts in the country since the inter-war period during his first term and had vowed before the election to cut a further £12 billion from the welfare bill. In March 2015, the Rousseff government in Brazil was faced with a huge demonstration, ostensibly against corruption but in fact directed against her presidency and the hold of the Workers' Party (PT) on government (Saad-Filho, 2015). Notably, the Lula and Rousseff administrations are among the few examples of governments with a strong track-record in reducing inequality.

All in all, it appears that we find ourselves in a situation of political impasse (cf. Gallas, 2014) between the social-political forces of continuity and the forces of change. Political critiques of inequality, on the whole, remain ineffective – despite the fact that there are many people who are discontent with the existing economic divides and the fact that those hit hardest by the current global economic crisis are those who benefited the least from the long, credit-induced boom that had preceded it. It appears that the political forces of the status quo – sustained by transnational financial capital, the managerial strata of multinational corporations and members of the global 'elite' – are deeply entrenched in the structures and institutions of neoliberal capitalism. There is need for a debate on how to advance an egalitarian agenda in this situation.

The need for counter-strategies

The inequality impasse has not been covered much in the social science literature on the topic. Whereas there are numerous analyses of the causes of rising inequality, there is little systematic research on how this rise can be contained or even on how inequality can be reduced. Likewise, there are few systematic reflections on the role of trade unions in the process – despite the fact that the labour movement is uniquely positioned to play an important role. After all, it has been acting as a force for equality for a long time and has a strong track record in the field. Correspondingly, various authors (Gago, 2013; Kimball and Mishel, 2015; Watt and O'Farrell, 2009) stress that the presence of organised labour in a country, measured in union density, is inversely correlated with the degree of inequality.

In light of these gaps in inequality research, this volume attempts to sustain the critique of inequality at the discursive level and to provide intellectual support to those inside the labour movement who are working to translate the critique into political action. It aims to:

- identify drivers of inequality;
- assess existing proposals on how to deal with the issue;

- develop alternative proposals that take into account the limits of existing proposals;
- discuss the political context of the debate;
- highlight opportunities, constraints and dilemmas for political forces fighting inequality;
- identify strategic paths for change.

On the whole, the objective of the book is to make a systematic contribution to debates on countermeasures and counter-strategies.

Defining and measuring inequality

There are different ways to define and measure economic inequality. In general, the term refers to the unequal distribution of economic resources (assets or income) within a specific social setting. Economic inequality can be distinguished from inequalities referring to other 'regions' of the social world, for example inequality before the law, which highlights differences in treatment by the judiciary, or political inequality, which refers to differences in influence over political decision-making. Inequalities emerging out of different 'regions' normally reinforce each other, and economic inequality tends to translate into legal and political inequality (cf. Gallas et al., 2014; Uslaner, 2008).

Economic inequality can be seen as representing a cleavage within populations, that is the cleavage between rich and poor. However, it can also be used to describe other such cleavages, namely those between ethnic groups, races, genders, town/country and so on. If this multiplicity of cleavages is considered, it also becomes possible to identify cross-cutting cleavages, that is cleavages explaining divides within certain social groups. Examples are the existence of an economic divide along gender lines among poor people, as well as economic inequality among women. For reasons of complexity reduction and consistency, this volume focuses on analysing the distribution of economic resources as such. Considering the multiplicity of existing cleavages, however, it may be worth expanding the scope of future research projects.

There are two main ways of measuring inequality: the Gini coefficient and inequality ratios. The Gini coefficient is a variable between zero and one, where zero denotes perfect equality (everyone has the same) and one denotes maximum inequality (one person owns everything). The lower the Gini coefficient, the more equal a society.[7] Denmark, for example, has the lowest Gini coefficient in the OECD with 0.249; Chile the highest one with 0.503.[8]

Inequality ratios are based on dividing people in a society into groups of equal size (percentiles) according to their economic resources. This in turn allows for comparing any two percentiles and determining the factor by which the lower value needs to be multiplied in order to equal the higher value. It is common to measure economic inequality by comparing the top and bottom 10 per cent in a society, but it is equally possible to compare the top 20 and bottom 20 per cent (cf. Wilkinson and Pickett, 2009: 15ff.), or to measure middle-class inequality by comparing the fourth decile from the top with the third decile from the bottom (ILO, 2015: 24). If the top/bottom 10 per cent ratio is used, economic inequality in the OECD is highest in the Mexico with a factor of 30.5 and lowest in Demark with a factor of 5.2.

When economic inequality is analysed, the units of comparison can be individuals or households. It is often argued that comparing households is preferable because individuals, in particular children, may live in a household with substantial economic resources, but they may not control them directly. If the household represents the unit of comparison, economic inequality is still measured on an individual basis, but the value of economic resources at the disposal of individuals is equalised for members of the same household (Atkinson and Morelli, 2014: 3; Hills et al., 2010: 34).

Pay inequality refers to the inequality emerging out of employment. However, a considerable share of people in any population are not in employment and many people possess economic resources that are not the result of their working for a wage. In other words, pay inequality only explains economic inequality within the group of the employed and only insofar as the inequality within that group is caused by employment. Profit income, which is market income not originating from work, can also be more or less unequally distributed. A society with a large number of small companies and a strictly controlled financial system has a profit distribution different from a country with big corporations owned by a few families and a deregulated financial system with a powerful rentier class.

Income inequality can be measured in two different ways: functional income distribution refers to the share of aggregate income from capital as opposed to the share of aggregate income from labour and therefore captures the capital/labour cleavage neatly, but does not show the internal differentiation of the groups thus defined; personal income distribution provides a more detailed picture of different income groups, but covers up this cleavage. Furthermore, it is necessary to distinguish between personal income or gross income and disposable income, that is net income after tax including social transfers. In other words, the difference between personal and disposable income distribution shows the direct effect of state redistribution on economic inequality.

Wealth refers to all assets possessed by individuals or households, which includes both financial assets (such as shares or savings) and property (such as businesses or real estate). The more unequal the distribution of wealth, the more unequal the profit distribution will become.

The various chapters of the book discuss different measures of income inequality and different indicators depending on the dimension of income they discuss. All of them converge insofar as they agree that rising inequality has detrimental economic, political and social effects.

The combating inequality research project

This book represents the final publication of the *Combating Inequality Research Project* – an undertaking that was launched in January 2013 and that ended in

May 2015, involving around 50 scholars and trade unionists from across the globe. The project was funded by the Hans Böckler Foundation, which is based in Düsseldorf and linked with the German trade union movement. It was hosted by the Global Labour University (GLU). The GLU is a network of universities offering MA programmes in global political economy and labour studies that are specifically designed for trade unionists. It has campuses in Brazil (University of Campinas), Germany (Berlin School of Economics and Law and University of Kassel), India (Jawaharlal Nehru University, New Delhi and Tata Institute of Social Sciences, Mumbai), South Africa (University of the Witwatersrand, Johannesburg) and the US (Pennsylvania State University, State College).

A whole range of publications emerged out of the research project, documenting the research findings of the scholars involved and providing analysis, political recommendations and strategic considerations. Apart from this book, they consist in a number of working papers,[9] a special issue of the *International Journal of Labour Research*[10] and a special issue of the *Global Labour Journal*.[11]

A global issue

Considering the global nature of the problem of inequality, it is impossible to grasp it fully if it is examined exclusively at the national level. At least two of the key drivers of inequality emerge out of global configurations: the ensemble of transnational production networks co-ordinated and controlled by multinational corporations;[12] and the global financial system.[13] In both cases, it has proven extremely difficult to regulate these configurations effectively at the national level. This suggests that achieving fundamental change in the area of inequality requires scholars and activists to explore transnational paths of intervention and linking them up with national campaigns.

At the same time, the uneven and combined development of global capitalism means that the transnational flows of capital, money and commodities are interiorised into national economies in different ways. Among the factors determining interiorisation are (a) the position of an individual country in the world market and the international division of labour; and (b) the economic and political institutions as well as the relations of forces between capital and labour particular to that country. The existence of national specificities means that the nature of inequality differs vastly between countries. Unsurprisingly, emerging economies tend to have levels of inequality considerably higher than countries in the Global North (ILO, 2015: 24f.; OECD, 2011: 49).

Nevertheless, seminal academic contributions to the debate on inequality, for example the books by Wilkinson and Pickett (2009), Stiglitz (2013) and Piketty (2014), display a certain 'northern' bias. To a degree, this reflects the easier accessibility and the higher reliability of economic data in the Global North. At the same time, it is obvious that a wider perspective is needed in order to grasp the multi-faceted character of inequality in present-day capitalism. Accordingly, this book includes analysis and reflections on inequality both in the Global North and South.

The labour perspective

Traditionally, the organised working class and trade unions have been at the forefront of the struggle against economic inequality. In the post-war period in Western Europe, economic inequality was comparably low, which is at least in part a reflection of the strength of the unions and their political leverage. Conversely, attacks on unions and attempts to curb worker militancy were part and parcel of the neoliberal projects emerging in many countries in the Global North and South from the 1970s onwards, which – combined with the privatisation of state-owned industries, tax and benefits cuts, the liberalisation of financial markets and the switch to the shareholder-value system of corporate governance – led to significant increases in inequality.

The global financial and economic crisis has not resulted in a weakening of neoliberalism. In fact, the prevalent pattern of crisis management consists in a deepening of neoliberalisation and fresh attacks on labour – notably in the countries of the European South that are hit hard by the economic, social and political troubles in the Eurozone, but also elsewhere: trade unionists and labour scholars from different parts of the world are speaking of authoritarian state responses to labour activism and strikes (cf. Alexander, 2014; Montoya, 2012; Nowak, 2015; Satgar, 2012).

Against this backdrop, it is unsurprising that inequality remains an issue high on the agenda of trade unions from around the globe. Edlira Xhafa (2014: 39) shows in her study on the views of unions from 37 countries that most are very much concerned with inequality: 79.3 per cent of her respondents (94 trade union officials) attached a very high importance to inequality for society as a whole. At the same time, trade unions have significant resources to combat inequality: due to their long history, they constitute stores of knowledge concerning past struggles with egalitarian aims; as organisations actively involved in wage bargaining, they can influence wage dispersion to a certain degree; and as mass organisations, they potentially have considerable political leverage.

However, it also needs to be considered that the neoliberal offensives have had effects that are difficult to reverse. The fact that in most countries neither organised labour nor any other social or political forces have been capable of challenging the dominant modes of managing the global crisis shows that the defenders of neoliberalism are in a position of strength. Against this backdrop, a fundamental political shift will only occur if there is a broad movement demanding change. However, this requires unions to widen their appeal beyond their core constituency: building broad alliances requires strategies that take into account different types of discrimination and a variety of anti-egalitarian tendencies.[14]

In-depth analysis and a political-strategic narrative

Corresponding with its aims, this book can be divided into two larger sections. Whereas Parts I to III focus on analysing different aspects and different national configurations of economic inequality, Parts IV to VI are mostly concerned with political interventions aimed at addressing the issue and discussing strategic preconditions for change. Put differently, Chapters 2 to 11 prepare the 'analytical' ground out of which a political-strategic narrative emerges in Chapters 12 to 20.

Part I emphasises the impact of increasing inequality on macroeconomic and political processes as well as people's everyday lives. The contributors highlight (a) that economic inequality has detrimental social, economic and political consequences and (b) that it is always also conditioned by political choices. Along these lines, Tandiwe Gross, Frank Hoffer and Pierre Laliberté debunk myths peddled by the apologists of inequality, notably the assumption that it is the price to be paid for rapid growth. Akua O. Britwum shows that trade unions in their effort to curb economic inequality have failed to tackle adequately the connected problem of gender inequality. Edward Webster and Christopher Morris highlight that labour movements made an important contribution to decreasing inequality in the twentieth century, adding that trade unions need to operate in the framework of broad coalitions if they want to challenge the neoliberal orthodoxy.

Part II takes up this line of argument by providing in-depth analyses of the drivers of inequality and showing how political interventions in the last 40 years have contributed to unleashing the forces behind rising inequality. Looking at data on the OECD countries plus Brazil, India and South Africa, Hansjörg Herr and Bea Maria Ruoff contend, that all in all, the profit share and wage dispersion have increased in recent years, and that the liberalisation of finance, the deregulation of labour markets and the weakening of trade unions have played an important role in these processes. Similarly, Trevor Evans provides a comparative analysis of the effects of financial liberalisation in the US, Brazil, Germany and India, showing that there are diverging development paths: whereas inequality has increased significantly in recent years in India and the US due to liberalisation, a similar trend in Germany is more than anything a reflection of the liberalisation of the labour market. In Brazil, despite liberalisation efforts in the area of finance, a rise did not occur because the government chose to introduce financial inclusion programmes and social policy measures. Mark Anner and Jakir Hossain conclude the part by analysing the impact of multinational corporations and demonstrating, with reference to the textile industries in Bangladesh and Honduras, that whereas firms located at the top of global supply chains benefit from the weak bargaining position of the supplier base, the workers at the bottom lose out.

Part III looks more specifically at national economies in the Global North and South, backing up the general claims made in Part II with detailed country case studies. These show that economic models producing massive inequality are not just unsustainable because of the social and political upheaval they cause, but also in a plain economic sense. Thomas I. Palley shows that the neoliberal doctrine guiding US economic and social policy in recent decades has not only resulted in substantial increases in inequality, but has also proved incapable of addressing the root causes of the Great Recession, producing the economic stagnation that characterises the current situation in the country. Eckhard Hein and Daniel Detzer take a similar view on Germany: again, this is a case of a country dominated by an economic model (in this case export-led mercantilism) that has resulted in rather low gross domestic product (GDP) growth and vulnerability, accompanied by a marked growth in inequality. Jayati Ghosh looks at India and argues that in recent years there has been an expansion of the Indian economy based on a credit-induced bubble, which has driven up inequality, as well as exposing India to economic, social and political instability. Marcelo Manzano, Carlos Salas and Anselmo Santos analyse the situation in Brazil and come to the conclusion that whereas the accumulation regime in the country has lifted millions out of poverty, the global crisis has revealed its fragility.

Part IV opens the political-strategic section. It demonstrates the limits of the standard political responses to growing inequality. Birgit Mahnkopf criticises the 'green growth' agenda promoted by business associations, trade unions and political parties for assuming that it is possible to limit resource extraction and emissions while defending the notion of 'growth'. Heike Solga shows how education is presented as an appropriate response to growing inequality by protagonists of the 'social investment state', and how the notion of 'meritocracy' used in this context serves as a justification for inequality rather than as an effective countermeasure. Lena Lavinas highlights with reference to Brazil that under the slogan of 'financial inclusion', a financialisation of social policy is taking place, which makes people in need of a social safety net vulnerable to macroeconomic shocks.

Against the backdrop of the limits of standard responses to inequality, the contributions in Part V set out an alternative agenda. Hansjörg Herr rebuts the neoclassical defence of the free market by showing that unregulated markets do not lead to 'maximum welfare' and calls for macroeconomic demand management as well as the comprehensive regulation of financial and labour markets. Christoph Hermann criticises the dominant political and academic discourses on the public sector for solely focusing on questions of efficiency and highlights its redistributive effects, which make it an important instrument in the struggle for a more equal society. Sarah Godar, Christoph Paetz and Achim Truger argue that there is considerable room of manoeuvre for introducing a more progressive taxation regime, which should be used for redistributive purposes.

Part VI is concerned with the strategic question, more specifically with the political context within which activists promoting an egalitarian agenda operate, as well as with the question of how to campaign for a more equal society and which concepts to use for strategic calculations. Christoph Scherrer provides a detailed account of the economic and political context in which the trade unions operate when they develop egalitarian strategies. Michelle Williams traces the path of campaigns originating both inside and outside the labour movement that have successfully challenged inequality. She shows that in many cases, they used creative tactics expanding beyond the traditional repertoire of trade unions. Christoph Scherrer, again, and Timm Schützhofer develop a conceptual 'toolbox' that allows for categorising the different policy proposals made throughout the book according to their scope and strategic preconditions. The resulting classifications facilitate thinking about the opportunities for intervention available to unions in specific political conjunctures. The chapter by Scherrer and Schützhofer thus sums up and concludes the volume.

Remaining challenges

This volume shows that there is no shortage of ideas on how to deal with inequality and that there are opportunities for change. Nevertheless, there remain numerous challenges that have not been addressed in detail, and most of them are both academic and political in nature.

The first and foremost challenge consists in understanding and responding politically to the persistence of neoliberalism. Free-market policies have contributed both to reinforcing crisis tendencies that erupted into the global financial and economic crisis after 2007 and to increasing inequality considerably. Nevertheless, they still dominate government agendas in many parts of the world. Following Scherrer (2014), it may be useful to see this persistence as a 'matter of class'. The fact that many avenues for change remain blocked at the political level reflects the fact that pushes for reregulation or reform go against financial capital plus 'private property holders' more broadly (Scherrer, 2014: 349). Furthermore, once the global financial and economic crisis reached public finances, it gave the forces in favour of the status quo the opportunity to launch the next round of attacks against labour – with the aim of implementing changes that they had been demanding for a long time, notably further welfare state retrenchment and further privatisations in the public sector.

Against this backdrop, I contend that a key academic challenge consists in connecting the issue of inequality with the relations of economic, political and ideological class domination structurally inscribed in capitalism. This may go a long way towards explaining the intensity, intractability and durability of economic inequality. At the political level, this translates into the challenge of 'bringing class back' into the labour movement, as Sam Gindin (2015) has demanded recently. This should not be taken to imply that simply reverting to the 'traditional' language of class is the way forward for the labour movement. Rather, I argue that successful strategies against inequality are based on understanding the power relations and the socio-political forces underpinning the status quo and on identifying those social groups who will benefit materially, as well as those who will not, from an egalitarian social model.

Moreover, there are at least two other key challenges that the book only discuses in passing: first of all, the different forms of inequality and the range of cleavages existing in contemporary capitalism, which often reinforce each other; and second, the fact that there are not just massive inequalities between people within national spaces, but even more substantial inequalities if the global level is considered.

That said, it is worth stressing that the events in recent years show how quickly fundamental economic and political shifts can happen. Even if it does not seem as if there will be a decisive push towards a less divisive society any time soon, new opportunities for change are arising all the time. In light of this, it is worth discussing how to combat inequality.

Notes

1 I would like to thank Norma Tiedemann for proofreading and formatting the final manuscript and bringing it into line with the Routledge house style; as well as Andy Humphries and Laura Johnson at Routledge for their consistent support of our book project.

2 See Herr and Ruoff's chapter in this volume.

3 Correspondingly, F.A. Hayek remarked in his last book, *The Fatal Conceit*, that '[m]ankind could neither have reached nor could now maintain its present numbers without an inequality that is neither determined by, nor reconcilable with, any deliberate moral judgements' (1988: 118). When pressed by the Liberal Democratic MP Simon Hughes in November 1990 on the fact that inequality had increased during her tenure as prime minister, Margaret Thatcher famously retorted: 'The hon. Gentleman is saying that he would rather that the poor were poorer, provided that the rich were less rich. That way one will never create the wealth for better social services, as we have. What a policy.'

4 See also the chapters by Herr and Ruoff and Herr in this volume.

5 See Gross et al.'s chapter in this volume and Wilkinson and Pickett (2009, 2014).

6 See also Scherrer's chapter in this volume.

7 For a concise account of how the Gini coefficient is calculated, see Sen (1997: 29ff.).

8 All OECD numbers refer to the last year where data are available (2011 in the case of Chile, 2013 or later in the case of Denmark and Mexico) and household disposable income (see below) (OECD, 2015: 56).

9 See www.global-labour-university.org/302.html.

10 See www.ilo.org/wcmsp5/groups/public/---ed_dialogue/---actrav/documents/publication/wcms_247981.pdf.

11 See https://escarpmentpress.org/globallabour.

12 See Anner and Hossain's chapter in this volume.

13 See Herr and Ruoff's and Evans's chapter in this volume.

14 See also Williams's chapter in this volume.

References

Alexander, P. (2014) Marikana Shows Gap in Piketty Thesis. *Mail & Guardian*, 25 July 2014. Available at: http://mg.co.za/article/2014-07-24-marikana-shows-gaps-in-piketty-thesis (accessed 30 May 2015).

Atkinson, A.B. and Morelli, S. (2014) *Chartbook of Economic Inequality*. ECINEQ Working Paper Series No.2014-324. Available at: www.chartbookofeconomicinequality.com/wp-content/uploads/Chartbook_Of_Economic_Inequality_complete.pdf (accessed 29 May 2015).

Gago A. (2013) Trade Unions' Collective Bargaining Efforts Have Serious Implications for Social and Economic Equality in European Countries. European Politics and Policy Blog, London School of Economics. Available at: http://bit.ly/1bgm5k3 (accessed 25 May 2015).

Gallas, A. (2014) Editorial: The Inequality Crisis. *International Journal of Labour Research* 6(1): 9–16.

Gallas, A., Scherrer, C. and Williams, M. (2014) Inequality – The Achilles Heel of Free Market Democracy. *International Journal of Labour Research* 6(1): 143–161.

Gindin, S. (2015) Bringing Class Back In. *Global Labour Journal* 6(1): 103–115.

Hayek, F.A. (1988) *The Fatal Conceit: The Errors of Socialism*. London: Routledge.

Hills, J. et al. (2010) *An Anatomy of Economic Inequality in the UK: Report of the National Equality Panel*. London: Government Equalities Office.

ILO (2015) *Global Wage Report 2014/15: Wages and Income Inequality*. Geneva: International Labour Organization (ILO).

Kaufmann, S. and Stützle, I. (2015) *Kapitalismus: Die ersten 200 Jahre*. Berlin: Berz & Fischer.

Kimball, W. and Mishel, L. (2015) Unions' Decline and the Rise of the Top 10 Percent's Share of Income, Economic Policy Institute. Available at: www.epi.org/publication/unions-decline-and-the-rise-of-the-top-10-percents-share-of-income/ (accessed 28 May 2015).

Krugman, P. (2011) Oligarchy, American Style. *New York Times*, 3 November 2011. Available at: www.nytimes.com/2011/11/04/opinion/oligarchy-american-style.html (accessed 25 May 2015).

Montoya, N. (2012) Es scheint, als ob mit dem Streik eine vereinte Bewegung enstanden ist. In Gallas, A., Nowak, J. and Wilde, F. (eds) *Politische Streiks im Europa der Krise*. Hamburg: VSA: 156–164.

Nowak, J. (2015) Massenstreiks und Straßenproteste in Indien und Brasilien. *Peripherie* 137: 74–102.

OECD (2011) Divided We Stand: Why Inequality Keeps Rising, Paris: Organisation for Economic Co-operation and Development (OECD). Available at: http://dx.doi.org/10.1787/9789264119536-en (accessed 1 June 2015).

OECD (2015) *In It Together: Why Less Inequality Benefits All*. Paris: Organisation for Economic Co-operation and Development (OECD).

Ostry, J.D., Berg., A. and Tsangarides, C.G. (2014) Redistribution, Inequality and Growth. IMF Staff Discussion Note. Washington, DC: International Monetary Fund (IMF). Available at: www.imf.org/external/pubs/ft/sdn/2014/sdn1402.pdf (accessed 26 May 2015).

Piketty, T. (2014) *Capital in the Twenty-First Century*. Cambridge, MA: Harvard University Press.

Saad-Filho, A. (2015) Brazil: The Débâcle of the PT. *Socialist Project E-Bulletin*, No. 1097. Available at: www.socialistproject.ca/bullet/1097.php#continue (accessed 25 May 2015).

Satgar, V. (2012) Beyond Marikana: The Post-Apartheid South African State. *Africa Spectrum* 47(2–3): 33–62.

Scherrer, C. (2014) Neoliberalism's Resilience: A Matter of Class. *Critical Policy Studies* 8(3): 348–351.

Sen, A. (1997) *On Economic Inequality*. Expanded edition. Oxford: Oxford University Press.

Standard & Poor's (2014) How Increasing Income Inequality Is Dampening U.S. Economic Growth, and Possible Ways to Change the Tide. Global Credit Portal. Available at: www.globalcreditportal.com/ratingsdirect/renderArticle.do?articleId=1351366&SctArtId=255732&from=CM&nsl_code=LIME&sourceObjectId=8741033&sourceRevId=1&fee_ind=N&exp_date=20240804-19:41:13 (accessed 26 May 2015).

Stiglitz, J.E. (2013) *The Price of Inequality: How Today's Divided Society Endangers Our Future*. New York: W.W. Norton.

Thatcher, M. (1990) House of Commons Speech, 22 November 1990. Hansard HC [181/445-53]. Available at: www.margaretthatcher.org/document/108256 (accessed 25 May 2015).

Uslaner, E. (2008) *Corruption, Inequality and the Rule of Law: The Bulging Pocket Makes the Easy Life.* Cambridge: Cambridge University Press.

Watt, A. and O'Farrell, R. (2009) Are Trade Unions a Force for Greater Equality in Europe or the Champions of Privileged Insiders? *Intereconomics* November/December: 346–352.

Wilkinson, R. and Pickett, K. (2009) *The Spirit Level: Why More Equal Societies Almost Always Do Better.* London: Allen Lane.

Wilkinson, R. and Pickett, K. (2014) The World We Need. *International Journal of Labour Research* 6(1): 17–34.

Xhafa, E. (2014) Trade Unions and Economic Inequality: Perspectives, Policies and Strategies. *International Journal of Labour Research* 6(1): 35–56.

Part I
The challenge of inequality

2 The rise of inequality across the globe

Drivers, impacts and policies for change

Tandiwe Gross, Frank Hoffer and Pierre Laliberté

Overcoming poverty is not a task of charity; it is an act of justice. Like slavery and Apartheid, poverty is not natural. It is man-made and it can be overcome and eradicated by the actions of human beings.

(Nelson Mandela)

Introduction

Inequality is nothing new. What changes over time are the justifications for, and the varying degrees of inequality. Legitimising discourses are most effective when the poor accept inequality as a functional necessity, and when the rich have no doubts that they deserve to be at the top. In reality many factors beyond individual control or merit like the country of birth, skin -colour, gender, family fortune and class, as well as talent, beauty and so on, are major determinants of position and income in society. For this reason most rich people cannot claim their income is exclusively deserved because they have worked so much harder than others. Progressive taxation is therefore to a large extent about sharing the accidental windfall gains of inheritance, upbringing and other non-meritocratic wealth determinants in an equitable way.

Recently the Great Recession has challenged the hegemonic pre-crisis discourse on inequality. Complacent indifference over the growing income gap has given way to growing concern and anger but has yet to translate into a concerted movement for real policy change. Looking at the drivers of inequality and the discourses justifying it, we argue that inequality is not an irreversible phenomenon, but one that stems from political choices of the past and can be remedied through appropriate policies. We offer a few policy proposals at the end of this chapter.

Drivers of inequality

Under conditions of unfettered globalisation, a shareholder-value approach to corporate governance and labour market deregulation, income among the top earners has sky-rocketed. At the same time, the ability of societies to create fairer outcomes through redistribution policies has not kept up and even declined.

Indeed, the promise of trickle-down economics has not materialised for many at the bottom. Today, the top 8 per cent of the world's population gets one half of the world's income (Milanovic, 2012: 8). Over 840 million people are still suffering from hunger (FAO, 2013), hundreds of millions are dying from insufficient health provisions (WHO, 2013), and even in rich societies 15 to 20 per cent of children grow up in poverty (UNICEF, 2007), while 19,000 children under the age of five die every day worldwide mainly from preventable, poverty-related causes (UNICEF, 2011).

The ability of workers to get a fair wage has also declined. Average wages have failed to follow productivity growth globally. For many workers, they have even been stagnant or falling in real terms. Furthermore, the wage share of GDP has been falling in favour of the profit share.

Presenting this situation as the inevitable outcome of technological change and a growing labour supply from emerging economies is comfortable for the beneficiaries of rising inequality but ignores the fact that distributional outcomes are always determined by politically motivated decisions and non-decisions. While technology has undeniably offered new possibilities for economic development, its development and use has been shaped by the deregulatory policy context in which it has been introduced.

Cheap communication and transport costs, the instant mobility of financial capital, higher educational levels and better infrastructure, and sophisticated supply chain and logistics management offer profit-maximising enterprises new opportunities to circumvent or undermine existing national regulations and institutions that used to modify distributional outcomes. However, transforming these possibilities into reality is not automatic. Neoclassical economic convictions combined with corporate interests created an intellectual and political hegemony for a new regulatory framework. This included the free convertibility of currencies, flexible exchange rates, independent central banks, trade liberalisation, international protection for property rights, obscure forms of shadow banking, tax havens, opaque tax regimes and regulatory arbitrage.

Global corporations are at once the key architects of this new global business environment and themselves the objects of the structural forces they have helped unleash. Under the imperative of competitiveness, policy space is gradually closed to help prevent social wrongs. Mutually reinforcing trade relations, deregulated capital markets as well as 'neo-classically' inspired interventions in the areas of fiscal, monetary and labour market policy have resulted in growing inequality in most countries. Profits have shifted from the real economy to the financial sector, the bargaining position of workers has been weakened and the capacity of governments to tax capital has been eroded. In the end, the mobility of capital has resulted in workers making wage concessions and governments making tax concessions (Stiglitz, 2013).

Capital mobility and myriad new financial instruments are used as powerful tools to demand concessions from workers and governments and generate the exorbitant profit rates in the financial sector. This has allowed financial profits to accrue 40 per cent of all corporate profits in the US (Stiglitz, 2012). The rising share of profits absorbed in the financial sector has resulted in a decline in real investment despite historically high levels of overall profitability. As Piketty (2014) highlights, the growing disconnection between the rate of return on capital and the real economy is a key cause of growing inequality and dysfunctions of our economies. This is no accident, but the outcome of 30 years of steady and coherent policy lobbying to free capital from rules and regulations determined by nation states. The increased structural and political power of insufficiently regulated capital markets resulted in increased pressure to further dissolve labour-market regulations that protect workers and support collective representation and collective bargaining. This has led to the growth of precarious and low-paid work resulting in a shrinking wage share as well as increasing inequality within the working class (ACTRAV, 2011).

Inequality needed to reduce poverty?

A standard argument to justify inequality is that it is the inevitable price for rapid growth, and that there is an inherent trade-off between growth and equality. As long as the 'rising tide lifts all boats', it is said, inequality should be seen as a negative side effect of a generally positive development. However, there is no empirical evidence for the existence of this trade-off. The World Bank's (2011) overview of studies that have examined the impact of greater equality on growth shows that it has either no impact or a positive one. This is particularly true for more equitable wealth distribution and redistributive government policies. Similarly, a recent publication from the International Monetary Fund (IMF) states: 'attention to inequality can bring significant longer-run benefits for growth. Over longer horizons, reduced inequality and sustained growth may thus be two sides of the same coin' (Berg and Ostry, 2011: 3).

In fact, for societies with similar per capita income there is no correlation between the levels of inequality and their competitiveness in a globalised economy with respect to trade or innovation. Moreover, countries with lower levels of inequality have been generally more successful in terms of translating growth into poverty reduction (Fosu, 2011). The more unequal the distribution, the higher the required growth rate to improve living conditions at the bottom of the income pyramid. Rapid growth without fair distribution – as the example of China shows – can lift millions of people out of absolute poverty, but countries with better distributional policies such as Brazil can achieve similar income growth for the poor with lower rates of growth.

Above a certain income threshold, when poverty is no longer a matter of survival, it becomes increasingly a question of relative income levels in a given society. In the European Union, for instance, people are considered poor and deprived of opportunity if they earn less than 60 per cent of the median income (Eurostat, 2014). As relative poverty depends on distribution and the income differentials within societies, it can increase while absolute poverty is reduced.

Relative poverty can by definition not be addressed without reducing distributional inequality. The idea that growing inequality can be ignored as long as it reduces poverty is therefore a false alternative. The reduction of relative poverty requires a reduction in inequality.

Inequality and social and economic risks

In their research on health and social effects of inequality, Wilkinson and Pickett (2010) show a strong and consistent correlation between most negative social outcomes and high levels of inequality. The average quality of life decreases in societies as inequality increases *even if the average level of income is growing.* Moreover, the quality of life is not only deteriorating for the poor but also for the rich. For instance, the life expectancy of wealthy people in unequal societies is lower than those living in more equal societies.

In addition to deteriorating welfare indicators, growing inequality carries considerable risks for equal opportunity, democracy, social stability, public safety, and even environmental sustainability.

Risks for equal opportunity

It is ironic that the apologists of the status quo should present inequality as the natural result of 'meritocracy'. Indeed, inequality is a sure obstacle to equal opportunity. If societies want to fully benefit from the creativity, intellectual capacity and potential of all members of society, social mobility and opportunities for everybody are indispensable. The de facto exclusion of the children of

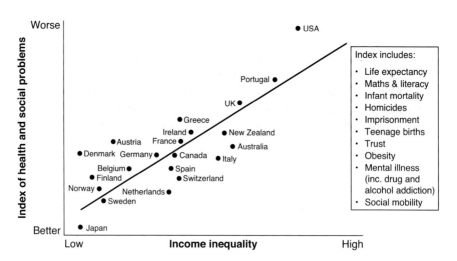

Figure 2.1 Health and social problems are worse in more unequal societies
Source: Wilkinson and Pickett (2010) cited in The Equality Trust (2013).

the poor, girls and second-generation migrants from quality education is not only a form of discrimination, but also a waste of development opportunities for society as a whole. Inequality of income and wealth inevitably translates into inequality of opportunity. Where parents cannot afford to send their children to school – or where public schools are so deprived that only those able to pay for private schooling can ensure quality education for their children – income inequality translates into education privileges. The probability of unequal educational outcomes rises with the unequal distribution of the initial assets. Therefore it is highly unlikely that inequality can be overcome or substantially reduced through the educational system, if this is not accompanied by policies to ensure greater income inequality. It is telling that one of the countries where inequality has most increased in recent years, the United States, once a beacon of social mobility, has become one of the industrialised countries with the least social mobility (Wilkinson and Pickett, 2010).

Risks for democracy

The massive concentration of wealth increases the risk of corrupting political parties, individual politicians and election campaigns. It creates a government 'of the 1 per cent, by the 1 per cent, for the 1 per cent' (Stiglitz, 2011). Think tanks that are funded by billionaires, media outlets that are controlled by private wealth and an endless supply of well-funded business lobbyists are a threat to democracy (Reich, 2012).

Risks for social stability

There is a correlation between growing social unrest or civil conflict on the one hand and the overall wealth share elites appropriate on the other hand (Milanovic, 2013). With growing concentrations of money and wealth in the hands of a few, the risk of social breakdowns and civil conflicts increases. As Stiglitz (2011) has put it:

> The top 1 per cent has the best houses, the best education, the best doctors, and the best lifestyles, but there is one thing that money doesn't seem to have bought: an understanding that their fate is bound up with how the other 99 per cent live. Throughout history, this is something that the top 1 per cent eventually do learn. Too late.

Risks for public safety

On average, unequal societies have more crimes and bear increased costs to deal with this insecurity. Not only are more people in jail (International Centre for Prison Studies, 2013), but also a growing number of those who can afford it retreats into gated communities and pays private security guards to protect them against the rest of society (El Nasser, 2002). Public spaces, where people can mingle, meet, debate and experience their commonality and diversity, disappear as a result. Inclusive societies cannot be built on the basis of segregation, fences and fear. The economic resources that are directed to the security industry constitute a pure waste from an economic and social point of view.

Risks for environmental sustainability

That conspicuous consumption induced by wealth concentration and income inequality should raise problems for sustainable development requires no complex explanation. When it comes to the environmental crisis, it is also clear that its consequences will add to global inequalities and will continue to do so even more in the future if left unchecked. To start with, countries that have contributed the least to greenhouse gases emissions are likely to be among the most affected by their effects with dire consequences on economic activities and those that have the least means to protect themselves. This is not only true between countries, but of course, within each country. For instance, a study of the impact of Hurricane Mitch on Central America demonstrated that relative losses were inversely proportional to families' income levels (UNDP, 2007).

If the impact of climate change will affect disproportionately low-income earners, it is also clear that they would also be those most impacted, relatively speaking, by increases in the price of fossil fuels and its indirect impact of the price of food staples. For those reasons, decisions concerning green taxation must be handled carefully and must be used as an opportunity to increase fairness. Addressing inequality is thus a pre-condition to finding durable solutions to environmental challenges.

The changing debate about inequality

If growing inequality was largely a 'non-issue' for a long time, in the aftermath of the Great Recession a debate on this issue became unavoidable. This was notably reflected in the new concern about inequality that can be found in such institutions as the Organisation for Economic Co-operation and Development (OECD) and the IMF. With the shift in public perception, the apologists of inequality have been on the defensive and have presented ever changing arguments to defend the indefensible.

A. *Inequality does not matter as long as it creates growth and lifts people out of poverty.*
    Not only is there no evidence that unequal societies grow faster, but they typically require higher rates of growth in order to have the same poverty-reducing effect than more equal societies. A moral case can be made for preferring greater equality to higher growth, but surely there is no argument for greater inequality if the same or higher growth rates can be achieved through lowering inequality. Indeed, higher inequality has ultimately led to

lower final consumption, lower real investment and lower aggregate demand on the one hand and a growing share of capital circulating constantly in the financial markets on the other hand (Stockhammer, 2012). This was disguised for a while by debt-fuelled consumption, but it became fully apparent when 'the music stopped' in 2008.

B. *Inequality is 'fair' because in a market-based meritocracy, unequal rewards are the fair expression of individual achievement.*

As outlined above, the position of people on the global income ladder is to a large extent not a result of personal achievement but of pre-determined factors such as class, gender or skin colour. Sixty per cent of inequality today is defined through inequality between countries (Milanovic, 2012). Within unequal societies, the barriers to social mobility are higher and the social status of parents becomes a major defining factor for individual success (Winship, 2011). As illustrated by Jäntti et al. (2006), the chances of someone ending up at the bottom of the income ladder in a country is always higher if their parents were at the bottom of that ladder themselves. However, the chances of moving up are considerably greater in countries that are more equal.

C. *Unequal wages might not be fair, but they reflect the marginal productivity of a worker. The reason one person earns more than another person is explained by the higher added value of his or her work to the profit of the company. Growing skills differentials are the reasons for growing inequality.*

Measuring individual marginal productivity in today's complex work environment is empirically impossible. Among top executives in particular, for whom the real income explosion took place in recent decades, marginal productivity theory seems to be an unlikely explanation for these wage developments: it is not to be expected that an executive's productivity is significantly higher if he earns $10 million instead of $5 million per year. According to marginal productivity theory, the pre-tax income should reflect the marginal productivity rate independently from the tax rate. In reality, as Piketty and Saez (2012) have shown, top income increases with lower top tax rates as the incentive for executives to bargain for higher wages grows. Additionally, no above average increase in productivity can be observed along with these pay increases. Wages at the very top, according to Piketty and Saez (2012) and Stiglitz (2012), are rather determined by rent-seeking and insider bargaining power of the management elite than by any objective economic criteria (see Herr and Ruoff in this volume).

D. *Inequality might be unfair and undesirable, but it is indispensable for motivating the most talented people to do their best.*

Productivity growth, the ultimate measure for innovation and entrepreneurship, is today lower than in the 1950s, 1960s and 1970s when top salaries were much lower in absolute and relative terms. Genuine innovators and entrepreneurs seem to be largely driven by intrinsic motivation, and beyond a certain level, additional motivation from more money becomes marginal. As wealth beyond a certain level is largely status relevant, an overall cut in top incomes would probably reduce the size of luxury mansions or yachts, but would have little impact on motivation.

E.   *Inequality is inevitable, because of globalisation and technological change differentials. These objective drivers are beyond political control and there is no alternative than to adapt.*

The great variety of capitalisms shows that countries integrate into the global economy through different strategies and approaches. Furthermore, globalisation itself is not an inevitable part of the market's development process, but the outcome of policies that aim at moving power and decision-making from the policy sphere into the market sphere (Eberhardt, 2014). By transferring policy decisions to global bodies like the World Trade Organisation (WTO), IMF or the European Union (EU), national decision-making – where the democratic influence of the people is stronger – is disempowered and national decision-makers are forced to subordinate their policy options under global market powers (Weizsäcker, 2003).

F.   *Inequality is not inevitable, but a consequence of skills differentials. It can only be overcome through investment in education.*

Turning education into the explanation for inequality shifts the debate from distributional policies towards a generational project. Nothing can be done to improve the poor income situation of the uneducated poor. The reasons for inequality are individualised as it is the personal lack of skill that is responsible for the low income. However, this line of argument is based on several implicit assumptions that are questionable: first, that the wage structure in a society is determined by skills and not other factors like tradition, policy decisions, bargaining power, discrimination, rent seeking; second, that remuneration corresponds to absolute and not relative skill levels and an improvement in overall skills will therefore compress the wage structure; and third, that it is possible to provide for equal educational opportunities in highly unequal societies. The persistent gender pay gap, which continues to exist despite increasing educational successes of women, is one of the most obvious examples to question that education is the silver bullet. High levels of education will not translate into greater income equality if the necessary labour-market institutions and regulatory measures are not in place (see Solga in this volume).

The way forward: using existing and regaining greater policy space

> If there is any law governing the distribution of income between classes, it still remains to be discovered.
>
> (Robinson, 1966 [1942]: 34)

Reducing inequality is good for societies as a whole, but it is not a win–win situation for everybody. The potential losers of greater equity are often the most powerful in society.

In most societies, the enrichment of the top 10 per cent appears to take place at the expense of the bottom 40 per cent. A comparative study of 132 countries (Palma, 2011: 22) shows that the fifth to ninth deciles typically capture about 50 per cent of national income. The success of the very rich in acquiring a bigger share of the pie thus appears to be more directly to the detriment of the bottom 40 per cent. While the multiple of D10 over D2 is growing from 3.6 to 33.2 over 134 countries the multiple of the D9 over D2 rises only from 2.3 to 15 and even more remarkable it is rather constant for the 100 least unequal societies (Palma, 2011: 23) This raises an important political question as to whether the middle class aligns itself with the wealthy against the poor by reducing the welfare state and by supporting an unprotected low-wage sector, or whether it aligns itself with the poor in raising taxes for a more comprehensive welfare regime, public services, higher progressive taxation and a living minimum wage for all workers.

Inclusive societies need policies attractive for the middle and lower classes. They cannot try to maintain a welfare state by taxing the middle class and allowing for a flying top. If the rich cannot be forced to share their prosperity, the middle class will sooner than later resist solidarity with the poor. This suggests that policies focussing only on redistribution within the current system might unwittingly help crystallise a conservative reaction orchestrated by the richest.

A policy package thus needs to address simultaneously the 'preferential' treatment of capital income versus income from labour; the equality of pre-tax earnings; the tax and redistribution systems; and of the role of public goods.

Many of the policies needed can be implemented at the national level but also require multilateral commitment to be successful. In addition, a universal commitment to pursuing these objectives would help create a mutual trust that good policies are not undercut by 'beggar thy neighbour' strategies. International Labour Organization (ILO) standards provide valuable guidance for the necessary policy co-ordination concerning labour and social policies for greater distributive justice.

Policies for faster income growth at the bottom

- *The right to organise: 'We are poor, but so many' (Bhatt, 2005)*
  Without pressure from below, policy opportunities in favour of the poor rarely arise. The self-organisation of the poor into trade unions and other membership-based organisations is an important step towards voice and representation with the aim of realising the crucial right to Freedom of Association (see ILO Convention 87 on Freedom of Association and Protection of the Right to Organise, 1948).
- *Full and productive employment*
  Full employment has been the exception in the history of capitalism. The level of unemployment has a direct impact on inequality, as the unemployed tend to be poorer. It also has an indirect impact on inequality as it leads to

a downward pressure on wages for those still in the workforce. Full employment should once again take policy precedence over other economic considerations.

- *A wage floor*
Compressing the bottom part of the wage structure through a living minimum wage as suggested in the ILO Constitution and in C.131 (Minimum Wage Fixing Convention, 1970) guarantees that enterprises do not compete by pushing down wages. It also ensures that highly inefficient enterprises over-exploiting labour make way for more efficient ones. A living minimum wage would, ceterus paribus, also change the wage structure: the real wages of low-income earners would grow as their salaries increase and the real wages of other workers who consume products and services provided by these workers would go down.

- *Solidarity-funded social protection floors*
Providing income security and health services for all through a welfare state has proven to be an efficient way of protecting people from poverty. Universal social protection floors as outlined in ILO Recommendation 202 (Social Protection Floors Recommendation, 2012) are the first step of an inclusive social security system offering basic security. They are essential for avoiding extreme poverty and total market dependency of the poor for income generation (see Herrmann in this volume).

- *Universally accessible public services and infrastructure*
Free or universally affordable, high-quality public services constitute a social wage and equalise opportunities. These services have the strongest income effect on poor households, enable women to enter the labour market and increase the social mobility of the next generation.

Polices for limiting high income growth

- *Progressive taxation*
Progressive taxation is not only fair and democratic since it helps to create the distributional preconditions for inclusive societies, but it also does not create any substantial welfare losses for the rich. High incomes are largely not about satisfying needs but about status consumption (*The Economist*, 2005). Applied universally, higher taxation for the rich will by and large not affect their incentive to work hard since the prime motivation of status competition remains the same: earning more than the others (see Godar et al. in this volume).

- *Regulating financial markets and strengthening the public banking sector*
Downsizing the financial sector, ensuring anti-trust policies and transparency, separating commercial and investment banking, and regulating investment banking are vital for creating more sustainable financial markets. This must be complemented by the creation of a well-regulated public banking sector and saving banks as financial public utilities (see Evans in this volume).

- *Linking the highest salaries in any company to the lowest salaries*
  The salary of a chief executive officer (CEO) should exceed the salary of the lowest paid employee by a reasonable factor. When reaching this ceiling, managers can only increase their salaries further if they simultaneously also improve the income of the lowest paid worker within the company.
- *Policies to avoid tax evasion*
  Tax havens should be closed and there should be co-ordinated efforts to avoid transfer pricing and other tax-evasion schemes of multinational companies and wealthy individuals (see Godar et al. in this volume).

Policies to strengthen and broaden the middle income group

- *Universal high-quality public services*
  Quality health, education, transport and other public services are indispensable for inclusive societies. The support for universal services requires quality standards that make it unattractive for people to look for private alternatives (see Lavinas in this volume).
- *A productivity-enhancing wage and employment policy*
  A regulatory environment that supports stable employment relationships and gives preference to internal enterprise flexibility over high employment volatility in unprotected labour markets is required. Research by Kleinknecht et al. (2013) has shown that stable employment leads to a much better productivity performance compared to flexible, precarious and informal labour markets.
- *Promotion and extension of collective bargaining*
  A comprehensive collective bargaining system is one of the most effective means to achieve equality. Indeed, bargaining coverage is inversely related to wage inequality and collective bargaining at the sectoral and national level is more effective at achieving greater equality than decentralised bargaining (see Herr and Ruoff in this volume). Legal provisions must be put in place to stop employers' aggression against workers who desire to create or join a trade union. Legal extension mechanisms have to be established to extend collective bargaining agreements – particularly also to those employed in small and medium enterprises (SMEs). This is necessary to prevent competition over wages and working conditions and force enterprises to compete through product quality and productivity gains.
- *Reduction of precarious forms of employment*
  Outsourcing, agency work, fixed-term contracts and subcontracting are methods used to undermine collective bargaining and individual labour rights. They are not an economic necessity for development, but rather aggressive instruments for creating a low pay sector (ACTRAV, 2011). The multifaceted abuse of labour-market power through employers can be stopped by introducing protection against unfair dismissal; recognising, at the legal level, de facto employment relationships; and giving part-time employees equal rights.

Clear limitations for the use of temporary employment and triangular employment relationships are required.

- *Public procurement policies, preferential public investment credits*
  Governments need to set an example as employers and use their role as the procurers and providers of subsidies and credits to secure fair remuneration and working conditions (see C.94 Labour Clauses [Public Contracts] Convention, 1949).
- *Non-discrimination*
  Equal pay for work of equal value and non-discrimination and equal rights for migrants are key policy measures to close discriminatory wage gaps (see Britwum in this volume).
- *Comprehensive social security systems*
  Social security systems that provide security and adequate income stability are needed. Mature social security systems are indispensable for inclusive societies at each level of development (see Lavinas in this volume).
- *Corporate governance*
  A narrow focus on shareholder value should be replaced by a stakeholder concept that limits the property rights of capital owners in favour of specific participatory rights of other groups like workers, local communities and society at large that are affected by company decisions and performance.
- *Economic democracy and empowerment*
  A fundamental lesson of the crisis and of corporate behaviour in the age of globalisation is that we need to explore new ways of organising production and ensuring that it better serves workers and their communities. Workers can harness the power of their own knowledge and capital (savings) to dispense with an increasingly unaccountable, wasteful and unfair system. The case of Mondragon in Spain, a co-operative with more than 250 subsidiaries and over 70,000 workers, demonstrates that this is both possible and sustainable. Mondragon businesses are more productive and twice as profitable as other Spanish enterprises, while the pay differential between executives and workers with the lowest wages is on average in the different subsidiaries one to five and not more than one to nine (Wilkinson and Pickett, 2010).

From policy proposals to policy solutions

Many of the policies suggested above were by and large practised by the industrialised countries during the long post-war recovery, and they had no negative impact on employment, growth or inflation – to the contrary.

However, in today's context of open economies, the situation has become more complicated and national policy options are more limited. The cross-border mobility of capital and trade liberalisation provide easier exit opportunities from national regulation and lead to so-called social system competition. The new context created by corporate globalisation has intensified deregulatory pressures, particularly on labour-market institutions. The Great Recession is used as a pretext for an even more radical attack on protective regulations and institutions.

Combating inequality requires a comprehensive multi-level policy response. This response has to include policy initiatives at the national and international level. In an ideal world this would happen in a co-ordinated and complementary way. However, sometimes the best is the enemy of the good. A strategic, piece-meal approach might be preferable to a more ambitious grand design.

Where global solutions are difficult to achieve, successful national policies that defend and strengthen labour-market institutions in one country also extend the policy space in other countries. The concept of the ILO standards is based on such a global win–win situation where the implementation of labour standards improves not only the working conditions under a government's own jurisdiction, but also the policy space for others. This philosophy is contrary to that of the WTO, where each round of trade liberalisation reduces the nations' policy space for the democratic decision-making of nations.

The focus on labour-market institutions and social policies as the traditional areas of trade union competency remains vitally important, but they need to be embedded in a broader set of policies aimed at reversing the trend of growing inequality. This concerns in particular the downsizing of the hypertrophic and dangerous financial sector, and measures against tax fraud. According to Barroso, the former president of the EU Commission, tax-evasion costs the EU member states €1 trillion a year (BBC, 2013), which equals twice the annual budget deficit of *all* member states. Oxfam (2013) estimates that developing countries lose $100–$160 billion a year due to tax-evasion strategies of multinational corporations.

Opinion polls in many countries confirm there is a majority in favour of bet-ter social protection systems; public investment in infrastructure, education and environmentally friendly technologies; greater equity; protective labour legislation and measures against tax evasion (ITUC, 2013). But these desires of the major-ity are not reflected in government policies.

Political systems that fail to respect and implement the ideas and aspirations of the people are flawed and unsustainable. Transferring decision-making to technocratic national or international institutions that lack democratic legitimacy is short-sighted and dangerous. Democracy cannot function if the *demos* is told that all vital decisions are taken elsewhere. Re-taking societies from the over-powering influence of big money requires a fundamental shift to greater equality and social inclusion. The arguments for a policy shift are overwhelming, but overcoming the vested interests of the status quo requires broad alliances for change. In increasingly diverse societies, it is a huge challenge to create and maintain a unifying movement within nation-states and across borders.

The rational assessment of power relations in any society at any time tends to lead to the adoption of the conservative view that the powerful will always prevail. However, historical experience contradicts the conservative utopia of a persisting status quo. Throughout history, popular movements have been the driving force behind the humanisation of capitalism. While they often have fallen short of their high ambitions and progress has not been linear, the positive changes and reforms achieved over time have been impressive.

References

ACTRAV (2011) *From Precarious Work to Decent Work: Policies and Regulation to Combat Precarious Employment*. Geneva: ILO (International Labour Organization). Available at: www.ilo.org/actrav/info/WCMS_164286/lang--en/index.htm (accessed 4 November 2013).

BBC (2013) EU tax: Barroso Urges Full Automatic Exchange of Data, 21 May. Available at: www.bbc.co.uk/news/world-europe-22599324 (accessed 20 October 2013).

Berg, A. and Ostry, J. (2011) Inequality and Unsustainable Growth: Two Sides of the Same Coin? IMF staff discussion note, SDN/11/08. Available at: www.imf.org/external/pubs/ft/sdn/2011/sdn1108.pdf (accessed 20 October 2013).

Bhatt, E. (2005) *We Are Poor but So Many: The Story of Self-Employed Women in India*. Chicago: Oxford University Press.

Eberhardt, P. (2014) Investment Protection at Cross Roads. In Scherrer, C. (ed.) *The Transatlantic Trade and Investment Partnership (TTIP) Implications for Labor*. Munich: Rainer Hampp Verlag: 100–119.

The Economist (2005) Inconspicuous Consumption, 20 December. Available at: www.economist.com/node/5323772 (accessed 7 January 2015).

El Nasser, H. (2002) Gated Communities More Popular, and Not Just for the Rich. *USA Today*, 16 December. Available at: http://usatoday30.usatoday.com/news/nation/2002-12-15-gated-usat_x.htm (accessed 20 October 2013).

The Equality Trust (2013) Why More Equality? Health and Social Problems Are Worse in More Unequal Countries. Figure 13. Available at: www.equalitytrust.org.uk/research (accessed 20 October 2013).

Eurostat (2014) Glossary: At Risk of Poverty Rate. Available at: http://ec.europa.eu/eurostat/statistics-explained/index.php/Glossary:At-risk-of-poverty_rate (accessed 6 January 2015).

Food and Agriculture Organisation of the United Nations (FAO) (2013) Global Hunger Down, but Millions Still Chronically Hungry. News Article, 1 October. Available at: www.fao.org/news/story/en/item/198105/ (accessed 20 October 2013).

Fosu, A.K. (2011) Growth, Inequality, and Poverty Reduction in Developing Countries Recent Global Evidence. UNU-WIDER Working Paper No.2011/01. Available at: http://www.wider.unu.edu/publications/working-papers/2011/en_GB/wp2011-001/ (accessed 4 November 2013).

International Centre for Prison Studies (2013) Entire world – Prison Population Rates per 100,000 of the National Population. Available at: www.prisonstudies.org/info/worldbrief/wpb_stats.php?area=all&category=wb_poprate (accessed 20 October 2013).

ITUC (2013) Global Poll 2013. Available at: www.ituc-csi.org/IMG/pdf/ituc_13_g20 labour_financeministers_july2013_12072013.pdf (accessed 9 January 2015).

Jäntti, M. et al. (2006) American Exceptionalism in a New Light: A Comparison of Intergenerational Earnings Mobility in the Nordic Countries, the United Kingdom and the United States. Institute for the Study of Labour, IZA Discussion Paper No. 1938. Available at: http://ftp.iza.org/dp1938.pdf (accessed 20 October 2013).

Kleinknecht et al. (2013) Labour Market Rigidities Can Be Useful: A Schumpeterian View. In Fadda, S. and Tridico, P. (eds) *Financial Crisis, Labour Markets and Institutions*. London: Routledge.

Milanovic, B. (2012) *Global Income Inequality by the Numbers: in History and Now. An overview*. Policy Research Working Paper Series No.6259. Washington, DC: World Bank. Available at: www-wds.worldbank.org/external/default/WDSContentServer/IW3P/IB/2012/11/06/000158349_20121106085546/Rendered/PDF/wps6259.pdf (accessed 2 November 2013).

Milanovic, B. (2013) The Inequality Possibility: Frontier Extensions and New Applications. Policy Research Working Paper Series No.62596449. Washington, DC: World Bank. Available at: http://elibrary.worldbank.org/doi/book/10.1596/1813-9450-6449 (accessed 2 November 2013).

Oxfam (2013) Tax Evasion Damaging Poor Country Economies. Press Release, 1 September. Available at: www.oxfam.org/en/pressroom/pressrelease/2013-09-01/tax-evasion-damaging-poor-country-economies (accessed 20 October 2013).

Palma, J.G. (2011) Homogeneous Middles Vs. Heterogeneous Tails, and the End of the 'Inverted-U': The Share of the Rich Is What it's All About. Cambridge Working Papers in Economics (CWPE) No. 1111. Available at www.econ.cam.ac.uk/dae/repec/cam/pdf/cwpe1111.pdf (accessed 20 October 2013).

Piketty, T. (2014) *Capital in the Twenty-First Century*. Cambridge, MA: Harvard University Press.

Piketty, T. and Saez, E. (2012) Top Incomes and the Great Recession: Recent Evolutions and Policy Implications. *IMF Economic Review*, 61(3): 456–478. Available at: http://piketty.pse.ens.fr/files/PikettySaezIMF2013.pdf (accessed 20 October 2013).

Reich, R. (2012) *Beyond Outrage: Expanded Edition: What Has Gone Wrong with Our Economy and Our Democracy, And How to Fix It*. New York: Vintage.

Robinson, J. (1966 [1942]) *An Essay on Marxian Economics*, 2nd edition. London: Macmillan. Available at http://digamo.free.fr/robimarx.pdf (accessed 20 October 2013).

Stigliz, J. (2011) Of the 1%, by the 1%, for the 1%. *Vanity Fair*, May. Available at http://www.vanityfair.com/society/features/2011/05/top-one-percent-201105 (accessed 20 October 2013).

Stiglitz, J. (2012) The 1 Percent's Problem. *Vanity Fair*, 31 May. Available at: www.vanityfair.com/politics/2012/05/joseph-stiglitz-the-price-on-inequality (accessed 20 October 2013).

Stiglitz, J. (2013) Inequality Is a Choice. *The New York Times Opinion Pages*, 13 October. Available at: http://opinionator.blogs.nytimes.com/2013/10/13/inequality-is-a-choice/?_r=1 (accessed 7 January 2015).

Stockhammer, E. (2012) Financialization, Income Distribution and the Crisis. *Investigación Económica*, vol. LXXI (279), Mexico: Facultad de Economía Distrito Federal: 39-70. Available at http://eprints.kingston.ac.uk/23226/1/Stockhammer-E-23226.pdf (accessed 7 January 2015).

United Nations Children's Fund (UNICEF) (2007) Child Poverty in Perspective: An Overview of Child Well-Being in Rich Countries. Innocenti Report Card 7. Florence: UNICEF Innocenti Research Centre. Available at: www.unicef-irc.org/publications/pdf/rc7_eng.pdf (accessed 20 October 2013).

United Nations Children's Fund (UNICEF) (2011) Millennium Development Goals. Goal: Reduce Child Mortality. Available at: www.unicef.org/mdg/index_childmortality.htm (accessed 20 October 2013).

United Nations Development Programme (UNDP) (2007) Climate Shocks: Risk and Vulnerability in an Unequal World. Available at: http://hdr.undp.org/en/media/HDR_20072008_EN_Chapter2.pdf (accessed 20 October 2013).

Weizsäcker, E.U. (2003) Globalisation, Democracy and the Role of NGOs. Available at: http://ernst.weizsaecker.de/en/globalisation-democracy-and-the-role-of-ngos/ (accessed 7 January 2015).

Wilkinson, R. and Pickett, K. (2010) *The Spirit Level: Why Equality Is Better for Everyone*. London: Penguin.

Winship, S. (2011) *Mobility Impaired*. Brookings Series: Social Genome Project Research, No.21. Available at: http://www.brookings.edu/research/articles/2011/11/09-economic-mobility-winship (accessed 20 October 2013).

World Bank (2011) *Growth and Inequality*. Available at http://go.worldbank.org/AKKLH75ES0 (accessed 20 October 2013).

World Health Organization (WHO) (2013) *Clean Care is Safer Care. The evidence for clean hands*. Available at: http://www.who.int/gpsc/country_work/en/ (accessed 20 October 2013).

3 Gender inequality and the labour movement

Akua O. Britwum

Introduction

The global economic crisis has been linked with rising inequality by numerous authors (e.g. Treeck and Sturn, 2012). A number warn of the danger rising inequality poses to development (IMF–ILO, 2010; Rubery, 2013; Sheldon et al., 2009; UN Commission of Experts, 2009). These studies tend to ignore other forms of inequality, in particular unequal gender relations. In contrast, feminist scholars highlight the negative impact of gender inequality on development (Arestis, et al., 2013; Cobble, 2012; Page and Conley, 2010; Ridgeway, 2009). Under UN leadership, the world community has instituted several instruments – some of which are binding – urging nations to address women's rights and gender inequality. The results have been mixed. While Ridgeway (2009) as well as Wright and Rogers (2011) celebrate the increasing presence of women in decision-making and critical areas of employment, Rubery (2013) laments the mismatch between achievements and investments. Fears of an emerging backlash that threatens limited gains are underscored by Britwum et al.'s (2012) conclusion that patriarchal norms continuously shape gender policy discourses and equality interventions.

This chapter discusses the connection between gender and inequality, utilising existing literature and data from the 13 country case studies[1] of the GLU Gender and Trade Union Research Group (G&TU). Members of the research group produced reports on gender relations and unions in their respective countries between 2009 and 2014, focusing on national labour markets and selected employment sectors. The role of unions is highlighted because of their particular location and role within economic systems. Paid employment is considered a vital tool for tackling gender equality and the existence of numerous legal arrangements guaranteeing women's rights supports this position. Unions have responsibility for promoting workers' rights in the workplace and beyond. Yet unions in many cases reflect and reinforce gender power relations within the structures of paid work and are implicated in occupational sex segregation and the gender pay gap. Recognising this failing, unions have over a period of time instituted gender equality measures with mixed outcomes. This situation raises far-reaching questions about how gender inequality shapes labour markets and the specific roles of unions in this phenomenon. Other issues of concern are how unions' contribution to equality strategies are facilitating women's activism to counter forces shaping labour-market inequalities. For unions, gender inequality is problematic because their core function is securing workers' rights; yet the workplace acts as a site for contesting male workers' entitlements.

Discussions in this chapter are organised in five sections. First, I provide a brief overview of existing discourses on gender and inequality and why this topic matters. Second, I discuss sources of gender inequality as located in women's reproductive roles in the sexual division of labour as well as other forms of inequality mediating women's experience of subordination. Third, I examine gendered labour markets and factors pushing women into insecure low-paying jobs with less access to social security. Fourth, I provide the contexts of gender equality agendas of the unions, forces shaping policies, practices used and their outcomes for women workers and women union members. Fifth, I explore union spaces that can be used by women to advance equality agendas. In the conclusion, I note that union attempts to establish gender equality have to be underpinned by women's activism.

Discussing gender and inequality

Gender inequality arises out of structured social disparities between women and men. Wright and Rogers explain that '[g]ender relations are the result of the way social processes act on specific biological categories and form social relations between them' (2011: 2). Over the years, dedicated attention to the socio-economic impact of inequality has weakened the foundations of the discourses and practices that legitimate discriminatory gender relations. There is global unity around commitments to eradicate gender inequality, but strategies to achieve them are still contentious. Disagreements have revolved around whether targets should focus on equality, difference or autonomy (Verloo, 2005) and there have been disputes over what to stress: liberal reforms or social transformation (Walby, 2005). Such altercations are creating a diversion by distracting attention away from a constant questioning of gender inequality (Verloo, 2005).

Feminists have long discounted explanations emphasising personality or individual propensities as causes of gender and other forms of inequality. Dominant analyses of gender inequality, however, assign considerable weight to economic factors such as individual access to productive resources and financial institutions (Arestis et al., 2013: 160). Out of the six factors Arestis et al. (2013) have identified as structuring household responses to economic shocks (an important element in the income inequality equation), only one is not gender-related. The other five are the functioning of labour markets; entry qualifications; educational systems; and monetary and fiscal policy responses to cyclical unemployment. Such observations, despite being derived from a one-sided, economistic analysis of inequality, have far-reaching implications for gender inequality. Numerous studies point out that gender determines the nature and quality of educational attainment and ensuing qualifications for accessing labour markets (e.g. Anker et al., 2003). Approaches critical of inequality insist that gender and other forms of discrimination result from power relations embedded in daily occurrences, which are normalised by the very systems that legitimise them (Arestis et al., 2013). This is saying that individual attributes or personal attainment granting access to labour markets are the result of social relations.

Production, reproduction and gender inequality

Our understanding of gender inequality is predicated on existing forms of labour-force participation and their support structures (Little, 1994). A major factor structuring women's inequality is their role in reproduction (Smith, 1997). Women's reproductive work within the domestic sphere is directly linked to capital's ability to extract surplus labour in the workplace. The family, the bed-rock of gender inequality, functions as an economic unit.[2] In the determination of wages, employers can afford to ignore the work carried out to reproduce labour power and the workforce because women offer these services for free. Yet such social reproductive roles impose immense demands on women's time and health and compromise their labour force participation.

All the 13 case studies from the G&TU reported women as bearing unequal responsibility for domestic work in addition to their income-earning activities. They noted deeply entrenched, patriarchal cultural settings. These were reinforced through:

- religion in the case of Turkey (Yilmaz, 2012);
- social, political and legislative actions in New Zealand (Jess, 2013) and South Korea (Kim, 2009), where women often have to withdraw from paid employment to take up caring roles;
- resistance to male participation in domestic work despite norms insisting on women assuming supposedly male roles like family provisioning in Ghana (Britwum, 2013), the Philippines (Certeza and Serrano, 2013) and South Korea (Kim, 2009);
- non-reciprocal access of husbands to their wives' labour in the highly informalised economies of Ghana, Nigeria (Odigie, 2013), Zambia (Phiri, 2011) and Zimbabwe (Chinguno, 2013); and
- the existence of a male breadwinner position granting Canadian men the right to withdraw from domestic work if they so wish (Chong, 2009).

Increased labour-force participation and improved technology for reducing the time and drudgery involved in housework has not limited women's reproductive role; in fact, reproduction still remains their primary responsibility (Smith, 1997; Young, 2001). Young's work in Germany (2001) noted male resistance to redistributing of house and care work. A situation which led upper- and middle-class women to adopt methods that do not demand a change in men's attitude to domestic work, but rather to offload domestic responsibilities onto paid domestic workers. In contrast, poorer women carry a greater burden in their attempt to resolve the conflict between their productive and reproductive roles. Smith (1997) concludes that altering existing sexual stereotypes by increasing male involvement in reproductive work should be accompanied by access to high-quality, institutionalised childcare. Though both approaches are important, the former serves to address women's real needs by drawing attention to male participation in domestic work. The impact of class differences highlights the variations among women's lived experiences arising out of other forms of inequalities.

Different historical and cultural contexts create social structures with distinct privileges and corresponding disadvantages beyond gender relations. Significant differences in women's experiences of gender inequality, according to Chong (2009), limit the universal applicability of the term 'woman'. According to the G&TU case studies, other forms of inequality mix with gender inequality, further disadvantaging certain groups of women. Existing discriminatory systems highlighted in the case studies were caste, race, ethnicity and religion: race privileges some women in New Zealand (Jess, 2013) and Canada (Chong, 2009), as well as exacerbating – together with ethnicity in the case of New Zealand (Jess, 2013) – gendered disadvantage for others. Intersections of gender and caste in India further marginalise women, preventing them from accessing the paltry state benefits available to workers generally and women workers in particular. The Nigerian case study (Odige, 2013) shows that ethnicity and religion determine the acquisition of pre-labour market skills.

A striking observation is the role women's sexuality plays in their experience of inequality. Here I draw on the WHO's definition as provided by Esplen (2007) which outlines sexuality as encompassing sex, gender identities and roles, sexual orientation, eroticism, pleasure, intimacy and reproduction. Sexuality is socially constructed and rooted in definitions of gender identities and what is considered the proper place of women and men in society (Ilkkaracan and Jolly, 2007). Besides housework, sexuality is an added factor structuring women's participation in paid employment (Barnes, 2007). Sexuality through commercial and transactional sex, as well as sexual harassment and other forms of violence, impact on women's participation in labour markets, furthering their disadvantage (Barnes, 2007; Smith, 1997; Walby, 2007). The cases noted the existence of sexual harassment as a condition for employment or participation in union activities. In their weak workplace position women succumb to pressures from male superiors to trade sex for merit-based employment and workplace benefits. The case studies from India (Chatterjee, 2013), South Africa (Munakamwe, 2013), Turkey (Yilmaz, 2012) and Ghana (Britwum, 2013) mention victim-blaming and a loss of self-esteem for the women caught in this sexual economy bind.

Gendered labour markets and inequality

According to Anker et al., labour-market access is influenced by the ideological perceptions underlying gender differences, which create 'occupational sex segregation – the separation of men and women into different occupations' (2003: 1). Thus, women are heavily represented in precarious and insecure sections of the labour markets and they dominate the informal sector. In the formal labour market, they tend to be located in the public sector pandering to known stereotypes captured by Çağatay and Erturk as the five Cs: caring, cashiering, catering, clerical and cleaning (2004). For Anker et al. (2003), this uneven distribution of women and men is one of the most pernicious aspects of inequality in the labour market, since it is generally accompanied by lower pay and worse working conditions in female occupations. It is also one of the most enduring aspects of labour markets around the world. It exists at all levels of development, under all political systems, and in diverse religious, social and cultural settings (Anker et al., 2003: 1).

Britwum et al. (2012) maintain that the bail-outs taking place in the Global North as a response to the banking crisis tend to favour financial systems rather than workers. The resulting cuts in state expenditure have resulted in the shrinking of sectors with secure employment. Such measures lead to more insecure employment, buffer jobs and 'flexible' labour (Rubery, 2013). Arestis et al. point out that 'cuts in production costs translate into higher unemployment', weakening labour's ability to fight for working rights (2013: 154). In the US and Western Europe, for example, the recession is said to have intensified precarious employment, leading to the expansion of what Standing (2011) describes as the 'precariat'. As a result of women's social and organisational positioning and their location in the precarious sectors of the labour market, they are the first to be attacked by mitigating strategies. Austerity measures diminish women's public sector employment advantages in the form of 'professional career opportunities and [. . .] higher minimum standards at the lower end of the job ranking' (Rubery, 2013: 33). This process leads to the 'feminisation of work': women become overwhelmingly represented in precarious employment sectors such as agriculture, domestic work and export processing zones – areas where poor working conditions are the norm rather than the exception (Fudge and Owens, 2006).

All the countries covered by the G&TU are located within the world capitalist system. The case studies confirmed the existence of segmented labour markets with women located in the lower ranks of public and private services and heavily represented in the informal economy (where it exists). According to Chong (2009), as far back as 2004 one out of every four women falls in the lower tier of retail trade and consumer services in Canada. Women constitute 66 per cent of the precarious workforce in South Korea (Kim, 2009). In New Zealand, women dominate in the outsourced sections of the service and public sectors (Jess, 2013).

One similarity shared by the case countries is the presence of labour-market regulations that lead to cost-cutting on the side of employers and predispose women to low-paying, insecure jobs. They all report shrinking public sector employment, which is significant because women-sensitive labour legislation tends to be enforced better in the public sector. In transition economies like Brazil (Lins, 2011), India (Chatterjee, 2013), South Africa (Munakamwe, 2013), Turkey (Yilmaz, 2012), the Philippines (Certeza and Serrano, 2013), and developing ones like Ghana (Britwum, 2013), Nigeria (Odigie, 2013), Zambia (Phiri, 2011) and Zimbabwe (Chinguno, 2013), women are located to a large degree in the informal economies. These are areas well known for their decent work deficits and weak or non-existent legal protection (Webster, 2005). Women here are less likely to be in waged employment. In Ghana, for example, over 80 per cent of working women are in the informal economy – and the figure for Zimbabwe (Chinguno, 2013) is 90 per cent. They form over 60 per cent of the Nigerian peasant labour force. Labour-force participation therefore forms an important structure through which perceived gender differences are legitimised and reinforced (Little, 1994; Rubery, 2013). The gendered nature of women and men's labour-force participation thus poses a problem for national and global efforts at eradicating gender inequality. The fact that labour markets are determined by the ideological perceptions highlights the social and economic basis of gender inequality.

Gendered earnings and workplace benefits

Segmented labour markets produce forms of disadvantage that further entrench gender inequality such as income disparities. Lower earnings reproduce inequality, a reason why distributional strategies, in the main, target income. The gender pay gap underscores that there is a gender regime of household production favouring the male breadwinner role as well as the structural exclusion of women from leadership and power roles within the workplace and labour movements. All case studies report gaps between average earnings of women and men despite legislation making pay discrimination illegal. In Turkey (Yilmaz, 2012), for example, there is a widening gap, with women earning about 83 per cent of men's wages. In the case of South Korea (Kim, 2009), women's average earnings stood at 69 per cent of men's while that of female precarious workers was 39 per cent. In Canada (Chong, 2009), women formed 60 per cent of minimum wage earners, and their earnings were 71 per cent of men's. The case of the Philippines (Certeza and Serrano, 2013), however, shows a reversal of the trend concerning the national average basic pay for women: it was lower than men's in 2006, but by 2010 they were earning more. Close scrutiny of the report shows a more nuanced situation with lower averages for women in industries where they dominate such as retail; hotels and restaurants; public administration; the health sector; and social and domestic work.

Added to extremely low wages is the differential access to legislative protection and the absence of social wages. Women, who are often located in less secure jobs like part-time or outsourced work or jobs in the informal economy, lose access to employment-based social protection schemes such as pensions and health insurance. In Ghana (Britwum, 2013), women constitute 29 per cent of contributors to the state pension scheme and 15 per cent of its beneficiaries. Women are more likely to lack safeguards against the sudden loss of income or drastic reductions. It is precisely to avoid social security contributions that employers embark on labour-force deregulation. A contradictory trend emerging from the case studies was an observed drop in earnings in the face of women's increasing levels of employment. One case study that confirms this trend is the Canadian report: it quotes Trisha and Yalnizyan's concept of a 'he-cession' to explain this phenomenon (2009; cited in Chong, 2009).

All the case studies point to deepening labour-market segmentation and occupational segregation with supporting ideologies that justify women's employment in low-paying jobs. This, together with the shrinking of secure employment forms for women, raises deep questions about the empowering potential of waged work for women and the drive to use paid employment as a tool for ending gender inequality. The workplace is a reflection of segmented labour markets and occupational segregation grounded in unequal gender relations. The legitimating logic is based on perceived female and male in/capabilities used to qualify or disqualify them for certain jobs. Thus for Britwum et al. (2012), women's increasing entrance into paid employment is not accompanied by a corresponding improvement in employment conditions including wages. Rather, women workers, they contend, are competing with men for low paid jobs – a situation that serves to push down wage levels since such jobs are based in insecure labour markets and workers' bargaining power is further weakened by such unusual competition. Arestis et al.'s (2013) analysis of the US, for example, reveals that while the pay gap is narrowing in less secure jobs, it is widening in more secure, full-time jobs. The persistence of gender inequality in this case serves to weaken unions by lowering workers' bargaining power. It further fragments the labour force by giving males a sense of being entitled to self-perpetuating labour-market privileges (Jackson, forthcoming).

Trade unions and the shape of equality policies and practices

Several studies highlight grave disparities in women and men's trade-union experiences. Britwum et al. (2012) note that across the globe women form less than one third of union membership while Briskin (2013) discerns an even smaller proportion in union leaderships. Earlier studies have questioned the democratic credentials of organised labour with reference to these low numbers (Cockburn, 1996; Cook et al., 1992; Creese, 1999; Deslippe, 2000; Graham, 2001; McBride, 2001). The conclusion was that unions exhibited a gender democracy deficit. Other authors tried to understand how unions can surmount internal challenges to successfully tackle gender democratic deficits (Briskin, 2013; Colgan and Ledwith, 2002; Franzway, 2001).

The case studies all reported that patriarchal cultures still dominate unions, supporting notions that union leadership positions are the preserves of men. Striking cases were Canada (Chong, 2009) and Zimbabwe (Chinguno, 2013), where men controlled the leadership in unions with women as the majority in membership. Furthermore, women were less likely to have access to union education and be part of negotiating teams. These observations support Ledwith's

(2006) and Hensman's (2002) position: according to them, unions reproduce existing social inequalities that workers bring into the workplace and, by extension, into their unions. Hensman (2002) concludes in her examination of the Indian caste system that unions absorbed without resistance the existing social stratification. For Ledwith (2006), the selectivities inherent in union structures grant some members greater legitimacy to access secluded spaces like the union leadership.

Globally, unions have instituted several initiatives to address their internal deficits that are based on three main strategies. First of all, representational strategies target women as a group. Second, promotional initiatives support individual women trying to access union power through affirmative action provisions like reserved seats and quotas. Third, there are also attempts to alter union rules in order to anchor gender democracy strategies firmly within union structures (Britwum, 2013; Britwum et al., 2012; Ledwith, 2006). These strategies have a common premise: they aim to ensure that the consistent pursuit of women's concerns is a legitimate part of union agendas and thus transform patriarchal structures inside unions. Union provisions are informed by existing national legislations and policies that seek to protect women's workplace rights and promote their participation in political decision-making. Gender inequality is addressed by special provisions such as affirmative action, gender mainstreaming and oversight organs.

All countries without exception had institutional mechanisms designed to improve the position of women. Brazil (Lins, 2011) and South Africa (Munakamwe, 2013), with their history of oppression, have incorporated in their nation-building efforts equality provisions. These establish organs are tasked with overseeing the implementation of measures that foster equality and ensuring compliance. The case studies mention quotas for employment and political representation. Labour legislation in various countries, taking a cue from the provisions of the International Labour Organization (ILO), tends to provide special protection and support women during pregnancy and childbirth. Beyond legislative and constitutional provisions, there are specific gender equality policies in Brazil (Lins, 2011). In South Africa (Munakamwe, 2013), a women's equality bill is under consideration. These national provisions for women's rights at work are effective only through enforcement. This is where unions play an important role: they ensure the translation of rights into realisable benefits for workers.

There is evidence that unions are addressing democratic deficits. All the case studies reported the existence of equality provisions of some sort instituted by unions. In Canada (Chong, 2009) and Brazil (Lins, 2011), the mandates of equality organs extended to sexual, race and ability differences. Separate women's conferences and quotas were other strategies adopted by unions in Ghana (Britwum, 2013), Nigeria (Odigie, 2013), South Africa (Munakamwe, 2013) and Zambia (Phiri, 2011). Others strategies were quotas for all union activities including education and training and special representation in union leaderships. The constitutional changes needed had been effected.

After decades of targeting gender democracy deficits, a number of studies have analysed the effectiveness of strategies (Briskin and McDermott, 1993; Britwum, 2007; Creese, 1999; Cook et al., 1992; McBride, 2001). Their verdicts acknowledge successes such as increased numbers of women in the membership and leadership of unions. However, observations also warn of a persistent backsliding noting that strategies are yet to transform union structures and their patriarchal ideology (Briskin, 2013; Parker and Douglas, 2010; Pillinger, 2010). Women's organs remain on the margins of mainstream union power structures. In a number of cases, such as Ghana (Britwum, 2013) and Nigeria (Odigie, 2013), these organs were severely underfunded. Unions in Brazil (Lins, 2011), Ghana (Britwum, 2013) and Zambia (Phiri, 2011) were relying on external partners for financial support.

National provisions for women's rights at work are effective only if they are enforced. All unions with the exception of Canada (Chong, 2009) relied on national legislation for framing women workers' rights. In light of this, collective bargaining becomes crucial. The case studies highlight that the implementation of measures was strongly contested in union circles. This suggests that the bargaining strategies of unions decide over how women benefit from legal allowances. The general trend in the case studies is that unions are reluctant to pursue such provisions; they are usually not seen as core concerns. In all cases, women's workplace issues rarely figured in collective bargaining, and there was a marked absence of women in union bargaining teams. Their concerns were rarely present at the negotiating table – and if they were, they were more likely to be dropped than other issues. Where unions responded, the issues they pursued were limited to mandated legislative provisions. In India (Chatterjee, 2013), the gender neutral formulation of primary work rights was forcing the exclusion of women's rights during negotiations. Provisions contingent on employer support for implementation were being used to deny women access to jobs or employment benefits in India (Chatterjee, 2013), Nigeria (Odigie, 2013), Turkey (Yilmaz, 2012) and, to some extent, Ghana (Britwum, 2013). Women workers on probation were being forced to forgo maternity leave with pay in Ghana and Nigeria. Employers in Turkey (Yilmaz, 2012) used the provisions as an excuse to refuse hiring females. Weak monitoring made legislative gains in South Africa (Munakamwe, 2013) ineffective. Only Canada (Chong, 2009) had a policy of structuring bargaining in such a manner that working women's rights and equity were advanced. Where women were present in negotiating teams, their issues were more likely to be present, tabled and secured. Thus the Brazilian experience is important: if women were active in bargaining, they achieved higher benefits for childcare and maternity leave and greater access to union decision-making positions (Lins, 2013). Progress for women's working rights was patchy: faster for the public and slower in private sector-based unions. Patriarchal norms constrained the use of collective bargaining as a gender equality tool and failed in the task of translating national legislative provisions for women's rights in the workplace. Union refusal to pursue gender equality provisions was counter-productive for women's employment security.

Women's activism and union space for gender equality

Moving beyond the issues of strategic adequacy and union resistance to working women's rights we arrive at the deeper question of women developing the appropriate consciousness to frame and pursue their independent claims with attention to changing patriarchal union structures. Women's activism is recognised as a significant ingredient in increasingly advancing union gender equality. According to Koch-Baumgarten (2002), a litmus test for ascertaining the power and effectiveness of organs of gender democracy consists in their ability to mobilise a broad power base of women union members and to serve as spaces for women where they can voice their concerns. This raises an additional question posed by both Ledwith (2006) and Hensman (2002): who qualifies best to represent women, and how women union activists can make labour movements respond to their needs. According to Koch-Baumgarten (2002) and Hensman (2002), these problems revolve around issues of identity and interest. They emerge from the marked differences in women's concerns arising out of their varied experiences of subordination. McBride (2001) discusses them in terms of the challenge of transforming representative democracy into participatory democracy. Women leaders should be capable of identifying with all women members and of devising a set of common concerns.

Therefore, the potential of increased women presence in unions in terms of providing sufficient empowerment to counter male hegemony is of concern here. Suggestions include greater collaboration between women leaders and union staff and building bridges across unions with social groups.[3] Such a potential was examined in the case studies and they showed evidence of female leadership bringing gains to working women in Brazil (Lins, 2011), Canada (Chong, 2009), India (Chatterjee, 2013), South Africa (Munakamwe, 2013) and the Philippines (Certeza and Serrano, 2013). Notably, this was connected to struggles for equality that went beyond the workplace. This connection was visible in Brazil (Lins, 2011), Turkey (Yilmaz, 2012), Ghana (Britwum, 2013), Botswana (Maruping, 2013) and South Africa (Munakamwe, 2013). While the synergies were stronger in Brazil (Lins, 2011) and South Africa (Munakamwe, 2013), legislative gains were dampening women's activism, which raised concerns about how to sustain gains once achieved.

Conclusion

The discussions reveal how the reproductive role of women and stereotypical notions of gender differences justify labour-market segmentation and wage gaps. Inequality in labour-market positions is further heightened by economic restructuring. In light of this, there needs to be greater attention to the gender dimensions of inequality. Increased labour-market participation and higher earnings do not reduce women's responsibility for domestic work. Neither does women's increased labour-force participation alter existing notions of gender differences that feed into women's subordination. In fact, the issue of domestic work and traditional perception of gender roles threaten to undermine the potential of paid employ-ment for a transformation of gender relations. Men do not relieve women of domestic responsibilities with the same ease as women, who actively contribute to household income. And yet, women's differential social positions belie the assumption that there is a uniform experience of gendered inequality. There are two important questions emerging against this backdrop: how to structure inter-ventions that minimise women's reproductive burden across the board, and how to justify the claim that only women can be true representatives of the women's cause? The deeper issues of power differences among women undermining gen-der equality strategies remains a prime concern, since patriarchy, as the base of women's subordination, operates in tandem with other forms of inequality. An exclusive focus on one form of inequality to the neglect of others may render strategies aimed at combating inequality sterile and doomed to fail.

Legal provisions, however limited they are in their effectiveness, are major steps towards equality. They do not automatically translate into social equality, but they provide unions with the new opportunities for achieving better outcomes. Beyond women's presence in the leaderships of unions, it is their participation in negotiating teams that leads to women workers' rights being enforced. Strat-egies for union democratisation hold great potential for fostering women's activ-ism and confronting gender inequality as well as other forms of inequality. For the moment, unions are yet to make a mark in this direction.

Table 3.1 GLU Gender and Trade Union Research Group case study reports

Country	Author/s	Title and Date
Botswana	Mpho S. Maruping	The Response from Botswana Federation of Trade Unions (BFTU) (2013)
Brazil	Juçara Portilho Lins	Trade Union Leadership and Gender: Brazilian Banking Workers' Inequalities (2011)
Canada	Patricia Chong	Trade Union Equality Policies: Canada (2009)
Ghana	Akua O. Britwum	The Female Factor in Ghana's Trades Union Congress (2013)
India	Rhea Aamina Chatterjee	Margins within Margins: A Study of Street Cleaners in Mumbai (2013)
New Zealand	Carol Jess	New Zealand: A Case Study of Women Workers (2013)
Nigeria	Joel Odigie	Nigeria GLU Gender Research Paper (2013)
Philippines	Ramon Certeza, Melisa Serrano	Gender, Unions and Collective Bargaining in the Philippines: Issues and Critical Factors (2013)
South Africa	Janet Munakamwe	South African Case Study Report (2013)
South Korea	Mijeoung Kim	South Korea Case Study Report (2009)
Turkey	Gaye Yilmaz	Turkey Evaluation Report Synthesis (2012)
Zambia	Boniface Phiri	Zambia Gender Case Study (2011)
Zimbabwe	Crispen Chinguno	Trade Unions Leadership and Gender: Cases from Zimbabwe (2013)

Notes

1 The list of authors and cases is provided in Table 3.1.
2 The conception of the family as an economic unit can be compared in some measure to Rajan's (2010) (as quoted in Treeck and Sturn, 2012) notion of the family as a 'consumption unit'. The difference lies in its primary function – whether it is conceived as a production or a consumption entity. I insist it is a production unit.
3 Ledwith (2006) describes this as rainbow politics, a variation of Munck's (2002) social movement unionism.

References

Anker, R., Melkas, H. and Korten, A. (2003) *Gender-Based Occupational Segregation in the 1990s*. Geneva: International Labour Organization (ILO).

Arestis, P., Charles, A. and Fontana, G. (2013) Financialization, the Great Recession, and the Stratification of the US Labor Market. *Feminist Economics* 19(3): 152–180.

Barnes, T. (2007) Politics of the Mind and Body: Gender and Institutional Culture in African Universities. *Feminist Africa* 8: 8–25.

Briskin, L. (2013) Merit, Individualism and Solidarity: Revisiting the Democratic Deficit in Union Women's Leadership. In Ledwith, S. and Hansen, L.L. (eds) *Gendering and Diversifying Union Leadership*. London: Routledge: 138–161.

Briskin, L. and McDermott, P. (1993) *Women Challenging Union: Democracy, and Militancy*. London: University of Toronto Press.

Britwum, A.O. (2007) The Gender of Trade Union Democratic Participation. In Kester, G. (ed.) *Trade Unions and Workplace Democracy in Africa*. Aldershot: Ashgate: 227–251.

Britwum, A.O. (2013) Female Union Leadership, Power, Dynamism and Organised Labour in Ghana. In Ledwith, S. and Hansen, L.L. (eds) *Gendering and Diversifying Union Leadership*. London: Routledge: 265–284.

Britwum, A.O., Douglas, K. and Ledwith, S. (2012) Women, Gender and Power in Trade Unions. In Mosoetsa, S. and Willliams, M. (eds) *Labour in the Global South: Challenges and Alternatives for Workers*. Geneva: International Labour Organization: 41–64.

Çağatay, N. and Erturk, K. (2004) *Gender and Globalization: A Macroeconomic Perspective*. World Commission on the Social Dimension of Globalization, Policy Integration Department. Geneva: International Labour Organization (ILO).

Cobble, D.S. (2012) *Gender Equality and Labor Movements: Toward a Global Perspective*. New Brunswick: Department of Labor Studies and Employment, Rutgers University.

Cockburn, C. (1996) Strategies for Gender Democracy: Strengthening the Representation of Trade Union Women in the European Social Dialogue. *European Journal for Women's Studies* 3: 7–26.

Colgan, F. and Ledwith, S. (2002) Gender and Diversity: Reshaping Union Democracy. *Employee Relations* 24(2): 167–189.

Cook, A.H., Lorwin, V.R. and Daniels, A.K. (1992) *The Most Difficult Revolution: Women and Trade Unions*. London: Cornell University Press.

Creese, G. (1999) *Contracting Masculinity: Gender Class, Race in a White Collar Union 1944–1994*. London: Oxford University Press.

Deslippe, D.A. (2000) *"Rights not Roses" Unions and the Rights of Working Class Feminism, 1945–80*. Chicago: University of Illinois Press.

Esplen, E. (2007) *Gender and Sexuality*. Brighton: Institute of Development Studies, University of Sussex.

Franzway, S. (2001) *Sexual Politics and Greedy Institutions*. Melbourne: Pluto Press.

Fudje, J. and Owens, R. (2006) *Precarious Work, Women and the New Economy: The Challenge to Legal Norms*. Oxford: Hart Publishing.

Graham, Y. (2001) Changing the United Brotherhood: An Analysis of the Gender Politics of the Ghana Trades Union Congress. In Tsikata, D. (ed.) *Gender Training in Ghana: Politics, Issues and Tools*. Accra: Woeli Publishing Services: 293–320.

Hensman, R. (2002) Organisational Strategies of Women Workers in India. In Clogan, F. and Ledwith, S. (eds) *Gender, Diversity and Trade Unions: International Perspectives*. London: Routledge: 95–112.

Ilkkaracan, P. and Jolly, S. (2007) *Gender and Sexuality: Overview Report*. Sussex: Institute of Development Studies.

IMF–ILO (2010) *The Challenges of Growth, Employment and Social Cohesion*. Joint ILO–IMF Conference. Oslo: IMF–ILO.

Jackson, R.M. (forthcoming) *Down so Long*.

Koch-Baumgarten, S (2002) Changing Gender Relations in German Trade Unions: From 'Workers' Patriarchy' to Gender Democracy? In Clogan, F. and Ledwith, S. (eds) *Gender, Diversity and Trade Unions: International Perspectives*. London: Routledge: 132–153.

Ledwith, S. (2006) The Future is Female? Gender, Diversity and Global Labour Solidarity. In Phelan, C. (ed.) *The Future of Organised Labour: Global Perspectives*. Oxford: Peter Lang: 91–134.

Ledwith, S. (2013) Doing, Un-Doing and Re-Doing Gendered Union Leadership. In Ledwith, S. and Hansen, L.L. (eds) *Gendering and Diversifying Trade Union Leadership*. London: Routledge: 91–116.

Little, J. (1994) *Gender Planning and the Policy Process*. Oxford: Pergamon.

McBride, A. (2001) *Gender Democracy in Trade Unions*. Aldershot: Ashgate.

Munck, R. (2002) *Globalization and Labour: The New "Great Transformation"*. London: Zed Books.

Page, M. and Conley, H. (2010) *Between Compliance and Conviction – Gender Mainstreaming as Contested Practice*. Keele University: Gender and Work Organisation.

Parker, J. and Douglas, J. (2010) Can Women's Structures Help New Zealand and UK Trade Unions' Revival? *Journal of Industrial Relations 52* (4): 439-458.

Pillinger, J. (2010) *From Membership to Leadership: Advancing Women in Trade Unions*. Brussels: European Trade Union Confederation.

Ridgeway, C.L. (2009) Framed Before We Know It: How Gender Shapes Social Relations. *Gender and Society* 23(2): 145–160.

Rubery, J. (2013) From 'Women and Recession' to 'Women and Austerity': A Framework for Analysis. In Karamessini, M. and Rubery, J. (eds) *Women and Austerity: The Economic Crisis and the Future for Gender Equality*. IAFFE Advances in Feminists Economics. London: Routledge: 17–36.

Sheldon, R., Platt, R. and Jones, N. (2009) *Political Debate about Economic Inequality: An Information Resource*. York: Joseph Rowntree Foundation.

Smith, S. (1997) Engels and the Origin of Women's Oppression. *International Socialist Review* 2. Available at: http://www.isreview.org/issues/02/engels_family.shtml.

Standing, G. (2011) *The Precariat: The New Dangerous Class*. London: Bloomsbury.

Treeck, T. and Sturn, S. (2012) *Income Inequality as a Cause of the Great Recession? A Survey of Current Debates*. Geneva: International Labour Organization.

United Nations (2009) *Report of the Commission of Experts of the President of the United Nations General Assembly on Reforms of the International Monetary and Financial System*. New York: United Nations.

Verloo, M. (2005) Displacement and Empowerment: Reflections on the Concept and Practice of the Council of Europe Approach to Gender Mainstreaming and Gender Equality. *Social Politics International Studies in Gender, State and Society* 12(3): 344–365.

Walby, S. (2005) Gender Mainstreaming: Productive Tensions in Theory and Practice. *Social Politics* 12(3): 1–25.

Walby, S. (2007) Gender (In)equality and the Future of Work. *Transforming Work* (55). Working Paper Series No. 55. Lancaster University.

Webster, E. (2005) New Forms of Work and the Representational Gap: A Durban Case Study. In Webster, E. and Von Holdt, K. (eds) *Beyond the Apartheid Workplace: Studies in Transition*. University of KwaZulu: Natal Press: 387–405.

Wright, E.O. and Rogers, J. (2011) *American Society How it Really Works*. New York: W.W. Norton and Company.

Young, B. (2001) The 'Mistress' and the 'Maid' in the Globalized Economy. *The Socialist Register* 37: 315–327.

4 Trade unions and the challenge of economic inequality

An unresolved debate

Edward Webster and Christopher Morris

Introduction

Contemporary labour studies reveal a paradox: in a context where traditional trade unions in advanced industrialising countries are in decline, the study of global labour is flourishing. This paradox emerged at the 9th Global Labour University (GLU) conference, 'Inequality Within and Among Nations: Causes, Effects and Responses', held in Berlin in 2014. What the 88 papers demonstrated is the ferment of ideas, initiatives and policies that are emerging in response to deepening inequality and the growing numbers of the working poor worldwide. Jennifer Chun suggests there is a

> growing interest in a new political subject of labour, women, immigrants, people of colour, low-paid service workers, precarious workers, groups that have been historically excluded from the moral and material boundaries of union membership. Rather than traditional scholarship on industrial relations, new labour scholars are exploring transformations occurring at the periphery of mainstream labour movements.
>
> (2012: 40)

The clearest example of this emerging field of global labour studies is the increasing interest amongst academics in the study of global labour. In 2002, the American Sociological Association established a special section on labour and labour movements, and in the United Kingdom a Critical Labour Studies network was launched. The Labour Movements section of the International Sociological Association (ISA), also known as Research Committee 44, has become one of the most active sections of the ISA. Similarly, we have seen the emergence of labour geography and global labour history as key specialisations within their disciplines. A key text in history, for example, is Marcel van der Linden's *Workers of the World: Essays toward a Global Labour History*.

A number of journals devoted to global labour have been established – or in some cases, revitalised – over the past decade: *Labour, Capital and Society*; *Labour Studies Journal*; *International Journal of Labour Research*; *Globalizations*; *Work, Organisation, Labour and Globalisation* and *Global Labour Journal*.

In this chapter, we reflect on the strategies and policies for combating inequality that are emerging amongst trade unionists and labour scholars. We divide the chapter into three sections: in the first section, we discuss three major studies on inequality to show how the study of inequality is being mainstreamed. In the second section, we examine a range of demands and policy instruments emerging from within the labour movement that provide an alternative to the dominance of neoliberal economic and social policies. In the third section, we identify five unresolved issues that the labour movement will have to tackle in the near future. We suggest that the central challenge facing labour is how to build a broad alliance that combines 'initiatives for change from within government structures with support for developing wider, more radical sources of power outside' (Wainwright, 2013: 139). We conclude by pointing to the need for trade unions to be part of a broader movement designed to challenge the dominance of neoliberal economic and social policies.

Studies on inequality

'Inequality', Gustav Horn from the German Macroeconomic Policy Institute declares, 'is now a topic of the economic mainstream' (2014). Indeed, it could be said that mainstream economic research is informing the left's long-term critique of trickle-down economics. Thomas Piketty, in his best-selling book *Capital in the Twenty-First Century* (2014), confirms that market-led growth deepens inequality and good redistributive policies improve growth. By analysing tax records in Western Europe and the United States he shows that until 1910 (the eve of the First World War), wealth and income were concentrated in the hands of the top share of owners and earners. These top shares' incomes dropped from then until 1970–1980 and have been increasing ever since, to levels last seen in the early 20th century. Thanks mainly to the effects and after-effects of the 'shocks' of war during the first half of the twentieth century, inequality of share of income decreased. Through unionisation, higher incomes for the middle classes, a progressive tax and nationalisations, the divergence in income was stemmed. This process was reversed in the 1980s and now the top owners and earners are once again taking in a greater share of income.

Research by Kate Pickett and Richard Wilkinson shows that among the richest countries, it is the more unequal ones that do worse according to almost every quality of life indicator (Pickett and Wilkinson, 2014: 18). They trace the changes in inequality since 1921, showing how the income share of the richest 1 per cent follows a 'u-shape' when plotted on a graph. So until the 1930s, the richest 1 per cent's share was high. It then started a steady decline (and with it, inequality also declined) that ended in the 1970s. Subsequently, it began to rise again until it reached levels somewhere near or at 1920s levels. They go on to show how relative income plays an important role in key indicators of quality of life (Pickett and Wilkinson, 2014: 19–21). What emerges from their study is that life expectancy is closely tied to one's relative income in a society. Other societal problems caused by high inequality include ill-health, violence, poor education, high infant mortality, higher homicide rates, higher proportions of the population in prison, teenage pregnancy, how much people feel they can trust each other, mental illness (including substance abuse) and lack of social mobility (Pickett and Wilkinson, 2014: 18).

An important voice in the inequality debate is the re-emergence of Keynesian arguments against inequality (Dullien et al., 2011). In a more recent study, Herr et al. argue that financialisation is part of a neoliberal *political project* designed to increase the share of income going towards profits, thereby increasing inequality (2014: 51). In addition, the size and speed of financial transactions has grown exponentially since the 'neoliberal revolution', and this process wreaks havoc with whole industries world-wide. The fact that capital can move across the world while labour is locked into the nation-state means that capital can easily discipline labour and push down wages by threatening to move elsewhere (Herr et al., 2014: 63–64).

Three broad conclusions can be drawn from these studies of inequality. First, levels of inequality were reduced between the 1920s and 1970s by the use of policy instruments such as progressive taxation and nationalisation, as well as the growth and development of trade unions. Second, inequality has a negative effect on the quality of life, including life expectancy, levels of violence and other societal problems. Third, the growth in levels of inequality since the 1970s is the result of a political project designed to increase the power of capital – and finance capital in particular – over labour. This 'neoliberal revolution' has not only increased the share of income going to profits; it has weakened trade unions and eroded the institutional gains made by workers in advanced capitalist countries after the Second World War. Against this backdrop, we turn now to an examination of the demands emerging from the labour movement on how to address these developments and overcome inequality.

Trade-union views

The most comprehensive account of union views on inequality can be drawn from a survey by Edlira Xhafa (2014) of 94 trade unionists from 37 countries. What emerged from the interviews is that the main indicators of increasing economic inequality are (in rank order): increasing job insecurity and precarisation; increasing wage gaps in the labour market; declining real wages; increasing profit margins for companies and reductions in welfare benefits (Xhafa, 2014: 37).

The survey identified the policies and strategies adopted by unionists to counter economic inequality. Xhafa divides them into three areas: (1) wage and income strategies; (2) social security and protection strategies; and (3) labour-market policies and strategies (2014: 41). Under (1), unionists identified three main policies and strategies pursued to tackle inequality. The first is the minimum wage; the second the expansion of collective bargaining coverage; and the third the living wage. Under (2), there are demands for countries to ratify ILO conventions on social security. Aside from this, interventions consist mainly of efforts to establish or adjust benefits to prevailing living standards or to expand existing schemes in order to provide more comprehensive coverage to all citizens, without conditionality. Area (3) was the one least frequently mentioned by respondents (less than half of them did so). The top policies proposed are employment policies for women, policies to tackle unemployment, policies for youth employment and policies providing job security (Xhafa, 2014: 43). Overall, when unionists were asked to identify the most successful policy proposals, 56 per cent identified the minimum wage, 54 per cent said pensions, 52 per cent picked out wages and income, 52 per cent mentioned social protection proposals and 52 per cent made note of the increasing coverage of Collective Bargaining Agreements (Xhafa, 2014: 46).

As suggested in the survey above, the demand for a national minimum wage emerges as the most consistent response to inequality by trade unions. In a comprehensive Political Report to the 2012 congress of COSATU, South Africa's largest trade-union federation, the then general secretary, Zwelinzima Vavi, argued for following the Brazilian example:

> At the heart of the gains in [Brazil's] labour market, is the consolidation of national minimum wages and collective bargaining, with a deliberate strategy driven by progressive governments, to substantially increase the real level of minimum wages, and address the plight of the working poor. The other key leg of this strategy to raise people's incomes is the introduction of social protection measures to ensure that all the poor, including unemployed, have access to a basic income. These redistributive policies have been effectively combined with state-driven industrial and investment strategies.
>
> (COSATU, 2012: 1)

One of the most successful policy instruments introduced in Brazil is a conditional cash transfer scheme, the Bolsa Família (family grant), which provides low-income families with a basic grant provided their children of school-going age attend school (Moretto, 2014: 161). Bolsa Família focuses on poor and extremely poor families that fall below the poverty line (140 Reais per capita per month) and the extreme poverty line (70 Reais), respectively. The value of the total grant varies according to family characteristics. The Brazil sem Miséria programme (BSM) was introduced by President Dilma Roussef's government in 2011 to overcome some of the difficulties faced in implementing Bolsa Família. A crucial challenge is the public education system that has not managed to adequately prepare children for employment. As Moretto argues:

> It is impossible to reduce social inequality and poverty with such schemes alone. Together with such programmes, there must be a set of other public policies aimed at eliminating or reducing the social risks faced by

contemporary societies. Such risks – such as those related to health and transport – often cannot be attributed exclusively to low household income. Hence, it is recognised that poverty and extreme poverty cannot be reduced to insufficient income alone.

(2014: 166)

Increasingly, international observers have suggested that there may be lessons in Brazil's recent growth, offering an alternative that links growth to improved living conditions for all. As senior ILO economists Janine Berg and Stephen Tobin conclude: 'Experiences of Brazil serve as an important case study in how income policies can play a critical role in mitigating economic downturn, and how, rather than jeopardising economic growth, they can drive economic recovery' (2011: 1). However, Vavi's endorsement of Brazil's income-led growth path was a cautious one: 'These major advances in Brazil', he went on to say, 'don't mean that it has solved its fundamental problems. It remains a capitalist society, with high levels of inequality, poverty, violence and landlessness' (COSATU, 2012: 2). COSATU's invocation of Lula's success is a pragmatic one: 'If workers in Brazil can do it, so can we', Vavi remarked at a round table on the Lula moment (Webster, 2014: 9). Lula achieved this transformation in people's lives by:

- Creating more and better jobs;
- Increasing the proportion of formal employment;
- Defending, together with the unions, a development model that distributes income;
- Ensuring improved labour law compliance while contributing to increased formality.

(COSATU, 2012: 3–4)

In his second term of office (2007–2010), Lula embarked on what Giorgio Romano Schutte, a former adviser to the presidential office, terms a 'neo-developmentalist approach' (2014: 21). This approach constituted a move away from the Washington Consensus: it was based on increasing the minimum wage as well as promoting policies that favoured job creation. The trigger for this 'virtuous circle' was the expansion of credit fuelled by an increase in commodity prices. But the real change came about, Schutte (2014: 21) argues, through the dynamics provoked in the internal market: increased incomes and credit for poor and lower-middle-class households created new demand for locally produced consumer goods, which in turn spurred more economic growth and more jobs.

While Romano Schutte emphasises Lula's policy innovation in his second term (2014: 19–26), Gay Seidman suggests that Lula's success also built on some innovations introduced by the Cardoso government in the 1990s – especially its emphasis on both macroeconomic stability and greatly improved tax collection (2014: 40).

Above all, however, Seidman emphasises the way Lula's government created a social safety net for Brazil's poor households, mainly by raising and enforcing minimum wages and expanding pension programmes for retired workers, especially in rural areas (2014: 41–42). 'Most importantly', Seidman suggests, 'Brazil has:

- dramatically increased the real value of Brazil's legal minimum wage;
- increased the value of pensions to older Brazilians, especially for poor rural workers who had long been excluded from formal pension schemes;
- linked the minimum wage to pensions;
- moved many more workers from precarious or temporary status into formally-regulated employment contracts.'

(2014: 42)

Further, she suggests, increased funding for Brazil's labour department has strengthened labour law enforcement, in ways that have improved both workers' conditions and small enterprises' productivity. She quotes Brazilian labour expert Roberto Pires, who concluded:

When the labour department works well with business and unions, compliance raises wages, ensures better health and safety for workers, and can also improve the sustainability of businesses. This is because inspectors can help employers find new strategies to improve productivity.

(Cited by Seidman, 2014: 44)

Ruy Braga, a Brazilian left academic, questions the notion of a Lula moment. Describing conditions for workers in São Paulo's call centres, Braga points to the limits of a 'precarious development model based on cheap and unskilled labour', arguing that 'the current development model has created access to social rights at the cost of low wages and precarious working conditions' (2014: 38).

In February 2013, when the roundtable was held, Braga's presentation seemed rather pessimistic. But only four months later, his critique of the Brazilian developmental model proved to be prescient, as a million Brazilians – including many young workers drawn from relatively educated but poor paid industries such as call centre workers – took to the streets in June and July.

While Brazil's 2013 street protests were triggered by increases in fares on public buses and trains, the protests soon took on a range of amorphous issues and diverse groups of social actors, including sections of the middle class. As two astute observers put it:

The dissatisfaction is quite real: urban transportation, health care provision, and public education are in shambles. Despite the progress of recent years, there is a sense that things are not as good as they should be – that more of the population should benefit from prosperity and growth, that services should be better, and that regular citizens are left out of decisions that matter to them.

(Teixeira and Baiocchi, 2013: 2)

The expansion of citizenship has benefited the very poor creating a social floor, but other observers agree with Braga that by dramatically expanding university education, the PT may have raised expectations further: the middle class want more (Saad Filho, 2013).

Whether Lula's successor Dilma Rousseff can win over the middle classes and push for progressive policy change remains to be seen. What is clear is that the massive expenditure on state-of-the-art football stadiums for the 2014 World Cup fuelled a sense of disillusionment, giving rise to demands for improved public services for all Brazilians.

Unresolved issues

While there has been widespread discussion in recent years of policy instruments such as conditional cash transfers (CCTs), the basic income grant (BIG) and increasing taxes on the rich including a financial transaction tax, a number of debates remained unresolved.

The first is around social policy. Armando Barrientos and David Hulme (2009) suggest that a 'quiet revolution' is taking place in social policy in the Global South. They argue:

> Social protection is now better grounded in development theory, and especially in an understanding of the factors preventing access to economic opportunity and leading to persistent poverty and vulnerability. The initially dominant conceptualisation of social protection as social risk management is being extended by approaches grounded in basic human need and capabilities.

(2009: 439)

In practice, this has involved the 'rapid up-scaling of programmes and policies that combine income transfers with basic services, employment guarantees or asset building' (Barrientos and Hulme, 2009: 451). Many of these programmes and policies have been dismissed by the left as neoliberal (Barchiesi, 2011; Satgar, 2012) and tokenistic (Bond, 2014). The question is whether, as Ferguson provocatively puts it:

> Can we on the left do what the right has, in recent decades, done so successfully, that is, to develop new modes and mechanisms of government? And (perhaps more provocatively) are the neoliberal 'arts of government' that have transformed the way that states work in so many places around the world inherently and necessarily conservative, or can they be put to different uses? To ask such questions requires us to be willing at least

to imagine the possibility of a truly progressive politics that would also draw on governmental mechanisms that we have become used to terming 'neoliberal'.

(2009: 173)

The growing institutionalisation of social assistance as a right through intense political struggle is the story in India, Brazil and South Africa. James Ferguson (2009: 167) suggests that this 'redefines groups in poverty as citizens (social citizens). A deepening of democracy follows'. The Mahatma Gandhi National Rural Employment Guarantee Scheme (MGNREGS) in India entitles every rural household to one hundred days of work per year. The budget for this imaginative guarantee of employment in 2006–2007 was 0.33 per cent of GDP (Chakraborty, 2007). The Community Work Programme (CWP) in South Africa provides two days a week of public employment, in a scheme similar to the MGNREGS in India.

These emerging welfare regimes are different from the European welfare state that was constructed around the equal contribution of three pillars: permanent full-time employment, a strong professional public service and the nuclear family. Instead, the emerging welfare regimes of the South are what Ian Gough (2004) calls informal security regimes. They rely on informal work as well as a variety of livelihood strategies such as street trading, the extended family, and the villages and communities within which they are embedded. However, these schemes merely temporarily alleviate the conditions of the poor; they do not enable the poor to escape poverty. Unlike the social assistance schemes in South Africa and India, the focus of Bolsa Família is not on providing jobs for the unemployed poor. Instead this scheme and its predecessors focus on a combination of income grant and means to enhance 'human capital' development. This means-tested cash benefit is attached to certain conditions, mainly school attendance and health checks for children.

The second unresolved issue is over the relationship between economic growth and the environment. Contrary to business, who argue that there is a trade-off between preservation of the environment and employment, commentators argue that 'green jobs' can mean more jobs. Devan Pillay and Vishwas Satgar describe this approach as the eco-socialist option, citing the 'revenge of nature' as the greatest danger facing humankind (Pearce, 2007).[1]

Satgar has been developing the notion of a 'solidarity economy' over the past 15 years through the creation of co-operatives and a non-governmental organization (NGO), the Co-operative and Policy Alternative Center (COPAC). This has evolved into building a locally controlled food system and promoting the notion of food sovereignty, which is popular in Bolivia, Venezuela and Brazil (Satgar, 2014a). Pillay, on the other hand, traces the roots of eco-socialism to Marx and demonstrates how the impact of the 'eco-logic of fossil capitalism' is reaching its 'natural limits' (2014: 160).

The initiative of the National Union of Metal Workers of South Africa (NUMSA) for socially owned renewable energy is an example of an attempt by a trade union to influence policies in the direction of renewable energy [Satgar, 2014b]. Their spokesperson announced:

> As a union we . . . are convinced of the potential of renewable energy – if structured properly – to address energy inequality and poverty and lead to alternative forms of industrialisation. As a union we have been calling for a socially-owned renewable energy sector where renewable energy generating companies will be cooperatives, municipal – owned farm winds, energy parastatals and energy community trusts.
>
> (Ngobese, 2013)

A third issue is the role of multinational corporations (MNCs) in reproducing inequality and the question of how to 'tame' corporate power. It is widely acknowledged that the US corporate model is driving global supply chains. In this context, Mark Anner and Jakir Hossain acknowledge the complexities in MNCs' structures and dynamics, and their potential role in transferring knowledge and upgrading productive structures. However, they add that MNCs may create jobs, but the benefits created by these jobs are not distributed evenly along global supply chains (see their chapter in this volume).

The Bangladesh accord entered into in May 2013 is an example of an attempt to 'tame' multinationals (IndustriALL, 2013). It was entered into after the tragic deaths of over a thousand garment workers who were crushed to death when the building they were working in collapsed. The agreement is legally binding and enables factory inspectors of factories to check whether workplaces are safe. It was signed by over 150 apparel corporations from twenty countries in Europe, North America, Asia and Australia. The signatories included two global trade unions, IndustriALL and UNI, as well as numerous Bangladeshi unions and numerous local unions. A number of international NGOs, such as the Clean Clothes Campaign, were witnesses to the Accord, with the ILO as the independent chair.

John Miller (2003) has challenged mainstream economists who defend sweatshops. Contrary to conventional wisdom, it has been estimated by the Worker Rights Commission that introducing a programme of safer working conditions would only increase the cost of the price of a garment from Bangladesh by 10 cent if spread over five years (Dudley, 2012). It is worth noting that these figures have even convinced Nobel Prize-winning economist Paul Krugman who in 1997 defended sweatshops but now believes that imposing 'modestly higher [safety] standards for all countries' can be achieved without undermining competitive position of the export industries in the developing world (Krugman, 2013).

A disturbing feature of the power of these large multinational corporations is their ability to evade the taxation laws of countries in the developing world. According to a report by a Washington, DC research and advocacy group, the developing world lost $6.6 trillion in illicit outflows between 2003 and 2012. In real terms, these flows increased at 9.4 per cent per annum. After a brief slowdown during the financial crisis, illicit outflows are once again on the rise, hitting a new peak of $991.2 billion in 2012 (Kar and Spanjers, 2014: 1). Furthermore, 'the $991.2 billion that flowed illicitly out of developing countries in 2012 was greater than the combined total of foreign direct investment and net official development assistance, which these economies received that year' (Kar and Spanjers, 2014: 2). The biggest problem is trade misinvoicing:

> Trade misinvoicing is possible due to the fact that trading partners write their own trade documents. Usually through export under-invoicing and import over-invoicing, corrupt government officials, other criminals, and commercial tax evaders are able to move assets easily out of countries and into tax havens, anonymous companies, and secret bank accounts.
>
> (Kar and Spanjers, 2014: 2)

A fourth unresolved issue is how to develop a coherent alternative to neoliberalism. On the one hand, we have seen a growing movement of young economists calling for universities worldwide to reform the way they teach economics. Founded in 2012, the Rethinking Economics network is demanding a broader range of approaches to economics than the dominant quantitative methods of the neoclassical school (Jones, 2014: 10). On the other hand, in thinking about an alternative to neoliberalism, labour will need to learn a lesson from the right, and how it successfully led a counter-revolution to Keynesian economics after the Second World War through the creation of think tanks (Cockett, 1994; Peck, 2010).

The process began, Cockett (1994) argues, in 1944 with the publication of Friedrich Hayek's *Road to Serfdom*, a critique of the state interventionism in the vogue at the time. It was a passionate plea for 'market freedom' and was largely ignored until Hayek met with Milton Friedman and established a think tank, the Mont Pelerin Society. In a similar analysis, Jamie Peck (2010) focuses on the complex way in which this group of right-wing intellectuals were able to gradually position themselves through their writings and professional work to enable neoliberalism to be adopted as a policy framework – first by Margaret Thatcher in 1979 and then Ronald Reagan in 1980.

The lesson we draw from this right-wing counter-revolution is to follow what Antonio Gramsci (1971: 229) called the 'war of position'. Confronted with societies in which capitalism is dominant and the bourgeoisie holds sway, the task of activist intellectuals is to create a counter-hegemony through the propagation of alternative ideas, norms and values. But change, Stephen Gill (2009: 98; cf. Gramsci, 1971: 175) maintains, within 'the limits of the possible'. The challenge is, therefore, not for just any type of reform, but reforms that connect the immediate concerns of the present with a long-term vision of the future.

John Saul captured this strategic point best through his distinction between 'mere reformism' and 'structural reform'. Structural reform links the present to the future through two key attributes. For any reform to be structural it must not be comfortably contained but must, instead, be part of 'an emerging and on-going project of structural transformation in a coherently left-ward direction'. Second, it 'must root itself in popular initiatives in such a way as to leave a residue of further empowerment' (Saul, 2011: 94).

A final key unresolved issue is an identification of the social forces that will align with the union movement to implement these policies. It is important to note that fundamental differences in the perceptions of the role of trade unions exist – differences that have divided the trade-union movement since unions first emerged in nineteenth-century Europe. The division lies between those who discern significant potential in trade union activity, and those who argue that such activity does not in itself facilitate (indeed, some hold that it may even inhibit) the transformation of capitalist society. Hyman (1972) refers to the former as the optimistic tradition and the latter as the pessimistic tradition. Could the surge of worker and popular resistance worldwide provide the global trade-union movement with an opportunity for the optimistic tradition to re-emerge? Could global labour take the lead in developing a broad coalition of social forces that combines 'initiatives for change from within government structures with support for developing wider, more radical sources of power outside' (Wainwright, 2013: 139)?

If the labour movement is to play this broader role, new forms of organisation, new sources of power and new forms of worker solidarity will need to be constructed. Ingemar Lindberg (2014: 136) suggests that 'union solidarity has a constitutive element of mutual self-interest'. He adds:

> Solidarity in a union context means moving from an individual self-interest, or the self-interest of a smaller group to a broader self-interest, perhaps of all metalworkers in Sweden or all dockworkers in Europe, perhaps eventually to the mutual self-interest of a global working class. But even so, union solidarity will always have an element of shared self-interest. Unions are interest-based organisations.
>
> (Ibid.)

A broader role for labour will require reviving and redefining the role of labour as a 'sword of justice' in the fight against inequality and not as a 'defender of vested interest' (Flanders, 1970: 15). Globalisation must be seen not only as a constraint, but also an opportunity for new forms of transnational networks to build a movement at various levels, worker to worker, worker to communities, union to union and between labour scholars.

Conclusion

A new global labour studies has emerged that is rich with ideas and policy proposals that could provide the basis for a broad alliance to overcome inequality. But it is important to be aware of the limits of trade unions. Trade unions are not the institutions that revolutionaries hope; neither are they the institutions that conservatives fear. As Tony Lane observed some forty years ago: 'Trade unions are not to be equated with socialism though, as an enduring expression of the irreconcilability of capital and labour, trade unions point in that direction. But point is all they do' (1974: 27).

The key challenge unions face in challenging inequality in the age of neoliberalism is to resolve the question of how to connect trade unions in the workplace with movements of the dispossessed. This requires creating an active civil society, committed to a struggle for an alternative to neoliberalism. As the newly appointed editors of the *Global Labour Journal* argue:

> In the contemporary era of multiple global crises, we no longer appear to be grappling with the question of whether labour should contest neoliberal capitalism through struggles against exploitation or commodification, but how labour should connect these two types of struggles. Likewise, the issue is no longer whether labour should embrace transnational forms of organisation, but how to do it.
>
> (Agarwala et al., 2015: 1)

Note

1 The 'revenge of nature' is the prediction that man-made global warming is on the verge of unleashing unstoppable planetary forces. Biological and geological monsters are being woken, and will consume us. We are, Pearce (2007) dramatically predicts, the last generation to live with any kind of climatic stability. In response, it has been argued that the metaphor is misleading as 'nature' is not a subject.

References

Agarwala, R., Chan, J., Gallas, A. and Scully, B. (2015) Editors' Introduction. *Global Labour Journal* 6(1): 1–3.

Barchiesi, F. (2011) *Precarious Liberation: Workers, the State and Contested Citizenship in Post-apartheid South Africa.* New York: State University Press.

Barrientos, A. and Hulme, D. (2009) *Social Protection for the Poor and Poorest in Developing Countries: Reflections on a Quiet Revolution.* Oxford: Development Studies.

Berg, J. and Tobin, S. (2011) Income-Led Growth as a Crisis Response: Lessons from Brazil. In *The Global Crisis: Causes, Responses and Challenges.* Geneva: International Labour Organization (ILO): 181–192.

Bond, P. (2014) 'Talk Left, Walk Right' in South African Social Policy – Tokenistic Extension of State Welfare Versus Bottom-Up Commoning of Services. *Transformation: Critical Perspectives on Southern Africa* 86: 48–77.

Braga, R. (2014) Brazil: Limits of a Precarious Developmental Model. In Webster, E. and Hurt, K. (eds) *A Lula Moment for South Africa: Lessons from Brazil.* Johannesburg: Chris Hani Institute: 33–38.

Chakraborty, P. (2007) Implementation of the National Rural Employment Guarantee Act in India: Spatial Dimensions and Fiscal Implications. Working Paper No. 505, Bard College, Levy Economics Institute.

Chun, J. (2012) The Power of the Powerless: New Schemas and Resources for Organizing Workers in Neoliberal Times. In Suzuki, A (ed.) *Trade Unions: Past, Present and Future.* Berlin: Peter Lang.

Cockett, R. (1994) *Thinking the Unthinkable: Think tanks and the Economic Counter Revolution, 1931–1983*. New York: HarperCollins.

COSATU (2012) *Political Report*. Johannesburg: COSATU.

Dudley, R. (2012) Bangladesh Fire Safety to Cost Retailers $3 Billion, Group Says. *Bloomberg Businessweek*, 10 December. Available at: www.bloomberg.com/news/articles/2012-12-10/bangladesh-safety-would-cost-retailers-3-billion-group-says (accessed 21 May 2015).

Dullien, S., Herr, H. and Kellermann, C. (2011) *Decent Capitalism: A Blueprint for Reforming our Economies*. London: Pluto Press.

Ferguson, J. (2009) The Uses of Neoliberalism. *Antipode* 49: 166–184.

Flanders, A. (1970) *Management and Unions*. London: Faber and Faber.

Gough, I. (2004) Welfare Regimes in Developing Contexts: A Global and Regional Analysis. In Gough, I. and Wood, G. (eds) *Insecurity and Welfare Regimes in Asia, Africa, and Latin America: Social Policy in Development Contexts*. Cambridge: Cambridge University Press: 15–48.

Gill, S. (2009) Pessimism of the Intelligence, Optimism of the Will: Reflections on Political Agency in the Age of 'Empire'. In Francese, J. (ed) *Perspectives on Gramsci: Politics, Culture and Social Theory*. Abingdon: Routledge: 97–109.

Gramsci, A. (1971) *Selections from the Prison Notebooks*. London: Lawrence & Wishart.

Herr, H., Ruoff, B. and Salas, C. (2014) Labour Markets, Wage Dispersion and Union Policies. *International Journal of Labour Research* 6(1): 57–72.

Horn, G. (2014) Inequality: A Price that Needs to be Paid. Panel One, 9th Global Labour University Conference 'Inequality Within and Among Nations: Causes, Effects and Responses', 15 May. Berlin: Friedrich Ebert Foundation.

Hyman, R. (1972) *Marxism and the Sociology of Trade Unionism*. London: Pluto Press.

IndustriALL (2013) *Accord on Building and Safety in Bangladesh*. Washington, DC: IndustriALL.

Jones, C. (2014) Change of Course. *Financial Times*, 17 May.

Kar, D. and Spanjers, J. (2014) *Illicit Financial Flows from Developing Countries: 2003–2012*. Washington, DC: Global Financial Integrity.

Krugman, P. (1997) In Praise of Cheap Labor: Bad Jobs at Bad Wages Are Better than No Jobs at All. *Slate*, 27 March.

Krugman, P. (2013) Safer Sweatshops, *New York Times*, 8 July.

Lane, T. (1974) *The Union Makes Us Strong*. London: Arrow Books.

Lindberg, I. (2014) Unions and Trade: What kind of Solidarity? *Globalizations* 11(1): 131–141.

Miller, J. (2003) Why Economists Are Wrong about Sweatshops and the Antisweatshop Movement. *Challenge* 46(1): 93–112.

Moretto, A. (2014) Brazil's Strategy Against Poverty: The Bolsa Familia and Brazil Sem Miseria. In Fakier, K and Ehmke, E. (eds) *Socio-Economic Insecurity in Emerging Economies: Building New Spaces*. London: Routledge: 160–173.

Ngobese, C. (2013) NUMSA's Response to Metal Pension Fund Investment in Renewable Energy. *Cosatu*, 25 April. Available at: www.cosatu.org.za/show.php?ID=7220 (accessed 30 April 2015).

Pearce, F. (2007) *The Last Generation: How Nature Will Take Her Revenge for Climate Change*. London: Random House Group.

Peck, J. (2010) *Constructions of Neo-liberal Reason*. Oxford: Oxford University Press.

Pickett, K. and Wilkinson, R. (2014) The World We Need. *International Journal of Labour Research* 6(1): 17–34.

Piketty, T. (2014) *Capital in the Twenty-First Century*. London: Harvard University Press.

Pillay, D. (2014) Marx and the Eco-Logic of Fossil Capitalism. In Williams, M. and Satgar, V. (eds) *Marxisms in the Twenty-First Century: Crisis, Critique and Struggle*. Johannesburg: Wits University Press: 143–164.

Saad Filho, A (2013) The Mass Protests in Brazil in June–July 2013. *The Bullet: Socialist Project*, 15 July.

Satgar, V. (2012) Beyond Marikana: The Post-Apartheid South African State. *Africa Spectrum* 47(2–3): 33–62.

Satgar, V. (2014a) *The Solidarity Economy Alternatives: Emerging theory and Practise*. Pietermaritzburg: University Kwa-Zulu Natal Press.

Satgar, V. (2014b) *Developing a Trade Union Approach to Climate Justice: The Campaign Strategy of the National Union of Metal Workers of South Africa (NUMSA)*. 9th Global Labour University Conference 'Inequality Within and Among Nations: Causes, Effects, and Responses', 15 May. Berlin: Friedrich Ebert Stiftung.

Saul, J. (2011) *Liberation Lite: The Roots of Recolonization in Southern Africa*. New Delhi: Three Essays Collective.

Schutte, G.R. (2014) Brazil: Ten Years of a Workers' Party Government. In Webster, E. and Hurt, K. (eds) *A Lula Moment for South Africa: Lessons from Brazil*. Johannesburg: Chris Hani Institute: 15–32.

Seidman, G. (2014) New Citizenship Rights for the Poor. In Webster, E. and Hurt, K. (eds) *A Lula Moment for South Africa: Lessons from Brazil*. Johannesburg: Chris Hani Institute: 39–46.

Teixeira, A.C. and Baiocchi, G. (2013) Who Speaks for Brazil's Streets. *Boston Review*, 31 July.

Wainwright, H. (2013) Transformative Power; Political Organization in Transition, *Socialist Register* 49: 137–158.

Webster, E. (2014) Introduction. In Webster, E. and Hurt, K. (eds) *A Lula Moment for South Africa: Lessons from Brazil*. Johannesburg: Chris Hani Institute: 7–14.

Xhafa, E. (2014) Trade Unions and Economic Inequality. *International Journal of Labour Research* 6(1): 35–55.

Part II
Drivers of inequality

5 Labour and financial markets as drivers of inequality

Hansjörg Herr and Bea Ruoff

Introduction

A more unequal income distribution is one of the key attributes of the type of capitalism that came to prevail from the 1970s onwards. The background for this development can be found in the regime change that took place in the 1970s and 1980s when finance-driven forms of capitalist development started to emerge (Dullien et al., 2011: 11ff.). In this chapter, we will focus on one aspect of finance-driven capitalism: the dynamics of market income distribution.

Income distribution primarily reflects the share of labour (wages) and the share of capital (profits) in annual income creation (functional income distribution). Profits include interest, dividends, rents, money income that is not redistributed and so on. In contrast, personal income distribution tells us how income is distributed between households. Households usually obtain incomes from both labour and capital. This implies that the market income distribution of households depends on functional income distribution and the dispersion of capital income and wage income. Furthermore, the state influences income distribution via taxes and transfer payments. Disposable income distribution reflects the impact of such redistributive measures. Last but not least, public goods provided by governments also impact distribution. However, our chapter mainly focuses on market income distribution.

Table 5.1 provides an overview of the development of personal income distribution in selected countries between the mid-1980s and early 2010s. In almost all Organisation of Economic Co-operation and Development (OECD) countries market income distribution and disposable income distribution changed substantially, but market income distribution on average changed more. Among the most unequal OECD countries in terms of market income distribution are the USA, the UK, Germany and Italy. Looking at disposable income distribution in the same year, the USA, the UK, Canada and Japan belong to the most unequal countries. In the BRICS countries, the development of market income distribution is diverging. While Brazil has been showing high but decreasing levels of inequality since the mid-1980s, India and especially Russia and China have moved from a low level of inequality in the mid-1980s to a substantially higher level in recent years. In South Africa, the level of inequality remained high – despite the fact that the Apartheid regime fell.

Table 5.1 Market and disposable incomes (Gini, selected countries)

Country	Market income					Disposable income				
	Year	Value	Year	Value	Change in %	Year	Value	Year	Value	Change in %
Selected OECD countries										
Canada	1985	0.395	2011	0.438	10.89	1985	0.293	2011	0.316	7.85
Denmark	1985	0.373	2011	0.431	15.55	1985	0.221	2011	0.253	14.48
France	1996	0.473	2011	0.512	8.25	1996	0.277	2011	0.309	11.55
Germany	1985	0.439	2011	0.506	15.26	1985	0.251	2011	0.293	16.73
UK	1985	0.469	2010	0.523	11.51	1985	0.309	2011	0.344	11.33
Italy	1984	0.387	2011	0.502	29.72	1984	0.291	2010	0.341	17.18
Japan	1985	0.345	2009	0.488	41.45	1985	0.304	2009	0.336	10.53
Netherlands	1985	0.473	2012	0.424	-10.36	1985	0.272	2012	0.278	2.21
Sweden	1983	0.404	2011	0.435	7.67	1983	0.198	2011	0.273	37.88
USA	1984	0.436	2011	0.508	16.51	1985	0.34	2011	0.389	14.41
OECD Average	1985	0.421	2011	0.474	12.59	1985	0.287	2011	0.312	8.71
BRICS countries										
Brazil	1981	0.579	2001	0.599	3.45	1981	0.579	2012	0.527	-8.98
China*	1980	0.320	1998	0.403	25.94	1981	0.291	2010	0.421	44.67
India	1975	0.405	2005	0.480	18.52	1983	0.311	2009	0.339	9.00
Russia	1988	0.264	2006	0.451	70.83	1988	0.238	2009	0.397	66.81
South Africa*	1990	0.630	1995	0.590	-6.35	1993	0.593	2011	0.650	9.61

Sources: Disposable income, OECD countries, BRICS: OECD (2014a); market income, BRICS: UNU-WIDER (2014), OECD countries: OECD (2014a).
Note: * More recent data not available.

Table 5.2 shows that whereas the bottom half of the population in Europe obtained 25 per cent of total income in 2010, in the USA the figure was only 20 per cent. In the same year, the top 10/1 per cent received 35/10 per cent in Europe and 50/20 per cent in the USA.

In order to explain personal market income distribution, we will look at functional income distribution, wage dispersion and profit dispersion. We will conclude our chapter with discussing policies aimed at combating inequality. We focus on the OECD, South Africa, India and Brazil.

Functional income distribution

Empirical development

Figure 5.1 reveals that the wage share declined in the OECD from over 60 per cent in the 1960s to less than 60 per cent after the Great Recession which hit the world economy in 2009. The decline was particularly strong in Japan and continental Europe. In the USA and other Anglo-Saxon countries, it was less pronounced. Because of the huge small enterprise and informal sector, wage shares in the Global South are usually much lower than in developed countries. In India, the wage share – around 30 per cent – has been stable from the 1990s onwards. In South Africa, it declined in the same period from around 50 per cent to 45 per cent. In Brazil, the wage share increased slightly and reached around 50 per cent in the early 2010s (ILO, 2012).[1]

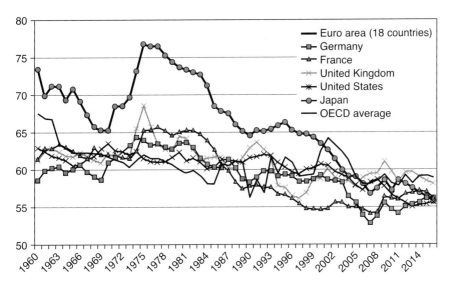

Figure 5.1 Adjusted wage share of selected countries (wages as a percentage of net domestic product at current market prices)

Source: AMECO (2014), authors' calculations.

Notes: Data for Germany refer to West Germany until 1990. Data for 2014 onwards are projections.

Table 5.2 Total Income Inequality (selected countries, different periods)

Shares in total income (labour and capital)	Low inequality (Scandinavian countries, 1970–1980)	Medium inequality (Europe, 2010)	High Inequality (USA, 2010; Europe 1910)	Very high inequality (USA, 2030?)
Top 10% (upper class)	**25%**	**35%**	**50%**	**60%**
Including the top 1% (dominant class)	7%	10%	20%	25%
Including the next 9% (well-to-do-class)	18%	25%	30%	35%
Middle 40% (middle class)	**45%**	**40%**	**30%**	**25%**
Bottom 50% (lower class)	**30%**	**25%**	**20%**	**15%**
Corresponding Gini coefficient	0.26	0.36	0.49	0.58

Note: Europe including the EU, Russia and the Ukraine (Piketty 2014: 62).
Source: Piketty (2014: 249, table 7.3)

The Keynesian explanation

To discuss functional income distribution, it is useful to show in an algebraic way the factors that determine the wage share. Income (Y) equals the wage sum (W) and the profit sum (Q). With profits as profit rate (q) multiplied with the stock of capital (K), it follows that $W = Y - q \cdot K$. Dividing both sides of the equation by Y and using the definition of the capital coefficient k as $\left(k = \dfrac{K}{Y} \right)$

provides the follow useful definition of the wage quota (W/Y): (equation 1)

$$\frac{K}{Y} = 1 - q \cdot k.$$

This suggests that, first of all, the wage share (and thus functional income distribution) depends on the profit rate.[2] The latter is influenced by the profit claims of institutions and actors in the financial system. The lowest profit rate is the long-term (money) interest rate. After all, firms investing with borrowed money have to earn enough to service their debt. In addition, there would be no incentive to invest if equity would earn less than the interest rate. However, the financial system demands more from an investment in capital. How much higher the general profit rate is than the long-term interest rate is not given by objective factors. It depends on the power of financial systems to set conventions concerning the profit rate.[3]

Falling wage shares can be explained, first of all, with reference to market deregulation, which increased the power of the financial system. The change in the corporate governance system from a stakeholder to a shareholder system from the 1980s onwards symbolises this development. In a stakeholder system, management has to find compromises between owners, unions, lenders and the local community and does not dare pay itself high wages (Galbraith, 1967). In a shareholder system, owners press management to increase short-term profits without limits. Pioneers for the new corporate governance philosophy were Alfred Rappaport (1999) as well as Jack Welch, CEO of General Electric. Management salaries became linked to profits to create clear incentives for profit-oriented management behaviour. These changes were only possible because unions were weakened by the deregulation of the financial system, the deregulation of labour markets and hostile governments, in particular in the Anglo-Saxon countries. When management in an increasing number of firms tries to increase profitability at any cost, and there is only limited resistance from unions, the profit rate will go up and the wage share down (Boyer, 2000; Zalewski and Whalen, 2010).

A second argument for increasing profit rates is provided by Kalecki (1954). He stresses the importance of monopoly power. If firms pursue a strategy of rent-seeking through the creation of monopolies, collude in cartels or enter non-price forms of competition (for example through the creation of brand names or opaque pricing systems), profits will go up. Stiglitz (2012) convincingly argues that in recent years rent-seeking behaviour especially in the financial system has become epidemic and has increased profits (Hein, 2014). The increasing power of the financial system and rent-seeking behaviour are interwoven and stimulate each other.

Third, the stock of capital striving for profit increases when the government privatises companies. The worldwide trend towards privatisation after the 1970s was the result of neoliberal strategies and recommendations by international financial institutions. In equation (1), privatisation increases the profit-seeking capital stock and thus the capital coefficient $\left(k = \dfrac{K}{Y} \right)$, which also means that the wage share is reduced.

Finally, there are various other reasons for a changing capital coefficient. New technologies can increase, decrease or, by chance, keep the capital coefficient unchanged. The so-called 'two Cambridges debate' showed that changes of the profit rate also influence the capital coefficient and thus the functional income distribution. A decrease (increase) of the profit rate can increase or decrease the capital coefficient.[4] It is an empirical question whether the capital coefficient increases or not. Piketty (2014: 113ff.) argues that the capital coefficient increased during the last decades, which reduces the wage share.

To sum up this section: there are many possible factors reducing the wage share. At the empirical level, it is difficult to keep the different factors apart. However, it appears that neoliberal policies of financialisation and privatisation together with widespread rent-seeking play a key role.

Wage dispersion

Empirical development

Among OECD member countries, wage dispersion differs greatly. Figure 5.2 shows the development of ratio of the 9th and the 1st decile (D9/D1) for selected countries from the 1970s until 2011. Italy shows the lowest level of wage dispersion – even if it has been increasing recently. In France and Japan, declining (D9/D1) ratios can be observed. All other countries show a distinctive upward trend with the USA and the UK showing both the highest level and increase.

Figure 5.3 shows D9/D5 ratio for selected countries. The USA and the UK show the highest figures as well as a considerable increase. France, Germany and Japan show lower figures and not much change. Figure 5.4 displays the (D5/D1) ratio. In France, and to a lesser extent in Japan and the UK, wage levels were compressed from below. This means that the lowest decile gained in relation to the middle. Wage dispersion at the bottom of the wage structure increased in Germany and especially in the USA.

If we look at wage dispersion in OECD countries, no uniform development can be detected. In the USA, for example, there are exploding low-wage and high-wage sectors. The German case is different: whereas the low-wage sector expanded considerably, the difference between the middle decile and the highest decile remained stable. In France, the wage structure was compressed from below.

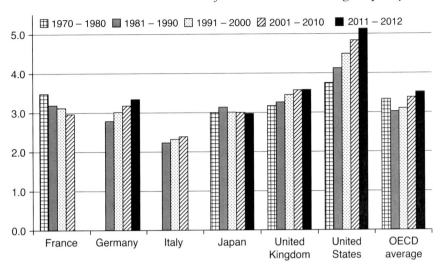

Figure 5.2 Wage dispersion (market income) in selected OECD countries – ninth decile to first decile (D9/D1)

Source: OECD (2014), authors' calculations.
Note: Calculations based on full-time earnings. The figure for Germany (1981–1990) is taken from OECD (2004: 141).

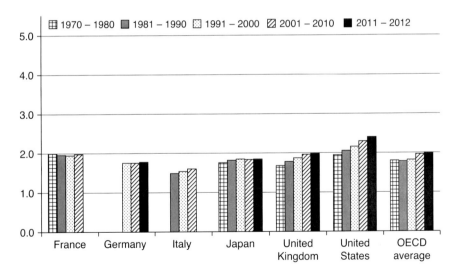

Figure 5.3 Wage dispersion (market income) for selected OECD countries – ninth decile to fifth decile (D9/D5)

Source: OECD (2014a), authors' calculations.
Note: Calculations based on full-time earnings.

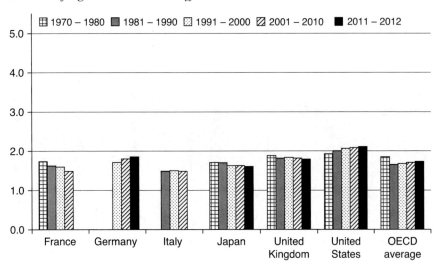

Figure 5.4 Wage dispersion (market income) for selected OECD countries – fifth decile
    to first decile (D5/D1)
Source: OECD (2014a), author's calculations.
Note: Calculations are based on full-time earnings.

Figure 5.5 shows that in the late 2000s, wage dispersion in developing countries was usually higher than in OECD countries – this is at least the case for
Brazil, India and South Africa. In the period between the early 1990s and late
2000s, wage dispersion increased dramatically in India. In South Africa, there
was a compression from below of wage levels. Only Brazil managed to notably
decrease the dispersion of wages over the whole wage structure even though the
(D9/D1) ratio is still very high.

Comparisons of deciles do not show the differentiation within deciles. In
particular, the entry level of wages of the 9th decile does not show the extent of
high wages. Following the calculations of Piketty (2014: 247), the top 10 per
cent wage earners in Europe in 2010 received 25 per cent of total labour income.
In the USA, the number was 35 per cent and is expected to increase further. The
top 1 per cent in Europe obtained 7 per cent of labour income; in the USA, the
figure was 12 per cent. The bottom 50 per cent of workers got a meagre 30 per
cent of total labour income in Europe and only 25 per cent in the USA. Especially
in Anglo-Saxon countries, the income of top wage earners exploded. However,
top wages increased much more than average wages also in other countries
(Piketty, 2014: 304ff.).

Summarising the empirical development of wage dispersion, it appears that
there are notable differences in the analysed countries. Between the 1970s and
2011, wage dispersion increased in 16 out of 23 of OECD countries. In contrast,
wage dispersion declined in France and Spain; South Korea, Belgium, Finland,
Japan and Ireland showed no substantial change (OECD, 2011: 88). In most

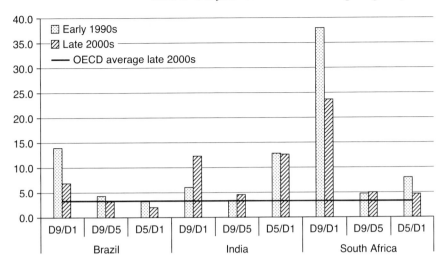

Figure 5.5 Wage dispersion (market income, selected BRICS countries)
Source: OECD (2011: 58), Divided We Stand, Figure 0.7.
Notes: The OECD average refers to the D9/D1 decile ratio of full-time wage workers across 23
OECD countries. Data for the early 1990s generally refer to 1993; data for late 2000s generally refer
to 2008. For Brazil and South Africa, the age group is 15–64, for India it is 15–59.

countries, top wage earners were the main winners of increasing wage dispersion
(OECD, 2011: 86). In Brazil and South Africa, wage dispersion decreased; in
India, it increased.

The neoclassical explanation

The neoclassical paradigm assumes, at the level of theory, that workers are
remunerated according to their marginal physical productivity. The latter decreases,
ceteris paribus, the more labour is employed.[5] A more productive labour force
will earn a higher real wage and the wage share will increase. A more productive
new technology can increase the physical productivity of capital and the profit
share. Thus, the marginal productivity theory of distribution argues that each
factor of production is remunerated according to its marginal productivity, which
in turn explains functional income distribution. It follows that the productivity
of workers has increased when their wages increase, no matter whether they are
nurses or professors. But what exactly is the marginal productivity of a nurse or
a professor? It is impossible in this framework to provide a definition of marginal
productivity that goes beyond its simple equation with wage levels.

Importantly, the marginal productivity theory of distribution turns out to be
inconsistent as soon as two capital goods exist that are produced with different
capital intensities. As has been mentioned, the value of the capital stock depends
on the distribution of income. Any alteration in distribution will lead to a change
in value. But the value of the capital stock has to be known to define marginal

productivity and income distribution. It is impossible to escape from this circle.[6] In sum, marginal productivity is used to explain both functional income distribution and wage dispersion in the neoclassical paradigm, but in neither case is the explanation provided convincing.

At the empirical level, the neoclassical story on the development of income distribution in recent years goes like this: Due to a specific type of technological development, capital productivity has been increasing faster than labour productivity. This development has increased capital's share of national income and has changed functional income distribution at the expense of the wage share. According to the neoclassical school, technological developments have also led to a substantial increase in the demand for highly skilled specialists. Due to a shortage of such specialists, real wages in this segment have exploded, reflecting their high marginal productivity. To make matters worse for low-skilled workers, technological change has created ample opportunities for carrying out low-skilled tasks with the help of machines. Furthermore, globalisation has shifted low-skilled jobs to developing countries, notably China, the new workshop of the world. In the Global North, the lower demand in the segment of low-skilled jobs under conditions of an unchanged labour supply has brought down equilibrium wages and has turned unskilled workers into a social group losing out in the process of globalisation. In addition, the argument goes, many routine jobs requiring a medium level of skills have been replaced thanks to the use of information technology (IT), for example in the area of accountancy. Usually, it is emphasised in this context, insufficient investment in education has intensified the trend of increasing wage dispersion (cf. Kierzenkowski and Koske, 2012).[7]

This story is only convincing at first glance. As we have shown, countries affected by the same technological developments and the same globalisation processes show highly diverging levels and developments of wage dispersion. It is wishful thinking to believe that marginal productivity explains the fact that the CEO-to-worker compensation ratio of the biggest 350 US companies increased from below 30 in the 1970s to over 200 in the 2010s (Mishel and Sabadish, 2013).

The Keynesian explanation

According to Keynesian thinking, it is not personal factors such as marginal productivity that explain wage dispersion. It is worthwhile quoting John Maynard Keynes:

> the struggle about money-wages primarily affects the distribution of the aggregate real wage between different labour-groups, and not its average amount per unit of employment which depends [. . .] on a different set of forces. The effect of combination on the part of a group of workers is to protect their relative real wage. The general level of real wages depends on the other forces of the economic system.
>
> (1936: 14)

Following Keynes, wage dispersion depends on the relative power of different groups of workers.

Certainly, supply and demand are contributing to the relative power of different groups of workers, but this has nothing to do with marginal productivities. Besides market forces, wage dispersion depends on country-specific labour-market institutions, wage bargaining systems, and the social and political situation of a country. The role of statutory minimum wages, union density, the strength of employers' associations, the existence of extension mechanisms making wage-bargaining outcomes binding for all companies in a sector, the regulation of working conditions, social conventions concerning justice and fair wages and other factors determine wage dispersion.

This leads to the next important difference between the neoclassical and Keynesian paradigm. 'Allocation, allocation! That is Moses and the prophets!' – this is the neoclassical credo. In the neoclassical world, almost all economic variables are determined together with the structure of relative prices, which in turn reflect the structure and volume of production and consumption, investment and savings, the dispersion of wages and the level of employment and income distribution. Aggregate demand plays no role in determining the volume of production and employment, only the supply side. Any intervention in the free play of markets disturbs the market-given structure of relative prices including the structure of wages, the argument goes, and will reduce welfare. For example, a compression of the wage structure from below via statutory minimum wages or wage bargaining will lead – so the argument goes – to unemployment.[8]

In the Keynesian paradigm, allocation and the level of output and employment are independent from each other. The structure of relative prices depends on wage dispersion, which not just reflects all the institutional and social factors mentioned above, but also functional income distribution, technologies and many other factors. The level of production and employment results from aggregate demand. The independence of allocation from the level of production and employment explains why there are countries with approximately the same unemployment rate that diverge hugely in terms of wage dispersion. The Scandinavian countries, for example, show both a low level of wage dispersion compared with the USA and a completely different structure of relative prices.

As has been demonstrated, wage dispersion has been increasing in most of the analysed countries since the 1970s. These are the main explanations for this trend (cf. Herr and Ruoff, 2014): In Europe, average union density has declined from 51.3 per cent in 1980 to 40.9 in 2013. France and Poland, for example, have lost more than a half of their union density since 1980 (OECD, 2014). In the OECD countries, union density on average declined from 33.7 per cent in 1970 to 16.7 in 2013 (OECD, 2014). There is a range of factors behind this decline. First, governments – in particular in the USA and the UK – turned hostile against unions after the 1970s. Second, in the OECD countries, sectors with low union density like the service sector gained in importance while well-organised branches of industry such as mining and metal lost out. In Brazil, union density underwent a sharp decline from 45 per cent in 1992 to 27.9 per cent in 2009. Since then, the figures have been relatively stable. In contrast, union density has increased substantially both in India (from 16.7 per cent in 1980 to 32.9 in 2005) and in South Africa (from 39.3 per cent in 1988 to 57.8 per cent in 1993) (ILO, 2014). There is wide empirical evidence of a close correlation of falling union density and increasing wage dispersion.[9]

Wage bargaining coverage did not change much in many OECD countries during the 1990s and 2000s. In some European countries, for example in France, there were almost universal legal extension mechanisms. In Austria, employers are forced by law to join employers' organisations, which means that they have to participate in industry-level bargaining. Continental Europe displays a high wage bargaining coverage with more than 76 per cent in 2006 – in spite of low union density in some countries. In Germany, wage-bargaining coverage has been declining recently. Overall, the USA and UK show a low wage-bargaining coverage, which is less than 25 per cent (Caju et al., 2008). The Great Recession with its long-term negative employment effects and the pressure to deregulate labour markets in the countries affected by the Eurozone crisis will certainly reduce this percentage.

The level of wage bargaining and wage co-ordination are of importance for explaining differences in wage dispersion between countries. Firm-based wage negotiations result in a higher wage dispersion within an industry and a country because usually they only consider the profitability and productivity of individual units (Soskice, 1990). Labour-market institutions that tend to lead to low wage dispersion are those ensuring that all firms and all industries pay wages that follow the medium-term, macroeconomic development of productivity. Vertical wage co-ordination among different firms within one industry and horizontal wage co-ordination between different industries seem to be the best mechanisms for keeping wage dispersion low. Wage co-ordination is facilitated through the existence of centralized wage bargaining. However, sector-level bargaining and, to a lesser extent, firm-level bargaining can be combined with a high degree of wage co-ordination. This is the case when important industries (as in Germany) or firms (as in Japan) kick-start the wage round by setting a standard for other industries or firms. Scandinavian countries are a good example for how vertical and horizontal wage co-ordination leads to a low level of wage dispersion (Caju et al., 2008; Soskice, 1990). In contrast, a high degree of wage dispersion can be found in South Africa, where the mining industry pays relatively high wages but wage negotiations are not co-ordinated with other industries. In Brazil, to give another example, a tendency can be observed in recent years of moving wage negotiations from the firm- to the industry-level and of facilitating wage co-ordination (Coleman, 2013; Leubolt, 2014a).

The deregulation of labour markets after the 1970s in the spirit of the dominating neoliberal regime substantially added to increasing wage dispersion in many countries. Precarious working conditions (temporary and part-time work, fixed-term contracts and low-income forms of self-employment) were made legal in many countries and became widespread. For example, whereas the degree of protection of regular workers tends to be similar among the OECD countries and has been relatively stable, it has declined drastically in 11 out of 23 countries (OECD, 2011: 101). Furthermore, neoliberal policies have fostered declining statutory minimum wages in many OECD countries (ILO, 2013). Overall, in many countries dual labour markets have emerged with precarious and low-paid jobs in one segment and secure forms of employment in the other. Under such conditions, regulation arbitrage is leading to outsourcing inside the country. In developing countries, a large segment of the labour market is offering nothing but precarious working conditions and low wages. In many cases, labour-market policies including minimum wages do not reach this segment. However, there are also countervailing developments. In Brazil, the newly elected President Lula da Silva increased substantially statutory minimum wages in 2002. As a result, wage dispersion was reduced (Leubolt, 2014b).

Importantly, the existence of a high-wage segment is adding to increasing wage dispersion. In the late 1970s and early 1980s – and against the backdrop of the emergence of a shareholder-value approach to corporate governance – wages including rewards from bonus payments increased to extreme heights, especially in the Anglo-Saxon countries. Hikes in income started in the financial sector and spread to all big companies. Conventional judgement of fairness changed and extraordinarily high wages became socially acceptable (Lemieux et al., 2009). But it was not only senior management that began to receive obscenely high salaries; today's incomes of professional athletes, movie and pop stars, lawyers, and so on, were not imaginable 30 years ago. Mass communication and the social role of celebrities are additional explanations for the existence of very high salaries (Rosen, 1981).

Profit and wealth dispersion

In this section, we discuss how income that does not stem from labour is distributed among households. If wealth would be evenly distributed among all households, profit dispersion would be small and would only depend on the different rates of return of different forms of wealth. Let us look first at the empirical level.

Developments at the empirical level

Wealth is distributed very unequally. Table 5.3 shows that with the exception of Scandinavia in the 1970s and 1980s, the bottom 50 per cent of the population tends to own only 5 per cent total wealth – that is, almost nothing. In Europe in 2010, the top 10/1 per cent owned 60/25 per cent of total wealth; in the USA in the same year, the top 10/1 per cent owned 70/35 per cent. Roughly from the beginning of the First World War, wealth concentration in Europe and the USA started to fall. In the 1970s, it started to increase again – slowly but steadily (Piketty, 2014: 347ff.). Against this backdrop, Piketty (2014: 514) points out that 'the risk of a drift towards oligarchy is real and gives little reason for optimism about where the United States is headed'. Similarly, Joseph Stiglitz (2011) speaks

Table 5.3 Wealth inequality (selected countries, different times)

Shares of different groups in total capital	Medium inequality (Scandinavian countries, 1970s–1980s)	Medium high inequality (Europe, 2010)	High inequality (USA, 2010)	Very high inequality (Europe, 1910)
Top 10% (upper class)	**50%**	**60%**	**70%**	**90%**
Including the top 1% (dominant class)	20%	25%	35%	50%
Including the next 9% (well-to-do-class)	30%	35%	35%	40%
Middle 40% (middle class)	**40%**	**35%**	**25%**	**5%**
Bottom 50% (lower class)	**10%**	**5%**	**5%**	**5%**
Corresponding Gini coefficient	0.58	0.67	0.73	0.85

Source: Piketty (2014: 248), table 7.2.
Note: Europe includes the EU, Russia and the Ukraine (Piketty 2014: 62).

about the danger of the USA drifting towards oligarchy and Paul Krugman (2009: 21ff.) refers to a plutocracy dominating the country.[10]

Theoretical explanation

The reasons for the concentration of wealth from the 1970s onwards are not a big secret. It represents the result of a cumulative market process. The higher the concentration of wealth, the faster it will increase. This is because the concentration of wealth is accompanied by the concentration of high income from profits in a small number of households, which allows them to accumulate wealth faster and faster. Without inheritance taxes or other taxes on high wealth or income, endogenous wealth concentration cannot be stopped (see Herr's chapter in this volume).

Importantly, market income distribution depends on a variety of factors. When we list policy recommendations below, it should be kept in mind that they have to be specified according to the situations in specific countries.

Summary and options for reform

Importantly, market income distribution depends on a variety of factors. When we list policy recommendations below, it should be kept in mind that they have to be specified according to the situations in specific countries.

Functional income distribution and profit dispersion

The concentration of profit flows to an increasingly smaller number of households shows why changes in functional income distribution without doubt have been contributing to a more unequal personal income distribution (Daudey and García-Peñalosa, 2007). In our opinion, there is a range of measures that can be taken to decrease the concentration of profit flows.

First of all, *financial markets* have to be regulated strictly in order to reduce the power of financial capital. Commercial banking should be focused on financing companies and private and public households. Banks should be required to hold more equity, while risk models should play only a limited role. Financial entities specialising in speculation should not to be funded by commercial banks. Financial products should be standardised, and financial innovations should only be allowed if they have social advantages (see Evans's chapter in this volume).

Second, the abolition of the shareholder-value system of corporate governance is needed for a variety of reasons, for example in order to avoid a one-sided focus on the interests of owners and to prevent short-sightedness and overly risky management decisions that tend to reduce long-term growth and productivity. Instead, a stakeholder system should be introduced. In this system, unions would be able to influence management decisions. For example, they could thwart management attempts to phase in low wages and precarious working conditions and block the payment of obscenely high salaries and bonuses to senior managers. Furthermore, unions could become involved in investment decisions, including the decision to use outsourcing strategies. In our view, such strategies should be prevented in cases where they are based on regulation arbitrage. They can be stopped more easily if as many employees as possible are covered by collective bargaining and horizontally co-ordinated wage bargaining.

Third, competition policy should be used to reduce rent-seeking. And governments can create transparency through standardisation and placing the obligation on institutions and firms to provide clear and full information on their assets and activities.

Last but not least, keeping natural monopolies like water, public transport and energy in public hands increases the wage share.

Wage dispersion

The increasing wage dispersion is the most important factor explaining changes in personal market income distribution. In most countries, wages account for more than 60 per cent of market income. This means that changes in wage dispersion have significant effects on the distribution of market income. The OECD calculated that between the mid-1980s and the mid-2000s, over 70 per cent of changes in disposable income distribution in member countries were caused by increasing wage dispersion.[11]

A variety of measures are needed to reduce wage dispersion (cf. Herr and Ruoff, 2014). First of all, making the union movement stronger constitutes a key element of any strategy aimed at reducing wage dispersion. Increases in union density are desirable, but even in countries with relatively low union density, the wage bargaining system can contribute to containing wage dispersions. In our view, firm-based wage bargaining should be phased out. Theoretically, pattern bargaining can work in a system with firm-based wage negotiations, but it is not very likely that this will have the desired effects. Industry-based bargaining is preferable, combined with extension mechanisms for the whole sector. The Austrian system of a compulsory membership of firms in employers' associations is an interesting approach, but of course there are other effective extension mechanisms. In any case, strong employers' organisations are needed; otherwise unions have no relevant counterpart for negotiations. In this context, it is important to be aware of the fact that industry-level negotiations do not automatically lead to low wage dispersion. In fact, it should be complemented by the vertical and horizontal co-ordination of wage development. Medium-term productivity at the macroeconomic level, among other factors, should be the yardstick for wage negotiations.

Second, statutory minimum wages are significant because they compress wage dispersion from below. Minimum wages below 40 per cent of median wages must be considered unexceptionally low. The best way to fix minimum wages is to establish a tripartite body responsible for setting them at the national level. The number of minimum wages within a country should be as small as possible and adjustment should happen on a yearly basis. However, the minimum wage should not be linked to increases in pensions and benefits in order to avoid budgetary constraints. Instead, the minimum wage should represent a percentage of average wages. This is preferable to basing it on a basket of goods, which can never be defined with the precision needed. Crucially, state institutions have to enforce minimum wages (cf. Benassi 2011; Herr and Kazandziska, 2011).

Third, labour-market regulations have to prevent precarious work and restrict the use of contractual models like temporary employment.[12]

Overall, we conclude that functional income distribution and wage dispersion cannot be explained with the help of the (marginal) productivities of the different factors of production and the skill levels of workers. Market income distribution depends on power relations and institutions. In fact, the increasing power of the financial system plays a key role in changing functional income distribution. Weaker trade unions, the deregulation of labour markets, the processes of outsourcing taking place both within and between countries, the explosion of precarious jobs, and changes in conventions and values are the key factors explaining the increasing wage dispersion. These developments *can* be changed *if* the radical free-market globalisation project that has been unfolding since the 1970s is abandoned and replaced with a project establishing a more regulated type of capitalism with a better protection of workers and increased power for labour.

Notes

1 For OECD countries, we use adjusted wage shares, for other countries unadjusted wage shares.
2 'The rate of profits [. . .] is [. . .] susceptible of being determined from outside the system of production, in particular by the level of the money rate of interest' (Sraffa, 1960: 33; cf. Keynes, 1936: Chapter 17 and 18). In the classical paradigm, real wages determine profits and the profit rate. This argument is not convincing. After all, actors in labour markets negotiate over nominal wages. It follows that changes in the nominal wage level do not change functional income distribution but only the price level (see Herr, 2009).
3 Long-term interest rates (i) depend on short-term interest rates (is), which are determined by the central bank, plus a risk premium (l). We obtain is $+ l = i$. If b expresses the power of institutions and agents in the financial system to force companies to realise a certain profit rate (q) above the interest rate, we get $q = i + b$ or $q = is + l + b$.
4 Given different industries with different capital intensities, any change in wages leads to unequal profit rates. These can only be equalised again if the whole structure of relative prices changes. One consequence of this analysis is that changes in distribution and technology alter the value of capital stock in an unpredictable way. This suggests that its value cannot be interpreted as the result of the historical values of past savings (Harcourt, 1972).
5 Increasing returns to scale can lead to increasing marginal productivities and must be excluded in this framework.
6 In addition, the marginal productivity theory of distribution only works under the condition of constant returns of scale. In the case of increasing returns to scale more income is distributed than produced. Decreasing returns to scale do not distribute all income to the factors of production (see Heine and Herr, 2013).

7 For a critique of this position, see Solga's chapter in this book.
8 An exception is a monopsony, that is, a situation where a company can influence wages but not the price of the products it produces.
9 See, for example, Koeniger et al. (2007).
10 The concentration in developing countries is difficult to measure due to a lack of data.
11 The OECD (2011: 240) includes in its analysis Australia, Canada, Finland, Germany, Israel, the Netherlands, Norway, Sweden, Switzerland, the UK and the US.
12 This chapter is focused on market income distribution. But it should be mentioned that tax policy plays an important role altering disposable income (see Godar et al.'s chapter in this volume). The same is true for state expenditure and the provision of public goods (see Hermann's chapter in this volume).

References

AMECO (2014) Annual Macro-Economic Database of the European Commission's Directorate General for Economic and Financial Affairs (DG ECFIN). Available at: http://ec.europa.eu/economy_finance/ameco/user/serie/SelectSerie.cfm (accessed 22 May 2015).

Benassi, C (2011) The Implementation of Minimum Wage: Challenges and Creative Solutions. Global Labour University working papers No. 12. Geneva: International Labour Organization (ILO).

Boyer, R. (2000) Is a Finance-Led Growth Regime a Viable Alternative to Fordism? A Preliminary Analysis. *Economy and Society* 29(1): 111–145.

Caju, P.D., Gautier, E., Momferatou, D. and Ward-Warmedinger, M. (2008) Institutional Features of Wage Bargaining in 23 European Countries, the US and Japan. European Central Bank Working Paper Series No. 974. Frankfurt: European Central Bank (ECB).

Coleman, N. (2013) Towards New Collective Bargaining, Wage and Social Protection Strategies in South Africa – Learning from the Brazilian Experience. Global Labour University Working Paper No. 17.

Daudey, E. and García-Peñalosa, C. (2007) The Personal and the Factor Distribution of Income in a Cross-Section of Counties. *Journal of Development Studies* 43(5): 812–829.

Dullien, S., Herr, H. and Kellermann, C. (2011) *Decent Capitalism: A Blueprint for Reforming our Economies*. London: Pluto Press.

Galbraith, J.K. (1967) *The New Industrial State*. Boston: Houghton Mifflin.

Harcourt, G. (1972) *Some Cambridge Controversies in the Theory of Capital*. Cambridge: Cambridge University Press.

Hein, E. (2014) *Distribution and Growth After Keynes: A Post-Keynesian Guide*. Cheltenham: Edward Elgar.

Heine, M. and Herr, H. (2013) *Volkswirtschaftslehre: Paradigmenorientierte Einführung in die Mikro und Makroökonomie*. 4th edition. Munich: Oldenburg Verlag.

Herr, H. (2009) The Labour Market in a Keynesian Economic Regime: Theoretical Debate and Empirical Findings. *Cambridge Journal of Economics* 33(5): 949–965.

Herr, H. and Kazandziska, M. (2011) *Principles of Minimum Wage Policy – Economics, Institutions and Recommendations*. Global University Working Paper No. 11.

Herr, H. and Ruoff, B. (2014) Wage Dispersion as Key Factor for Changing Personal Income Distribution. *Journal of Self-Governance and Management Economics* 2(3): 28–71.

ILO (2012) Data Collection on Wages and Income. Geneva: International Labour Organization (ILO). Available at: www.ilo.org/travail/areasofwork/wages-and-income/WCMS_142568/lang--en/index.htm (accessed 22 May 2015).

ILO (2013) Global Wage Report 2012/13: Wages and Equitable Growth. Geneva: International Labour Organization (ILO). Available at: www.ilo.org/global/research/global-reports/global-wage-report/2012/lang--en/index.htm (accessed 22 May 2015).

ILO (2014) *UNIONS 2014: Trade Union Membership Statistics Database.* Geneva: International Labour Organization (ILO). Available at: http://laborsta.ilo.org/applv8/data/TUM/UNIONS2014.xls (accessed 22 May 2015).

Kalecki, M. (1954) Theory of Economic Dynamics: An Essay on Cyclical and Long-Run Changes in Capitalist Economy. *Revue Économique* 5(5): 809–811.

Keynes, J.M. (1936) *The General Theory of Employment, Interest and Money.* Cambridge: Cambridge University Press.

Kierzenkowski, R. and Koske, I. (2012) Less Income Inequality and More Growth – Are they Compatible? Part 8. The Drivers of Labour Income Inequality – A Literature Review. OECD Economic Department Working Papers No. 931. Paris: OECD Publishing.

Krugman, P. (2009) *The Conscience of a Liberal.* New York: Norton.

Lemieux, T., MacLeod, W. and Parent, D. (2009) Performance Pay and Wage Inequality. *Quarterly Journal of Economics* 124(1): 1–49.

Leubolt, B. (2014a) Social Policies and Redistribution in South Africa. Global Labour University Working Paper No. 25.

Leubolt, B. (2014b) Social Policies and Redistribution in Brazil. Global Labour University Working Paper No. 26.

Mishel, L. and Sabadish, N. (2013) CEO Pay in 2012 Was Extraordinarily High Relative to Typical Workers and Other High Earners. Economic Policy Institute. Available at: www.epi.org/publication/ceo-pay-2012-extraordinarily-high/ (accessed 22 May 2015).

OECD (2004) Employment Outlook: Wage-Setting Institutions and Outcomes. Paris: OECD (Organisation for Economic Co-operation and Development). Available at: www.oecd-ilibrary.org/employment/oecd-employment-outlook-2004_empl_outlook-2004-en (accessed 22 May 2015).

OECD (2011) Divided We Stand: Why Inequality Keeps Rising. Paris: Organisation for Economic Co-operation and Development (OECD). Available at: http://dx.doi.org/10.1787/9789264119536-en (accessed 22 May 2015).

OECD (2014) *Income Distribution and Poverty Statistics.* Paris: Organisation for Economic Co-operation and Development (OECD).

Piketty, T. (2014) *Capital in the Twenty-First Century.* Cambridge, MA: Harvard University Press.

Rappaport, A. (1999) New Thinking on How to Link Executive Pay with Performance. *Harvard Business Review* 77(2): 91–101.

Rosen, S. (1981) The Economics of Superstars. *American Economic Review* 71(5): 845–858.

Soskice, D. (1990) Wage Determination: The Changing Role of Institutions in Advanced Industrialized Countries. *Oxford Review of Economic Policy* 6(4): 36–61.

Sraffa, P. (1960) *Production of Commodities by Means of Commodities.* Cambridge: Cambridge University Press.

Stiglitz, J. (2011) Of the 1%, by the 1%, for the 1%, *Vanity Fair.* May.

Stiglitz, J. (2012) *The Price of Inequality.* New York: W.W. Norton & Company.

Zalewski, D. and Whalen, C. (2010) Financialization and Income Inequality: A Post Keynesian Institutionalist Analysis. *Journal of Economic Issues* 44(3): 757–777.

6 The impact of the financial sector on inequality

A comparison of the USA, Brazil, Germany and India

Trevor Evans[1]

Introduction

The basis of a capitalist economy is that money is advanced to make more money. This rests on the production and distribution of commodities by industrial and commercial enterprises. However, banks and other financial institutions play a very special role in this process: they manage the advance and circulation of money. Since the emergence of capitalism, financiers have through their strategic position been able to appropriate an impressive share of the economic surplus. As a result of the influence that the financial sector has exerted over activities in the rest of the economy, it has played a major role in shaping the pattern of inequality under capitalism.

Modern Western banking originated in the city states of northern Italy from the twelfth century, first in Venice, then in Florence and Genoa. By the fifteenth century, the Medici bank had become the largest in Europe, generating enormous wealth – and political power – for its owners. In the seventeenth century, the locus of commercial capitalism shifted to the Netherlands and, as Italian bankers moved their business to Amsterdam, the city became for a time the richest in the world. Following the so-called Glorious Revolution of 1688 in Britain, the Dutch King William assumed the British crown. Bankers from Amsterdam followed the new king to London, and the City established itself in the eighteenth century as the leading commercial and financial centre in the world, creating the conditions for the industrial transformation which took off in the nineteenth century. In the late nineteenth century, giant banks emerged in Germany and, above all, in the United States, where banking dynasties became the centre of huge blocks of financial and economic power.[2]

In the aftermath of the 1929 financial crash, there was a major shift in the position of the financial sector. Governments sought to constrain the power of financial capital and, unusually, for several decades its wealth and influence was subject to strict limits, both in the USA and the other major capitalist states. Significantly, the initial post-war decades were characterised by a much reduced level of inequality. In many countries, governments introduced limits on interest rates and established programmes to direct the allocation of credit, while publically owned development banks were set up to promote investment. This approach was especially significant in many developing countries, where governments were struggling to overcome debilitating levels of poverty amongst wide sectors of the population.

In the 1970s, when the strong post-war rates of economic growth slowed, government regulation of the financial system began to be challenged by a resurgent school of neoclassical economists and, since the 1980s, the influence and impact of the financial sector has re-emerged with a vengeance in many countries. This chapter will outline the arguments used to justify the lifting of constraints on the financial sector and, drawing on a broadly Marxian and post-Keynesian approach, will examine the impact that this has had in the USA, Brazil, Germany and India. The chapter concludes with some brief suggestions for how the financial sector might be transformed so as to serve broader social interests.

'Unshackling' the financial sector

During the initial post-war years, financial policy was strongly influenced by the ideas of Keynesian economists. Following Keynes, it was believed that low interest rates were desirable to encourage investment and so to promote growth and employment. In the early 1970s, this approach was challenged by two neoclassical writers, Ronald McKinnon (1973) and Edward Shaw (1973), who were highly critical of the impact it had had in developing countries. They argued that limits on interest rates together with government-directed credit programs – policies that they characterised as 'financial repression' – had had a negative impact on economic development. According to McKinnon and Shaw, limits on interest rates had discouraged saving and, therefore, the funds available to finance investment. They argued that financial liberalisation would, by eliminating such controls, allow interest rates to rise. This would make it more attractive to postpone consumption and save, thereby increasing the funds available to invest in production and growth. McKinnon and Shaw also argued that higher interest rates would raise the quality of investments, by ensuring that only projects with a high rate of return would obtain financing.

McKinnon and Shaw's analysis won considerable influence in academic and policy-making circles, but was also subject to criticism on both theoretical and empirical grounds. A key theoretical criticism concerned the neoclassical argument that higher interest rates will lead to more savings. From a Keynesian or Marxian perspective, higher interest rates will tend to lead to lower investment, and this will have a negative effect on national income and thus on the level of national savings (Burkett and Dutt, 1991).

An influential empirical criticism of the policy of financial liberalisation by Carlos Días-Alejandro (1985) focused on the case of Chile after the military coup in 1973. Following the advice of the so-called Chicago boys (young economists who had studied at the University of Chicago under Milton Friedman and his monetarist colleagues), General Pinochet's military dictatorship had privatised the banking system, eliminated interest-rate controls and removed all restrictions on international capital transactions. Chilean banks borrowed extensively abroad in foreign currencies and lent the money at much higher interest rates to domestic firms. This was initially highly profitable, but the sharp rise in US interest rates in the early 1980s led to a flight of capital out of the country in 1981. This led to a sharp depreciation of the Chilean currency and, as a result, a marked rise in the real debt burden of domestic debtors who had borrowed in foreign currency. The banking system was faced with a collapse and the government, for all its neoliberal bravura, was obliged to take over large parts of the financial system.

The policy of financial liberalisation was also questioned by an influential survey of econometric evidence by Rudiger Dornbusch and Alejandro Reynoso (1989). This concluded that, while some studies did appear to lend support to the arguments for financial liberalisation, there were many others which did not, and that the strong claims made for policies of financial liberalisation were not supported by the evidence.

Significantly, Ronald McKinnon (1993) subsequently distanced himself from some of his earlier positions. Responding to developments in Chile and other countries, he argued that financial liberalisation should only be implemented in carefully timed phases, which should depend on the specific conditions in each country. He also accepted that savings did not respond to interest-rate rises in the way he had anticipated in his earlier work and even argued that, in view of 'information deficiencies', there was a case for governments to introduce ceilings on interest rates.

Although some mainstream academic economists adopted a somewhat more qualified approach, the international financial institutions continued for some time to be influenced by the more radical ideas advanced in support of financial liberalisation. In the 1980s, when the International Monetary Fund (IMF) first introduced so-called programme lending, one of the conditions that it attached to providing countries with loans was the introduction of policies of financial liberalisation. In 1989, the World Bank dedicated its annual development report to finance and development, strongly criticising state intervention in the financial system, and calling for policies of privatisation and deregulation. The World Bank has since stepped back from some of the more radical claims it made for the benefits of liberalisation, but the policies that it and other international institutions insist on have continued to stress the broad benefits of financial liberalisation.

The expansion of financial capital in the United States

The United States was one of the first developed capitalist countries to introduce widespread policies of financial liberalisation (for details see Sherman, 2009). The first step occurred in 1980 under the Carter government. In response to rising inflation, the legal ceiling on interest rates, which had been introduced in 1933, was abolished. It was, however, only after the Reagan government took office in 1981 that a more far-reaching process of financial liberalisation began.

One of the first steps, in 1982, was to lift many of the restrictions on the activities of savings and loans associations (S&Ls) – banks which enabled households to save and then receive a loan to buy a home. Liberalisation enabled ambitious S&Ls to branch out into many new areas of finance – including drilling for new oil and gas deposits – but resulted in huge losses at the end of the decade, and eventually required the government to intervene to the tune of some $150 billion to rescue the sector.

In 1987, the Reagan government did not renew the tenure of Paul Volcker as Chair of the Federal Reserve. Instead, it appointed Alan Greenspan, an active proponent of the policies of financial deregulation favoured by the government. Under Greenspan, the Fed adopted an increasingly flexible interpretation of the 1933 Bank Act, allowing banks to expand step by step into activities that had been prohibited. This process was continued after the Clinton government took office in 1993 and culminated in a new banking act in 1999. This ended the legal separation between commercial and investment banks, and opened the way for the re-emergence of giant financial conglomerates in the early years of the new century.

From the early 1980s, the position of the financial sector became increasingly important in the US economy. First, there was a strong growth of financial institutions. This included banks; institutional investors, in particular mutual funds that were increasingly used by the middle class to hold their savings; and, from the 1990s, smaller more speculative institutions including hedge funds and private equity funds. Second, there was a strong growth of financial markets, as financial institutions adopted much more active trading strategies in markets for bonds, shares and derivatives. Third, there was a rapid process of innovation, leading to the creation of ever more complex securities, including the notorious collateral debt obligations, whose failure sparked the crisis in 2007–2008.

Financial developments were accompanied by a weakening of US unions. In response to rising inflation, US interest rates were raised sharply at the end of 1979 and in the early 1980s. This 'monetarist offensive' resulted in a deep recession and, while inflation declined, it led to a sharp rise in unemployment. In what two mainstream economists have called the 'frightened worker' effect (Blinder and Yellon, 2001), many employees accepted declining real wages in the hope of hanging on to their jobs. The position of trade unions was also weakened by the policies of the Reagan government, which, on taking office in 1981, responded to a strike of air-traffic controllers by simply sacking the staff involved and installing military and other personal until new staff could be trained (McCartin, 2011).

The developments in the financial sector had a major impact on non-financial sectors of the US economy. Institutional investors began to take a far more active role in managing their share-holdings in non-financial companies. In what came to be known as promoting 'share-holder value', companies were pressured to give priority to raising profitability so as to increase the dividend payments accruing to shareholders and so to the value of shares. This in turn pressured companies to focus on activities with the highest rate of return, to eliminate less profitable units through closure or sale, and to outsource tasks to other companies in the USA or abroad which could complete tasks more cheaply – principally through lower wage costs. Companies were expected to announce regular projections for future profits and, if they failed to meet these, they were threatened with the prospect that investors would sell their shares. This would mean a fall in the share price, making a company vulnerable to a takeover bid, and the likelihood that senior management would lose their jobs. To avoid this, companies embarked on a major programme of 'buying back' their own shares, so as to push up their price. Within companies, internal funds were allocated between divisions according to which could achieve the highest rate of return, and non-financial companies themselves began to invest in financial assets, which appeared to offer especially attractive returns.

The persistent pressure to cut costs and the increasing allocation of funds to financial investments rather than investments in expanding production has, in the context of a weakened union movement, resulted in a notable increase in inequality in the USA since the early 1980s. According to figures published by the Economic Policy Institute, real wages for the lowest paid and for middle-income groups increased only very slightly between 1980 and 2007 (before the impact of the crisis), while the incomes of the top 20 per cent, and most especially the top 1 per cent, increased very strongly (Mishel et al., 2012). According to the widely cited figures published by Thomas Piketty and his colleagues (Piketty, 2014), the share of the top 1 per cent in US national income increased from 9 per cent in the later 1970s to around 20 per cent in 2007.

The growth of the financial sector in the USA since the 1980s has been associated with a major increase in inequality. Top incomes in the financial sector and in the non-financial sector have increased very markedly, while those of the majority of workers and middle-class employees have at best increased only very slightly. With wages failing to rise in line with productivity, the economy became dependent on credit-financed consumer spending (Rajan, 2011). But this was unsustainable. Much borrowing was linked to rising house prices and, when the bubble in house prices burst, the economy was faced by a major financial crisis in 2007–2008. As credit expansion collapsed, the US economy was hit by the deepest recession since the 1930s.

Promoting 'financial inclusion' in Brazil

Brazil has a financial system that is predominantly bank-centred with conglomerate groups based around large public and private banks.[3] Following the debt crisis in the early 1980s and the subsequent period of very high inflation, the government launched the so-called Real Plan in 1994. This was successful in ending the very high inflation and was followed by a series of measures directed at transforming the financial system. These included a policy of deregulation and a partial privatisation of the banks; at the same time, foreign banks were allowed to enter the country in order to promote greater competition. This was followed by a wave of mergers and takeovers amongst private, nationally owned banks in the later 1990s and early 2000s as they sought to consolidate their position in the new, more competitive environment. Public banks, however, continued to play an important role in the economy, and include two universal banks, the national development bank (BNDES) and two regional banks. The public banks are responsible for managing government-assigned credit programmes, which provide lending to households and businesses at reduced interest rates. In 2011, the public and nationally owned private banks each accounted for just over 40 per cent of the banking sector's assets while foreign-owned private banks accounted for just under 20 per cent.

Following the process of deregulation and privatisation, banks initially continued to favour purchases of short-term treasury bills, which were indexed to the central bank interest rate, and which, despite falling inflation, still paid interest rates that were high in real terms. As a result, between 1994 and 2002, the volume of bank-lending to households and business actually declined in relation to GDP. This changed in 2003, however, following the election of Lula da Silva, the Workers' Party candidate, as president, and the beginning of a period of strong economic growth. The economy benefited from a rising demand for its primary commodity exports, in particular from China, and there was a significant inflow of foreign capital which contributed to lower interest rates – although also to a higher exchange rate.

The Lula government raised the level of the minimum wage and of pensions, and introduced the Bolsa Família, a programme of cash grants for poor families which had a major impact on reducing poverty (Leubolt, 2014). There was also a significant expansion of bank lending to the business sector and an even larger expansion of lending to private households. Lending to households was encouraged by the government as part of a policy of 'financial inclusion' by which loans to workers and pensioners could be repaid through deductions from payrolls. This was intended to enable lower-income households to purchase homes and consumer durables, and it made a significant contribution to the growth of domestic demand.

The expansion of credit between 2003 and 2008 was led by the private national and foreign banks. However, from 2008 the growth of private lending declined sharply as a result of the impact of the international financial crisis, and the public banks increased their lending as part of the government's anti-cyclical policies. The national development bank (BNDES) in particular increased its lending strongly in 2009 in order to support investment, with around half the funding intended for micro-, small and medium enterprises. From 2011, as the impact of the crisis receded, private and foreign banks began to increase their lending again, while the public banks reduced the scale of their programmes.

The restructuring of the banking sector in the 1990s had led initially to a decline in employment, but this was partially recuperated after 2003, when new branches were set up to facilitate the policy of financial inclusion. Furthermore, bank staff benefited from the strong rise in real wages. More generally, the strong economic growth and the high price for export commodities resulted in a growth of employment and of real incomes, especially for low-income groups. In this way, despite the shift to a more liberalised financial system in the 1990s, the policies introduced by Workers' Party governments, including the policy of financial inclusion, contributed to an appreciable reduction in poverty in Brazil.

The longevity of Germany's bank-based system of finance

Germany has long had a bank-based financial system in which universal banks combine commercial and investment banking activities.[4] However, unlike the other major capitalist states, private profit-oriented banks account for only a minority of banking assets (38 per cent in 2012), and this sector is dominated by four large banks, of which one – Deutsche Bank – is far larger than the others. A notable feature of the German banking system is the existence of a significant publically owned sector (29 per cent of assets in 2012), which consists of local savings banks owned by city and county governments and regional *Landesbanken*. The savings banks are very efficient by standard banking criteria and, while they are required to avoid losses, their priority is not to make profits but rather to serve the businesses and households in the communities where they are based.[5] There is also a third sector of co-operative banks (12 per cent of assets in 2012) which includes local banks and two regional organisations.[6] Historically, the profit-oriented banks were mainly involved in providing finance for large companies, in which they also had significant shareholdings, while the savings and co-operative banks provided finance for Germany's important small and medium enterprise sector.

In the 1990s, the German government launched a series of financial reforms intended to promote a more active role for financial markets in the country (Financial Market Promotion Acts of 1990, 1995 and 1998). This had been strongly promoted since the mid-1980s by the big private banks, which were keen to develop their investment-banking activities. Their traditional lending business had declined as big companies had become largely self-financing. The growth of financial markets was also actively encouraged through a programme of privatising publically owned enterprises, including a major publicity campaign to encourage purchases of shares in the national telecommunications company. However, a limited extension of share ownership was sharply curtailed after stock-market prices collapsed in 2000 and many small investors made significant losses. A further encouragement for financial market activity was the elimination of a tax on capital gains in 2001, which made it attractive for banks to sell off their large share-holdings in non-financial companies, and a law introduced in 2002 which reduced the ability of companies to defend themselves against hostile takeovers.

Despite these initiatives, the size of the financial sector in Germany has not increased in relation to the size of the economy. While the financial sector's share of value-added has tended to fluctuate, the overall tendency since the turn of the century has been a slight decline. Since the early 1990s, earnings in the financial sector have increased roughly in line with economic growth and, while top incomes have increased considerably, this has been in line with the rise in top salaries in other sectors of the German economy. There has, however, been a significant change in the pattern of share-ownership. In the 1990s, the proportion of shares held by insurance companies and pension funds increased considerably, and, in both the 1990s and the following decade, there was an even stronger rise in the proportion of shares held by foreign investors, in particular institutional investors based in the USA and Britain. According to a survey of the managers of German firms, this resulted in greater attention being paid to meeting the demands of shareholders for higher returns (Achtleiter and Bassen, 2000). The new environment also led to a rise in the activities of hedge funds and private equity funds, which invested in companies and then put pressure on them to raise their returns, usually resulting in workers being laid off in order to reduce costs.

The German financial system has continued to be predominantly bank-based despite the attempts to promote more market-based forms of finance. There has not been a significant shift in the sources of company finance to more market-based instruments but the changes that were introduced have led to greater pressure on firms to raise their returns. Furthermore, the changes coincided with a marked deterioration in the distribution of income in Germany, most notably in the first decade of the 2000s, when real wages did not increase for most workers and the share of wages in national income declined. However, these developments affected all sectors of the economy, and not only those affected by the increased shareholdings of institutional investors or the intervention of hedge funds and private equity funds.

The main reason for the deterioration in the distribution of income in Germany does not appear to be due to developments in the financial system, but rather to labour-market reforms introduced by the Social Democratic–Green coalition government in the early 2000s. These measures involved curtailing the country's relatively generous unemployment insurance system. As a result, the prospect of becoming unemployed presented a much greater threat, and unions responded by shifting the main focus of their bargaining away from demands for higher wages to obtaining guarantees of job security for their members. This was accompanied by the expansion of employment in non-unionised sectors and a marked rise in the number of workers in low-paid jobs.[7]

Favouring the well-off in India

The Indian financial system consists of a so-called organised sector, made up of public and private banks together with various development institutions, and a large 'unorganised' informal sector, which provides loans to those without access to the formal sector, but at much higher rates of interest.[8]

The organised sector, much of which had been inherited from the former colonial regime, was subjected to a major transformation in 1969. The government nationalised 14 banks which, it argued, had focussed on the interests of big industrial firms and failed to provide finance in rural areas, thereby leaving large parts of the population without access to financial services. This was followed by the creation of two development banks, the Regional Rural Bank in 1975 and the National Bank for Agricultural and Rural Development in 1982. Under a 'lead bank' scheme, districts throughout the country were allotted to one of the public banks, and these were required to focus on priority lending programmes to agricultural producers and small industries. This scheme was subsequently broadened to include lending to retailers and to professional and self-employed people, and loans for housing and consumption. At the same time, banks were required to expand their network of rural branches and a central bank directive in 1980 required banks to direct 40 per cent of their loans to priority lending programmes.

In 1991, following a serious financial crisis, there was a major shift in the economic policies of the Indian government. As part of this, the financial system was subjected to a policy of liberalisation, the aim of which was to create a more efficient and competitive financial system that could strengthen growth. This was a response to concerns about the low returns of the public banks and revelations that programmes intended to reduce poverty had been used in part for loans to public functionaries. After the introduction of the liberalisation programme, the priority-lending targets were relaxed, there was a reduction in targeted lending to small farmers and businesses, and the number of rural bank branches declined. At the same time, the liberalisation programme resulted in the creation of new private banks and allowed foreign private banks to enter the country. However, both types of banks focussed their business on entrepreneurs and corporations rather than rural lending, which was viewed as unprofitable.

Despite this change in policy, the most important bank remained the publicly owned State Bank of India, which is by far the largest bank in the country, with more than 14,000 branches and some quarter of a million employees. In 2012, public-sector banks still accounted for 76 per cent of lending, while private banks were responsible for 19 per cent and foreign banks 5 per cent. Although the private and foreign banks pay higher salaries than the public-sector banks, jobs in the public sector are highly prized as a stable source of employment and are much sought after.

Following the introduction of policies of liberalisation in India in 1991, the economy for a time registered higher economic growth. However, there was also a very marked increase in inequality. Real wages for the great majority of the urban and rural poor did not increase, and the benefits of higher economic growth appear to have accrued overwhelmingly to the middle- and especially upper-income groups. Developments in the financial sector appear to have contributed to this increase in inequality by shifting the availability of credit to the business sector and the better-off, while leaving many rural and small-scale producers facing higher interest rates and less access to finance.[9]

A democratisation of Finance

The policies of financial liberalisation, argued for by neoclassical economists and strongly promoted by financial interests, have been introduced widely since the 1980s. In the countries considered here, financial liberalisation was associated with a marked increase in inequality in the USA and India; by contrast, while inequality has increased in Germany, this was primarily due to labour-market policies, and in Brazil inequality actually declined, at least for a time, due to the impact of the progressive redistributional policies introduced by Workers' Party governments.

Developments in the different countries indicate that there is a need for wide-ranging changes in the organisation of the financial sector in order to contribute to reducing inequality. The most appropriate policies will depend on the specific conditions in different countries, but the following guidelines could provide the basis for discussions about the measures which should be adopted.

Co-operative, municipal and other public banks should be actively promoted. These should ensure that access to financial services is available to both men and women and, of particular importance for developing countries, to residents of both urban and rural districts. The experience of Germany's local savings banks, where every citizen has a right to open an account, demonstrates how it is possible to ensure that all citizens have access to financial services.

Public development banks should ensure that financing is available for socially and environmentally desirable investment projects. Private banks have shown that they are often unwilling to provide longer-term finance for investment projects. By contrast, development banks in Brazil and Germany have made an important contribution to ensuring the availability of long-term finance for investment, including for small and medium enterprises.

The size of private commercial banks should be limited, and there should be strict provisions to ensure that they can fail without endangering the stability of the financial system. In the USA, where the situation is perhaps most acute, the biggest banks have emerged in an even more dominant position following the 2007–2008 crisis and, because of the potential danger to the rest of the financial system, the authorities are faced with the problem that they are 'too big to fail'.

The regulation of commercial banks, both public and private, should involve direct controls on the expansion of credit. This should be built around a democratically agreed investment and development strategy. The 'arm's length' regulation based solely on capital requirements and, more recently, liquidity requirements, allows banks to encourage forms of lending that appear highly profitable but which do not promote social development and which lead to a build-up of dangerously high levels of systemic risk.

There should be a clear separation between commercial banks, which accept deposits and make loans, and investment banks, which are active in capital markets. Such a separation contributed to greater financial stability in the US between 1933 and 1999 and, although such a legal division did not exist in Germany, big banks were not engaged in significant investment banking activity until the 1990s – after which Germany's biggest banks again built up highly dangerous positions, particularly in the USA.

Investment banks, together with hedge funds, private equity funds and all other 'shadow-banking' institutions should be subject to tight restraints. They should not be allowed to operate with borrowed money, and they should be required to open all their activities to public scrutiny. These institutions, operating with high levels of leverage (borrowed money), have exerted major pressure on firms to rationalise and cut jobs so as to raise short-term profitability, often at considerable long-term costs to firms' productive capacity, while extracting large amounts of profit for themselves.

All financial securities should be traded on public platforms. The growth of securities trading by financial institutions through private transactions that are not subject to public scrutiny has led to greater opacity and, in the event of one party failing, exposes the financial system to greater risk.

A transactions tax should be levied on all financial transactions, including foreign-exchange transactions. This should contribute to stabilising financial markets by reducing the volume of short-term speculative activity, as argued by Keynes (1973 [1936]) and, more recently, Tobin (1978). In the event that exchange-rate fluctuations threaten economic stability, or current account imbalances become too large, international capital flows should be restricted through the use of capital controls.

Financial derivatives should be standardised, and all new financial securities should be subject to testing by a public authority; financial institutions should have to prove that an instrument is of benefit to non-financial sectors of the economy before it is approved. The huge array of divergent derivatives is largely the result of attempts to obscure the specific characteristics of particular instruments, to make it difficult to compare one with another and to avoid tax payments.

The use of offshore financial centres should be prohibited. Their use only benefits rich individuals, institutional investors and transnational corporations who wish to evade taxation and national regulation.

The general aim of the proposals is to strengthen democratic control of the financial system, to make finance more widely available and to prevent financial institutions from building up dangerous positions which, in the event of failure, could threaten financial stability and impose extensive costs on society.

Notes

1 This chapter draws on Evans (1998), (2009) and especially (2014). I am grateful to Hansjörg Herr and Christoph Scherrer for their helpful comments on an earlier draft.
2 The shifting locus of financial power is described by Arrighi (1994); the classic study of concentrated financial power at the turn of the twentieth century is Hilferding (1981 [1919]).
3 This section is based on Prates and Ferreira (2013); see also Manzano et al.'s chapter in this volume.
4 This section is based on Detzer (2014).
5 Some of the *Landesbanken*, by contrast, made significant losses on investments in complex US securities in the period prior to the 2007–2008 financial crisis.
6 The remaining bank assets are mainly accounted for by specialized mortgage banks.
7 See Herr and Ruoff's chapter in this volume.
8 This section is based on Bedekar (2013).
9 See Ghosh's chapter in this volume.

References

Achtleiter, A. and Bassen, A. (2000) Entwicklungsstand des Shareholder-Value-Konzepts in Deutschland – Empirische Befunde. EBS Finance Group Working Paper 00–02. Oestrich-Winkel: EBS Finance Group.

Arrighi, G. (1994) *The Long Twentieth Century: Money, Power and the Origins of Our Times.* London: Verso.

Bedekar, A. (2013) An Overview of the Indian Financial System and Its Policy Implications for Financial Inequality. Paper prepared for the Global Labour University Combating Inequality Research Project.

Benassi, C. (2011) The Implementation of Minimum Wage: Challenges and Creative Solutions. Global Labour University Working Paper No. 12. Geneva: International Labour Organization (ILO).

Blinder, A. and Yellon, J. (2001) *The Fabulous Decade: Macroeconomic Lessons from the 1990s.* New York: Century Foundation.

Burkett, P. and Dutt, A.K. (1991) Interest Rate Policy, Effective Demand and Growth in LDCs. *International Review of Applied Economics* (5)2: 127–153.

Detzer, D. (2014) Inequality and the Financial System: The Case of Germany. Global Labour University Working Paper No. 23.

Días-Alejandro, C. (1985) Goodbye Financial Repression, Hello Financial Crash. *Journal of Development Economics* 19(1–2): 1–24.

Dornbusch, R. and Reynoso, A. (1989) Financial Factors in Economic Development. *American Economic Review* 79(2): 204–209.

Evans, T. (1998) *Liberalización financiera y capital bancario en América Central.* Managua: CRIES.

Evans, T. (2009) The 2003–2007 US Economic Expansion and the Limits of Finance-Led Capitalism. *Studies in Political Economy* 83: 33–59.

Evans, T. (2014) The Impact of Financial Liberalisation on Income Inequality. *International Journal of Labour Research* 6(1): 129–142.

Hilferding, R. (1981 [1919]) *Finance Capital: A Study of the Latest Phase of Capitalist Development.* London: Routledge.

Keynes, J.M. (1973 [1936]) *The General Theory of Employment, Interest and Money.* London: Macmillan.

Leubolt, B. (2014) Social Policies and Redistribution in Brazil. Global Labour University Working Paper No. 26.

McCartin, J. (2011) *Collision Course: Ronald Reagan, the Air Traffic Controllers, and the Strike that Changed America.* Oxford: Oxford University Press.

McKinnon, R. (1973) *Money and Capital in Economic Development.* Washington, DC: Brookings Institute.

McKinnon, R. (1993) *The Order of Economic Liberalization: Financial Control in the Transition to a Market Economy.* Baltimore, MD: Johns Hopkins University Press.

Mishel, L., Bivens, J., Gould, E. and Shierholz, H. (2012) *The State of Working America*, 12th edition. Washington, DC: Economic Policy Institute.

Piketty, T. (2014) *Capital in the Twenty-First Century.* Cambridge, MA: Harvard University Press.

Prates, D. and Ferreira, A. (2013) The Brazilian Credit Market: Recent Developments and the Impact on Inequality. Paper prepared for the Global Labour University Combating Inequality Research Project.

Rajan, R. (2011) *Fault Lines: How Hidden Fractures Still Threaten the World Economy*. Princeton, NJ: Princeton University Press.

Shaw, E. (1973) *Financial Deepening in Economic Development*. Oxford: Oxford University Press.

Sherman, M. (2009) *A Short History of Financial Deregulation in the United States*. Washington, DC: Centre for Economic and Policy Research.

Tobin, J. (1978) A Proposal for International Monetary Reform. *Eastern Economic Journal* 4(3–4): 153–159.

World Bank (1989) *World Development Report: Financial Systems for Economic Development*. Oxford: Oxford University Press.

7 Multinational corporations and economic inequality in the Global South

Causes, consequences and countermeasures in the Bangladeshi and Honduran apparel sector

Mark Anner and Jakir Hossain

Introduction

Multinational corporations (MNCs) have increasingly linked countries of the Global South to global markets through a complex mix of intra- and inter-organisational networks. For some, they hold the promise of providing host countries with new opportunities to accelerate growth and development. Yet, as will be illustrated in this chapter, MNCs also pose challenges to and impose constraints on economic management. Most notably, the distribution of gains for workers at the bottom relative to those at the top of MNC supply chains is often not equitable in terms of income relative to worker productivity nor does the treatment of workers often meet basic criteria for decent work.

The MNC-led growth model, which in most cases is incentivised by considerable tax and tariff breaks, raises the question as to whether workers in MNCs might even, under some circumstances, earn less than they might have done if tax and other incentives had been used to favour local businesses over foreign investors. Hence, the most relevant question is how the gains from MNC investment are distributed. As Amarty Sen eloquently has argued, 'even if the poor were to get just a little richer, this would not necessarily imply that [they] were getting a fair share of the potentially vast benefits of global economic interrelations' (2002: 5). Indeed, this chapter argues that recent MNC-led economic integration often has increased inequality.

The chapter first gives an overview of MNCs and explores the debate on MNCs and inequality. In the section that follows, we provide global data on shifts in MNCs' investment dynamics and patterns of inequality. The chapter then reviews current arguments and evidence on the dynamics of MNC investment in the Global South and its causal links to inequality through inherent power imbalances in global supply chains. Next we draw on the global apparel industries in Bangladesh and Honduras as important examples of the distributional consequences of MNCs operating in buyer-driven global supply chains and examine countermeasures, including domestic and transnational labour strategies.

MNCs and the inequality debate

The relationship between multinational investment and inequality has often been portrayed as paradoxical and inconclusive. Some scholars have suggested that, depending on regions or a country's level of development, an increasing flow of foreign direct investment (FDI) may reduce income inequality (Chintrakarn et al., 2010; Figini and Gorg, 2006; Pan-Long, 1995). The assumption behind these arguments is that MNCs bring greater technological know-how, pay high wages relative to domestic employers and provide governments with needed tax revenue that can be used to pay for social programmes.

Another common argument in favour of FDI is that it helps to create an industrial base in society (Markusen and Venables, 1997). The assumption of this argument is that FDI will complement local industry and thus help it to grow. However, in a model of FDI based on cost-cutting outsourcing in apparel global supply chains, it is also likely that foreign apparel manufacturers producing for export and receiving generous tax and tariff incentives can displace local manufacturers who do not receive the same incentives. In the process, higher-paying domestic manufacturing jobs are displaced by lower-paying apparel export jobs. In some cases, the displacement caused by the FDI-friendly market-oriented reforms can result in a net loss of manufacturing jobs (Anner, 2008).

A number of other studies also demonstrate that FDI inflows in general are conducive to higher levels of income inequality (Basu and Guariglia, 2007; te Velde, 2003). This view is reflected in the 'race to the bottom' argument, which sees capital increasingly able to play workers, communities and states off against one another, as it demands tax, regulation and wage concessions (Barnet and Müller, 1974). One account suggests that there is 'the climb to the top' when there is direct ownership by MNCs of their suppliers in which competition induces countries to provide high skill workers and quality infrastructure and a race to the bottom when there is MNC outsourcing through global supply chains that favour cost reductions (Mosley, 2011).

The view that we present here acknowledges the complexities in MNCs' structures and dynamics and their potential role in transferring knowledge and upgrading productive structures. However, without proper state policies – as well as strong local and international labour union organising, bargaining and leveraging through strike actions – MNCs may create jobs in the Global South, but the benefits they generate will not be equitably distributed along global supply chains. Due to inherent power imbalances in the relationship between lead firms and their suppliers and between suppliers and their workers, the benefits of MNC-driven growth accumulates to those at the top of the supply chains at the expense of those at the bottom – who disproportionately include women, migrant workers and other sectors of society that have faced historic exclusion.

MNCs and the Global South

There is little debate in the literature concerning the predominance of MNCs in the Global South; they have grown exponentially in recent decades. In 1998, there were approximately 63,459 MNCs that owned a total of 689,520 foreign affiliates (UNCTAD, 2000). A decade later, 82,000 MNCs controlled around 810,000 foreign affiliates (UNCTAD, 2009). The number of people employed in these affiliates rose substantially too, from approximately 21 million in 1990 to 72 million in 2012. Approximately 425,000 of these affiliates are located in countries of the Global South. Together, parent firms and their foreign affiliates account for about 28 per cent of global gross exports; value-added trade contributes at least 30 per cent to Global South countries' gross domestic product (GDP) on average, as compared with 18 per cent in developed countries (UNCTAD, 2013).

The patterns of value-added trade in global value chains are shaped to a significant extent by the investment decisions of MNCs. An estimated 35 per cent of world trade takes place within MNCs (intra-firm trade). MNCs with cross-border trade of inputs and outputs within their networks of affiliates and with contractual partners and arm's-length suppliers currently account for some 80 per cent of global trade in terms of gross exports (UNCTAD, 2013).

FDI is the mechanism through which MNCs establish affiliates and acquire or merge with existing firms located abroad. The last decade was characterised by record global FDI inflows with sharp fluctuations. In 2007, global flows reached close to $2 trillion and currently amount to around $1.35 trillion. While developed countries historically have accounted for the vast majority of FDI inflows, by 2012 for the first time, the value of FDI in developing economies surpassed that of developed economies, with FDI flows to the Global South reaching over $700 billion (see Figure 7.1) Of this, China accounts for $121 billion and Brazil accounts for $65 billion. The share going to least developed countries rose from $19 billion in 2010 to $26 billion in 2012 (UNCTAD, 2013).

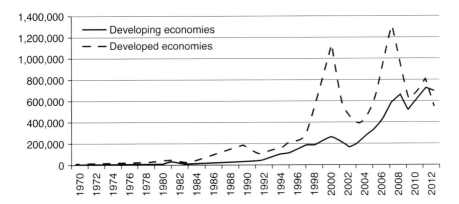

Figure 7.1 Inward foreign direct investment flows, annual US dollars (millions)
Source: World Development Indicators

MNCs and inequality dynamics

Inherent in most global supply chains are powerful imbalances between lead firms and their suppliers. Economists refer to this as supply chain monopsony, where a buyer can dictate production contract terms to multiple suppliers much in the way a monopolistic firm controls the price of goods for a large number of consumers. Since, for example, tens of thousands of suppliers compete for a contract with a major buyer such as Wal-Mart, Wal-Mart is largely able to set the price of production contracts for suppliers. This is because the bargaining power of suppliers relative to such large buyers is so limited.

This allows Wal-Mart to accumulate significant profits while suppliers are forced to look for numerous ways to keep costs down to remain economically active, which often includes keeping wages low and unions out (Anner, 2011a). Wal-Mart's monopsony power allowed it to bring in over $450 billion in revenue and almost $17 billion in profits in 2012 (see Figures 7.2 and 7.3).

Two additional examples help to illustrate the power imbalance within MNC controlled supply chains and the resulting impact on inequality. In the electronics sector it is sometimes argued that the power imbalance between suppliers and lead firms is not as significant as is suggested by critics (Locke et al., 2009). For example, while Apple had a revenue of $108.3 billion in 2011, its main supplier, Foxconn, had a revenue of $111.1 billion. Yet, subsequent research on gross profits reveals the true nature of the power imbalance. Apple's gross profits in 2011 were $43.8 billion compared with $2.2 billion for Foxconn (Locke, 2013). That is, while Apple's revenue was less than Foxconn's revenue, its profits were approximately 20 times greater.

In the running shoe industry, the impact of supply chain power imbalances can also be seen. For running shoes that sell for $100, the MNC share is $84 while the share going to labour in the shoe assembly plant is $2. Other segments of the supply chain receive the remaining $14 in value. Undoubtedly, costs for product design, advertising and distribution are included in the $84 share that goes to the lead firm. Yet, even while accounting for these expenses, Nike

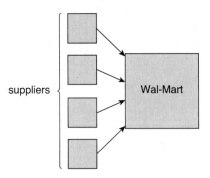

Figure 7.2 Monopsony

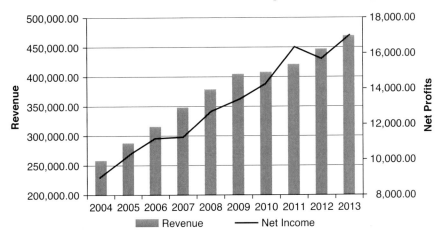

Figure 7.3 Wal-Mart: revenue and income ($ millions)
Source: Hoovers

Table 7.1 Revenue and profits of buyers and suppliers

	Revenue (Billions)	*Gross Profits*
Buyer		
HP	$127.20	$29.70
Apple	$108.30	$43.80
Supplier		
Foxconn	$111.10	$2.20
Flextronics	$30.30	$1.60

Source: Locke 2013; data correspond to 2011

accumulated approximately $2.5 billion in net profits in the fiscal year ending in May 2013 (see Figure 7.4). The link between high prices and low production worker wages in MNC-controlled supply chains has a resulted in steady decline in the price US MNCs paid per square meter for imported apparel, which dropped by 46.2 per cent between 1989 and 2011. During this same period the cost-savings to US consumers were on average 7.5 per cent, suggesting most of the savings resulting from supply chain power imbalances benefited MNCs, not consumers (Anner et al., 2013).

Multinationals and the apparel sector

The global apparel industry represents a case of a 'buyer-driven' global supply chain in that brands and retailers have the most significant control over supply chains dynamics (Gereffi, 1994). The greatest value-generating stages of the supply chain are intangible services that occur before and after the apparel production process. The most profits result not from production, but rather from

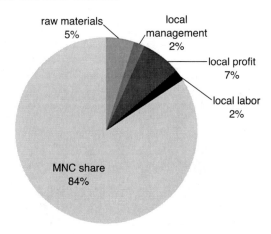

raw materials 5%
local management 2%
local profit 7%
local labor 2%
MNC share 84%

Figure 7.4 Supply chain breakdown $100 running shoes
Source: Tran, 2011

high-value research, design, sales and marketing (Gereffi and Memedovic, 2003). There is thus a double squeeze placed on production workers. First, the geographic fragmentation of the production and distribution de-links them from greater value generating activities. And second, the power imbalance at the point of production reducing their share of the gains even at this low tier in the value chain.

What is also notable about supply chains is that, if we look more deeply at employment relations dynamics in each segment, we can find core, contingent and informal workers. For example, in cotton (as in much of agriculture), there are permanent workers who work and maintain the field, contingent workers who are employed seasonally and informal (or undocumented) workers, including child labourers. Similarly in the production realm, there are core workers employed by the principal contractor, contingent workers employed either temporarily or by an unauthorised sub-contractor and there are informal workers who may include homeworkers. And in retail, there are permanent retail store workers, growing numbers of part-time and temporary retail store workers and informal sector workers who sell apparel in unauthorised shops or as street vendors (see Figure 7.5).

The extreme power imbalances in apparel global supply chains challenge the notion that MNCs always pay higher wages than domestic employers. A close examination of census data from El Salvador revealed that garment workers, who mostly worked for Asian-owned MNCs, earned less during their regular hours of work than workers in almost every other sector of the domestic economy. Indeed, El Salvador established a differentiated minimum wage system where the hourly minimum wage rate for the service sector was $1.01, $0.99 for non-apparel manufacturing and $0.85 for workers in export processing zones (EPZs). The law thus codifies the higher wages paid to workers for domestic firms relative to wages paid to apparel workers in MNCs (Anner, 2011a).

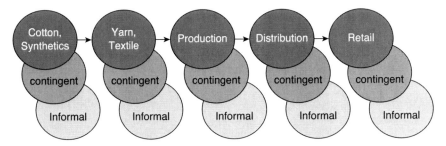

Figure 7.5 Embedded employment relation dynamics in value chains

Table 7.2 Wages and productivity; apparel manufacturing, 1998

	Hourly Compensation	*Productivity Index*	*% of U.S. Wages*
U.S.	8	100	100%
Dominican Republic	1.15	70	14%
Malaysia	1.15	65	14%
Mexico	0.85	70	11%
Guatemala	0.65	70	8%
Thailand	0.65	65	8%

Source: Kurt Salmon Associates, cited in *Business Week*, May 3, 1999, p. 189

Over time, this power imbalance plays out through the failure of wages to rise with productivity gains. This provides a clear illustration of what we mean when we indicate that workers do not receive a 'fair' share of the gains from economic globalisation. One of the earliest studies on the apparel sector revealed this gap between productivity and wage gains, highlighting the fallacy in the argument that workers' wages in developing countries will rise once they achieve productivity levels approaching those of developed countries. The studied revealed, for example, that workers in the Dominican Republic achieved 70 per cent of the productivity rate of US workers, but only 14 per cent of their compensation level. The gap between productivity and wages is even more dramatic in Malaysia, Mexico, Guatemala and Thailand (see Table 7.2).

This wage/productivity gap can also be seen over time between 1990 and 2009 in El Salvador where, in the manufacturing sector (which is dominated by the apparel export sector), labour productivity rose by 78.1 per cent while real-dollar unit labour costs declined by 60.8 per cent (Alvarado Zepeda, 2010).

Honduras: the impact of MNC apparel investment on inequality

Like many small developing countries, Honduras sought economic development through the promotion of EPZs largely dedicated to apparel exports for the US market. And while civil wars in the 1980s in El Salvador, Nicaragua and Guatemala kept most investors away, EPZ production boomed in Honduras partly due to the absence of a full-scale war and because infrastructural advantages, such as good highways and a deep water port, facilitated FDI growth. By the late 1990s, the value added from EPZ sector exports surpassed the combined value of coffee and banana exports, Honduras's most important products for overseas markets during the previous century. And by 2008, Honduras apparel exports to the US market had surpassed those of all other countries in Latin America, including Mexico.

MNC investors in the apparel sector have received millions of dollars in tax breaks, low-interest loans and tariff waivers (Anner, 2011b). The question is whether these generous government incentives contributed to development by increasing the income of the poor and by lowering inequality. Looking first at national poverty rates, we find that the percentage of the population living on less than $2 per day did indeed drop from 47.7 per cent in the 1990s to 35.5 per cent in the 2000s (2005 international prices). But if we look at value added in the EPZ sector from the 1990s to 2012, we see the most significant growth in the 1990s and then considerable volatility and a lower rate of growth in the 2000s. Where growth was far steadier and considerably more significant was in family remittances, particular in the 2000s, the period in which poverty declined. Remittances are funds received by Hondurans from family members living outside the country, mostly in the USA (see Figure 7.6).

Some 493,000 adult immigrants in the United States sent on average $5,231 to Honduras in 2012, which accounted for 15.7 per cent of GDP (Cohn et al., 2013). In contrast, in 2011 some 118,000 apparel export workers earned on average in straight wages $2,949 per year. These wages declined in real dollar terms over the course of the 2000s by 8.76 per cent and only covered 47 per cent of basic living expenses (WRC, 2013). That is, migrants contributed 6.4 times more to Honduran family income than apparel workers and remittances were distributed to a far greater number of Honduran families than apparel wages were distribution to Honduran families. Hence, what these data suggest is that

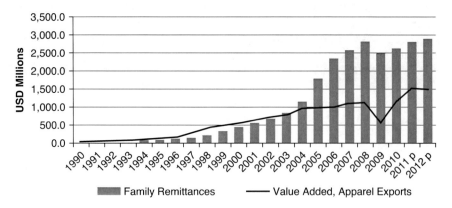

Figure 7.6 Honduras: apparel exports vs. remittances income
Source: Central Bank of Honduras; p = preliminary

the reduction in poverty in Honduras in the first decade of the twenty-first century is far more tied to remittances than to MNC investment.

Turning to the issue of inequality, if we look first at the most traditional indicator of inequality, the Gini Index, we see a rise from 0.546 to 0.580. Using another measure of inequality, we took the share of all income received by the lower 40 per cent of the society as a ratio of the share received by the upper 20 per cent. Here we see the bottom 40 per cent receiving an average of 17.33 per cent of what the top 20 per cent received in the 1990s. In the 2000s, the bottom 40 per cent received an average of only 13.36 per cent of what the top 20 per cent took home. Put differently, the top 20 per cent took home 5.8 times what the bottom 40 per cent received in the 1990s and 7.49 times what they took home in the 2000s (see Figure 7.7).

The reason why MNC investment has not reduced inequality is because Honduras remains stuck in a low-wage, low-skill form of production: wages have not kept pace with inflation and they cover less than half of a family's basic needs. Thus, not only were wages too low to provide decent human development, but over time living conditions declined. At the same time, labour laws and practices have worked to keep unions weak in the sector. While many of the laws were favourable to unionisation (much more so than, for example, US labour law), the underfunding of the Ministry of Labour resulted in an inability of the state to enforce its labour laws. In the years in which apparel production boomed, there were only 17 workplace inspectors for the entire San Pedro Sula region, the heart of EPZ production with hundreds of factories (Anner, 2008). Numerous anti-union practices became prevalent in the sector, such as employer blacklisting of workers who had tried to form unions (U.S. Department of State, 2009). And the ILO Committee of Experts on the Application of Conventions and Recommendations (CEACR) found that the penalties in the Honduran Labour Code for persons who interfere with the right to freedom of association were 'insufficient and a mere token'.[1]

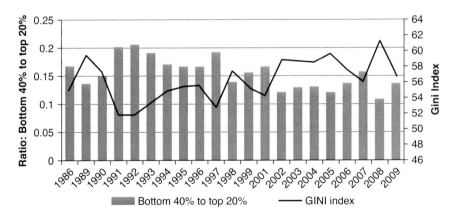

Figure 7.7 Inequality in Honduras
Source: World Development Indicators

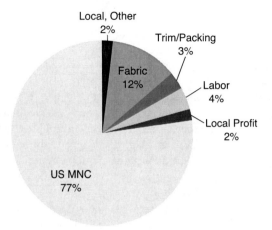

Figure 7.8 Honduras: cotton jeans cost structure
Source: O'Rourke Group Partners, 2011

There was an expectation that the relatively pro-labour agenda of President Manuel Zelaya (2006–2009) would stem some of the more systematic labour abuses. But those hopes diminished on 28 June 2009 when Zelaya and his ministers were removed from office in a coup d'état. Labour unionists who took to the streets in large protests were often subjected to repression. In the coup aftermath, Honduras became one of the most violent countries in the world and this climate of fear and intimidation has impacted on unionisation. The consequence of a weak state labour relations regime and of employer anti-union discrimination is a system in which MNC investment, rather than bringing benefits to workers and their families, results in the largest share of wealth generated going to the MNC in its home country. The dynamic can be seen by breaking down the cost structure of cotton jeans produced in Honduras. For these jeans, which sell in the United States for $37.91, apparel assembly workers take home $1.72, or 4 per cent of the sale price. In contrast, the share going to the MNC is $29.04, or 77 per cent (see Figure 7.8). A model based on such a skewed distribution of value can only deepen and not address the problem of inequality.

Addressing inequality in MNC supply chains through corporate campaigns[2]

Given the context of cost-squeezing pressures in the apparel global supply chain, weak local labour law enforcement and a fragmented labour movement, the range of countermeasures available to workers appears limited in the Honduran case. Yet in 2009, Honduran workers achieved perhaps their most significant success in defending workers' rights and significantly improving wages and working conditions at the country's largest private sector employer, Russell Athletic, a Fruit of the Loom/Warren Buffett apparel division. On 19 November 2009,

Russell accepted the re-hiring of 1,200 Honduran workers, recognised the workers' union and agreed to begin collective bargaining. This favourable outcome was the result of rigorous domestic organising and cross-border solidarity.

The campaign began in 2007 when management had dismissed 145 workers at the plants due to their union activity (WRC, 2008). The action motivated activists in the Global North, including student activists organised in United Students Against Sweatshops (USAS), to organise a campaign in co-ordination with Honduran unionists demanding Russell rehire the fired unionists. The worker–student alliance made sense for an additional reason: Russell was one of the largest producers of US collegiate apparel. This gave the students a source of economic leverage that they could exploit by demanding universities cut their contracts with Russell until the company demonstrated it respected internationally recognised workers' rights. US trade unionists also became involved in the campaign. Notably, the AFL–CIO's American Center for International Labor Solidarity provided support to the Honduran union and offered training activities.

The USAS protests escalated and the students organised three speaking tours of fired Russell unionists, which covered influential universities from the east to west coast of the United States. In December 2008, the University of Miami had become the first school to cut its contract with Russell. Later, other universities cut their ties, some soon after the workers visited their campuses. Eventually, major US universities terminated their licensing agreement with Russell.

USAS targeted not only Russell's collegiate consumers, but also non-collegiate business relations. For example, when USAS learned about Russell's subsidiary, Spalding, which had a long-standing relationship with the National Basketball Association (NBA), it went to the play-offs and hung a four-storey-high banner that denounced Russell's sweatshop practices and demanded the NBA terminate the deal. Activists also went to Russell's headquarters in Kentucky and travelled to Warren Buffett's home to express their discontent with the billionaire's investment in the company. Adding to the corporation's discomfort were USAS Twitter 'bombs' and Facebook 'wall attacks' that bombarded these social media sites with messages such as 'Did you know that Russell just closed a factory and illegally destroyed 1,800 jobs?' Russell responded by shutting down its Facebook wall.

On 17 November 2009, after years of union organising efforts and an intense one-year transnational campaign, Russell announced it would re-open the factory and re-hire all the fired unionists and dismissed workers. Russell also agreed to recognise the union, begin collective bargaining and adhere to a union neutrality clause for all of its other seven factories in Honduras (Hobbs, 2009; Russell Athletic, 2009).

It is important to note that the cross-border solidarity campaign would not have been successful without the persistent local activism of labour organisers in Honduras. This fits a pattern of cross-border campaigns in the region over the last 20 years. Research has shown that the most successful campaigns integrate strategic international activist pressure with local slowdowns, strikes and pressure on government offices. Campaigns that only had an international component failed to provide sustained improvements for workers (Anner, 2011b). What this indicates is that international solidarity can complement but cannot supplant good local organising and bargaining. When these two elements are well combined, as they were in the Russell campaign, the result is often stronger unions and improved wages and benefits, and thus one step in the direction of more equitable distribution of income in MNC controlled supply chains.

Bangladesh's apparel sector and the consequence to MNC investment

The impetus for the relocation of apparel industries to Bangladesh included the adoption of the Multi-Fibre Arrangement (MFA) in 1974, which regulated exports of textiles and clothing of the developing world through restraining the rate of export growth, along with an 'anti-surge' provision safeguarding sudden increases by a particular country to a specific market (Raffaeli, 1994). By capitalising on the opportunities offered by the MFA and pursuing favourable domestic policies to stimulate the sector, Bangladesh has turned into the second largest exporter of apparel in the global market after China and has held that position despite the termination of the MFA in 2004. The quota-based system helped Bangladesh gain a foothold in the global apparel industry, and low costs and scale allowed Bangladesh to continue to grow after the MFA phase-out.

This has happened within a relatively short period. The export earnings from apparel reached $21.5 billion in 2012–2013. The share of apparel in total merchandise exports has grown remarkably over the years; from a meagre 4 per cent of total merchandise exported in 1983–1984 to 2012–2013 when it captured more than 79 per cent of the share. For global brands that move from country to country in order to benefit from the cheapest labour costs, Bangladesh has been attractive, especially as wages have risen in China.

Foreign investment has played a central role in establishing the apparel industries in Bangladesh, with MNCs contracting production to locally owned firms, which now dominate the industry. The textile, garment and leather industry is prevalent in EPZs, accounting for one fifth of Bangladesh's total export value. While in 1984–1985 only 120,000 people were employed in the sector, three decades later the number reached four million. Noticeably, women represent over 80 per cent of the workforce.

Notwithstanding work opportunities, particularly for women, the integration of Bangladesh into the global apparel sector has produced several consequences leading to inequality (Titumir and Hossain, 2005). Bangladesh's manufacturing success continues to depend on the country having among the lowest labour costs in the world. The apparel sector minimum wage rates were set for years at around $39 per month, until they were increased in January 2014 to $68 following the local and global outrage at the Rana Plaza building collapse that killed over 1,100 workers. Yet, the race to the bottom in terms of wages and benefits continues. If one looks at the various components from the viewpoint of buyer/company,

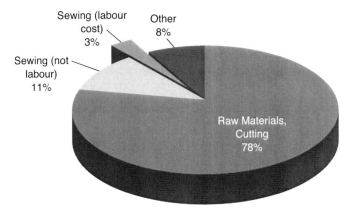

Figure 7.9 Cost breakdown of a polo shirt costing $3.46 to produce
Source: World Bank, 2013

wages only account for 0.5 to 1 per cent of the ultimate sale price of the product, while marketing and advertising as well as profit for the company amounts to over 25 per cent of the end sale price (Clean Clothes Campaign, 2008).

A value chain analysis of a polo shirt also reveals the small share of income that goes to labour (World Bank, 2013). The study shows that the unit cost of a shirt in Bangladesh is approximately $3.46, excluding margins and the cost of transportation to port. The highest cost component in polo shirt production is fabric in Bangladesh representing 77.5 per cent. The second-highest cost component is sewing and assembly, which represent 14.1 per cent of costs. Labour for the sewing and assembly stage is 23 per cent of total costs, which amounts to around 3 per cent of total production costs (see Figure 7.9).

Under the operation of subcontracting rules, workers are at the mercy of brokers who determine production and compensation procedures. This creates confusion for workers regarding to whom they should direct their demands. As a result, work and working conditions within the supply chain are often not properly addressed, as was seen by the November 2012 Tazreen Fashions factory fire and the April 2013 Rana Plaza building collapse.

Bangladesh's active policy stance towards greater FDI has led to the installation of differential labour standard regimes in the country. While most industrial workers, including those of the garment sector, are currently under the purview of the Bangladesh Labour Act (BLA) of 2006, coverage has not been extended to the workers in EPZs. The flexibility of labour laws, particularly the exemption from national legislation, is just one facet of the incentives given to foreign investors in EPZs. Differential labour law regimes in EPZs outline several phases for implementation with complicated and cumbersome procedures at each stage – posing significant restrictions and delays in relation to the workers' right to organise. In sum, the law continues to deny workers' full rights to organize in EPZs.

Addressing inequality in MNC supply chains in Bangladesh

There are a number of initiatives and campaigns currently in place to address the unequal power of MNCs in Bangladesh's apparel sector. These initiatives range from labour-law reform to labour solidarity campaigns for setting standards of enforcement and ensuring MNC supply chains improve work and working conditions through credible, transparent and legally binding mechanisms. Campaigns in the country and abroad are widespread, calling for brands and retailers not only to establish and implement responsible sourcing practices, but also to prohibit the use of factories in the supply chain that do not comply with applicable laws, regulations and internationally accepted labour standards. These standards include workers' right to unionise, negotiate legally binding collective agreements and refuse dangerous work, as well as ensuring that supply chain workers earn enough wages to lift themselves and their families out of poverty.

There is also a call for brands and retailers to go beyond voluntary social auditing practices that have failed to protect workers from deadly safety hazards and move towards legally binding workplace inspection and remediation processes. Brands and retailers in producing areas are being pressured to develop a multi-stakeholder engagement approach that entails the establishment of close links with workers' organisations.

The Accord on Fire and Building Safety in Bangladesh – a legally binding and enforceable agreement between companies and unions – provides a good countermeasure. It includes independent safety inspections with public reports; mandatory repairs and renovations to address all identified hazards; and a central role for workers and unions, which includes worker-led safety committees and union access to factories to educate workers on how they can protect their rights and their safety, such as their right to refuse unsafe work.[3] At its centre, there is the commitment by companies to work with their suppliers to secure financing, maintain orders and ensure factory renovations and repairs to make buildings in Bangladesh safe.

Trade unions and labour rights activists have demanded buyers provide full compensation to the victims. This demand indicates that the multinationals – despite their complex structural relationships across different national jurisdictions and contexts – are responsible for their own internal corporate network as well as other actors in the supply chain. Labour's second key demand relates to the call for all brands and retailers to sign on to the Bangladesh Safety Accord. As of May 2015, the Accord had been signed by over 200 apparel corporations from 20 countries, mostly in Europe.[4] Labour signatures included IndustriALL, which represents 50 million workers in 140 countries in the mining, energy and manufacturing sectors, and UNI, which represents over 20 million workers in the services sector. Several Bangladeshi unions also signed.

The European Clean Clothes Campaign, the US Workers' Rights Consortium, the International Labor Rights Forum and the Canadian Maquila Solidarity Network are witnesses to the Accord. The International Labour Organization (ILO) holds the position of an independent chair. However, key companies including

Gap, Wal-Mart and Arcadia Group have not signed the Accord. Wal-Mart, the single largest buyer from Bangladesh, and Gap announced their own rival safety plan, which is not legally binding, does not commit companies to pay for the cost of safe buildings and does not include major national and international trade unions (Appelbaum and Lichtenstein, 2014).

Trade unions have also been vocal about reforming the Bangladesh Labour Act and forcing the government to implement its commitments under the 'National Tripartite Plan of Action on Fire Safety and Structural Integrity'. Their goal is to increase the number of government inspectors, improve the quality of their training and expand the resources available to the inspectorate. Concerned by domestic and international pressure following the collapse of the Rana Plaza building and other tragedies, the Bangladesh parliament made 87 amendments to the 2006 Bangladesh Labour Act. However, the amendments fall short of providing enough protections for workers to organise trade unions and of bringing EPZ employment relations practices into conformity with international standards.[5] As a result, labour unions and their allies continue to organise and mobilise within Bangladesh for better laws, more effective enforcement and stronger unions with the goal of ensuring safer building and better wages. In the process, they hope to reduce historic patterns of inequality that have plagued apparel global supply chains.

Conclusion

MNC investment in developing countries has grown exponentially over the last several decades and now surpasses the value of MNC investment in developed countries. Some 80 per cent of world trade now takes place within supply chains. Their impact depends on the structure of their investment. Much of MNC investment now is not done directly by wholly owned enterprises but rather through networks of suppliers that are placed in competition with each other in bidding wars to see who can produce for MNCs at the lowest costs and in the shortest time. At the end of these hyper-competitive supply chains are the workers, who face low wages, reduced benefits, production speed-ups and an array of union-avoidance strategies. To keep costs even lower, many suppliers resort to contingent workers and informal sub-contracting networks, which often rely on women, child labour and marginalised sectors of society as the work becomes more precarious.

In examples from the apparel industry in Bangladesh and Honduras, we saw how different structures of supply chains often result in similar forms of downward pressure on workers. MNC supply chains in developing countries often work to keep wages low and unions out. But we also identified several effective countermeasures. In Bangladesh, in the aftermath of the Rana Plaza disaster, labour developed alliances with international solidarity groups and global union federations to pressure MNCs into signing the binding Accord on Fire and Building Safety. Through the accord, MNCs were forced to commit to paying a price to contractors that would allow for production in safe buildings. Labour also worked to reform national labour laws and to improve state building inspection capacity. In Honduras, workers of Russell, who faced dismissal because they had attempted to form a union and bargain with the company, also sought out cross-border alliances with student and labour groups in the United States. The campaign resulted in over 110 cut contracts for the company and forced it to re-hire the union leaders and members and to begin good faith bargaining. The results are significantly improved wages and benefits and the formation of what is becoming the largest private sector union in the country.

The challenge posed by inequality remains considerable. MNC investments generate massive amounts of wealth and they do provide jobs. Yet it is not enough to provide workers with low-wage jobs that come with temporary or part-time contracts; the wealth generated by MNCs needs to be more equitably shared down the supply chain. MNCs will not, on their own accord, commit to a more equitable distribution of their wealth. Rather, they will continue to operate according to market dictates and opportunities so long as there are no considerable countervailing forces. What these findings suggest is that alternatives to market mechanisms – such as better state policies, stronger international regulations and more effective local and international trade union strategies – are crucial for ensuring that the poor get a fair share of the vast benefits of global economic interrelations.

Notes

1 www.ilo.org/dyn/normlex/en/f?p=1000:13100:0::NO:13100:P13100_COMMENT_ ID:3085010 (accessed 23 April 2015).
2 This sections draws on Anner (2013).
3 Bangladesh Accord, 2013. The Accord on Fire and Building Safety in Bangladesh, www.bangladeshaccord.org/wp-content/uploads/2013/10/the_accord.pdf.
4 Bangladesh Accord, Signatories, http://bangladeshaccord.org/signatories/ (accessed 16 January 2015).
5 This observation is based on field research by Jakir Hossain in Bangladesh in January 2014.

References

Alvarado Zepeda, C.A. (2010) *Análisis de la Productividad y los Costos Laborales Unitarios Reales en El Salvador 1990–2009: Aspectos Teóricos e Implicaciones en la Competitividad.* San Salvador: Banco Central de Reserva de El Salvador.
Anner, M. (2008) Meeting the Challenges of Industrial Restructuring: Labor Reform and Enforcement in Latin America. *Latin American Politics and Society* 50(2): 33–65.
Anner, M. (2011a) The Impact of International Outsourcing on Unionization and Wages: Evidence from the Apparel Export Sector in Central America. *Industrial & Labor Relations Review* 64(2): 305–322.
Anner, M. (2011b) *Solidarity Transformed: Labor's Responses to Globalization and Crisis in Latin America.* Ithaca, NY: ILR Press, imprint of Cornell University Press.
Anner, M. (2013) Workers' Power in Global Value Chains: Fighting Sweatshop Practices at Russell, Nike and Knights Apparel. In Fairbrother, P., Hennebert, M.A. and

Lévesque, C. (eds) *Transnational Trade Unionism: Building Union Power*. New York: Routledge: 23–41.

Anner, M., Bair, J. and Blasi, J. (2013) Toward Joint Liability in Global Supply Chains: Addressing the Root Causes of Labor Violations in International Subcontracting Networks. *International Labor Law & Policy Journal* 35(1): 1–43.

Appelbaum, R. and Lichtenstein, N. (2014) An Accident in History. *New Labor Forum* 23: 58–65.

Barnet, R.J. and Müller, R.E. (1974) *Global Reach: The Power of the Multinational Corporations*. New York: Simon & Schuster.

Basu, P. and Guariglia, A. (2007) Foreign Direct Investment, Inequality, and Growth. *Journal of Macroeconomics* 29(4): 824–839.

Chintrakarn, P., Herzer, D. and Nunnenkamp, P. (2010) *FDI and Income Inequality: Evidence from a Panel of US States*. Kiel: Institute for the World Economy.

Clean Clothes Campaign (2008) Who Pays for Our Clothing from Lidl and KiK? Available at: www.cleanclothes.org/resources/national-cccs/lidl-kik-eng.pdf/view (accessed 23 April 2015).

Cohn, D., Gonzalez-Barrera, A. and Cuddington, D. (2013) *Remittances to Latin America Recover, But Not to Mexico*. Washington, DC: Pew Research Center.

Figini, P. and Gorg, H. (2006) Does Foreign Direct Investment Affect Wage Inequality? An Empirical Investigation. IZA Discussion Paper No. 2336. Bonn: Institute for the Study of Labour (IZA).

Gereffi, G. (1994) The Organization of Buyer-Driven Global Commodity Chains: How U.S. Retailers Shape Overseas Production Networks. In Gereffi, G. and Korzeniewicz, M. (eds) *Commodity Chains and Global Capitalism*. Westport, CT: Praeger: 95–122.

Gereffi, G. and Memedovic, O. (2003) *The Global Apparel Value Chain: What Prospects for Upgrading for Developing Countries*. Vienna: United Nations Industrial Development Organization.

Hobbs, S.R. (2009) Russell Factory in Honduras to Reopen in Response to U.S. Student Pressure. *BNA Daily Labor Report*, 23 November.

Locke, R. (2013) *The Promise and Limits of Private Power: Promoting Labor Standards in a Global Economy*. New York: Cambridge University Press.

Locke, R., Amengual, M. and Mangla, A. (2009) Virtue out of Necessity? Compliance, Commitment, and the Improvement of Labor Conditions in Global Supply Chains. *Politics & Society* 37(3): 319–351.

Markusen, J.R. and Venables, A.J. (1997) Foreign Direct Investment as a Catalyst for Industrial Development. Working Paper No. 6241. Cambridge: National Bureau of Economic Research.

Mosley, L. (2011) *Labor Rights and Multinational Production*. New York: Cambridge University Press.

O'Rourke Group Partners (2011) Benchmarking the Competitiveness of Nicaragua's Apparel Industry. Ventnor: O'Rourke Group Partners, LLC.

Pan-Long, T. (1995) Foreign Direct Investment and Income Inequality: Further Evidence. *World Development* 23(3): 469–483.

Raffaeli, M. (1994) Some Considerations on the Multi-Fibre Arrangement: Past, Present, and Future. In Meyanathan, S.D. (ed.) *Managing Restructuring in the Textile and Garment Subsector: Examples from Asia*. Washington, DC: World Bank: 59–84.

Russell Athletic (2009) *Athletic and Union Announce Landmark Agreement*. Available at: www.workersrights.org/linkeddocs/RussellPublicAnnouncement.pdf (accessed 23 April 2015).

Sen, A. (2002) How to Judge Globalism. *American Prospect* 13(1): 1–14.

te Velde, D.W. (2003) *Foreign Direct Investment and Income Inequality in Latin America: Experiences and Policy Implications*. London: Overseas Development Institute.

Titumir, R.A.M. and Hossain, J. (2005) *Bangladesh: Poverty and Employment: Lost in the Queue?* Dhaka: Unnayan Onneshan.

Tran, A.N. (2011) The Vietnam Case: Workers Versus the Global Supply Chain. *Harvard International Review* 33(2): 60–65.

UNCTAD (2000) *World Investment Report: Cross Border Mergers and Acquisitions and Development*. Geneva: United Nations Conference on Trade and Development (UNCTAD).

UNCTAD (2009) *World Investment Report: Transnational Corporations, Agricultural Production and Development*. Geneva: United Nations Conference on Trade and Development (UNCTAD).

UNCTAD (2013) *World Investment Report: Global Value Chains: Investment and Trade for Development*. Geneva: United Nations Conference on Trade and Development (UNCTAD).

U.S. Department of State (2009) *2008 Human Rights Report: Honduras*. Washington, DC: U.S. Department of State, Bureau of Democracy, Human Rights, and Labor.

World Bank (2013) *Bangladesh: Diagnostic Trade Integration Study*. Washington, DC: World Bank.

WRC (2008) *Worker Rights Consortium Assessment: Jerzees de Honduras (Russell Corporation) Findings and Recommendations*. Washington, DC: Worker Rights Consortium.

WRC (2013) *Global Wage Trends for Apparel Workers, 2001–2011*. Washington, DC: Worker Rights Consortium.

Part III
Country case studies

8 The US economy

Explaining stagnation and why it will persist

Thomas I. Palley

The crisis and the resilience of neoliberal economic orthodoxy

The financial crisis that erupted in 2008 challenged the foundations of orthodox economic theory and policy. At its outset, orthodox economists were stunned into silence as evidenced by their inability to answer the Queen of England's simple question to the faculty of the London School of Economics as to why no one foresaw the crisis (Greenhill, 2008). Six years later, orthodoxy has fought back and largely succeeded in blocking change of thought and policy. The result has been economic stagnation.

This chapter examines the major competing interpretations of the economic crisis in the USA and explains the rebound of neoliberal orthodoxy. It shows how US policy-makers acted to stabilise and save the economy, but failed to change the underlying neoliberal economic policy model. That failure explains the emergence of stagnation in the US economy – and stagnation is likely to endure. Current economic conditions in the USA smack of the mid-1990s. The 1990s expansion proved unsustainable and so will the current modest expansion. However, this time it is unlikely to be followed by a financial crisis because of the balance sheet cleaning that took place during the last crisis.

Competing explanations of the crisis

The Great Recession, which began in December 2007 and included the financial crisis of 2008, was the deepest economic downturn in the USA since the Second World War. The depth of the downturn is captured in Table 8.1, which shows the decline in GDP and the peak unemployment rate. The recession has the longest duration and the decline in GDP is the largest. The peak unemployment rate was slightly below the peak rate of the recession of 1981–1982. However, this ignores the fact that the labour-force participation rate fell in the Great Recession (i.e. people left the labour force and were not counted as unemployed) whereas it increased in the recession of 1981–1982 (i.e. people entered the labour force and were counted as unemployed).[1]

Table 8.2 provides data on the per cent decline in private-sector employment from business cycle peak to trough. The 7.6 per cent loss of private sector jobs

Table 8.1 Alternative measures of the depth of US recessions

Recession dates	Duration	GDP decline (peak to trough)	Peak unemployment rate
Nov 1948–Oct 1949	11 months	–1.7%	7.9% (Oct 1949)
July 1953–May 1954	10 months	–2.6%	6.1% (Sep 1954)
Aug 1957–April 1958	8 months	–3.7%	7.5% (July 1958)
April 1960–Feb 1961	10 months	–1.6%	7.1% (May 1961)
Dec 1969–Nov 1970	11 months	–0.6%	6.1% (Dec 1970)
Nov 1973–March 1975	16 months	–3.2%	9.0% (May 1975)
Jan 1980–July 1980	6 months	–2.2%	7.8% (July 1980)
July 1981–Nov 1982	16 months	–2.7%	10.8% (Nov 1982)
July 1990–March 1991	8 months	–1.4%	7.8% (June 1992)
March 2001–Nov 2001	8 months	–0.3%	6.3% (June 2003)
Dec 2007–June 2009	18 months	–4.3%	10.0% (Oct 2009)

Source: http://en.wikipedia.org/wiki/List_of_recessions_in_the_United_States

Table 8.2 US private employment cycles, peak to trough

Peak date (year – month)	Employment peak (thousands)	Trough date (year – month)	Employment trough (thousands)	Percent change	Peak to trough duration (months)
1948 – 9	39,489	1949 – 7	37,568	–4.8%	10
1953 – 7	43,813	1954 – 8	41,933	–4.3%	13
1957 – 4	45,537	1958 – 6	42,986	–5.5%	14
1960 – 4	46,278	1961 – 2	44,969	–2.8%	10
1969 – 12	58,763	1970 – 11	57,579	–2.0%	11
1974 – 6	64,363	1975 – 4	61,668	–4.2%	10
1980 – 3	74,695	1980 – 7	73,414	–1.7%	4
1981 – 8	75,448	1982 – 12	72,775	–3.4%	16
1990 – 4	91,274	1992 – 2	89,557	–1.9%	22
2000 – 12	111,681	2003 – 7	108,231	–3.1%	31
2008 – 1	115,610	2010 – 2	106,772	–7.6%	25

Source: Bureau of Labor statistics and author's calculations.

in the Great Recession dwarfs other recessions, providing another measure of its depth and confirming its extreme nature.

Broadly speaking, there exist three competing perspectives on the crisis (Palley, 2012a). Perspective one is the hardcore-neoliberal position which can be labelled the *government failure hypothesis*. In the USA, it is identified with the Republican Party and with the economics departments of Stanford University, the University of Chicago and the University of Minnesota. Perspective two is the softcore-neoliberal position, which can be labelled the *market failure hypothesis*. It is identified with the Obama administration, the Wall Street and Silicon Valley wing of the Democratic Party, and economics departments such as those at Massachusetts Institute of Technology, Yale and Princeton. In Europe it is identified with 'Third Way' politics. Perspective three is the progressive position, which is rooted in Keynesian economics and can be labelled the *destruction of shared prosperity hypothesis*. It is identified with the New Deal wing of the Democratic Party and the labour movement, but it has no standing within major economics departments owing to their suppression of alternatives to economic orthodoxy.

The hardcore-neoliberal *government failure* argument is that the crisis is rooted in the US housing bubble and its bust. The claim is that the bubble was due to excessively prolonged loose monetary policy and politically motivated government intervention in the housing market aimed at increasing ownership. With regard to monetary policy, the Federal Reserve pushed interest rates too low for too long following the recession of 2001. With regard to the housing market, government intervention via the Community Reinvestment Act and Fannie Mae and Freddie Mac drove up house prices and encouraged home-ownership beyond people's means.

The softcore-neoliberal *market failure* argument is that the crisis is due to inadequate financial sector regulation. First, regulators allowed excessive risk-taking by banks. Second, regulators allowed perverse incentive pay structures within banks that encouraged management to engage in 'loan pushing' rather than 'sound lending'. Third, regulators pushed both deregulation and self-regulation too far. Together, these failures contributed to financial misallocation, including misallocation of foreign savings provided through the trade deficit, which led to financial crisis. The crisis in turn deepened an ordinary recession, transforming it into the Great Recession, which could have become the second Great Depression if there had not been the extraordinary policy interventions of 2008–2009.

The Keynesian *destruction of shared prosperity* argument is that the crisis is rooted in the neoliberal economic paradigm that has guided economic policy for the past 30 years. An important feature of the argument is that, though the USA is the epicentre of the crisis, all countries are implicated as they all participated in the adoption of a systemically flawed policy paradigm. That paradigm infected finance via inadequate regulation, enabling financial excess that led to the financial crisis of 2008. However, financial excess is just one element of the crisis, and the full explanation is far deeper than just financial market regulatory failure.

According to the Keynesian *destruction of shared prosperity* hypothesis, the deep cause is generalised economic policy failure rooted in the flawed neoliberal economic paradigm that was adopted in the late 1970s and early 1980s. For the 1945–1975 period, the US economy was characterised by a 'virtuous circle' Keynesian growth model built on full employment and wage growth tied to productivity growth. This model is illustrated in Figure 8.1, and its logic was as follows: Productivity growth drove wage growth, which in turn fuelled demand growth and created full employment. That provided an incentive for investment, which drove further productivity growth and supported higher wages. This model held in the USA and, subject to local modifications, it also held throughout the global economy – in Western Europe, Canada, Japan, Mexico, Brazil and Argentina.

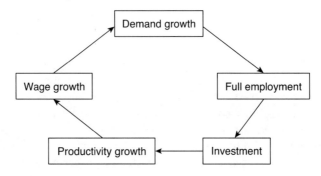

Figure 8.1 The 1945–75 virtuous circle Keynesian growth model

After 1980 the virtuous-circle Keynesian growth-model was replaced by a neoliberal growth-model. The reasons for the change are a complex mix of economic, political and sociological reasons that are beyond the scope of the current paper. The key changes wrought by the new model were: (1) abandonment of the commitment to full employment and the adoption of commitment to very low inflation, and (2) severing of the link between wages and productivity growth. Together, these changes created a new economic dynamic. Before 1980, wages were the engine of US demand growth. After 1980, debt and asset price inflation became the engine.

The new economic model was rooted in neoliberal economic thought. Its principal effects were to weaken the position of workers, strengthen the position of corporations, and unleash financial markets to serve the interests of financial and business elites. As illustrated in Figure 8.2, the new model can be described as a neoliberal policy box that fences workers in and pressures them from all sides. On the left-hand side, the corporate model of globalisation put workers in international competition via global production networks that were supported by free trade agreements and capital mobility. On the right-hand side, the 'small' government agenda attacked the legitimacy of government and pushed persistently for deregulation regardless of dangers. From below, the labour-market flexibility agenda attacked unions and labour-market supports such as the minimum wage, unemployment benefits, employment protections and employee rights. From

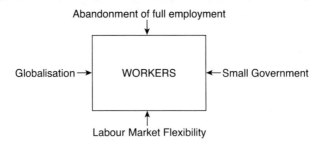

Figure 8.2 The neoliberal policy box

above, policy-makers abandoned the commitment to full employment – a development that was reflected in the rise of inflation targeting and the move towards independent central banks influenced by financial interests.

Corporate globalisation is a key feature. Not only did it exert downward inward pressures on economies via import competition and the threat of job offshoring, it also provided the architecture binding economies together. Thus, globalisation reconfigured global production by transferring manufacturing from the USA and Europe to emerging market economies. This new global division of labour was then supported by having US consumers serve as the global economy's buyer of first and last resort, which explains the US trade deficit and the global imbalances problem. This new global division of labour inevitably created large trade deficits that also contributed to weakening the aggregate demand (AD) generation process by causing a haemorrhage of spending on imports (Palley, 2015).

An important feature of the Keynesian hypothesis is that the neoliberal policy box was implemented on a global basis, in both the North and the South. As in the USA, there was also a structural break in policy regime in both Europe and Latin America. In Latin America , the International Monetary Fund (IMF) and the World Bank played an important role as they used the economic distress created by the 1980s debt crisis to push neoliberal policy. They did so by making financial assistance conditional on adopting such policies. This global diffusion multiplied the impact of the turn to neoliberal economic policy, and it explains why the Washington Consensus enforced by the IMF and the World Bank has been so significant. It also explains why stagnation has taken on a global dimension.

The role of finance in the neoliberal model

Owing to the extraordinarily deep and damaging nature of the financial crisis of 2008, financial market excess has been a dominant focus of explanations of the Great Recession. Within the *neoliberal government failure* hypothesis, the excess is attributed to ill-advised government intervention and Federal Reserve interest-rate policy. Within the *neoliberal market failure* hypothesis, it is attributed to ill-advised deregulation and failure to modernise regulation. According to the Keynesian *destruction of shared prosperity* hypothesis neither of those interpretations grasps the true significance of finance. The government failure hypothesis is empirically unsupportable (Palley, 2012a: Chapter 6), while the market failure hypothesis has some truth but also misses the true role of finance.

That role is illustrated in Figure 8.3 which shows that finance performed two roles in the neoliberal model. The first was to structurally support the neoliberal policy box. The second was to support the AD generation process. These dual roles are central to the process of increasing financial domination of the economy that has been termed 'financialisation' (Epstein, 2004: 3; Krippner, 2004, 2005; Palley, 2013).

The policy box shown in Figure 8.2 has four sides. A true box has six sides and a four-sided structure would be prone to structural weakness. Metaphorically

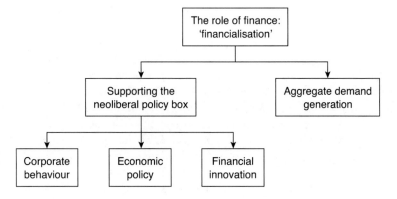

Figure 8.3 The role of finance in the neoliberal model

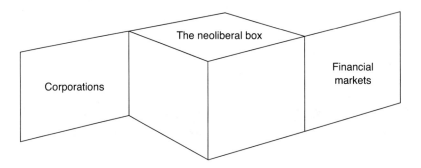

Figure 8.4 Lifting the lid on the neoliberal policy box

speaking, one role of finance is to provide support on two sides of the neoliberal policy box, as illustrated in Figure 8.4. Finance does this through three channels. First, financial markets have captured control of corporations via enforcement of the shareholder-value-paradigm of corporate governance. Consequently, corporations now serve financial market interests along with the interests of top management. Second, financial markets in combination with corporations lobby politically for the neoliberal policy mix. The combination of changed corporate behaviour and economic policy produces an economic matrix that puts wages under continuous pressure and raises income inequality. Third, financial innovation has facilitated and promoted financial market control of corporations via hostile takeovers, leveraged buy-outs and reverse capital distributions. Financial innovation has therefore been key for enforcing Wall Street's construction of the shareholder-value paradigm.

The second vital role of finance is the support of AD. The neoliberal model gradually undermined the income and demand generation process, creating a growing structural demand gap. The role of finance was to fill that gap. Thus, within the USA, deregulation, financial innovation, speculation and mortgage lending fraud enabled finance to fill the demand gap by lending to consumers and by spurring asset price inflation. Financialisation assisted with this process by changing credit market practices and introducing new credit instruments that made credit more easily and widely available to corporations and households. US consumers in turn filled the global demand gap, along with help from US and European corporations who were shifting manufacturing facilities and investment to the emerging market economies.

Three things should be emphasised. First, this AD-generation role of finance was an unintended consequence and not part of a grand plan. Neoliberal economists and policy-makers did not realise they were creating a demand gap, but their laissez-faire economic ideology triggered financial market developments that coincidentally filled the demand gap. Second, the financial process they unleashed was inevitably unstable and was always destined to hit the wall. There are limits to borrowing and to asset price inflation – and all Ponzi schemes eventually fall apart. The problem is the impossibility of predicting when they will fail. Third, the process went on far longer than anyone expected, which explains why critics of neoliberalism sounded like Cassandras (Palley, 1998: Chapter 12). However, the long duration of financial excess made the collapse far deeper when it eventually happened. It has also made escaping the after-effects of the financial crisis far more difficult as the economy is now burdened by debts and destroyed credit-worthiness. That has deepened the proclivity to economic stagnation.

Evidence

Evidence regarding the economic effects of the neoliberal model is plentiful and clear. Figure 8.5 shows productivity and average hourly compensation of non-supervisory workers (that is non-managerial employees who are about 80 per cent of the workforce). The link with productivity growth was severed almost 40 years ago and hourly compensation has been essentially stagnant since then.

Table 8.3 shows data on the distribution of income growth by business cycle expansion across the wealthiest top 10 per cent and bottom 90 per cent of households. Over the past 60 years there has been a persistent decline in the share of income gains going to the bottom 90 per cent of households ranked by wealth. However, in the period 1948–1979 the decline was gradual. After 1980 there is a massive structural break and the share of income gains going to the bottom 90 per cent collapses. Before 1980, on average the bottom 90 per cent received 66 per cent of business cycle expansion income gains. After 1980, on average they receive just 8 per cent.

Figure 8.6 shows the share of total pre-tax income of the top 1 per cent of households ranked by wealth. From the mid-1930s, with the implementation of the New Deal social contract, that share fell from a high of 23.94 per cent in 1928 to a low of 8.95 per cent in 1978. Thereafter it has steadily risen, reaching 23.5 per cent in 2007 which marked the beginning of the Great Recession. It then fell during the Great Recession owing to a recession-induced fall in profits,

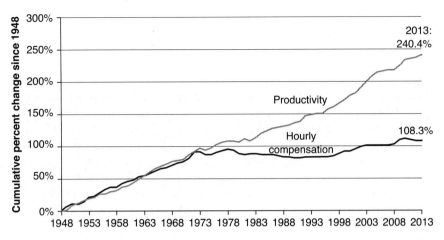

Figure 8.5 Productivity and real average hourly compensation of US non-supervisory
workers, 1948–2013

Note: Data are for compensation of production/non-supervisory workers in the private sector and
net productivity of the total economy. 'Net productivity' is the growth of output of goods and services
less depreciation per hour worked.

Source: Economic Policy Institute analysis of unpublished Total Economy Productivity data from
Bureau of Labor Statistics (BLS) Labor Productivity and Costs program, wage data from the BLS
Current Employment Statistics, BLS Consumer Price Index and Bureau of Economic Analysis
National Income and Product Accounts.

Table 8.3 Distribution of income growth by business cycle expansion across the
wealthiest top 10 percent and bottom 90 percent of households

	'49–'53	'54–'57	'59–'60	'61–'69	'70–'73	'75–'79	'82–'90	'91–'00	'01–'07	'09–'12	*Average Pre-1908*	*Average Post-1980*
Top 10%	20%	28	32	33	43	45	80	73	98	116	34%	92%
Bottom 90%	80%	72	68	67	57	55	20	27	2	–16	66%	8%

Source: Tcherneva (2014), published in The New York Times, September 26, 2014.

but has since recovered most of that decline as income distribution has worsened
again during the economic recovery. In effect, during the neoliberal era the US
economy has retraced its steps, reversing the improvements achieved by the New
Deal and post-Second World War prosperity, so that the top 1 per cent's share
of pre-tax income has returned to pre-Great Depression levels.

As argued in Palley (2012a: 150–151), there is a close relationship between
union membership density (i.e. the percentage of employed workers that are
unionised) and income distribution. This is clearly shown in Figure 8.7, which
shows union density and the share of pre-tax income going to the top 10 per
cent of wealthiest households. The neoliberal labour-market flexibility agenda
explicitly attacks unions and works to shift income to wealthier households.

Table 8.4 provides data on the evolution of the US goods and services trade
balance as a share of gross domestic product (GDP) by business cycle peak.

Figure 8.6 US pre-tax income share of top 1 percent (1913–2012)
Source: http://inequality.org/income-inequality/. Original source: Thomas Piketty and Emanuel Saez (2003), updated at http://em.lab.edu/users/saez

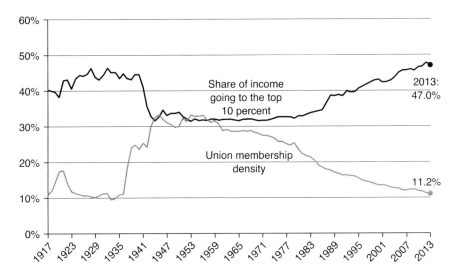

Figure 8.7 Union membership and the share of income going to the top ten percent of wealthiest households, 1917–2013
Source: Data on union density follows the composite series found in Historical Statistics of the United States; updated to 2013 from unionstats.com. Income inequality (share of income to top 10%) from Piketty and Saez, 'Income Inequality in the United States', 1913–1998, *Quarterly Journal of Economics*, 118(1), 2003, 1–39. Updated and downloadable data, for this series and other countries, is available at the Top Income Database. Updated January 2015.

Comparison across peaks controls for the effect of the business cycle. The data show that through to the late 1970s, US trade was roughly in balance, but after 1980 it swung to a massive deficit, which increased during each business cycle. These deficits were the inevitable product of the neoliberal model of globalisation

Table 8.4 The U.S. goods and services trade deficit/surplus by business cycle peaks, 1960–2007

Business cycle peak year	Trade balance ($ millions)	GDP ($ billions)	Trade balance/ GDP (%)
1960	3,508	526.4	0.7
1969	91	984.6	0.0
1973	1,900	1,382.7	0.1
1980	−25,500	2,789.5	−0.9
1981	−28,023	3,128.4	−0.9
1990	−111,037	5,803.1	−1.9
2001	−429,519	10,128.0	−.2
2007	−819,373	13,807.5	−5.9

Sources: Economic Report of the President, 2009 and author's calculations.

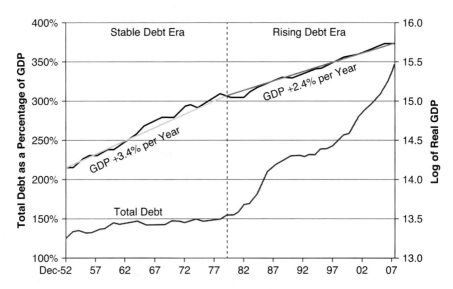

Figure 8.8 Total domestic debt and growth (1952–2007)
Source: Grantham, 2010.

(Palley, 2015), and they undermined the AD generation process in accordance with the Keynesian hypothesis.

Finally, Figure 8.8 shows total domestic debt relative to GDP and growth. This figure is highly supportive of the Keynesian interpretation of the role of finance. During the neoliberal era, real GDP growth has actually slowed but debt growth has exploded. The reason is that the neoliberal model did nothing to increase growth, but it needed faster debt growth to fill the demand gap created by the model's worsening of income distribution and creation of large trade deficits. Debt growth supported debt-financed consumer spending, and it supported asset price inflation that enabled borrowing, which filled the demand gap caused by the neoliberal model.

The debate about the causes of the crisis: why it matters

The importance of the debate about the causes of the crisis is that each perspective recommends its own different policy response. For *hardcore-neoliberal government failure* proponents, the recommended policy response is to double-down on the policies described by the neoliberal policy box and further deregulate markets; to deepen central bank independence and the commitment to low inflation via strict rules based monetary policy; and to further shrink government and impose fiscal austerity to deal with increased government debt produced by the crisis.

For *softcore-neoliberal market failure* proponents, the recommended policy response is to tighten financial regulation but continue with all other aspects of the existing neoliberal policy paradigm. That means continued support for corporate globalisation, so-called labour-market flexibility, low inflation targeting and fiscal austerity in the long term. Additionally, there is a need for temporary large-scale fiscal and monetary stimulus to combat the deep recession caused by the financial crisis. However, once the economy has recovered, policy should continue with the neoliberal model.

For proponents of the *destruction of shared prosperity* hypothesis, the policy response is fundamentally different. The fundamental need is to overthrow the neoliberal paradigm and replace it with a 'structural Keynesian' paradigm. That involves repacking the policy box as illustrated in Figure 8.9. The critical step is to take workers out of the box and put corporations and financial markets in so that they are made to serve a broader public interest. The key elements are to replace corporate globalisation with managed globalisation, thus blocking the 'race to the bottom' trade dynamics and stabilising global financial markets; restoring a commitment to full employment; replacing the neoliberal anti-government agenda with a social democratic government agenda; and replacing the neoliberal labour-market flexibility with a solidarity-based labour-market agenda. The goals are the restoration of full employment and the restoration of a solid link between wage and productivity growth.

Lastly, since the neoliberal model was adopted as part of a new global economic order, there is also need to recalibrate the global economy. This is where

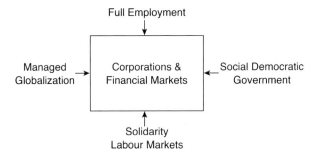

Figure 8.9 The structural Keynesian box

the issue of 'global rebalancing' enters: emerging market economies need to shift away from export-led growth strategies to domestic demand-led strategies, which poses huge challenges for many of them because they have configured their growth strategies around export-led growth based on selling to US consumers.

From crisis to stagnation: the failure to change

Massive policy interventions, unequalled in the post-war era, stopped the Great Recession from spiralling into a second Great Depression. The domestic economic interventions included the 2008 Troubled Asset Relief Program (TARP) that bailed out the financial sector via government purchases of assets and equity from financial institutions; the 2009 American Recovery and Reinvestment Act (ARRA) that provided approximately $800 billion of fiscal stimulus, consisting of approximately $550 billion of government spending and $250 billion of tax cuts; the Federal Reserve lowering its interest target to near-zero (0–0.25 per cent); and the Federal Reserve engaging in quantitative easing (QE) transactions that involve it purchasing government and private-sector securities. At the international level, in 2008 the Federal Reserve established a temporary $620 billion foreign exchange (FX) swap facility with foreign central banks. That facility provided the global economy with dollar balances, thereby preventing a dollar liquidity shortage from triggering a global wave of defaults on short-term dollar loans that the financial system was unwilling to roll over because of panic.[2] Additionally, there was unprecedented globally co-ordinated fiscal stimulus arranged via the G-20 mechanism.

Despite their scale, these interventions did not stop the recession from being the deepest since 1945, and nor did they stop the onset of stagnation. Table 8.5 shows how GDP growth has failed to recover since the end of the Great Recession, averaging just 2.1 per cent for the five-year period from 2010 to 2014. Furthermore, that period includes the rebound year of 2010 when the economy recovered from its massive slump owing to the extraordinary fiscal and monetary stimulus measures that were put in place.

Table 8.6 shows employment creation in the five years after the end of recessions, which provides another window on stagnation. The job-creation numbers show that the neoliberal model was already slowing in the 1990s with the first episode of 'jobless recovery'. It actually ground to stagnation in the 2001–2007 period, but this was masked by the house-price bubble and the false prosperity it created. Stagnation has persisted after the Great Recession, but the economic

Table 8.5 U.S. GDP growth

1961–1970	1971–1980	1981–1990	1991–2000	2001–2007	2008–2009	2010–2014
4.2%	3.2%	3.3%	3.5%	2.5%	−1.6%	2.1%

Source: Statistical Annex of the European Union, Autumn 2014 and author's calculations. The growth rate for 2014 is that estimated in October 2014.

Table 8.6 U.S. private sector employment creation in the five year period after the end of recessions for six business cycles with extended expansions

Recession end date	Employment at recession end date (millions)	Employment five years later (millions)	Per cent growth in employment
Feb 1961	45.0	52.2	16.0%
Mar 1975	61.9	74.6*	20.5%
Nov 1982	72.8	86.1	18.3%
March 1991	90.1	99.5	10.4%
Nov 2001	109.8	115.0	4.7%
June 2009	108.4	117.1	8.0%

Source: Bureau of labor statistics and author's calculations. * = January 1980 (the beginning of the next recession).

distress caused by the recession has finally triggered awareness of stagnation among elite economists. In a sense, the Great Recession called out the obvious, just as did the little boy in the Hans Andersen story about the emperor's new suit.

The persistence of stagnation after the Great Recession raises the question 'why?'. The answer is policy has done nothing to change the structure of the underlying neoliberal economic model. That model inevitably produces stagnation because it produces a structural demand shortage via (i) its impact on income distribution, and (ii) via its design of globalisation, which generates massive trade deficits, wage competition and offshoring of jobs and investment.

In terms of the three-way contest between the *government failure* hypothesis, the *market failure* hypothesis and the *destruction of shared prosperity* hypothesis, the economic policy debate during the Great Recession was cast as exclusively between government failure and market failure. With the Democrats controlling the Congress and Presidency after the 2008 election, the market failure hypothesis won out and has framed policy since then. According to the hypothesis, the financial crisis caused an exceptionally deep recession that required exceptionally large monetary and fiscal stimulus to counter it and restore normalcy. Additionally, the *market failure* hypothesis recommends restoring and renovating financial regulation, but other than that the neoliberal paradigm is appropriate and should be deepened.

In accordance with this thinking, the incoming Obama administration affirmed existing efforts to save the system and prevent a downward spiral by supporting the Bush administration's TARP, the Federal Reserve's first round of QE (November/December 2008) that provided market liquidity and the Federal Reserve's FX swap agreement with foreign central banks.

Thereafter, the Obama administration worked to reflate the economy via the passage of the ARRA (2009), which provided significant fiscal stimulus. With the failure to deliver a V-shaped recovery, candidate Obama became even more vocal about fiscal stimulus. However, reflecting its softcore-neoliberal inclinations, the Obama administration then became much less so when it took office.

Thus, the winners of the internal debate about fiscal policy in the first days of the Obama administration were those wanting more modest fiscal stimulus.[3] Furthermore, its analytical frame was one of temporary stimulus with the goal of long-term fiscal consolidation, which is softcore-neoliberal speak for fiscal austerity.

Seen in the above light, after the passage of ARRA (2009), the fiscal policy divide between the Obama administration and hardcore-neoliberal Republicans was about the speed and conditions under which fiscal austerity should be restored. This attitude to fiscal policy reflects the dominance within the Democratic Party of 'Rubinomics', the Wall Street view associated with former Treasury Secretary Robert Rubin, that government spending and budget deficits raise real interest rates and thereby lower growth. According to that view, the USA needs long-term fiscal austerity to offset social security and Medicare.

Side-by-side with the attempt to reflate the economy, the Obama administration also pushed for a major overhaul and tightening of financial sector regulation via the Dodd–Frank Act (2010). That accorded with the market failure hypothesis's claim about the economic crisis and Great Recession being caused by financial excess permitted by the combination of excessive deregulation, lax regulation and failure to modernise regulation.

Finally, and again in accordance with the logic of the market failure hypothesis, the Obama administration has pushed ahead with doubling-down and further entrenching the neoliberal policy box. This is most visible in its approach to globalisation. In 2010, free-trade agreements modelled after NAFTA were signed with South Korea, Colombia and Panama. The Transpacific Partnership (TPP) and the Transatlantic Trade and Investment Partnership (TTIP), two mega-agreements negotiated in secrecy and apparently bearing similar hallmarks to prior trade agreements, are also being pushed by the Obama administration.

The Obama administration's softcore-neoliberalism would have likely generated stagnation by itself, but the prospect has been further strengthened by Republicans. Thus, in accordance with their point of view, Republicans have persistently pushed the government failure hypothesis by directing the policy conversation to excessive regulation and easy monetary policy as the causes of the crisis. Consequently, they have consistently opposed strengthened financial regulation and demands for fiscal stimulus. At the same time, they have joined with softcore-neoliberal Democrats regarding doubling-down on neoliberal box policies, particularly as regards trade and globalisation.

Paradoxically, the failure to change the overall economic model becomes most visible by analysing the policies of the Federal Reserve, which have changed the most dramatically via the introduction of QE. The initial round of QE (QE1) was followed by QE2 in November 2010 and QE3 in September 2012, with the Fed shifting from providing short-term emergency liquidity to buying private sector financial assets. The goal was to bid up prices of longer-term bonds and other securities, thereby lowering interest rates on longer-term financing and encouraging investors to buy equities and other, riskier financial assets. The Fed's reasoning was lower long-term rates would stimulate the economy, and higher financial asset prices would trigger a positive wealth effect on consumption spending. This makes clear the architecture of policy. The Obama administration was to provide fiscal stimulus to jump start the economy; the Fed would use QE to blow air back into the asset price bubble; the Dodd–Frank Act (2010) would stabilise financial markets; and globalisation would be deepened by further NAFTA-styled international agreements. This is a near-identical model to that which failed so disastrously. Consequently, stagnation is the logical prognosis.

Déjà vu all over again: back to the 1990s but with a weaker economy

The exclusion of the *destruction of shared prosperity* hypothesis, combined with the joint triumph of the *market failure* and *government failure* hypotheses, means the underlying economic model that produced the Great Recession remains essentially unchanged. That failure to change explains stagnation. It also explains why current conditions smack of 'déjà vu all over again', with the US economy in 2014–2015 appearing to have returned to conditions reminiscent of the mid-1990s. Just as the 1990s failed to deliver durable prosperity, so too current optimistic conditions will prove unsustainable without deeper change.

The déjà vu similarities are evident in the large US trade deficit that has started to again deteriorate rapidly; a return of the over-valued dollar problem that promises to further increase the trade deficit and divert jobs and investment away from the US economy; a return to reliance on asset-price inflation and house-price increases to grow consumer demand and construction; a return of declining budget deficits owing to continued policy disposition toward fiscal austerity; a return of the contradiction that has the Federal Reserve tighten monetary policy when economic strength triggers rising prices and wages that bump against the ceiling of the Fed's self-imposed 2 per cent inflation target; and a renewal of the push for neoliberal trade agreements.

All of these features mean both policy context and policy design look a lot like the mid-1990s. The Obama administration saved the system but did not change it. Consequently, the economy is destined to repeat the patterns of the 1990s and 2000s. However, the US economy has also experienced almost 20 more years of neoliberalism, which has left its economic body in worse health than the 1990s. That means the likelihood of delivering another bubble-based boom is low, and stagnation tendencies will likely reassert themselves after a shorter and weaker period of expansion.

This structurally weakened state of the US economy is evident in the further worsening of income inequality that has occurred during the Great Recession and subsequent slow recovery. As shown in Figure 8.10, national income data show that the labour share has continued to fall during this period, hitting new post-war lows. Furthermore, earlier, Table 8.3 showed how the top 10 per cent of wealthiest households garnered 116 per cent of the income gains during the recovery period 2009–2012, implying that the bottom 90 per cent experienced falling income during this period.

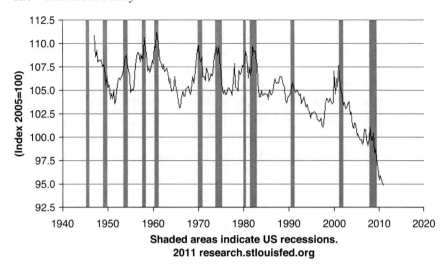

Figure 8.10 Labour share of US non-farm business GDP (%), 1945–2011
Source: Economist's View, June 16, 2011. Labour share consists of wages, salaries and pension benefits of non-supervisory workers.

This worsening of income distribution has multiple negative implications that promote stagnation via direct and indirect effects. With regard to direct effects, worsened income distribution shifts income from poorer low-saving households to richer high-saving households. That shift reduces consumption spending and aggregate demand. With regard to indirect effects, by lowering the incomes of poorer households (which tend to be borrowers), it reduces their borrowing capacity, which in turn reduces credit expansion via consumer- and mortgage-borrowing. This indirect effect helps explain why credit and mortgage growth have been sluggish despite much lower interest rates. QE aimed to stimulate household borrowing, but continued worsening of income distribution has under-mined middle-class households' ability to do so. Furthermore, at the start of the recovery in 2009, households already had more debt that was accumulated over the 2000–2007 period than they did in the 1990s. That combination of further worsened income distribution and increased debt makes the possibility of another 1990s-style extended debt-driven expansion unlikely.

A second problem is the macroeconomic restraining effects of the Dodd–Frank Act (2010) financial sector reforms and increased regulation. These measures were necessary to limit the scope and space for financial excess that was a threat to the economy's stability. However, the neoliberal economic model needs asset-price inflation and borrowing to fill the demand gap created by worsened income distribution, the trade deficit and fiscal austerity. Ironically, the Dodd-Frank reforms of the financial sector limit the financial system's capacity to generate asset-price inflation and borrowing to fill that gap. That is another difference from the 1980s and 1990s, when the system was being deregulated to facilitate this demand-filling mechanism (see Palley, 2012a: Chapter 5). This is

Table 8.7 Contributions to per cent change in real GDP

	2008	2009	2010	2011	2012	2013	2014
1. Government consumption & investment spending	0.54	0.64	0.02	−0.65	−0.30	−0.39	−0.03
2. Net exports of goods & services	1.11	1.19	−0.46	−0.02	0.04	0.22	−0.22
3. Gross private investment spending	−1.71	−3.52	1.66	0.73	1.33	0.76	0.95
4. Consumption spending	−0.23	−1.08	1.32	1.55	1.25	1.64	1.72
GDP growth (= 1 + 2 + 3 + 4)	−0.3%	−2.8%	2.5%	1.6%	2.3%	2.2%	2.4%

Source: Bureau of Economic Analysis, GDP Report, Table 1.1.2.

an additional reason why the system is less capable of generating another credit bubble to drive economic expansion.

Lastly, weakness in the global economy resulting from the spread of the export-led growth model (Palley, 2012b) promises to weaken demand for exports by US firms; increase the intensity of import competition as foreign firms try to capture an increased share of the US market to compensate for weakness in their own domestic markets; and increase the grinding downward pressure on US wages via global wage competition as the threat of unemployment compels workers to accept lower wages.

These adverse developments combine with and amplify the existing structural drags inherent to the neoliberal model (that is, wage stagnation, deteriorated income distribution, proclivity to fiscal austerity, trade deficits, global wage competition, job and investment offshoring, etc.). The 1990s boom proved unsustainable despite more favourable conditions. Worsened current conditions suggest any new expansion will again prove unsustainable, will peter out in stagnation, and will be much weaker and of shorter duration.

These tendencies are already visible. Table 8.7 shows the contributions to GDP growth from different sources for the 2008–2014 period. Having been positive in the 2008–2010 period because of ARRA, government spending has begun to contract and become a drag on growth. The collapse of imports during the Great Recession helped strengthen growth by lowering the trade deficit, but as the economy and the dollar have strengthened, that impetus has fallen and reversed. Investment spending has made a positive contribution but the contribution has been weaker than in the 1990s. The one strengthening area is consumption spending, but the past two business cycles (1991–2001, 2001–2007) have shown that that alone is not sustainable.

Conclusion: stagnation rather than another financial crisis

The Great Recession has been followed by stagnation which is likely to endure. That is because of failure to change the structure of the underlying economic policy model. Policy saved the model but did not change it. The policy mix constituting the neoliberal model failed in the 1990s and 2000s under more favourable conditions (that is, less debt hangover, less destroyed consumer credit-worthiness, financial innovation that was beginning and had room to grow, and equity and house prices that were at a lower base with more room for increases, etc.). That suggests the model is destined to fail again.

However, this time it is less likely the expansion will end in a financial crisis because the resolution of the last crisis compelled the financial sector to massively strengthen its balance sheet. Instead, the expansion is likely to end with a stock-market correction and evaporation of growth, but that may take a couple of years to play out. That said, there are two scenarios that may end in financial crisis. The first is if the euro implodes as a result of the exit of an economically depressed and politically stressed member country. The second is if the Federal Reserve continues to pump up financial asset prices and the economy eventually hits an inflation threshold that triggers higher interest rates, which could then trigger an asset price melt-down.

Stagnation without financial crisis seems the most likely outcome for the US economy. The neoliberal economic model is unchanged and exhausted. That is symbolically paralleled by the political system in which the 2016 presidential election may well be between Hillary Clinton and Jeb Bush. One is the wife of former President Bill Clinton, while the other is the brother of former President George W. Bush. Together, Presidents Clinton and Bush presided over the entrenchment and implosion of the neoliberal model. Paralleling the economy, US politics also smacks of déjà vu all over again.

Notes

1 Over the course of the 1981–1982 recession, labour-force participation rose from 63.8 per cent to 64.2 per cent, thereby likely increasing the unemployment rate. In contrast, over the course of the Great Recession the labour-force participation rate fell from 66 per cent to 65.7 per cent, thereby likely decreasing the unemployment. The decrease in the labour-force participation rate was even sharper for prime-age (25–54 years old) workers, indicating that the decrease in the overall participation rate was not due to demographic factors such as an ageing population. Instead, it was due to a lack of job opportunities, which supports the claim that labour force exit lowered the unemployment rate.

2 The FX swaps with foreign central banks have been criticised as being a bail-out for foreign economies. In fact, they saved the US financial system which would have been pulled down by financial collapse outside the US. Many foreign banks operating in the USA had acquired US assets financed with short-term dollar borrowings. When the US money market froze in 2008, they could not roll over these loans in accordance with normal practice. That threatened massive default by these banks within the US financial system, which would have pulled down the entire global financial system. The Federal Reserve could not lend directly to these foreign banks and their governing central banks lacked adequate dollar liquidity to fill the financing gap. The solution was to lend dollars to foreign central banks, which then made dollar loans to foreign banks in need of dollar roll-over short-term financing.

3 Since 2009 there has been some evolution of policy positions characterised by a shift to stronger support for fiscal stimulus. This has been especially marked in Larry Summers, who was the Obama administration's chief economic adviser when it took office. This

shift has become a way of rewriting history by erasing the memory of initial positions. That is also true of the IMF, which in 2010–2011 was a robust supporter of fiscal consolidation in Europe.

References

Epstein, G. (2004) Introduction. In Epstein, G. (ed.) *Financialization and the World Economy*. Northampton, MA: Edward Elgar: 3–16.

Grantham, J. (2010) Night of the Living Fed. *GMO Quarterly Letter*.

Greenhill, S. (2008) It's Awful – Why Did Nobody See It Coming? *Daily Mail*, 5 November 2008.

Krippner, G. (2004) *What Is financialization?* Mimeo, Department of Sociology, UCLA.

Krippner, G. (2005) The Financialization of the American Economy. *Socio-Economic Review* 3: 173–208.

Mishel, L., Gould, E. and Bivens, J. (2015) *Wage Stagnation in Nine Charts*. Washington, DC: Economic Policy Institute.

Palley, T.I. (1998) *Plenty of Nothing: The Downsizing of the American Dream and the Case for Structural Keynesianism*. Princeton, NJ: Princeton University Press.

Palley, T.I. (2012a) *From Financial Crisis to Stagnation: The Destruction of Shared Prosperity and the Role of Economics*. Cambridge: Cambridge University Press.

Palley, T.I. (2012b) The Rise and Fall of Export-led Growth. *Investigación Económica*, LXX, 280: 15–35.

Palley, T.I. (2013) *Financialization: The Macroeconomics of Finance Capital Domination*. Basingstoke: Macmillan/Palgrave.

Palley, T.I. (2015) The Theory of Global Imbalances: Mainstream Economics vs. Structural Keynesianism. *Review of Keynesian Economics* 3(1): 45–62.

Tcherneva, P.R. (2014) Reorienting Fiscal Policy: A Bottom-Up Approach. *Journal of Post Keynesian Economics* 37(1): 43–66.

9 Financialisation, redistribution and 'export-led mercantilism'

The case of Germany

Eckhard Hein and Daniel Detzer[1]

Introduction

The erosion of the 'golden age' of the 1950s and 1960s and the neoliberal 'counter-revolution' in the late 1970s and early 1980s provided the conditions for the emergence of 'financialisation' or 'finance-dominated capitalism'. The neoliberal advance started in the USA and the UK and spread over the developed and, subsequently, also the developing world. It has been characterised by the expansion of financial markets, the introduction of new financial instruments and the increasing dominance of financial motives in economic activity. Over the last 30 years, finance came to dominate industry and non-financial corporations have been increasingly engaged in financial as opposed to productive activities. At the level of the firm, the alignment of management with shareholder interests reflected a shift in focus towards the maximisation of short-term 'shareholder-value' instead of long-term growth objectives. What followed was a period of distinctly lower rates of capital accumulation in advanced capitalist economies, accompanied by rising income inequality. In order to sustain consumption or to follow rising consumption norms by higher income groups, households in some countries, for example in the USA or the UK, relied increasingly on credit to finance their consumption expenditure, creating the problems of private household over-indebtedness. Eventually, this triggered the financial crisis and the Great Recession in 2007–2009. In other countries, for example in Germany and Japan, weak investment and weak income-financed consumption demand was (partly) compensated for by rising net exports and current account surpluses, contributing to regional and global imbalances and to the latent over-indebtedness of the counterpart deficit countries.[2] This constellation provided the conditions for the severity of the global financial crisis and the Great Recession.

As analysed in detail in Detzer et al. (2013), the most important changes in the German financial sector that contributed to the increasing dominance of finance took place not before the 1990s: the abolition of the stock exchange tax in 1991; the legalisation of share buybacks in 1998; the abolition of capital gains taxes for corporations in 2002; and the legalisation of hedge funds, among others financial entities, in 2004. While financialisation is often associated with an increase in the share of the financial sector in value-added, employment and profits, this was not the case in Germany. The increased dominance of finance, however, was signalled by other indicators. Stock-market capitalisation and trading activity have grown strongly, even though they are still moderate compared with Anglo-Saxon, and other European countries. At the same time, the importance of institutional investors in Germany has increased strongly and the financial activity of non-financial firms has also expanded, which is indicated by an increasing share of financial profits in total profits in those firms.

In this chapter we will focus on the effects of these developments on income distribution and on the overall macroeconomic development in Germany. Against this background, we will then take a look at the economic and financial crisis in Germany, the main reasons for the quick recovery and the persisting problems before we draw some brief conclusions concerning economic policy.

Redistribution and rising inequality in Germany since the early 1980s

The period since the early 1980s has been associated with a massive redistribution of income. First, if we look at cyclical averages in order to eliminate cyclical fluctuations, the labour income share in the developed capitalist economies considered here showed a falling trend between the early 1980s and the Great Recession (see Table 9.1). In Germany the fall was considerable, in particular from the cycle of the 1990s to the cycle of the early 2000s.

Second, personal income distribution became more unequal in most countries between the mid-1980s and the mid-2000s. Taking the Gini coefficient for the distribution of market income, Germany is amongst those countries showing a considerable increase in inequality, with the Gini coefficient rising from 0.439 in 1985 to 0.499 in 2004 (OECD, 2012). In Germany, redistribution via taxes and social transfers has been considerable and has not been decreasing over time. However, this did not prevent the Gini coefficient for disposable income from increasing, too. While it was at 0.251 in 1985, it increased to 0.285 in 2004 (OECD, 2012). In fact, according to the OECD (2008), which applied further indicators for inequality, Germany is one of the countries where in the early 2000s the inequality of disposable income increased the most. And as can be seen in Table 9.2, this redistribution was mainly at the expense of people with very low incomes. While the P90/P10 ratio for disposable income rose significantly, the P90/P50 ratio hardly changed.

Third, as data based on tax reports provided by Alvaredo et al. (2014) have shown, there has been an explosion of the shares of the very top incomes since the early 1980s in the USA and the UK. Germany has not yet seen such an increase for the top 1 per cent, top 0.1 per cent or top 0.01 per cent income shares. However, if we take a look at the top 10 per cent income share, including capital gains, a rising trend from the early 1980s until 2007 can be observed, too. In total, their income share increased by five percentage points from 31.9 to 36.9 per cent in this period.

Table 9.1 Labour income share as percentage of GDP at current factor costs, average values over the trade cycle, early 1980s–2008

	1. Early 1980s– early 1990s	*2. Early 1990s– early 2000s*	*3. Early 2000s–2008*	*Change (3.–1.), percentage points*
Austria	75.66	70.74	65.20	−10.46
Belgium	70.63	70.74	69.16	−1.47
France	71.44	66.88	65.91	−5.53
Germany[a]	67.11	66.04	63.34	−3.77
Greece[b]	67.26	62.00	60.60	−6.66
Ireland	70.34	60.90	55.72	−14.61
Italy	68.31	63.25	62.37	−5.95
Netherlands	68.74	67.21	65.57	−3.17
Portugal	65.73	70.60	71.10	5.37
Spain	68.32	66.13	62.41	−5.91
Sweden	71.65	67.04	69.16	−2.48
UK	72.79	71.99	70.67	−2.12
US	68.20	67.12	65.79	−2.41
Japan[b]	72.38	70.47	65.75	−6.64

Notes: The labour income share is given by the compensation per employee divided by GDP at factor costs per person employed.
The beginning of a trade cycle is given by a local minimum of annual real GDP growth in the respective country.
[a] West Germany until 1990
[b] adjusted to fit into three-cycle patterns
Data: European Commission (2010)
Source: Hein (2012: 13)

Table 9.2 Percentile ratios for disposable income in Germany, 1985–2008

	1985	*1990*	*1995*	*2000*	*2004*	*2008*
P90/P10	3	3	3.3	3.2	3.4	3.5
P90/P50	1.7	1.8	1.8	1.8	1.8	1.8
P50/P10	1.7	1.7	1.8	1.8	1.9	1.9

Notes: The P90/P10 ratio is the ratio of the upper bound value of the ninth decile (i.e. the 10% of people with highest income) to that of the upper bound value of the first decile.
The P90/P50 ratio is the ratio of the upper bound value of the ninth decile to the median income.
The P50/P10 ratio is the ratio of median income to the upper bound value of the first decile.
Source: OECD (2014)

In what follows, we will focus on the determinants of functional income distribution and the falling wage or labour income share. This will also contribute to our understanding of the causes of the rising inequality in the personal or household distribution of income. The major reason why a falling labour income share contributes to rising personal and household income inequality is the fact that it is accompanied by an equivalent increase in the profit share. This means that (even more) unequal distribution of wealth-generating profit income feeds back, to a stronger degree than before, into the household distribution of income.

According to Grabka and Westermeier (2014), real and financial net wealth is distributed extremely unequally among households and individuals in Germany: the Gini coefficient for net wealth distribution among adults was at 0.777 in 2002, rose to 0.799 in 2007 and decreased slightly to 0.78 in 2012, but still is the highest among euro-area countries.

Following the Kaleckian theory of income distribution (Hein, 2014: Chapter 5; Kalecki, 1954: Part I), the gross profit share in national income, which includes retained earnings, dividends, interest and rent payments, as well as overhead costs (and thus also top management salaries), has three major determinants, which are listed at the top of Table 9.3:

First, the profit share is affected by firms' pricing in incompletely competitive goods markets, that is by the mark-up on unit variable costs. The mark-up itself is determined by:

(a) the degree of industrial concentration and the relevance of price competition relative to other instruments of competition (marketing, product differentiation) in the respective industries or sectors, that is, the degree of price competition in the goods market;
(b) the bargaining power of trade unions, because in a heterogeneous environment with differences in unit wage cost growth between firms, industries or sectors, the firm's or the industry's ability to shift changes in nominal unit wage costs to prices is constrained by competition of other firms or industries, which do not have to face the same increase in unit wage costs; and
(c) overhead costs and gross profit targets, because the mark-up has to cover overhead costs as well as distributed and undistributed profits.

Second, with mark-up pricing on unit variable costs, that is material plus wage costs, the profit share in national income is affected by unit (imported) material costs relative to unit wage costs. With a constant mark-up, an increase in unit material costs will thus increase the profit share in national income.

And third, the aggregate profit share of the economy as a whole is a weighted average of the industry- or sector-profit shares. Since profit shares differ among industries and sectors, the aggregate profit share is therefore affected by the industry- or sector-composition of the economy.

The changes in regulation, institutions and in particular economic and political powers associated with the rise of neoliberalism and financialisation since the 1980s and in Germany since the 1990s in particular have contributed to the fall in the labour income share and the rise in the profit share through three main channels.[3]

First, the sectoral composition of the economy has changed. In Germany, the share of the government sector in value-added has seen a tendency to decline, from 12 per cent in the mid-1990s to below 10 per cent in 2007 (Statistisches Bundesamt, 2012). This has meant a fall in the aggregate wage share and a rise in the aggregate profit share, because the government sector is a non-profit sector in the national accounts.

Table 9.3 Financialisation and the gross profit share – a Kaleckian perspective

Stylised facts of financialisation (1.–7.) and neo-liberalism (8.–9.)	Determinants of the gross profit share (including (top) management salaries)			2) Price of imported raw materials and semi-finished products	3) Sector composition of the domestic economy
	1) Mark-up				
	1.a) Degree of price competition in the goods market	1.b) Bargaining power and activity of trade union	1.c) Overhead costs and gross profit targets		
1. Increasing shareholder value orientation and short-termism of management	...	+	+	...	...
2. Rising dividend payments	...	...	+	...	...
3. Increasing interest rates or interest payments (in the 1980s)	...	...	+	...	...
4. Increasing top management salaries	...	...	+	...	...
5. Increasing relevance of financial to non-financial sector (investment)	...	+	...	...	+
6. Mergers and acquisitions	+	...	...	...	...
7. Liberalisation and globalisation of international finance and trade	−	+	...	+/−	+/−
8. Deregulation of the labour market	...	+	...	...	...
9. Downsizing of government	...	+	...	...	+

Notes:
+ positive effect on the gross profit share
− negative effect on the gross profit share
... no direct effect on the gross profit share
Source: Hein (2014a: 15)

Second, the increase in top management salaries and higher profit claims of financial wealth holders have contributed to a fall in the wage share of 'ordinary labour'. Dünhaupt (2011) has corrected the wage share from the national accounts for the labour income of the top 1 per cent by assuming that the latter represents top management salaries. The resulting wage share for direct labour shows an even steeper downward trend than the wage share from the national accounts (see Figure 9.1). Extending another analysis provided by Dünhaupt (2012), we also find that, in the long run, there is substantial evidence that the increase in the profit claims of rentiers came at the expense of the workers' share in national income (see Figure 9.2). In the 1980s, the fall in the wage share (compensation of employees as a share of national income, as retrieved from the national accounts) was accompanied by an increase of both the share of rentiers income (net property income consisting of interest, dividends and rents) and the share

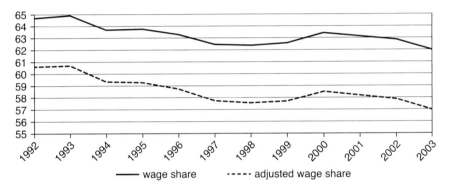

Figure 9.1 Wage share adjusted for the labour income of top 1 per cent, Germany, 1992–2003 (percentage of net national income)
Source: Dünhaupt (2011: 27).

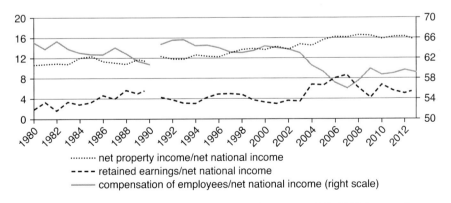

Figure 9.2 Income shares in net national income, Germany, 1980–2013 (per cent)
Source: Statistisches Bundesamt (2014), our presentation based on data provided by Petra Dünhaupt.
Note: West Germany until 1990.

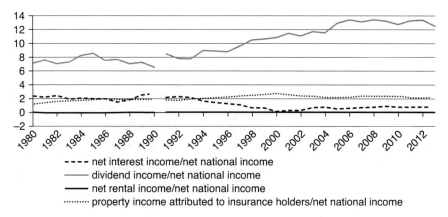

Figure 9.3 Components of rentiers' income as a share in net national income, Germany
1980–2013 (per cent)

Source: Statistisches Bundesamt (2014), our presentation based on data provided by Petra Dünhaupt.
Note: West Germany until 1990.

of retained earnings of corporations. However, from the 1990s until the Great
Recession, the fall in the wage share benefited mainly the rentiers' income share.
Only during the short upswing before the Great Recession did the share of retained
earnings also increase at the expense of the wage share. Decomposing the rentiers'
income share (see Figure 9.3), it becomes clear that starting in the mid-1990s,
the increase was almost exclusively driven by a rise in the share of dividends.
This is in the same period when we observe an increasing relevance of finance
and shareholders in the German economy.

Third, trade-union bargaining power has been weakened considerably. There
are several indicators for this. Starting in the early/mid-1990s, downsizing the
government sector and the switch towards restrictive macroeconomic policies
focussing exclusively on achieving low inflation and (close to) balanced public budgets meant low growth and rising unemployment, in particular in the
stagnation period of the early 2000s (cf. Bibow, 2005; Hein and Truger, 2005,
2007a; Herr and Kazandziska, 2011). There were policies of deregulation and
liberalisation targeting the labour market (the Hartz laws, Agenda 2010[4]), which
explicitly and successfully aimed at weakening trade-union bargaining power
by (a) lowering unemployment benefits, (b) establishing a large low-paid sector
and (c) reducing trade union membership, collective wage bargaining coverage
and the co-ordination of wage bargaining across sectors and regions (Hein and
Truger, 2005, 2007a). Table 9.4 summarises some data on these developments.
Furthermore, trade and financial openness of the German economy increased
significantly and put pressure on trade unions through international competition
in the goods and services markets and through the threat effect of delocalisation.
The foreign trade ratio (exports plus imports as a share of gross domestic product
– GDP), an indicator for trade openness, increased from 39.1 per cent in the
mid-1990s to 71.4 per cent in 2007, just before the Great Recession (Statistisches

Table 9.4 Indicators related to trade unions, labour market regulation and unemployment benefits, Germany 1990–2013

	1990–1994	1995–1999	2000–2004	2005–2009	2010–2013
Trade Unions					
Union density rate (per cent)	32.7	27.0	23.4	20.1	18.3
Union coverage of workplaces or establishments (per cent)	57.4	49.0		43.0	
Bargaining (or union) coverage, adjusted for occupations and sectors without right for bargaining (per cent)	85.0	74.2	67.9	63.9	61.1
Employment protection					
Strictness of employment protection – individual dismissals (regular contracts) (index)	2.6	2.7	2.7	2.9	2.9
Strictness of employment protection – collective dismissals (additional restrictions) (index)		3.6	3.6	3.6	3.6
Strictness of employment protection – temporary contracts (index)	3.3	2.6	1.7	1.0	1.0
Unemployment benefits					
Gross replacement rate (per cent of average production worker wage[1])	28.3	26.2	29.2	24.2	20.8
Gross replacement rate (per cent of average wage[2])			32.3	22.6	42.2
Net replacement rate summary measure of benefit entitlements (excl. social assistance and housing benefits) (per cent)			60.1	45.3	
Net replacement rate summary measure of benefit entitlements (incl. social assistance and housing benefits) (per cent)			63.1	57.6	53.7

Notes: Averages were calculated for the five-year periods indicated. Sometimes data were not available for all years; [1] refers to the average wage in sector D (Manufacturing) of the International Standard Industrial Classification of All Economic Activities (ISIC), Rev.3; [2] refers to the average wage in sectors B to N of the ISIC, Rev.4.
Sources: OECD (2014) for data on unemployment benefits and employment protection; Visser (2013) for data on trade unions; our calculations

Bundesamt, 2011). The foreign assets/foreign liabilities–GDP ratios, as indicators for financial openness, increased from 56/40 per cent in 1991 to 200/174 per cent in 2007 (Deutsche Bundesbank, 2014).

Finally, the shareholder-value orientation and short termism of management rose considerably, thus increasing the pressure on workers and trade unions. According to Detzer (2014a), the share of stocks directly held by private investors halved between 1991 and 2007, while the share held by institutional investors increased significantly. Similarly, strategic investors reduced their ownership share and investors who are more likely to have purely financial interests increased it. Also, there are fewer strategic block-holders, which could shield managers from market pressure. Additionally, activist hedge funds and private equity firms, which directly pressure management to favour shareholder value, have become more active in Germany. Furthermore, the development of a market for corporate control put pressure on managers to pursue shareholder value-friendly strategies in order to protect themselves against hostile takeovers. Notably, there are rising shares of financial incomes received in the operating surplus of German non-financial corporations, as well as a rising share of distributed profits, that is dividends and interest, in the operating surplus of these corporations. This is indicative of an increasing shareholder-value orientation of the management of non-financial corporations and an increasing preference for financial investment generating short-term profits at the expense of long-term oriented real investment (Hein and Detzer, 2014; Statistisches Bundesamt, 2012).

The German 'export-led mercantilist' type of development

Against the background of the increasing shareholder-value orientation of man-agement, which constrained investment in capital stock and the redistribution of income at the expense of the wage share and low-income households, average real GDP-growth over the cycle slowed down considerable with the increasing dominance of finance and the associated redistribution of income (see Table 9.5). Furthermore, whereas real GDP-growth in the cycles of the 1960s, 1970s and even the 1980s was mainly driven by domestic demand, in the trade cycles of the 1990s and early 2000s the growth contributions of net exports went up to considerably to 0.47 and 0.64 percentage points, respectively, which meant 33 and 40 per cent of real GDP-growth. In the course of this process, the degree of openness of the German economy exploded: the share of exports in GDP increased from 24 per cent in 1995 to 51 per cent in 2013 and the share of imports rose from 23 per cent in 1995 to 44 per cent in 2013 (European Commission, 2014). Growth was thus increasingly driven by net exports and the relevance of domestic demand declined dramatically.

The increasing relevance of net exports as the driver of growth since the early/mid-1990s finds its expression in the development of the financial balances of the main macroeconomic sectors (see Figure 9.4). The financial balance of the external sector (RoW) had turned positive in the 1990s after the German reuni-fication when Germany ran trade and current account deficits financed by capital

Table 9.5 Real GDP growth in Germany (in per cent) and growth contributions of the main demand aggregates (in percentage points), 1961–2013, cyclical averages

	1961–1966	1967–1974	1975–1981	1982–1992	1993–2002	2003–2008	2009–2013
Real GDP growth, per cent	4.49	3.82	2.40	2.77	1.40	1.59	0.66
Growth contribution of (percentage points)							
domestic demand including stocks	4.49	3.59	2.36	2.52	0.93	0.94	0.58
private consumption	2.47	2.25	1.55	1.42	0.72	0.28	0.60
public consumption	1.03	0.84	0.70	0.21	0.28	0.17	0.26
gross fixed capital formation	1.28	0.47	0.38	0.69	0.04	0.40	−0.10
change in inventories and net acquisition of valuables	−0.29	0.03	0.28	0.20	−0.11	0.10	−0.19
the balance of goods and services (net exports)	−0.01	0.23	0.04	0.25	0.47	0.64	0.08

Source: European Commission (2014), our calculations
Notes: The beginning of a trade cycle is given by a local minimum of annual real GDP growth, 1961–1966 and 2009–2013 are incomplete cycles.

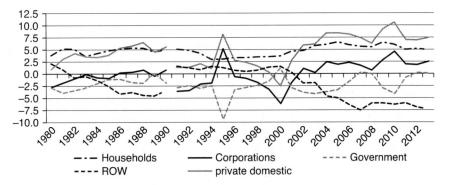

Figure 9.4 Financial Balances, Germany 1980–2013 (percentage of nominal GDP)
Source: European Commission (2014), our calculations.
Notes: West Germany until 1990. In 1995 the deficit of the 'Treuhandanstalt' was shifted from the corporate sector to the government sector. In 2000, the payments for UMTS licences from the corporate sector to the government sector are included. RoW is 'Rest of the world'.

inflows. It became negative in the early 2000s and decreased to –7.5 percent of nominal GDP in 2007. German growth was thus relying on current account surpluses – the counterpart of the deficits of the external sector – the extent of which had not been observed in German history before. The financial balances of the German private households have a long tradition of being in surplus. But these surpluses even increased in the early 2000s, indicating weak consumption demand and were accompanied by positive and rising financial balances of the corporate sector in this period, too, which indicates weak investment in capital stock. This meant large and increasing financial surpluses of the private sector as a whole, which were only temporarily and partly compensated by government sector deficits: the public sector was balanced in 2007, just before the Great Recession.

Therefore, the German type of development from the early/mid-1990s and from the early 2000s in particular, until the Great Recession can be classified as 'export-led mercantilist'.[5] This type of development was highly fragile, as became clear in the course of the financial and economic crisis. The moderate growth rates were dependent on the dynamic growth of export markets and hence on the expansion of the world economy. A collapse of the latter would therefore have major effects on German growth in particular. At the same time, increasing capital exports to the more dynamic economies carried the risk of contagion in the case of a financial crisis in these markets.

Before we move on to the crisis and the recovery in Germany, let us stress that we do not argue that the German type of export-led mercantilist development before the crisis was exclusively due to the increasing dominance of finance and associated redistribution of income. As has been analysed by Bibow (2005), Hein and Truger (2005, 2007a) and Herr and Kazandziska (2011) in more detail, restrictive macroeconomic policies have contributed significantly to depressed investment and consumption demand and hence to the mediocre growth and employment performance in Germany starting in the mid-1990s and, in particular, after the recession in the early 2000s. Increasing uncertainty, caused by policies of 'structural reform' and deregulation in the labour market (Agenda 2010 and Hartz-laws), subsidies for capital-based private pension schemes ('Riester'- and 'Rürup'-pensions) and redistribution at the expense of (low) labour income and in favour of profits and high income recipients associated with nominal wage moderation, have led to an increase in the propensity to save of private households since 2001. This contributed to weak consumption demand, which also affected investment in capital in the negative. Finally, high unemployment and pressures on trade unions caused moderate wage increases that not only contributed to redistribution at the expense of labour but also to inflation rates well below the euro-area average, leading to above average real interest rates. This made Germany particularly vulnerable to the 'anti-growth' bias (Bibow, 2007; Hein and Truger, 2007b) characterising the monetary policies of the European Central Bank (ECB) in the period from 1999 until the Great Recession. Moreover, the attempts of fiscal policy to balance the budget by means of expenditure cuts in periods of weak private demand, in particular in the period between the early 2000s and the Great Recession, reinforced weak domestic demand without directly reaching the consolidation target.

Deep crisis – quick recovery: Germany as a role model?

The 2008–2009 recession in Germany proved to be particularly strong (see Figure 9.5), also by international comparison. This was mainly due to the fact that, as a neo-mercantilist economy mainly driven by export demand, Germany

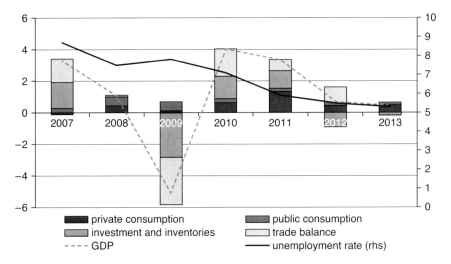

Figure 9.5 Real GDP growth, growth contributions of demand components and unemployment rate, Germany 2007–2013 (in percentage points (lhs), in per cent (rhs))

Source: European Commission (2014).

was particularly hard hit by the global slowdown and the dramatic decline in export demand. Although the recession was stronger in Germany than in many other economies, the loss in employment and the corresponding increase in the unemployment rate were much smaller (see Figure 9.5). This can be partially explained by a dramatic rise in short-time work, heavily subsidised by the government and the extensive use of the so-called working-time accounts, allowing firms to flexibly adjust their labour volume without sacking workers (OECD, 2010; SVR, 2009b; Will, 2011). Another striking feature was the fast recovery in Germany. After the large drop in GDP in 2009, growth picked up strongly in 2010 and 2011 and the unemployment rate fell to levels recently experienced only during the reunification boom.

The German Council of Economic Experts has identified two channels through which the crisis was transmitted into the German economy (SVR, 2009a): the foreign trade channel and the financial market channel. The foreign-trade channel became particularly effective because of the rapid increase in German dependence on exports and the specialisation in more volatile sectors and products (investment goods and cars in particular). The financial transmission channel is closely related to financial globalisation and the increasing German current account surpluses in the course of the early 2000s. Net foreign financial assets held by German wealth-owners rapidly increased up to €650 billion in 2007. Total foreign assets stood at €5 trillion. A large part of those assets were held by German banks (€2.5 trillion). While total foreign exposure had been standing at about 2.7 times banks' equity in 1995, it had increased to 7.6 at the end of 2007 (SVR, 2009a). Soon after the crisis started, German banks and other financial institutions registered heavy losses on those assets. The write-offs of large German financial institutions (banks and insurance companies) directly related to the financial crisis amounted to €102 billion in the period from 2007 to August 2009 (SVR, 2009a).

Germany's quick recovery from the crisis depended on three main favourable factors: the successful containment of the crisis in the financial sector, macroeconomic policies supporting recovery and dynamic export markets once again stimulating aggregate demand.

The losses in the financial sector rather swiftly translated into problems for large major banking institutions in Germany. At first public or partly public and later also increasingly private institutions were threatened with insolvency. However, the German government intervened on a massive scale to contain the problems in the financial sector, providing guarantees of up to €168 billion. It also recapitalised banks with almost €30 billion and allowed them to transfer their toxic assets to government-owned 'bad banks' (Bundesministerium der Finanzen, 2013). Additionally, there were costs for the budgets of the Länder (federal states) and municipalities related to the stabilisation of the Landesbanken (federal state banks) (Deutscher Bundestag, 2014). All together, these interventions contributed to the stabilisation of the German financial sector and the avoidance of a widespread banking crisis and a credit crunch in Germany. Another favourable factor was that, different from many of the internationally oriented big banks, the smaller locally oriented banks were not severely affected by the crisis and kept functioning well (Detzer, 2014b).

Macroeconomic policy, in particular fiscal policy, also helped to stabilise the German economy: a substantial stimulus package for 2009 and 2010 was enacted that amounted to 3.1 per cent of the 2008 GDP. This was certainly above the euro-area average. However, the US stimulus package had a volume of more than 5 per cent of GDP in the period 2008–2010, and was therefore substantially bigger (Hein and Truger, 2010; OECD, 2009).[6]

Therefore, on the domestic level, the fast stabilisation of the financial sector and the expansionary fiscal policies played a major role in stabilising the economy. However, looking at quarterly data, one can see that the recovery in 2009 only set in after a resumption of export demand (Statistisches Bundesamt, 2014) and that demand and growth in Germany after the crisis, in particular between 2010 and 2012, were again largely driven by net exports. Growth in investment activity in emerging markets sustained demand for German export goods and compensated for the reduction in exports to the euro area (Detzer and Hein, 2014).

However, this German type of recovery – increasingly considered as a role model for other countries – suffers from two major drawbacks. First, to the extent that it was driven by net exports, it relied on the neo-mercantilist type of development that had considerably contributed to global and regional imbalances and to the severity of the crisis in the first place. It therefore contained the seeds for further imbalances, fragilities and vulnerabilities of the German economy and it contributed significantly to the still persistent euro crisis (Cesaratto and Stirati, 2010; Hein, 2013–2014; Hein et al., 2012). Second, as a political precondition for the German fiscal stimulus packages, a so-called 'debt brake' was introduced into the German constitution and has been imposed on the other euro-area member countries as well. This will severely limit the room for manoeuvre for German fiscal policy in the future, prevent current account rebalancing and constrain aggregate demand management in the euro area as a whole (Hein and Truger, 2014).

Conclusions and economic policy implications

Based on the worldwide tendencies towards the increasing dominance of finance, which became important in Germany since the 1990s, we have traced the channels through which financialisation and a more neoliberal economic policy stance have contributed to the re-distribution of income at the expense of labour and to more unequal personal or household income distribution in Germany. Next, we have classified the German type of economic development under the conditions of financialisation and income re-distribution as export-led mercantilist. After this we have shown that this type of development showed vulnerability in particular in the course of the financial and economic crisis through the international trade and the financial contagion channels. Finally we have argued that, although the German economy managed to recover rapidly from the crisis through the successful containment of the problems in the financial sector, expansionary fiscal policies and the rapid recovery of German export markets in particular, the German economy cannot be considered a role model for other countries. On the contrary, the quick recovery to a major extent relied on German export-led mercantilism, which had contributed to the severity of the crisis in the first place.

This regime cannot be followed by too many other relevant countries, because it requires counterpart current-account deficit countries that have to accept rising foreign indebtedness in the long run. For this reason, this type of development is highly fragile and there are serious doubts regarding its sustainability, as has been confirmed by the recent crisis. Because of the unsustainability of both export-led mercantilist types of development and, as their counterpart, debt-led consumption ones, several authors have argued that a sustainable recovery strategy should focus on triggering 'wage-led' or 'mass income-led' growth based on rising wages – in particular in the lower segments – and a rising wage share (ILO, 2012; Lavoie and Stockhammer, 2013). Hein (2012: Chapter 7), Hein and Mundt (2012) and Hein and Truger (2012–2013) have suggested that such a wage-led recovery strategy should be embedded in a Global Keynesian New Deal, which more broadly would have to address the three main causes for the severity of the crisis: the inefficient regulation of financial markets, the increasing inequality in the distribution of income, and the rising imbalances at the global and the regional levels. The three main pillars of the policy package of a Global Keynesian New Deal are the following: first, the re-regulation of the financial sector in order to prevent future financial excesses and financial crises and to contribute to the re-distribution of income in favour of labour and capital invested in production; second, the re-orientation of macroeconomic policies towards stimulating and stabilising domestic demand, in particular in the current account surplus countries like Germany; and third, the re-construction of international macroeconomic policy co-ordination and a new world financial order in order to prevent export-led mercantilist, 'beggar thy neighbour' strategies.

Notes

1 This chapter is part of the results of the project Financialisation, Economy, Society and Sustainable Development (FESSUD). It has received funding from the European Union Seventh Framework Programme (FP7/2007–2013) under grant agreement no. 266800. (Website: www.fessud.eu). The chapter draws on Detzer and Hein (2014). We would like to thank Roel van Geijn for editing assistance.
2 On the macroeconomics of financialisation or financed-dominated capitalism, see Hein (2012).
3 See Hein (2015) for a review of the respective empirical literature based on different sets of countries and Hein and Detzer (2014) for a more detailed study on financialisation and distribution in Germany.
4 The Agenda 2010 of the early 2000s was meant to reform the German labour markets and welfare system. The Hartz laws were a key element of the Agenda 2010, increasing the pressure on the unemployed and reducing benefits in particular. Furthermore, labour laws were changed to legalise atypical types of employment such as 'mini' and 'midi' jobs as well as labour leasing.

5 For a classification of 'export-led mercantilist', 'debt-led consumption boom' and 'domestic demand-led' types of development or regimes and its application to different sets of countries, see, among others, Hein (2012: Chapter 6), Hein and Mundt (2012), Stockhammer (2010, 2012) and van Treeck and Sturn (2012), all of whom use slightly different terminologies.

6 For a more extensive analysis of the macroeconomic policies during the crisis see Hein and Truger (2010), Detzer et al. (2013: Chapter 17) and Detzer and Hein (2014).

References

Alvaredo, F., Atkinson, A.B., Piketty, T. and Saez, E. (2014) The World Top Incomes Database. Available at: http://g-mond.parisschoolofeconomics.eu/topincomes/ (accessed 7 May 2015).

Bibow, J. (2005) Germany in Crisis: The Unification Challenge, Macroeconomic Policy Shocks and Traditions, and EMU. *International Review of Applied Economics* 19: 29–50.

Bibow, J. (2007) The ECB – How Much of a Success Story, Really? In Hein, E., Priewe, J. and Truger, A. (eds) *European Integration in Crisis*. Marburg: Metropolis.

Bundesministerium der Finanzen (2013) Fünf Jahre Finanzmarktstabilisierungsfonds unter dem Dach der Bundesanstalt für Finanzmarktstabilisierung, Gastbeitrag der Bundesanstalt für Finanzmarktstabilisierung (FMSA), Monatsbericht Dezember 2013. Berlin: Bundesministerium der Finanzen. Available at: www.bundesfinanzministerium. de/Content/DE/Monatsberichte/2013/12/Downloads/monatsbericht_2013_12_deutsch. pdf?__blob=publicationFile&v=7 (accessed 7 May 2015).

Cesaratto, S. and Stirati, A. (2010) Germany and the European and Global Crises. *International Journal of Political Economy* 39(4): 56–86.

Detzer, D. (2014a) *Inequality and the Financial System – The Case of Germany*. Global Labour University Working Paper No. 23.

Detzer, D (2014b) The German Financial System and the Financial Crisis. *Intereconomics* 49(2): 56–64.

Detzer, D., Dodig, N., Evans, T., Hein, E. and Herr, H. (2013) *The German Financial System*. FESSUD Studies in Financial Systems No. 3, University of Leeds.

Detzer, D. and Hein, E. (2014) *Financialisation and the Financial and Economic Crises: The Case of Germany*. FESSUD Studies in Financial Systems No. 18, University of Leeds.

Deutsche Bundesbank (2014) *Time Series Data Base*. Available at: www.bundesbank.de/ Navigation/EN/Statistics/Time_series_databases/Macro_economic_time_series/macro_ economic_time_series_node.html (accessed 7 May 2015).

Deutscher Bundestag (2014) Drucksache 18/424.

Dünhaupt, P. (2011) *The Impact of Financialization on Income Distribution in the USA and Germany: A Proposal for a New Adjusted Wage Share*. IMK Working Paper 7/2011. Düsseldorf: Macroeconomic Policy Institute (IMK) at Hans Böckler Foundation.

Dünhaupt, P. (2012) Financialization and the Rentier Income Share – Evidence from the USA and Germany. *International Review of Applied Economics* 26: 465–487.

European Commission (2014) AMECO Database, Spring 2014. Available at: http://ec. europa.eu/economy_finance/db_indicators/ameco/index_en.htm (accessed 7 May 2015).

Grabka, M.M. and Westermeier, C. (2014) Anhaltend hohe Vermögensungleichheit in Deutschland. *DIW Wochenbericht* 9/2014: 151–164.

Hein, E. (2012) *The Macroeconomics of Finance-Dominated Capitalism – and its Crisis.* Cheltenham: Edward Elgar.

Hein, E. (2013–2014) The Crisis of Finance-Dominated Capitalism in the Euro Area, Deficiencies in the Economic Policy Architecture, and Deflationary Stagnation Policies. *Journal of Post Keynesian Economics* 36(2): 325–354.

Hein, E. (2014) *Distribution and Growth after Keynes: A Post-Keynesian Guide.* Cheltenham: Edward Elgar.

Hein, E. (2015) Finance-Dominated Capitalism and Re-Distribution of Income – A Kaleckian Perspective. *Cambridge Journal of Economics* 39(3): 907–934

Hein, E. and Detzer, D. (2014) Finance-Dominated Capitalism and Income Distribution: A Kaleckian Perspective on the Case of Germany. *Italian Economic Journal* 1(2): 171–191.

Hein, E. and Mundt, M. (2012) *Financialisation and the Requirements and Potentials for Wage-Led Recovery – A Review Focussing on the G20.* Conditions of Work and Employment Series No. 37. Geneva: International Labour Organization (ILO).

Hein, E. and Truger, A. (2005) What Ever Happened to Germany? Is the Decline of the Former European Key Currency Country Caused by Structural Sclerosis or by Macroeconomic Mismanagement? *International Review of Applied Economics* 19: 3–28.

Hein, E. and Truger, A. (2007a) Germany's Post-2000 Stagnation in the European Context – A Lesson in Macroeconomic Mismanagement. In Arestis, P., Hein, E. and Le Heron, E. (eds) *Aspects of Modern Monetary and Macroeconomic Policies.* Basingstoke: Palgrave Macmillan: 223–247.

Hein, E. and Truger, A. (2007b) Monetary Policy, Macroeconomic Policy Mix and Economic Performance in the Euro Area. In Hein, E. and Truger, A. (eds) *Money, Distribution and Economic Policy: Alternatives to Orthodox Macroeconomics.* Cheltenham: Edward Elgar: 216–243.

Hein, E. and Truger, A. (2010) Financial Crisis, Global Recession and Macroeconomic Policy Reactions – The Case of Germany. In Dullien, S., Hein, E., Truger, A. and van Treeck, T. (eds) *The World Economy in Crisis – The Return of Keynesianism?* Marburg: Metropolis: 191–220.

Hein, E. and Truger, A. (2012–2013) Finance-Dominated Capitalism in Crisis – The Case for a Global Keynesian New Deal. *Journal of Post Keynesian Economics* 35: 183–210.

Hein, E. and Truger, A. (2014) Fiscal Policy and Rebalancing in the Euro Area: A Critique of the German Debt Brake from a Post-Keynesian Perspective. *Panoeconomicus* 61(1): 21–38.

Hein, E., Truger, A. and van Treeck, T. (2012) The European Financial and Economic Crisis: Alternative Solutions from a (Post-)Keynesian Perspective. In Arestis, P. and Sawyer, M. (eds) *The Euro Crisis: International Papers in Political Economy.* Basingstoke: Palgrave Macmillan: 35–78.

Herr, H. and Kazandziska, M. (2011) *Macroeconomic Policy Regimes in Western Industrial Countries.* Abingdon: Routledge.

ILO (2012) *Global Wage Report: Wages and Equitable Growth.* Geneva: International Labour Organization (ILO).

Kalecki, M. (1954) *Theory of Economic Dynamics.* London: George Allen & Unwin.

Lavoie, M. and Stockhammer, E. (2013) Wage-Led Growth: Concept, Theories and Policies. In Lavoie, M. and Stockhammer, E. (eds) W*age-Led Growth: An Equitable Strategy for Economic Recovery.* Basingstoke: Palgrave Macmillan.

OECD (2008) *Growing Unequal? Income Distribution and Poverty in OECD Countries.* Paris: Organisation for Economic Co-operation and Development (OECD).

OECD (2009) *Economic Outlook*. Interim Report. Paris: Organisation for Economic Co-operation and Development (OECD).

OECD (2010) *OECD Employment Outlook: Moving Beyond the Job-Crisis*. Paris: Organisation for Economic Co-operation and Development (OECD).

OECD (2012) OECD.StatExtracts. Paris: Organisation for Economic Co-operation and Development (OECD). Available at: http://stats.oecd.org/ (accessed 13 August 2012).

OECD (2014) OECD.Stat. Paris: OECD (Organisation for Economic Co-operation and Development). Available at: http//stats.oecd.org (accessed 22 May 2015).

Statistisches Bundesamt (2011) *Export, Import, Globalisierung. Deutscher Außenhandel*. Wiesbaden: Statistisches Bundesamt. Available at: www.destatis.de/DE/Publikationen/ Thematisch/Aussenhandel/Gesamtentwicklung/AussenhandelWelthandel5510006127004. pdf?__blob=publicationFile (accessed 7 May 2015).

Statistisches Bundesamt (2012) *Sector Accounts – Annual Results 1991 onwards – 1991 to 2011*. Wiesbaden: Statistisches Bundesamt. Available at: https://www.destatis.de/DE/ Publikationen/Thematisch/VolkswirtschaftlicheGesamtrechnungen/Nationaleinkommen/ SectorAccountsAnnualresultsPDF_5812106.pdf (accessed 7 May 2015).

Statistisches Bundesamt (2014) Genesis-Online Data Base. May 2014. Wiesbaden: Statistisches Bundesamt.

Stockhammer, E. (2010) Income Distribution, the Finance-Dominated Accumulation Regime, and the Present Crisis. In Dullien, S., Hein, E., Truger, A. and van Treeck, T. (eds) *The World Economy in Crisis – the Return of Keynesianism?* Marburg: Metropolis: 63–86.

Stockhammer, E. (2012): Financialization, Income Distribution and the Crisis. *Investigación Económica* 71(279): 39–70.

SVR (2009a) *Deutschland im Internationalen Konjunkturzusammenhang. Expertise im Auftrag der Bundesregierung*. Wiesbaden: Statistisches Bundesamt.

SVR (2009b) *Die Zukunft nicht aufs Spiel setzen*. Jahresgutachten 2009/2010. Wiesbaden: Statistisches Bundesamt.

van Treeck, T. and Sturn, S. (2012) *Income Inequality as a Cause of the Great Recession? A Survey of Current Debates*. Conditions of Work and Employment Series No. 39. Geneva: International Labour Organization (ILO).

Visser, J. (2013) *ICTWSS: Database on Institutional Characteristics of Trade Unions, Wage Setting, State Intervention and Social Pacts in 34 countries between 1960 and 2012*. Amsterdam: Institute for Advanced Labour Studies at the University of Amsterdam. Available at: www.uva-aias.net/208 (accessed 21 May 2015).

Will, H. (2011) *Germany's Short Time Compensation Program: Macroeconom(etr)ic Insight*. IMK Working Paper 1/2011. Düsseldorf: Macroeconomic Policy Institute (IMK) at Hans Böckler Foundation.

10 Macroeconomic processes and economic inequalities in India

Jayati Ghosh

Introduction

Global perceptions of the Indian economy have been prey to swings that are almost as volatile – and as irrational – as the behaviour of unregulated financial markets. The celebration of India as one of the significant 'success stories' of globalisation along with China has more recently been replaced by a more pessimistic and negative assessment of its rampant crony capitalism, growing inequality and current tendencies towards stagflation. Yet both perceptions miss the point. Indeed, the extreme assessments on either side are not just inadequate but flawed: they fail to capture the basic tendencies that generated both growth and inequality and do not understand why the growth model that was so celebrated was unsustainable in the first place.

Exclusion through incorporation

Taking a long view, there are some clear achievements of the Indian economy since independence – most crucially the emergence of a reasonably diversified economy with an industrial base. The past 30 years have also witnessed rates of aggregate gross domestic product (GDP) growth that are high compared with the past and also compared with several other parts of the developing world. Significantly, this higher aggregate growth has thus far been accompanied by macroeconomic stability, with the absence of extreme volatility in the form of financial crises such as have been evident in several other emerging markets. There has also been some reduction (although not very rapid) in income poverty.

However, there are also some clear failures of this growth process even from a long-run perspective. An important failure is the worrying absence of structural change, in terms of the ability to shift the labour force out of low-productivity activities, especially in agriculture, to higher productivity and better remunerated activities. As Figure 10.1 indicates, the share of agriculture and allied activities in GDP fell from around 55 per cent in 1960–1961 to less than 18 per cent in 2011–2012 and the share of employment it accounted for declined much more slowly over the entire period (from 72 per cent in 1960–1961 to 48 per cent in 2011–2012). In the past decade, the agrarian crisis across many parts of the

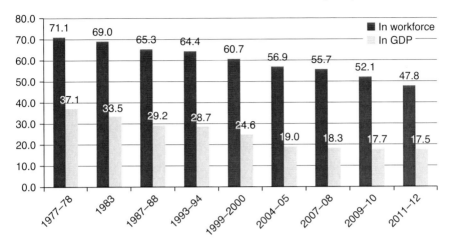

Figure 10.1 Share of agriculture
Sources: National Sample Survey Organisation, various large sample rounds and Central Statistical Organisation, National Income Accounts, various issues.

country has impacted adversely on the livelihood of both cultivators and rural workers, yet the generation of more productive employment outside this sector remains woefully inadequate. The lack of structural change specifically in terms of employment may prove to be the most critical failure of all. The share of manufacturing has stagnated at low levels of both output and employment – in 2011–2012 it accounted for only 14.4 per cent of GDP and 12.6 per cent of the work force. Ajit Singh and Sukti Dasgupta (2005) argue that India can successfully become a post-industrial 'service-driven' economy on the basis of modern services that are associated with rapid productivity increases. But it would be foolhardy to presume that the difficult but necessary stage of industrialisation can simply be bypassed in this manner, especially as the newer more productive services also generate very little additional employment. Indeed, the recent experience of the Indian economy is startling in the extent of its deviation from almost all of the expected features of the classic pattern that was outlined by Lewis (1954), Kuznets (1955) and Kaldor (1955).[1]

Other major failures, which are directly reflective of the still poor status of human development in most parts of the country, are in many ways related to this fundamental failure. These include: the persistence of widespread poverty; the sluggishness of employment, especially in the formal sector; the absence of basic food security (and growing food insecurity) for a significant proportion of the population; the inability to ensure basic needs of housing, sanitation, adequate health care to the population as a whole; the continuing inability to ensure universal education and the poor quality of much school education; and the sluggish enlargement of access to education and employment across different social groups and for women in particular. In addition there are problems caused by the very pattern of economic growth: aggravated regional imbalances, greater inequalities in the control over assets and in access to incomes, and the dispossession and displacement of people from land and livelihood without adequate compensation and rehabilitation.

Seen in this light, it becomes apparent that a basic feature of the process of economic development thus far has been exclusion: from control over assets, from the benefits of economic growth, from the impact of physical and social infrastructure expansion, from education and from income-generating opportunities. This exclusion has been along class or income lines, by geographical location, by caste and community and by gender. However, this has not meant exclusion from the system as such – rather, those who are supposedly marginalised or excluded have been affected precisely because they have been incorporated into market systems. We therefore have a process of exclusion through incorporation, a process that has actually been typical of capitalist accumulation across the world, especially in its more dynamic phases. Thus, peasants facing a crisis of viability of cultivation have been integrated into a market system that has made them more reliant on purchased inputs in deregulated markets and on volatile output markets in which state protection is completely inadequate. The growing army of 'self-employed' workers, who now account for more than half of our workforce, have been excluded from paid employment because of the sheer difficulty of finding jobs, but are nevertheless heavily involved in commercial activity and exposed to market uncertainties in the search for livelihood. Those who have been displaced by developmental projects or other processes and subsequently have not found adequate livelihood in other activities are victims of the process of economic integration, though excluded from the benefits.

This is largely because growth has not been associated with much employment generation. The expectation was that global competition would favour more labour-intensive activities. In fact the employment elasticities of output growth have actually declined as the economy has become more exposed to competition. This increase of labour productivity in traded goods sectors is a typical feature in several developing countries that felt the effects of external competition, which tends to force or incentivise the adoption of the latest labour-saving technologies from the North. In addition, a significant part of the increase in GDP has come from services that are not very employment-intensive, such as financial services and telecommunications.

The share of manufacturing in both output and employment has been stubbornly constant at relatively low levels. Low-productivity work continues to dominate in total employment, so in the aggregate there is little evidence of labour moving to higher productivity activities. Interestingly this is true across sectors, such that low-productivity employment co-exists with some high-value-added activities and there are extremely wide variations in productivity across enterprises even within the same sub-sector. The expected formalisation of work and the concentration of workers into large-scale production units has not occurred – rather, there has been a widespread persistence of informal employment and increase in self-employment in non-agricultural activities. Most striking of all is that the period of rapid GDP growth has been marked by low and declining workforce participation rates of women, in a pattern that is unlike almost any other rapidly growing economy in any phase of history over the past two centuries.

Remarkably, these features have persisted through different growth models and policy regimes in the post-independence period, whether Nehruvian mixed economy or open economy market-based strategies and through varying periods of slow growth, stagnation and rapid growth. The specific concern for our purposes is with the more recent period, when the significantly accelerated expansion of economic activity over the past two decades could have been expected to generate more significant structural changes as well.

The dominance of informal work

The period since the early 1990s has been marked by stagnation of formal employment growth despite accelerated output growth and lower intensity of employment in the most dynamic manufacturing and services sub-sectors (Arora, 2010; Kannan and Raveendran, 2009). Even within sectors that are perceived as more dynamic, the majority of workers persist in low-productivity activities, with only a small minority in each sector involved in highly remunerated and high productivity work. The most rapidly expanding activities in terms of GDP share, such as finance, insurance and real estate (FIRE), IT-related services and tele-communications which together now account for nearly 20 per cent of the GDP, still employ less than 2 per cent of the workforce. The persistence of the vast majority of workers in extremely low-productivity activities is therefore evident. Informal work overwhelmingly dominates total employment. In 2004–2005, informal workers were estimated to account for 96 per cent of all workers and there is little to suggest that the share of formal work would have increased greatly since then. This is in marked contrast to the experience of China, for example, where the period of rapid growth has been associated not only with industrialisation but particularly the emergence and preponderance of medium- and large-scale units that provide formal employment to workers. The persistence and continued domination of low-productivity work in all the major sectors despite several decades of rapid aggregate income growth suggests a particularly unusual growth pattern in India. The incidence of self-employment (most of it highly fragile and vulnerable) has actually increased as a proportion of non-agricultural work and the only reason for its overall stagnation is the decline in agricultural employment, particularly in the number of women workers self-employed in agriculture. Meanwhile, the share of the informal sector in GDP has fallen quite sharply during this period of high growth. Indeed, the recent period of most rapid acceleration of national income (NNP) was also the period marked by the sharpest fall in the share of unorganised incomes as shown in Figure 10.2. Thus, while the formal organised sector has substantially increased its share of national income, it has done so without drawing in more workers in the standard Lewisian trajectory, which involves a shift of workers from informal to formal activities in the course of development.

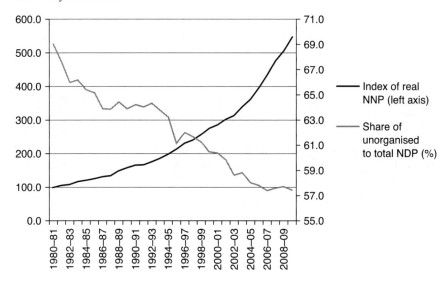

Figure 10.2 Unorganised sector in NDP
Source: CSO, Factor incomes in India, 2009–10.

The decline in female work participation

Another remarkable feature of the recent economic growth process in India is that, unlike most other cases of rapid economic growth that have been observed historically, recognised work-participation rates of women have not only not increased, but have actually declined. This is significant for several reasons. It is now generally accepted that most women work, even when they are not recorded as 'workers' by official and other data gatherers. The tasks associated with social reproduction and the care economy are largely (though not solely) borne by women, but in many societies these are not counted among economic or productive activities. Similarly many women are engaged in what is recognised otherwise as productive work, but as unpaid household helpers who are therefore only marginally seen as workers in their own right. The general invisibility of women's work is itself a mostly accurate reflection of their status in society: where women's official work participation is low, this is typically a sign of less freedom and mobility of women, lower status and lower empowerment. Indeed, where more women are active in the labour market and are employed (especially in formal activities), the share of unpaid work tends to come down and even the unpaid labour performed by women is more likely to be recognised and valued. This is why looking at the extent, coverage, conditions and remuneration of women's work is often a useful way of judging the extent to which their broader status in society has improved.

Female work participation rates (WPRs) in India have historically been significantly lower than male rates and are among the lower rates to be observed even in the developing world. What is more surprising is that despite three decades of relatively rapid GDP growth, these rates have not increased, but have actually fallen in recent times. The gap between male and female WPRs (for the 15+ age group) has grown, as male rates have remained stable and female rates have declined below their already very low levels (see Figure 10.3). The decline is particularly sharp for rural women (see Figure 10.4). The sharp decline in 2009–2010 was dismissed as a statistical aberration when it first emerged in the large survey of the National Sample Survey Office, but the subsequent large survey in 2011–2012 has revealed a further decline, implying that there is a real tendency at work that has to be understood and explained. In urban areas, WPRs have been very volatile (possibly reflecting the vagaries of the sample survey) but nonetheless over a mildly declining trend.

It is widely believed that the decline in work-participation rates is chiefly because of increasing participation in education, which is to be welcomed. It is

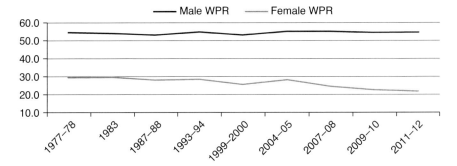

Figure 10.3 All India work participation rates (usual status, principal and subsidiary activities)
Source: NSSO Surveys of Employment and Unemployment.

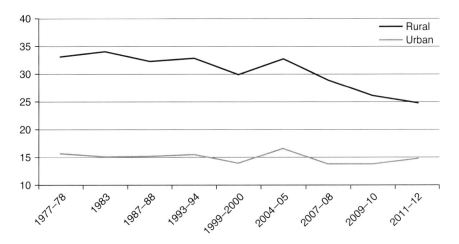

Figure 10.4 Female work participation rates
Source: NSSO Surveys of Employment and Unemployment.

certainly true that female participation in education has increased in both rural and urban areas and especially so since 2007. However, this still does not explain fully the total decline in female labour-force participation, which has been significantly greater (relative to the increase in those engaged in education) in rural India and somewhat greater in urban India. Also, the decline is clearly evident even for the age group 25 to 59 years, where there is little indication of increasing involvement in education. It is worth noting that labour-force participation rates (which include workers and those openly unemployed, i.e. searching but not finding jobs) closely track the work-participation rates, to the point that open unemployment rates of women have been falling because of declining labour-force participation. It may be that the 'discouraged worker' effect is particularly strong for women, or it may reflect other social causes that inhibit engagement in recognised work.

Accumulation through extraction

These tendencies have been reinforced by the nature of the growth strategy adopted in India over the past two decades. The focus of the Indian state (and of most state forces at the regional level) has been on generating growth through various incentives designed to encourage the expansion of private capital. It is now obvious that this can very quickly become prey to corruption, crony capitalism and the like. But it is possibly less obvious that this strategy in itself generates incentives for such private players that effectively militate against a more broadbased and egalitarian economic expansion. So new forms of capital certainly do emerge and proliferate as a result of this strategy, but they do so in a wider context in which capitalist accumulation is based essentially on extraction: of land and other natural resources, of the labour of differentiated workers, of the products of peasant cultivators and small producers of goods and services. This has reduced the incentives to focus on productivity growth and innovation as routes to more rapid growth, since state-aided primitive accumulation and socially determined extra-economic relationships provide easier and more reliable means of generating private surpluses. All this has actually been reinforced under globalisation, rather than being diminished by external competition.

The point is that these transactions in land, labour and product markets are not simply voluntary exchanges between equivalent parties. Instead, the game is played with dice that are heavily loaded in favour of capital, especially large capital, through various means: social institutions that allow for discriminatory labour-market practices, legal and regulatory institutions that can be and are mobilised to enhance the bargaining power of capital, and political forces that actively engage in supporting all of these. The process of capitalist accumulation in India has utilised the agency of the state to further the project of primitive accumulation through diverse means (including land-use change as well as substantial fiscal transfers) and has also exploited specific socio-cultural features, such as caste, community and gender differences, to enable greater labour exploitation and therefore higher surplus generation. These are in turn associated with various other more 'purely economic' patterns that pile on the imbalances: financial institutions, input and product markets that do not provide reasonable credit access and so on.

Accumulation and traditional identity

It can be argued (Harriss-White, 2005) that the greater part of the modern Indian economy is implicitly regulated or determined by social institutions derived from 'primordial identity' such as gender, caste and community. These interact with political forces, generating forms of patronage, control and clientelism that vary across regions. This makes the outcomes of government strategies, including those connected with liberalisation, privatisation and deregulation, different from those generally expected. Take the large bourgeoisie, for example, which is dominated by diversified joint family enterprises extending across different economic sectors. Even in the phase of globalisation, caste, region and linguistic community have been crucial in shaping these groups, determining their behaviour and influencing their interaction with each other as well as with global capital (Damodaran, 2008). The very emergence of such capital has often reflected Indian social forces: for example, there are no major business groups in the North and East that are not from 'traditional' business communities and nationally no Dalit (lowest or Scheduled Caste) business group of significance. Existing practices, such as gender discrimination in property ownership and control, have often been reinforced by corporate behaviour, such as the ability to utilise the existence of legal forms (such as the Hindu Undivided Family form of ownership) that deny any role to women (Das Gupta, 2012). These obviously added to the weight of socially discriminatory practices – and they affected how business houses at large and medium levels dealt with more purely economic forces and their attitudes to investment, employment and output.

Yet it could also be argued that these features of the Indian economic landscape are precisely what have been crucial in generating the recent phase of rapid growth, even as they have allowed the persistence of backwardness and accentuated inequalities in the course of that expansion. The complex nexus between politics and different levels of local, regional and national businesses has allowed for the appropriation of land and other natural resources that has been an integral part of the accumulation story and fed into the way that central and state governments have aided the process of private surplus extraction. More overt economic policies such as patterns of public spending and taxation are only one part of this – a substantial part relates to laws, regulations and their implementation (or lack of it) that provide the contours for the expansion of private capital.

These processes of direct and indirect underwriting of the costs of the corporate sector have been greatly assisted by the ability of employers in India to utilise social characteristics to ensure lower wages to certain categories of workers. Caste and other forms of social discrimination have a long tradition in India and they have interacted with capitalist accumulation to generate peculiar forms of labour-market segmentation that are unique to Indian society. Studies (such as Thorat, 2010) have found that social categories are strongly correlated with the incidence of poverty and that both occupation and wages differ dramatically across social categories. The National Sample Surveys reveal that the probability of being in a low-wage occupation is significantly higher for Scheduled Tribes (STs), Scheduled Castes (SCs), Muslims and Other Backward Castes (OBCs) in that order, compared with the general 'caste Hindu' population. This is only partly because of differences in education and level of skill, which are also important and which in turn reflect the differential provision of education across social categories.

While in many cases class and caste do overlap, the latter always supersedes the former at least in socio-economic factors. Caste is an extra-economic factor that acts in two forms, inequality of opportunity and inequality of outcome. Economic well-being cannot always overturn the inequalities of caste distinction, and that is reflected in the education levels, job opportunities, wage levels, access to social benefits and basic facilities, and so on. Caste clearly affects family income, consumption and other parameters like education, health, and so on. Such caste-based discrimination has operated in both urban and rural labour markets. One study of Delhi (Banerjee and Knight, 1985) found that significant discrimination against Dalit workers operating dominantly through the mechanisms of recruitment and assignment to jobs led to Dalits largely entering poorly-paid 'dead-end' jobs that are essential but significantly lower paid. Similarly, empirical studies of caste behaviour in rural India (Shah et al., 2006; Thorat, 2009) have found that there are many ways in which caste practices operate to reduce the access of the lower castes to local resources as well as to income-earning opportunities, thereby forcing them to provide their labour at the cheapest possible rates to employers. In addition to the well-known lack of assets, a large number of social practices effectively restrict the economic activity of lower caste and Dalit groups and force them to supply very low-wage labour in harsh and usually precarious conditions. These practices in turn can be used to keep wages of Dalit workers (who are extremely constrained in their choice of occupation) low, even in periods of otherwise rising wages. The persistence of such practices and their economic impact even during the period of the Indian economy's much-vaunted dynamic growth has been noted (Human Rights Watch, 2007).

Gender-based differences in labour markets and the social attitudes to women's paid and unpaid work are also reflections of this broader tendency. The widespread perception that women's work forms an 'addition' to household income and therefore commands a much lower reservation wage is common to both private and public employers. So for private employers, women workers within Dalit or other discriminated groups typically receive even lower wages for similar work. In public employment, the use of underpaid women workers receiving wages well below the legal minimum such as Anganwadi workers (those who work in the crèches financed by the Integrated Child Development Services Scheme for pregnant and lactating mothers and children below three years) or Accredited Social Health Activists (ASHAs) has become institutionalised. This applies to several flagship programmes that are designed to deliver essential public services in the areas of health, nutrition, support for early child development and even education. Further, the role played by the unpaid labour of women in contributing not only to social reproduction but also to what would be recognised as productive economic activities in most other societies has been absolutely crucial in enabling this particular accumulation process.

So it may not be surprising that private agents find little value in accumulation strategies that are designed to enable structural transformation. Indeed, such transformation may even be to the detriment of their short-term interests, if it reduces their bargaining power. The low tolerance levels of capitalists in India to anything that can even slightly improve the bargaining power of workers is evident in the growing impossibility of even forming workers unions in most activities controlled by the private sector. It is clearly indicated by the ferocious and orchestrated backlash against something as limited as the National Rural Employment Guarantee Act, only because it has provided some relief to rural workers who could at last begin to demand wages closer to the legal minimum from employers.

The point to note here is not simply that such practices continue to exist, but that they have become the base on which the economic accumulation process rests. In other words, capitalism in India, especially in its most recent globally integrated variant, has used past and current modes of social discrimination and exclusion to its own benefit, to facilitate the extraction of surplus and ensure greater flexibility and bargaining to employers when dealing with workers. So social categories are not 'independent' of the accumulation process – rather, they allow for more surplus extraction, because they reinforce low employment generating (and therefore persistently low wage) tendencies of growth. The ability to benefit from socially segmented labour markets in turn has created incentives for absolute surplus value extraction on the basis of suppressing wages of some workers, rather than requiring a focus on relative surplus value extraction resulting from productivity increases. High-productivity enclaves have not generated sufficient demand for additional workers to force an extension of productivity improvement to other activities; instead the accumulation process has relied indirectly on persistent low wages in supporting activities or on unpaid labour to underwrite the expansion of value added. So the particular (possibly unique) pattern of Indian inequality has led to a long-run growth process that generates further and continued inequality and does not deliver the expected structural change.

Increasing inequalities

This is the broader context within which recent measures of inequality must be interpreted. The only available large-scale survey data in India relate to consumption expenditure, which tend to understate the extent of inequality by underestimating the tails of the distribution (excluding the very rich and the very poor) and because the poor are more likely to consume as much or even more than their income while the rich are more able to save. Indeed, the first detailed income distribution estimates for India (Desai and Dubey, 2011) reveal quite high income inequality, with a Gini coefficient of 0.54 – or around the same as Brazil (based on survey estimates of gross income). Estimates based on village surveys derive even higher Gini coefficients: on average 0.645 across households and 0.595 across persons even within villages (Swaminathan and Rawal, 2011).

Even consumption data suggest increasing inequality of consumption, in both vertical and horizontal terms (Vanneman and Dubey, 2011). The national Gini coefficient for consumption increased from 0.31 in 1993–1994 to 0.36 in 2009–2010, while the ratio of urban to rural consumption went up from 1.62 to 1.96. The largest increases in consumption expenditure were concentrated in the top decile of the urban population: between 1993–1994 and 2009–2010, the income of the top urban decile went from 7.14 to 10.33 times that of the bottom urban decile and from 10.48 to 14.32 times that of the bottom rural decile. The movement of factor incomes corroborates the tendency towards greater inequality: the wage share of national income fell from 40 per cent at the start of the 1990s to only 34 per cent by 2009–2010, while in the organised sector the wage share fell from 69 per cent to 51 per cent in the same period. Meanwhile, even though the unorganised sector continues to account for the overwhelming majority of workers in the country, including the self-employed, its share of national income fell from 64 per cent to 57 per cent (Chandrasekhar and Ghosh, 2013).

So the gains from Indian growth were concentrated among surplus-takers, including profits, rents and financial incomes. A major reason for this is that the growth has not been generating employment sufficiently and therefore around half of the workforce continues to languish in low-productivity agriculture (even though that sector now accounts for less than 15 per cent of GDP) and in low-remuneration services. Recent high economic growth in India was related to financial deregulation that sparked a retail credit boom and combined with fiscal concessions to spur consumption among the richest sections of the population. The growth was driven by internal and external liberalisation measures that attracted global financial investors. Capital inflows sparked a domestic retail credit boom, which combined with fiscal concessions to spur consumption of the better-off sections.

Conclusion

The credit boom led to rapid increases in aggregate GDP growth, even as deflationary fiscal policies, poor employment generation and the persistent agrarian crisis reduced wage shares in national income and kept mass consumption demand low. There was a substantial rise in profit shares in the economy and the proliferation of financial activities. As a result, finance, insurance, real estate and business services accounted for more than 17 per cent of GDP in 2012–2013. This combined with rising asset values to enable a credit-financed consumption splurge among the rich and the middle classes especially in urban areas. And this in turn generated higher rates of investment and output over the upswing. The earlier emphasis on public spending – primarily in the form of public investment but also other spending designed to improve the living standards of the poor – as the principal stimulus for growth in the Indian economy was thus substituted in the past two decades with debt-financed housing investment and private consumption of the elite and burgeoning middle classes (Ghosh and Chandrasekhar, 2009).

The recent Indian growth story in its essentials was therefore not unlike the story of speculative bubble-led expansion that marked the experience of several other developed and developing countries and was therefore subject to similar problems of lack of sustainability. It is well known now that debt-driven bubbles usually end in tears, whether in rich, developed countries, in 'emerging markets' or in resource-rich, less developed countries. In the Indian case, the lack of sustainability is accentuated by the social and political problems that are increasingly emerging, driven by the unequal pattern of growth. Extremist movements are powerful and dominate in 150 backward and relatively undeveloped districts that are the location of extractive industries, lack of productive employment generation has given rise to powerful demands for regional autonomy and the exclusion of 'non-natives' within the different states, other forms of criminality are increasing and there is widespread public anger not only at the evident corruption that has been characteristic of this phase but also at the explicit ways in which state policy has favoured the rich. These create potent sources of instability that may rebound on the growth process in unpredictable ways.

Note

1 This classic pattern is one in which the share of industry (and particularly manufacturing) rises in both national income and employment in the early phases of industrialisation and is only subsequently overtaken by services at higher levels of per capita income.

References

Arora, A. (2010) *Economic Dualism, Openness and Employment in Manufacturing Industry in India.* New Delhi: Jawaharlal Nehru University.

Chandrasekhar, C.P. and Ghosh, J. (2013) India Still a Vast Informal Economy. *Businessline*, 28 October. Available at: www.thehindubusinessline.com/opinion/columns/c-p-chandrasekhar/india-still-a-vast-informal-economy/article5282078.ece (accessed 18 May 2015).

Damodaran, H. (2008) *India's New Capitalists: Caste, Business and Industry in a Modern Nation.* London: Palgrave Macmillan.

Das Gupta, C. (2012) Gender, Property and the Institutional Basis of Tax Policy Concessions: Investigating the Hindu Undivided Family. *MacroScan: An Alternative Economics Website*, 1 September. Available at: www.macroscan.net/index.php?view=search&kwds=Chirashree%20Das%20Gupta (accessed 29 December 2014).

Desai, S. and Dubey, A. (2011) Caste in 21st Century India: Competing Narratives. *Economic and Political Weekly* 46(11): 40–49.

Ghosh, J. and Chandrasekhar, C.P. (2009) The Costs of Coupling: The Global Crisis and the Indian Economy. *Cambridge Journal of Economics* 33(4): 725–739.

Harriss-White, B. (2005) *India's Market Economy*. New Delhi: Three Essays Collective.

Human Rights Watch (2007) *India: Hidden Apartheid: Caste Discrimination against India's 'Untouchables'*. Shadow Report to the UN Committee on the Elimination of Racial Discrimination. Available at: http://chrgj.org/wp-content/uploads/2012/07/IndiaCERDShadowReport.pdf (accessed 29 December 2014).

Kaldor, N. (1955) Alternative Theories of Distribution. *Review of Economic Studies* 23(2): 83–100.

Kannan, K.P. and Raveendran, G. (2009) Growth Sans Employment: A Quarter Century of Jobless Growth in Indian Organised Manufacturing. *Economic and Political Weekly* 44(10): 80–91.

Kuznets, S. (1955) Economic Growth and Income Inequality. *American Economic Review* 65(1): 1–28.

Lewis, W.A. (1954) Economic Development with Unlimited Supplies of Labour. *Manchester School* 22(2): 139–191.

Shah, G., Mander, H., Thorat, S., Deshpande, S. and Baviskar, A. (2006) *Untouchability in Rural India*. New Delhi: Sage Publications.

Singh, A. and Dasgupta, S. (2005) Will Services Be the New Engine of Economic Growth in India? ESRC Centre for Business Research Working Paper No. 310. London: ESRC.

Swaminathan, M. and Rawal, V. (2011) Is India Really a Country of Low Income-Inequality? Observations from Eight Villages. *Review of Agrarian Studies* 1(1): 1–22. Available at: https://ideas.repec.org/a/fas/journl/v1y2011i1p1-22.html (accessed 18 May 2015).

Thorat, A. (2010) Ethnicity, Caste and Religion: Implications for Poverty Outcomes. *Economic and Political Weekly* 45(51): 47–53.

Thorat, S. (2009) *Dalits in India: Search for a Common Destiny*. New Delhi: Sage Publications.

Vanneman, R. and Dubey, A. (2011) Horizontal and Vertical Inequalities in India. In Gornick, J. and Jantti, M. (eds) *Income Inequality: Economic Disparities and the Middle Class in Affluent Countries*. Stanford, CA: Stanford University Press: 439–458.

11 Brazil in the last 20 years

Searching for a new accumulation regime

Marcelo Manzano, Carlos Salas and Anselmo Santos

Introduction

After growing fast for almost two decades under the military regime, an external debt crisis at the beginning of the 1980s ended this growth cycle of the Brazilian economy. The debt crisis started a decade characterised by an inflation of over three digits. This economic scenario was the background to the transition back to democracy. Since 1994, the Brazilian economy has undergone two major periods marked by different economic and social policies, and thus major changes in the population's well-being.

In the first period, between 1994 and 2003 – under the two presidential terms of Fernando Henrique Cardoso, a centre-right politician – the Brazilian macroeconomic agenda was clearly oriented by the dictates of the Washington Consensus and by neoliberal policy prescriptions. The successful 1994 monetary stabilisation plan (Plano Real), the availability of foreign capital and the resultant surge in foreign direct investment (FDI), and the agenda of the governing political coalition resulted in a regime that was based, for the most part of those years, on pegging the national currency to a fixed and overvalued exchange rate; reducing the size of the state through privatisation; fighting discretion in the area of economic policy; and attempting to restrict the scope of social policies by focusing only on the most vulnerable groups. Despite being successful in terms of controlling inflation, this regime produced serious macroeconomic problems: slow gross domestic product (GDP) growth, a sizeable public debt that nearly doubled, an external account imbalance, a diminished industrial sector, a rise in unemployment, and so on.

This changed in 2004 with the formation of a new government under the leadership of José Inacio da Silva (Lula) from the centre-left Workers' Party (PT). At the time, there were major changes in the international economy (in particular the growing contribution of China to commodities demand). A slow but unequivocal reorientation of the direction of the Brazilian economy occurred, breaking the advance of neoliberalism and guiding the country towards a new stage of development. In spite of the view of some authors arguing that there was a return to developmentalism[1] in the first decade of the 2000s, we view this shift as a post-liberal turn: neither was neoliberalism abandoned completely, nor had a coherent and sustainable project been built that could have resulted in the emergence of a new development pattern.

In this chapter we will compare the two periods. The contrast between them will reveal the differences in economic and social outcomes and will also allow us to explain the reduction in poverty and inequality that occurred during the last 12 years. We will also show that during the presidencies of Lula (2003–2010) and Dilma Rousseff (from 2010) economic and social policies have departed, to a degree, from neoliberalism: there was a resumption of state leadership, with a wage-led model of sorts. However, a definite break with certain neoliberal elements of economic policy did not occur.

We see as evidence of the persistence of neoliberalism in macroeconomic policy the maintenance of what is called in Brazil the '*tripé*' (tripod): inflation targeting, flexible exchange rates and a primary fiscal surplus. On the one hand, the new government took important measures that ran contrary to neoliberal orthodoxy: state intervention in the economy (in particular through state banks); an end to privatisations; some stimuli for job creation; a sustained policy of increasing minimum and average real wages; and incentives for the registration of the self-employed and of workers in small businesses. Thus, this period can be characterised as being transitional: there were relevant advances of progressive forces. The new accumulation regime secured the capacity of the state to intervene and displayed dynamism resulting from a recovery of purchasing power (Carneiro et al., 2012; Fonseca et al., 2012; Silva, 2009). On the other hand, state intervention led to the enforcement of the social rights and institutions guaranteed by the 1988 constitution (Cardoso Jr., 2013; Krein and Manzano, 2014).

Towards a post-liberal regime: the macroeconomics of employment

In order to evaluate the economic outcomes in both periods, we have looked at the trajectory of GDP growth (see Figure 11.1). It is easy to see that there is – at least in the area of output growth – a change in the macroeconomic dynamic from the early years of the 2000s. Whereas in the neoliberal period (1994–2003) the annual average GDP growth was 2.5 per cent,[2] in the next period – which we call 'post-liberal' – there is an acceleration visible in an average growth rate of 3.5 per cent. It is noteworthy, however, that after the 2008 financial crisis, there was a considerable loss of dynamism (despite the exceptional growth of 7.5 per cent in 2010[3]), which reveals the limitations of the current macroeconomic regime and, in particular, the difficulty of making further gains under conditions of an adverse external environment.

Let us look closely at the main factors that explain the behaviour of the Brazilian economy throughout the period analysed.

We start from examining the trade balance. According to the data in Figure 11.2, there is a clear turn in foreign trade from the beginning of the 2000s, which is a result of the virtuous combination of two factors: the devaluations of the real in 1999 and 2002[4] and a rise in commodity prices induced, ultimately, by

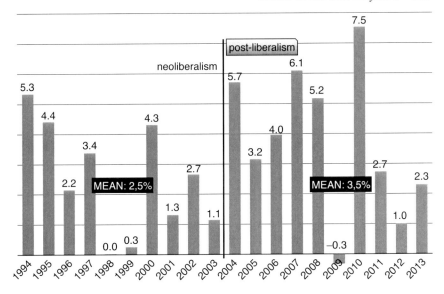

Figure 11.1 GDP growth rate – Brazil: 1994–2013
Source: IBGE/SCN-IPEADATA (2013).

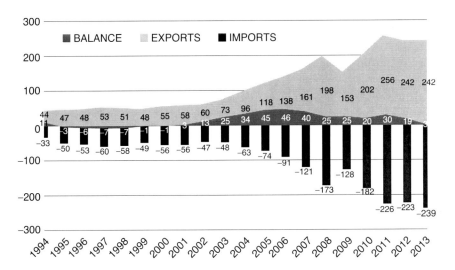

Figure 11.2 Trade balance evolution
Source: BACEN/IPEADATA.

the rapid growth of the Chinese economy, which led to a significant improvement in the terms of trade (Hiratuka et al., 2007).

In combination, these two factors not only contributed to the reversal of negative balances – which were present since 1995 – but also to the generation of high trade surpluses, which reached their peak in 2005–2006, when the Brazilian trade surplus was 23 per cent. In the post-crisis period, with the downturn in the

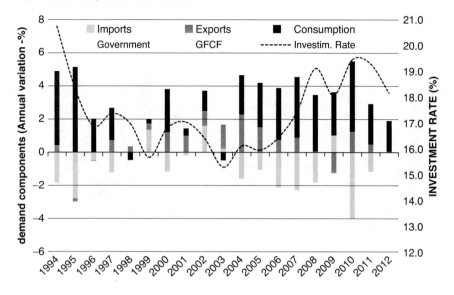

Figure 11.3 Contribution of the aggregate demand components to the GDP growth (annual variation)
Source: IBGE/SCN-IPEADATA (2013).

international economy and the valuation of the Brazilian currency, the economy has lost external competitiveness, resulting in a rather small trade surplus of $2.56 billion in 2013 – the equivalent of 0.5 per cent of current trade.

The importance of the external sector as a powerful growth engine during the first half of the 2000s is unquestionable. It is even more evident when we look at the contribution of different aggregate demand components to the GDP growth rate (see Figure 11.3). Nevertheless, it must be said that exports or the trade balance were not the only causes of the economic performance during those years. Unlike other emerging economies, Brazil still is a relatively closed economy with a low coefficient of external penetration. Therefore, it would be inappropriate to characterise the macroeconomic dynamics of this period as a typical example of export-led growth.

In fact, when we say the dynamics of the external sector were quite favourable due to the resumption of growth in the 2000s, it is also necessary to consider both the exceptional performance of the current account between 2003 and 2008 and, importantly, the stabilising effect of the high volume of foreign-exchange reserves accumulated during this period[5] (see Table 11.1). These factors opened up new opportunities for increases in output and investment and created space for expanding the public sector. In contrast to what happened in the 1990s, when the country alternated between short periods of growth and crisis (a classical stop-and-go dynamic), there were new prospects for the expansion of domestic demand from 2004, with growing foreign-exchange reserves and diminishing external risks. In this situation, consumption and investment boosted the GDP

Table 11.1 External accounts – Selected Indicators
Brazil: 1994–2013

Year	Exchange rate[1]	Current account	Capital account	FDI	Net Balance of Payments	Foreign-exchange reserves
	(em %)			*(em US$ Bilhões)*		
1994	0.84	−1.81	0.01	2.15	7.22	38.81
1995	0.97	−18.38	29.1	4.41	12.92	51.84
1996	1.04	−23.5	33.97	10.79	8.67	60.11
1997	1.12	−30.45	25.8	18.99	−7.91	52.17
1998	1.21	−33.42	29.7	28.86	−7.97	44.56
1999	1.79	−25.33	17.32	28.58	−7.82	36.34
2000	1.95	−24.22	19.33	32.78	−2.26	33.01
2001	2.32	−23.21	27.05	22.46	3.31	35.87
2002	3.53	−7.64	8	16.59	0.3	37.82
2003	2.89	4.18	5.11	10.14	8.5	49.3
2004	2.65	11.68	−7.52	18.15	2.24	52.93
2005	2.34	13.98	−9.46	15.07	4.32	53.8
2006	2.14	13.64	16.3	18.82	30.57	85.84
2007	1.77	1.55	89.09	34.58	87.48	180.33
2008	2.34	−28.19	29.35	45.06	2.97	206.81
2009	1.74	−24.3	71.3	25.95	46.65	239.05
2010	1.67	−47.27	99.91	48.51	49.1	288.57
2011	1.88	−52.47	112.38	66.66	58.64	352.01
2012	2.04	−54.25	70.01	65.27	18.9	378.61
2013	2.34	−81.37	73.78	64.05	−5.93	375.79

Source: BCB Boletim/BP
Note: (1) Referring to the last month of each year.

growth rate: as is evidenced by Figure 11.3 and Table 11.1, the investment rate started to grow more vigorously in 2004 – after four years of sustainable export growth, the reduction of the current account deficit and the growth of foreign-exchange reserves. From that moment, there were 19 consecutive quarters of investment growth, the majority of which were higher than GDP growth. This was the longest cycle of investment expansion since the mid-1980s (Carneiro, 2010).

At this point, a brief consideration of the evolution of the investment rate is needed. To a great extent, the recovery of investment since 2004 was followed by a rise in public sector investment, which expanded to 1.9 per cent of GDP mostly as a result of higher investment in state-owned companies (see Figure 11.4). Petrobras, for instance, the largest firm of Latin America, increased its annual average investment volume from $5.1 billion in 1995–2003 to $26.5 billion in the post-liberal period (2004–2012) (Petrobras, 2014).

Broadly, the macroeconomic dynamics in the 2000s are characterised by three expansive cycles of aggregate demand (external account–consumption–investment), which peaked in 2008 when they were partially interrupted by the international financial crisis. Since then, despite a marked recuperation of investment in 2010, the main engine of production has been consumption, which is

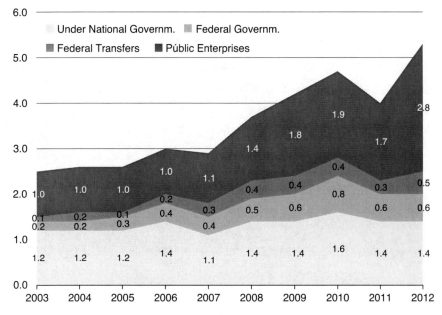

Figure 11.4 Public Investment as a proportion of GDP – Brazil 2003–2012
Source: STN/MF from: Ministério da Fazenda (2013, p. 26).

due to the persistent increases in real wages and the policy of issuing loans to the poorest members of the population. The positive performance has been maintained since 2004, though there is a downward trend lately.

In light of this, it is difficult or perhaps impossible to identify the post-liberal Brazilian macroeconomic regime as a pattern linked to a specific booster of aggregate demand. The good performance of exports, the resumption of investment and the expansion of consumption, are not, on their own, strong enough to explain the dynamic that started in this period. In order to understand the macroeconomic dynamic, we need to consider two other factors that had a central role: (1) redistributive social policies (which constituted an independent variable in the expansion of expenditure); and (2) the relative rigidity of the labour supply. A suitable label for the accumulation regime in the last few years may be 'macroeconomics of employment' – a wage-led growth regime in which the labour-market dynamic was at the centre of economic development, creating the necessary mix that allowed the other factors to become drivers of growth. In the next section, we will discuss how social policies and the labour market advanced in the period studied.

Social achievements: the hallmark of the Brazilian experience in recent years

As we have demonstrated, the resumption of growth, after two decades of GDP stagnation and chronic economic instability, is far from being a turnaround in

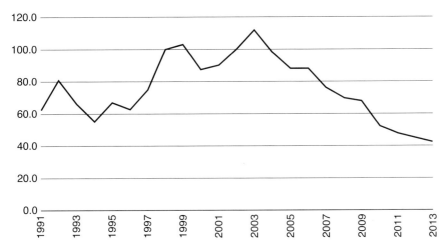

Figure 11.5 Evolution of the unemployment rate
        Brazil – Fixed Base Index: November/2002 = 100
Source: PME/IBGE

macroeconomic management or the emergence of a new accumulation regime. The prominence of the recent experience in Brazil in academic and political debates around the globe is a product of the social outcomes that were achieved (Fagnani, 2011; Krein et al., 2012; Oxfam, 2014; PNUD, 2014; Quadros, 2014) and of their macroeconomic implications (IMF, 2014).

Regardless of achieving lower economic growth than most emerging economies, the reduction in inequality and unemployment in the country has drawn attention to the fact that the public polices in the post-liberal period going beyond reluctant economic management and the retention of the 'macroeconomic tripod' have had effects almost counterbalancing the macroeconomic conservatism and going beyond the expectations of policy-makers.

One of the hallmarks of this period is the strong performance of the labour market and the growth in income of the poorest people. From 2004 up to 2012, Brazil created 10 million jobs, and average wages rose by 48 per cent (Leite and Salas, 2014). Those two factors had a major impact on income distribution, as we will discuss later. At the same time, unemployment has been going down since 2003, reaching a historic low in 2013 (see Figure 11.5). There has been a significant decrease in gender disparities as well; whereas in 2003, the female unemployment rate was 5.4 percentage points higher than the male rate, in 2013, this difference decreased to 1.8 percentage points (see Figure 11.6). Aside from job creation, there are several additional factors that explain the rigidity of the labour supply. First is the demographic structure that translates into a smaller family size; second is the increase in school enrolment levels, which is due to a greater access to education brought by specific government policies; and third is the higher average family income that meant lower participation rates of males.

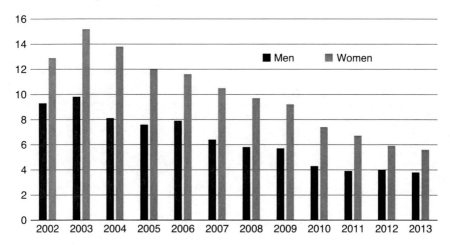

Figure 11.6 Evolution of the unemployment rate[1] – By gender
Source: PME/IBEGE.
Note: (1) reference month: november.

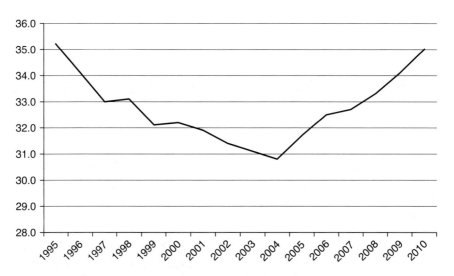

Figure 11.7 Wage share in GDP – Brazil: 2002–2010 (in %)
Source: IBGE/IPEADATA.

Other dimensions of the labour market also indicate relevant advances. The share of wages in GDP, which had fallen by almost five percentage points between 1995 and 2004, has recovered quickly and in 2010 returned to the level of 1995 (see Figure 11.7). With respect to the rate of formality – the share of wage workers holding a labour card – the change in numbers is similarly significant. Among the waged workers, the rate of formality grew by 11.3 percentage points between 1997 and 2012, mainly among non-whites (see Table 11.2). This is another indication that there has been a decrease of Brazil's historical inequalities.[6]

Table 11.2 Waged workers formality rate – By color/ethnicity[7]
Brazil: selected years (em %)

	1997	2001	2005	2009	2012	Variação
Total waged workers	55.8	54.9	56.8	61.7	67.1	*11.3*
Indigineous	36.9	51.3	54.3	58.9	60.4	*23.6*
White	63.2	61.6	63.6	68.2	73	*9.8*
Black	52.6	52.5	54.8	59.6	64.5	*12*
Asian	63.1	63	63.8	66.4	76.8	*13.7*
Brown	45.9	46	48.6	54.6	61.1	*15.2*

Source: PNAD/IBGE

The Gini index, which throughout the 1990s dropped by only 0.013 points, decreased by 0.096 points between 2001 and 2012, which is quite a significant development: it reached the lowest level since 1960 – 0.498.[8]

In conclusion, there has been an unequivocal improvement in the employment and income conditions of the Brazilian population in the last ten years, resulting in a significant decrease of inequality and contributing to overcoming some of the failings of the Brazilian economic and social structure that had been there from its origin.

Nevertheless, among analysts and observers, there are still disputes in relation to the factors within the accumulation regime that contributed to social improvement. Different hypotheses have been raised (Baltar et al., 2010; Carneiro et al., 2012), but the issue remains controversial. Our hypothesis is that the unprecedented socio-economic dynamism initiated with the advent of the twenty-first century was caused by a dual movement: On the one hand, objective conditions emerged for the stimulation of productive activities, resulting from both external

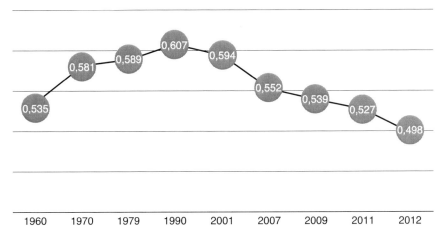

Figure 11.8 Gini Index – Brazil: selected years.
Source: IBGE/IPEA.

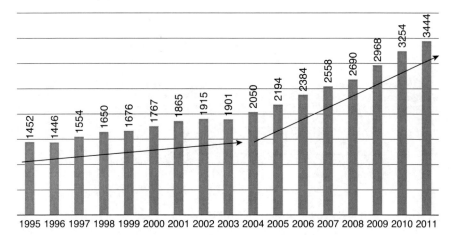

Figure 11.9 Social expenditure *per capita* of the Federal Government – Brazil 1995–2011
(prices of 2011)
Source: Siafi/STN, see: (Cardoso Jr. 2013).

and internal markets that had been constrained by 20 years of stagnating per capita income. This happened at the exact time that a new political coalition formed whose main demand was a decrease in inequalities and an emphasis on social policy. On the other hand, the institutions established by the 1988 Federal Constitution were being consolidated, which hitherto had been dormant – both because of the constraints produced by fiscal crisis of the 1990s and because the neoliberal government had no interest in developing the welfare state that had been enshrined in the constitution.

The following data help to clarify this matter. As shown by Castro (2012: 1023 f.), social expenditure has grown in the period analysed – from 19.2 per cent of GDP in 1995 to 21.9 per cent in 2005 and 25.2 per cent in 2010. In a period of 16 years, overall public expenditures grew by six percentage points in relation to the GDP, with a massive expansion of social expenditure by the federal government that alone accounted for an increase of 4.1 percentage points.

Considering social expenditure per capita of the federal government (see Figure 11.9), it can be observed that, despite continuous growth during the entire period, it has been increasing more since 2004: it grew by 31 per cent between 1995 and 2003 and by 81 per cent between 2004 and 2011. In 2011, it reached $1,852 per capita in 2011 prices. The development in the second period is due to the social policies pursued by the PT governments.

The conversion was made at the rate of purchasing power parity (PPP), at 2005 rates and then deflated by the U.S. (CPI-BLS) and in Brazil by the INPC / IBGE.

Importantly, the continuous expansion of social expenditure was strongly linked with the policy of raising the minimum wage in real terms. It is estimated that this was the principal cause for the decrease in inequality (Kerstenetzky, 2012;

Table 11.3 Evolution of the real minimum wage
In Brazilian Reais and Dollars (Purchasing Power Parity)
Brazil: 1994–2013

Year	Real Minimum Wage		Minimum Wage PPP[1]	
	Value in R$	*Index*	*Value in US$*	*Índx*
1995	262.92	**100**	100.99	**100**
1996	307.85	117.1	107.11	106.1
1997	318.02	121	111.86	110.8
1998	326.44	124.2	120.14	119
1999	345.74	131.5	119.03	117.9
2000	333.71	126.9	129.79	128.5
2001	351.4	133.7	143.57	142.2
2002	381.62	145.1	142.33	140.9
2003	364.5	**100**	157.64	**100**
2004	402.7	110.5	166.14	105.4
2005	412.11	113.1	188.73	119.7
2006	453.53	124.4	219.6	139.3
2007	514.07	141	235.99	149.7
2008	529.72	145.3	242.26	153.7
2009	543.57	149.1	267.81	169.9
2010	640.08	175.6	280.02	177.6
2011	636.19	174.5	290.44	184.2
2012	693.76	190.3	317.57	201.5
2013	709.19	194.6	332.84	211.1

Source: IPEADATA
Note: (1) The value in each month corresponds to the price of the same basket of goods that could be acquired with a minimum wage in Brazil.

PNUD, 2014). The minimum wage has been growing in Brazil since 1995, but growth accelerated from 2003 with the change of government.[9] Between 2003 and 2013, the minimum wage increased in real terms by 94.6 per cent (in reais) or 111.1 per cent (in purchasing power parity based on US dollars). Between 1995 and 2002, the increase was in 45.1 per cent (in reais) and 40.9 per cent (in USD/PPP (see Table 11.3).

The impact of a rising minimum wage goes beyond the workers who receive it, as it constitutes the basis for calculating the payment of some of the benefits that have a large impact in Brazil, namely the Regime Geral da Previdência Social (RGPS) and the Assistência Social. According to Castro (2012: 1024), the expenditure for the RGPS measured as a proportion of GDP rose by 2.43 percentage points (or about $48.4 million annually) for the whole period of 1995–2010, while the costs linked to welfare increased by 1.0 percentage points (approximately $22 billion). This demand stimulus helped to increase consumption for the poorest sectors of the Brazilian economy.

Expenditure for public health and public education also increased. These two items, along with the social benefits mentioned, constitute the largest portion of Brazilian social expenditure. After remaining stationary between 1995 and 2004, with a variation of 0.25 percentage points as a share of GDP in health and 0.09 percentage points in education, the expenditure rose in the period of 2005–2010, but more in education (0.95 percentage points) than in health (0.47 percentage points).

As a direct consequence of this increase in social expenditure, but also as a reflex of the consolidation of the institutions established in the 1988 Federal Constitution, the number of public workers employed in the direct administration increased to 3,645,579 – from 2,316,299 after 2003. This movement occurred also in public utility services: there was a minor drop between 1995 and 2002 (the period when these services were privatised), followed by a limited recuperation afterwards, increasing the total number of workers employed in this sector by 102,375 (see Table 11.4).

The increase in the number of public employees took place principally because of the expansion of municipal utilities – in fulfilment of government obligations under the 1988 Constitution and closely related to the increases in social spending in the recent period.[10] In fact, as is visible in the table below, public employment at the federal and the state level grew more slowly than the population and the labour force.[11] However, within the municipalities, there was an increase of 75 per cent between 1995 and 2007, with the 2.2 million new public sector jobs created. This corresponds to 91.3 per cent of the total number of public sector jobs created during the period analysed.

Moreover, analysing the dynamics of occupations at the federal level (see Table 11.6), one can see that between 1995 and 2012, although the number of statutory public workers of the executive branch did not vary much over the period (5.1 per cent), there was a significant increase in the number for the federal legislature (48.4 per cent) and in particular in the judiciary.

It should be noted that the expansion of employment in judiciary as well as the establishment of additional labour courts constitute important factors accounting for the formalisation of employment relations that has been occurring in recent years (Krein and Manzano, 2014).

Table 11.4 Number of workers in public sector, by type of contract
Public Administration and Public Utility Service Corporation (PUSC)
Brazil: selected years
(in thousands)

	1995		2002		2011	
	Public Admin.	*PUSC*	*Public Admin.*	*PUSC*	*Public Admin.*	*PUSC*
Private Regime	927,276	350,657	580,829	286,209	612,523	380,146
Public Regime	4,496,369	27,094	6,151,859	23,078	8,225,037	27,494
Others	34,377	457	54,614	1,079	266,041	5,101
Total	5,458,022	378,208	6,787,302	310,366	9,103,601	412,741

Source: RAIS/TEM web site (accesed on 23 February 2014)

Table 11.5 Personnel occupied in public sector* – By Federal Level
Brazil: selected years

	Federal	*Regional*	*Local*	*Total*
1995	1,437,296	3,426,320	2,970,131	7,833,747
2002	1,246,794	3,265,787	4,102,334	8,614,915
2007	1,574,161	3,502,156	5,205,329	10,281,646
Absolute Change				
2007/1995	136,865	75,836	2,235,198	2,447,899
2002/1995	−190,502	−160,533	1,132,203	781,168
2007/2002	327,367	236,369	1,102,995	1,666,731
Relative Change				
2007/1995	9.50%	2.20%	75.30%	31.20%
2002/1995	−13.30%	−4.70%	38.10%	10.00%
2007/2002	26.30%	7.20%	26.90%	19.30%

Source: PNAD, See Mattos, 2011, pp. 73–74.

Table 11.6 Number of federal public servants statutory – By Federal Power
Brazil: selected years

Poder	*1995*	*2002*	*2012*	*Absolute Change*	*Relative Change*
Federal Government	951,585	809,975	999,661	48,076	5.1%
Federal Legislative	17,402	20,501	25,828	8,426	48.4%
Federal Justice	64,561	81,716	104,971	40,410	62.6%
Total	1,033,548	912,192	1,130,460	96,912	9.4%

Source: SEGEP/M P, SOF/M P e STN/M F see: Ministério do Planejamento, 2013

Expanding credit also played an important role, supporting the hypothesis that the post-liberal accumulation regime period pushed – in an unprecedented way – the country's socio-economic dynamics. Due to advances in the formalisation of labour relations, employment growth, real wage gains and the facilitating and encouraging role of banking policy, consumer credits – especially those for durable goods – and subsidised housing credits have been growing strongly since 2002. This has amplified the effects of income expansion on demand primarily via consumption and secondarily via investment.

Final considerations

In the last decades, the Brazilian people have insisted on the government pursuing a macroeconomic arrangement placing the economy back on a development trajectory; that is, moving away from a neoliberal approach to a more heterodox model where social policies, state leadership and strategies for strengthening real wages gain increasing importance. During the past 12 years, a combination of

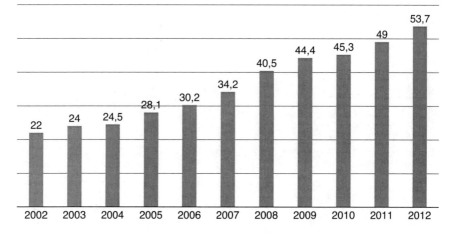

Figure 11.10 Credit as a proportion of GDP – Brazil – 2002–2012
Source: BACEN. See: BI&P (2013).

higher real wages, in particular minimum wages, and employment growth helped to stimulate consumption and economic growth. The indirect impact of the growing minimum wage consisted in increasing benefits, which helped many people to overcome poverty and thus reduced inequality.

However, since the 2008 financial crisis and, especially, its reappearance in Europe three years after, new obstacles have arisen, revealing some deficiencies overlooked in the boom period that question the sustainability of the new accumulation regime. With the reduction in commodity prices and pressure on the exchange rate,[12] the Brazilian economy has lost momentum, forcing the government to adopt a set of ad hoc measures aimed at supporting the consumption cycle and increasing investment in infrastructure. In this process, the difficulties of the industrial sector have become increasingly clear, particularly in the last five years: it has suffered strong competition from imported products and its share of output and employment has been decreasing.

Furthermore, the gaps and omissions in economic policy of the pre-crisis period bring to light issues that should have been addressed when the internal and external conditions were more favourable. Among these are: bottlenecks in the areas of infrastructure (roads, railways, ports and airports) and industrial utilities (energy, water and sanitation); the lack of an industrial policy and the growing separation of the Brazilian industry from international value chains; the difficulty to mobilise private sector investment in the context of a financial system that is not geared towards financing long-term projects; the persistence of inflationary pressures despite the overvaluation of the real and high interest rates, which are to the detriment of economic activity; the pressures on large urban centres caused by extensive real estate speculation; and the regressive and anti-competitive tax burden.

There are many obstacles to a move away from neoliberalism. Only a strong popular movement working at every level of society, from the grass-roots to the heart of the government, can help Brazil to move towards a more sustainable development path. To sum up, the analysis of the last 20 years in Brazil certainly permits us to say that neoliberalism is being questioned. Furthermore, there is a reasonable belief in the need for a co-ordinating role of the state in the economic development process that must have, as its first goal, a reduction of the enormous inequality that still tarnishes the country. Gradually, though in a reactive manner and with some shortcomings, the country has been moving towards an accumulation regime that is close to what the economic literature calls 'developmentalism'. However, despite the advances, we are still far away from a coherent and sustainable system of accumulation that can be recognised and defended as a political project.

Notes

1 See Bresser (2006), Mercadante (2010), Carneiro (2012) and Bastos (2012).
2 Note that the period average was positively affected by the high growth achieved in 1994–1995, which was caused by the income effect of a sharp drop in inflation. Consumption grew at high rates because of the recovery of the purchasing power of wages and a high rate of GDP growth ensued, which was facilitated by idle manufacturing capacities.
3 This is a result of the counter-cyclical policies adopted in Brazil to address the crisis and the statistical effect caused by the recession in the previous year.
4 In 1999, more than five years after the adoption of the 'exchange-rate band' system, which kept the currency fixed and overvalued, the Brazilian Central Bank allowed a devaluation to occur of approximately 50 per cent. It was pressed to act by increasing losses of foreign currency. Later, during the 2002 elections, political uncertainty about the rise of Lula as the opposition candidate caused a sharp depreciation of the Real, again at around 50 per cent.
5 Between 2002 and 2011, foreign-exchange reserves grew by 931 per cent. This was a result of favourable external conditions and, even more importantly, of a change in attitude of the new government: it started to acquire foreign currency in order to reduce the Brazil's exposure cyclical fluctuations in external market.
6 For an analysis of the decrease of gender and race inequality see Leite and Salas (2014).
7 Using data from the Monthly Employment Survey (PME/IBGE), which covers only the population from the six main Brazilian metropolitan areas, the formality rate reached 79.5 per cent of the wage workers in 2012 compared with 70.2 per cent in 2003 (Baltar, 2003).
8 National household income and expenditures surveys were first conducted in this year.
9 Having been a priority ever since the start of the Lula administration, the minimum wage policy from 2008 was based on an objective criterion of adjustment. The adjustment index is set by a formula that considers the GDP growth rate of the two previous years plus the inflation rate. For an analysis of the minimum wage policy during the Lula presidency see Souen (2013) and Kerstenetzky et al. (2013).
10 Note that in the Brazilian federalism emerged post-1988 Federal Constitution an important share of the social policy measures, although paid for by the central government budget, is executed by local governments.

11 The Brazilian population grew by 1.64 per cent a year in the 1990s and by 1.17 per cent a year in the 2000s. Importantly, the economically active population grew by 34.7 per cent over the same period.

12 This was an indirect result of the behaviour of central banks in developed countries – in particular, the 'quantitative easing' pursued by the US Federal Reserve.

References

Baltar, P. et al. (2010) Trabalho no Governo Lula: uma reflexão sobre a recente experiência Brazileira. Working Paper No. 9, Global Labour University. Campinas, SP: IE/Unicamp. Available at: www.global-labour-university.org/fileadmin/GLU_Working_Papers/GLU_WP_No._9_portuguese.pdf (accessed 23 April 2015).

Barros, R.P. et al. (2010) Determinantes da queda de desigualdade de renda no Brazil. Texto para Discussão, No.1460, Série Seminários. Brasília: IPEA. Available at: www.ipea.gov.br/portal/images/stories/PDFs/TDs/td_1460.pdf (accessed 23 April 2015)

Bastos, P.P.Z. (2012) A economia política do novo-desenvolvimentismo e do social desenvolvimentismo. *Economia e Sociedade* (21), Campinas: Número Especial: 779–810.

Cardoso Jr, J.C. (2013) *Mundo do trabalho e (des)proteção social no Brazil: ensaios de interpretação da história recente.* Tese (doutoramento). Campinas, SP: Unicamp.

Carneiro, R. (2010) O Desenvolvimento Brazileiro pós-crise financeira: oportunidades e riscos. *Observatório da Economia Global*, Texto No. 04. Campinas: Unicamp. Available at: www.centrocelsofurtado.com.br/arquivos/image/201108311439510.CARNEIRO1.pdf (accessed 23 April 2015).

Carneiro, R. (2012) Velhos e novos desenvolvimentismos. *Economia e Sociedade* (21). Campinas: Número Especial: 749–778. Available at: www.scielo.br/pdf/ecos/v21nspe/v21nspea03.pdf (accessed 23 April 2015).

Carneiro, R. et al. (2012) *O Desenvolvimento Brazileiro: temas estratégicos.* Texto para Discussão, Rede Desenvolvimentista, No. 01. Campinas, SP: Rede Desenvolvimentista.

Castro, J.A. (2012) Política Social e Desenvolvimento no Brazil. *Economia e Sociedade* (21), Campinas: Número Especial: 1011–1042.

Fagnani, E. (2011) *A política Social do Governo Lula (2003–2010): perspectiva histórica.* Texto para Discussão, IE/Unicamp, No. 192. Campinas, SP: Unicamp.

Fonseca, P.C.D., Cunha, A.M. and Bichara, J.S. (2012) *O Brazil na era Lula: Retorno ao Desenvolvimentismo?* Texto para Discussão, São Paulo, No. 04, (Rede Desenvolvimentista).

Hiratuka, C., Baltar C. and Almeida, R. (2007) Inserção Brazileira no comércio mundial no período 1995–2005. *Boletim Neit*, No. 09. Campinas: Unicamp.

IMF (2014) *Annual Report: from stabilization to sustainable growth.* Washington, DC: International Monetary Fund.

Kerstenetzky, C.L. (2012) Sobre a 'crise' do estado de bem-estar: retração, transformação fáustica ou o quê? *Dados – Revista de Ciências Sociais.*

Kerstenetzky, C.L. et al. (2013) A contribuição do salário mínimo para a redução recente da desigualdade na distribuição de renda no Brazil: uma aplicação do método RIF Regression. Texto para Discussão, CEDE/UFF, No. 87. Rio de Janeiro. Available at: www.proac.uff.br/cede/sites/default/files/TD87.pdf (accessed 23 April 2015).

Krein, J. and Manzano, M. (2014) Notas sobre Formalización – Estudio de caso: Brasil. Programa de promoción de la formalización en América Latina y Caribe. Lima: OIT.

Available at: http://ilo.org/wcmsp5/groups/public/---americas/---ro-lima/documents/publication/wcms_248256.pdf (accessed 23 April 2015).

Krein, D. et al. (2012) Trabalho no Governo Lula: avanços e contradições. Texto para Discussão, IE/Unicamp, No. 201. Campinas, SP: Unicamp.

Leite, M. and Salas, C. (2014) Trabalho e desigualdades sob um novo modelo de desenvolvimento. *Tempo social* (26)1: 87–100.

Mercadante, A. (2010) As bases do novo desenvolvimentismo: análise do governo Lula. Tese (Doutorado), Instituto de Economia da Universidade Estadual de Campinas: IE Unicamp.

Oxfam (2014) Governar para las élites: secuestro democrático y desigualdad económica. Informe de Oxfam No. 178. Oxford: Oxfam House. Available at www.oxfam.org/sites/www.oxfam.org/files/bp-working-for-few-political-capture-economic-inequality-200114-es.pdf (accessed 23 April 2015).

Petrobras (2014) Histórico de Investimentos Reais. *Destaques Operacionais*. Available at www.investidorpetrobras.com.br/pt/destaques-operacionais/investimentos/historico-de-investimentos-real/historico-de-investimentos-real.htm (accessed 23 April 2015).

PNUD (2014) *Humanidade Dividida: como hacer frente a la desigualdade em los países em desarrolho*. New York: PNUD. Available at: www.undp.org/content/dam/undp/library/Poverty%20Reduction/Inclusive%20development/Humanity%20Divided/Spanish_web_low.pdf (accessed 23 April 2015).

Quadros, W. (2014) No Brazil, avanços, apesar dos pesares. *Revista Carta Capital*, 6 February. Available at: www.cartacapital.com.br/revista/784/no-Brazil-avancos-apesar-dos-pesares-6121.html (accessed 23 April 2015)

Silva, B. (2009) *Desenvolvimento (sustentavel) no Brasil do Lula: Uma abordagem juridico-ámbiental*. Santa Cruz Do Sul: Edunisc.

Souen, J.A. (2013) A política do salário mínimo no governo Lula. Dissertação (Mestrado), Instituto de Economia da Universidade de Campinas. Campinas: IE/Unicamp.

Part IV

Critiques of conventional political responses

12 Greening inequality?

Limitations of the 'green growth' agenda

Birgit Mahnkopf

Introduction

The recent crisis of capitalism as a social-ecological world system indicates that 'the wall between human and natural history has been breached' (Chakrabarty, 2009: 221) and that human beings have become 'geological agents' who are destabilising the climate and many of the biophysical systems on which their livelihoods depend. Western nations and the capitalist system play the most important roles in destabilising the conditions that had previously functioned as the boundaries of human existence. And undoubtedly, the environmental damage linked to the ecological crisis will exacerbate inequalities across the globe.

The point of departure of this chapter is a critique of the widely shared assumption that growth is necessary for development. As will be discussed in the first section, the positive socio-economic effects of growth have been overrated. In fact, rapid growth has always gone hand in hand with massive deprivation. Since 'no growth' is not a viable political option within the framework of existing power structures, 'green growth' has been hailed as a win–win solution where green technologies and 'green jobs' replace the old 'brown' industries in capitalist societies. In the second section, it will be highlighted that the 'green growth' agenda rests on questionable assumptions, in particular the belief that economies can grow indefinitely, which are upheld despite the existence of 'planetary boundaries' (Rockström et al., 2009) that have already been exceeded. Unsurprisingly, the 'green promise', as will be argued in the third section, is met with reservations or even resistance in the Global South, where some political actors see it as a project that has emerged out of the Global North and is putting brakes on development. In the fourth section, three 'green' public policy areas will be presented where interventions could lead to both improved ecological sustainability and increased social equality: solid waste management and the 'greening' of agriculture and forestry in the Global South; as well as 'green jobs' in the Global North. As will be discussed in the conclusion, interventions such as these are necessary steps towards a 'just transition'. However, they can at best buy time, as profound changes in power relations between all stakeholders – including governments, the fossil fuel industry, workers and future generations – are required to avoid aggravating existing inequalities and to prevent violent ecological conflicts over scarce resources.

Growth and social inequality

Just as an orientation towards economic development at any cost was common in both capitalist and 'real-socialist' regimes in the post-war period, today's governments – be they left or right – share the assumption that economic growth is the remedy for most social problems. The only difference is that these days, governments tend to add that there is trade-off between a 'healthy', growth-based economy and a 'healthy' natural environment. The growth paradigm serves as a panacea alleviating class tensions, reducing the economic gaps between and within countries and providing political stability. Even though the purported positive effects of economic growth can be questioned, workers, trade unions and public-sector agencies also tend to take it as a given that 'no growth' is not a viable political option – both due to the existing huge social inequalities and the power relations sustaining the existing modes of production and living.

Thus, the ecological damage and the social problems caused by rapid industrialisation and urbanisation are still considered the price that has to be paid for 'development'. The dynamic of capitalism, in particular in those regions of the Global South where economies are based on resource extraction, makes it very difficult for political decision-makers to even consider a switch to sustainable forms of economic activity. A substantial reduction in output and foreign currency reserves, as well as drastic changes in world-market prices would emerge and this would damage the matrix of regional production. Ecological change is hard to achieve (if not impossible) as long as 'frontier movements' are going on that lead to the enclosing and plundering of natural resources for the purpose of exporting them.

As a result, the majority of countries in the Global North and South are dominated politically by supporters of the view that development is more or less equivalent to macroeconomic growth, material consumption, openness toward transnational corporations and financialisation. This view is particularly strong in the BRICS states, both among political and economic elites and trade unions (Dobrusin, 2014). Even in states where a 'green economy' agenda has been formally adopted, as is the case in Brazil and South Africa, the political elites tend to see it with scepticism, that is as a project reflecting the interests of Western countries. In defence of their 'right to develop', these countries forge a 'commodity consensus' (Svampa, 2013: 120), which parallels the 'Fordist consensus' in the North after the Second World War (Mathai and Parayil, 2013) as well as the 'export consensus' still existing in some Northern countries such as Germany.

However, it is worth remembering that long-term annual growth rates of 2.2 per cent in real terms have only been possible since the industrial-fossil revolution (cf. Maddison, 2001; Piketty, 2014). In the centuries and millennia before, the average growth rate was only about 0.2 per cent. Industrial production required more powerful sources of energy than those represented by biotic entities such as humans and animals as well as biomass, wind and water. The transition to fossil energies was of utmost importance – and this transition was only possible thanks to the emergence of rational organisation, modern science and technology on the one hand and the need for valorisation and capital accumulation on the other hand.

Nonetheless, it was not until the 1990s that economic growth became a political must and a 'fetish' (cf. Altvater, 2002). Today, growth rates are seen as the decisive 'benchmark' for 'good governance'. Admittedly, various economic problems can be resolved by fostering growth. However, the positive social effects of economic growth are dubious, particularly if we consider inequality. After all, rapid growth in many countries has gone hand in hand with the persistence of social deprivation on a mass scale. And even worse: in many countries, high growth rates have developed in parallel with growing inequality. Furthermore, growth resulting from rising labour productivity has created 'redundant populations' (David Ricardo), which means increasing unemployment and heightening economic insecurity in particular for those people who cannot afford to stay unemployed and thus have to make a living in the informal economy. Finally, growth-based development models are most of the time not conducive to an equal sharing of the burden of environmental pollution. In many emerging economies, growth and energy consumption have not been decoupled (not even in relative terms): despite their 'catching up' in terms of growth, they have not moved closer to 'clean pollution'.

'Green growth' as a panacea?

In many countries, workers, trade unions and public-sector organisations agree that the problems arising from the current financial, economic and ecological crises can be resolved by stimulating economic growth. At best, some argue in favour of 'sustainable' or 'green growth', maintaining that it is possible to decouple gross domestic product (GDP) growth from the consumption of raw materials and greenhouse-gas emissions. 'Green economy' or 'green growth' agendas – espoused, for example, by the United Nations (UN), the Organisation for Economic Co-operation and Development (OECD), the World Bank, the European Union (EU), the Independent Labour Organization (ILO) and numerous thinks tanks and lobby groups – tend to have the same starting point and objective: countering the impending threats of climate change and resource scarcity through the decarbonisation of the global economy.

Academics and organisations linked to the union movement more or less explicitly criticise the current phase of capitalism by emphasising the negative social consequences of financialisation, that is, the *finance-led growth* of the last few decades (see Evans's chapter in this volume). The 'green new deal' agenda raises hopes that the weak wage increases of recent years can be corrected by a *wage-led growth* strategy boosting domestic demand. It is assumed that this strategy, in combination with a new regime in tax and fiscal policy, can lead to a new and stable recovery (Green European Foundation, 2009, 2011; Green New

Deal Group, 2008, 2013; Pollin et al., 2008; UNEP, 2009). Proponents of a 'green new deal' are critical of other approaches that obscure or ignore the social and environmental costs of growth-based 'progress' and thus are sceptical towards using GDP as a benchmark for economic and social progress. They emphasise that the private sector fails to boost green growth as strongly and quickly as is required and suggest that governments play a more active and leading role. Nevertheless, they neither think it is possible nor desirable to disrupt the unholy alliance between profit maximisation and increasing consumption.

Among the proponents are numerous actors representing labour in one way or another – for example the ILO (2012a, 2012b), the ITUC (2012a, 2012b) or the ETUC (2012). All of these organisations focus on a possible net increase in jobs stimulated by a transformation towards a 'green economy'. Yet numerous corporate lobby groups such as the Global Green Growth Forum, the Global Green Growth Institute and the Green Growth Action Alliance are also dedicating themselves to promoting a 'green growth' model. The main purpose of these informal groups is to increase, with the help of a public–private-partnership model, the public resources dedicated to leveraging private investment in key sectors (for a critical review, see Alexander and Fuhr, 2012).

Despite marked political differences, all proponents of the 'green economy' share the following assumptions:

1   The ecosystems of the planet are being over-exploited, which means that the detrimental impact of human civilisations has to be limited.
2   Low carbon production, if based on appropriate technologies, can 'dematerialise' economic activity. In other words, 'environmentally friendly' growth is technically possible.
3   If unavoidable 'externalities' like carbon-dioxide and other pollutants were to be priced, the economy could keep on growing indefinitely.
4   Government interventions are both to compensate for market failures and to facilitate the green economic activity originating from the private sector.

Importantly, however, there are five important obstacles to 'green growth' that its promoters tend not to take into consideration:

1   the existing rules and regulations of free trade;
2   the existence of strong property rights;
3   the mode of operation of financial markets;
4   the constraints inscribed in the capitalist mode of production and exploitation;
5   the problems attached to treating biophysical and human nature as a *resource* that can be appropriated and exploited.

Undoubtedly, the vision of a low-conflict transition to a 'green economy', overcoming the economic crisis and the ecological limits to growth, is a very optimistic approach. Its central message is: a *sustainable* and *inclusive* type of growth, decoupled from environmental degradation and resource consumption, is possible through intelligent macroeconomic management, technical progress and the introduction of new products, processes and services. This message is based on an assumption inspired by Keynes, that is, that the present socio-economic order is capable of undergoing another (this time social-ecological) transformation and that 'decent capitalism' (Dullien et al., 2011) is both desirable and feasible.

Even if trade unions and leftist political activists tend to be aware of vested interests that obstruct progressive change (in particular the fuel and energy-intensive industries), they often believe that a global 'green new deal' may resolve the economic and social problems caused by the accumulation of capital. However, a basic question remains unanswered: How is it possible to limit resource extraction and emissions on a global scale while defending the commitment to growth?

In fact, the new discourse obscures many obstacles that impede a greening of the economy. At least five 'shades of green' are missing:

First, even if power generation was based solely on renewables (which is not compatible with a rising global demand for energy and a need for growth, even if it is only moderate growth), the physical limits of attempts to 'dematerialise' the economy would have to be taken into account. No increase in efficiency in the use of matter can replace matter itself (cf. Georgescu-Roegen, 2011 [1972]).

Second, 'rebound and backfire effects' of new technologies need to be considered. These consist in the additive rather than substitutive use of new technologies and in unintended consequences and 'normal accidents' (Perrow, 1999) associated with 'revolutionary' technologies.

Third, the problem of competition for resources, especially with regard to land, is largely ignored by the proponents of 'green growth'. They do not address the issue of growing competition between different patterns of land, for example the competition between biomass and food production. Put differently, a piece of land cannot be utilised simultaneously for wind turbines or solar panels, transport routes facilitating mass mobility, housing and organic farming (cf. Exner et al., 2013).

Fourth, the externalisation of environmental impact and the costs caused by trade-induced emission transfers plays only a minor role, if any, in the 'green growth' discourse. The transition to a low-emissions service economy – promoted mainly by Keynesian economists, trade unions and supporters of the European green and left parties – would be accompanied by growing emission transfers to developing countries.

Fifth, and most importantly, a 'green economy' is not in a better position to resolve the problems of global justice than its 'brown' fossil-nuclear counterpart. In particular, this applies to two issues: the extraction, processing and possession of resources; and the asymmetric relations of dependence between developed and developing countries in the area of scientific and technical know-how. Ultimately, the vision of a 'green economy' does not leave behind the traditional Western belief that the gap between the physical finiteness of resources and a sense of entitlement to profits and consumer goods can be bridged by technical innovation.

The 'green promise': reservations and resistance

The 'green economy' agenda in industrialised countries is promoting the further commodification of humanity's commons. In light of this, it can be expected that taking the 'green economy' path would result in a greater concentration of power and wealth and, consequently, in increasing social inequalities. Against this backdrop, it is not astonishing that numerous governments, trade unions and civil society organisations in the Global South perceive the agenda as providing a moral justification for extending the control of the 'Euro-Atlantic' core countries over natural resources on a global scale.

Around the globe, the move towards sustainable, low-carbon economic activities is compounded by the pressure to ensure that the transition to renewables is a 'just transition'. In other words, it is seen as an opportunity for achieving greater equality and social inclusion that should not be wasted, but this is by no means an automatic outcome. In developing countries that have built their industrial development strategies around cheap, carbon-based energy, the challenges posed by the transition to renewables are particularly difficult. In fact, the transition tends to provoke resistance. This is not only due to the fact that solar, wind and geothermal energy are still not affordable for many people. It is also because job losses in the conventional energy sector may not be compensated for by new 'green jobs'. Furthermore, there are cases of wind farms being built on indigenous estates, for example in Mexico (cf. Unmüßig, 2012), thus prohibiting traditional uses of the land; and of land needed for solar energy generation that is taken from most impoverished people, for example in India (cf. Gupta, 2012). As has been demonstrated by events in South Africa, Malawi and Mozambique, taking a 'green development' path causes significant economic and political costs and, in the short run, turns the poor into 'potential losers' (Resnick et al., 2012: 87) – even if such a shift may be reasonable and may eventually prove beneficial to the population.

Importantly, jobs in the renewables sector in the Global South are often not really 'green'. Hydroelectric power generation and agro-fuel production are associated with being 'green' and sustainable, but this can be questioned. In fact, hydroelectric power generation is harmful to the environment and agro-fuel production leads a loss in biodiversity and has a negative ecological impact on local populations. Furthermore, there is evidence that the growth of emerging economies, be it based on 'brown' or 'green' industries, correlates even more strongly than is the case in the old industrialised countries with increases in social inequality and processes of social exclusion.

In advanced industrialised countries, where most of the growth recorded in 'green jobs' has occurred, the potential for job destruction in non-green industries (such as transport, chemicals and pharmaceutics) is particularly high. In Germany or Sweden, 'green jobs' in the renewables sector and the recycling industry are neither particularly decent nor safe jobs. Very often, they are poorly paid and carried out by workers who are ill-trained and exposed to serious health risks, which are caused by the use of certain chemicals (Hermann, 2014; ILO, 2012b).

All of this suggests that the key question remains unanswered: how can social, gender and ecological justice be reconciled?

Public investment for social justice and environmental sustainability

A consensus exists that governments can contribute to 'greening' economies by reshaping and refocusing policies, investments and expenditure. At the same time, it is obvious that the financial and economic resources needed require a strong government prepared to stimulate and implement radical reforms that compete with more traditional economic and social concerns. Shifting to a 'green economy' agenda will, in the long run, have economic, social and ecological benefits. However, in the nearer future, it will not create a win–win situation, because in the short run, certain aspects of 'green policies' will cause economic and political costs. If an increase in inequality is to be avoided, it is of utmost importance that the costs of adaptation be disproportionally placed on those who can afford it.

Notably, actors such as political parties, businesses and even trade unions, in many cases face disadvantages from shifting away from their country's current development strategy. This is due to the fact that any 'green transition' project will not only create new investment and employment opportunities, but also make existing ones dispensable. Often, this affects (predominantly male) workers who are comparatively better paid, enjoy a higher rate of social and employment security and are more likely to be union members (for example, in mining, chemicals or manufacturing). At the same time, the three-fold challenge of establishing social, gender and ecological justice has to be taken seriously. In other words, the direct link between ecological degradation and poverty cannot be ignored: in the developing world, the poorest people depend disproportionally on the natural commons.

Consequently, three areas of public policy can be identified that not only increase sustainability, but also help improve the situation of the poor: investment in infrastructure (in particular the social infrastructure), in improvements in the livelihood of the rural poor and in services targeting ecosystems on which the extremely poor depend the most. As a number of projects across the world have demonstrated, there seems to be huge potential in urban areas of developing countries for improving equality and environmental outcomes through innovative government policy in solid waste management (SWM). In rural areas, in contrast, it is indisputable that policy instruments for stimulating a 'greening of agriculture' are of utmost importance for attempts to reduce inequality. In the Global North, the 'green jobs' agenda seems to be a useful target for public policy. A brief discussion of some relevant interventions in these three areas is provided below.

Solid waste management

In developing countries, huge numbers of informal workers work in recovering and recycling waste. SWM is a large industry that provides a livelihood for the weakest members of the community (in particular for women), allows local authorities to offload the responsibility for waste disposal and contains public health issues arising from the presence of waste in urban areas by removing it. However, it also creates other public health issues (affecting mostly the workers in the sector) and the usual problems connected to informal work: poor safety at work, no social protection and insecure incomes. A sector-specific problem is the high rate of child labour.

The environmental benefits of recycling and reuse are far more obvious than in other 'green' government projects, for example energy generation. The environmental impact of landfills is reduced, the demand for primary resources decreases and secondary resources are returned to the production cycle. The last two effects contribute to lower emissions. In addition, a unique opportunity for improving equality and environmental outcomes exists because there is still an absence of mechanised, privatised SWM systems in many developing countries. This creates space for government bodies to include informal workers in innovative SWM processes and help to improve working conditions in the sector as well as the social status and security of informal workers.

Currently, there is a window of opportunity in SWM policy: there is space for developing a system that responds to local social, economic and environmental demands and a wide variety of government interventions that could potentially contribute to decreasing inequality among workers (cf. Chikarname, 2012; CWG/GIZ, 2011; Gerdes and Gunsilius, 2010; Gunsilius et al., 2011; Zealand, 2013):

- strengthening the sector through excise, as well as other taxes and concessions;
- constituting boards with equal representation of waste pickers, traders and government officials;
- registering all waste pickers and itinerant buyers in order to create and provide contributory social security systems;
- offering credit to ensure the construction of safe, durable workshops;
- helping informal sector organisations involved in the contracting process by simplifying contractual terms;
- providing low-interest loans to co-operatives of waste pickers;
- reserving waste collection and small-scale processing for small- and medium-sized, informal waste collection enterprises;
- reserving land in development plans for the decentralised processing of organic waste and for recycling sheds, material recovery facilities, the storage of recyclables and intermediate processing;
- providing access to markets by building roads;
- guaranteeing that local councils refrain from imposing arbitrary fines and penalties;
- providing support services to upgrade the technology used.

Agriculture and forestry

Public policy for a 'green economy' in agriculture and forestry is far more controversial and contested than in the area of SWM. It is more likely in this area that there will be winners and losers, so priorities and value judgements play a more important role when proposals are appraised. Nonetheless, the two sectors are of key importance for 'green economy' agendas and thus deserve attention. It is uncontroversial that targeting agriculture is of the utmost importance for any serious attempt to reduce social inequality. With one billion people working in the sector (including subsistence farmers and the rural poor), agriculture is the biggest employer globally and represents the sector with the highest concentration of poor people. At the same time, agriculture and forestry account for 31 per cent of greenhouse gases if emissions are divided by sector (ILO, 2012a: 19, 21), which is a share far greater than any other sector's. Furthermore, agriculture contributes to the rapid loss in biodiversity and leads to top soil erosion and the exhaustion of ground water supplies.

The alternative to monocultures, which result in high-level emissions, is not an expensive technical fix, but a combination of measures, namely multi-cropping; mixed livestock and cereal production; rotational systems; and low-intensity input techniques. The required transition needs public policy support to generate socially and environmentally sustainable rural employment (cf. Cline, 2007). The ILO (2012a: 12) is promoting five key techniques that contribute to the 'greening' of agriculture:

- soil fertility management;
- more efficient water use;
- crop and livestock diversification;
- biological plant and animal health management;
- appropriate forms of farm-level mechanisation.

When done adequately, 'green' agricultural policy could improve environmental outcomes, food security and farmers' incomes as well as containing rural–urban migration. Some forms of a 'greener' agriculture are more labour-intensive than conventional methods and therefore can increase employment (though this does not guarantee 'decent work') (Altieri and Toledo, 2011; Martínez-Torres and Rosset, 2014; Pretty, 2006; Wichterich, 2012). Suitable policy instruments for stimulating agro-ecology in developing countries (cf. ILO, 2012a: 22–24; Pretty, 2006: 26) include:

- paying subsidies to farmers willing to abandon conventional farming;
- facilitating agro-ecological production by phasing out subsidies for conventional methods;
- guaranteeing access to land, water and seeds for small farmers;
- providing access to agro-ecological know-how, credit and local markets through supportive economic policies and, financial incentives;

- including agro-ecology in the agronomic curricula at schools and universities;
- investing in research and development (R&D) in the area of agro-ecological practices;
- creating public spaces for social movements and non-governmental organisations (NGOs) that generate and spread theoretical and practical agro-ecological knowledge;
- supporting the certification of agro-ecological products;
- facilitating the formation of farmers' associations (here, the dissemination of agro-ecological knowledge and technology is fastest);
- identifying businesses willing to buy smallholders' products at a price favourable to the producers;
- negotiating with supermarket chains over the sale of smallholders' products;
- encouraging the formation of relationships between smallholders (or middlemen) and the service sector such as restaurants, hotels, educational facilities and hospitals;
- subsidising agribusinesses that train and transfer appropriate technologies to smallholders;
- offering development credits for smallholders.

In addition, it is clear that many agricultural workers lack even basic social protection. As part of the transition towards sustainable agriculture, improving social services for the rural population can be an important means for achieving minimal income security, that is mitigating the risks of lower yields and migration (ILO, 2012a: 31).

However, there are a number of obstacles to 'greening' agriculture and fighting inequality at the same time. If a switch from conventional to organic production takes place, there is often a short-term fall in yields. Therefore, support is required during the transition period. Furthermore, safety, pay and work conditions as well as gender discrimination are issues in the agricultural sector – and a 'greener' agriculture does not automatically address any of these (cf. Matthei, 2014; UNRISD, 2011). The most important barriers are not technological but social and political. These include:

- systematic violations of the rights of agricultural workers;
- the power and reach of transnational 'agro-food' corporations (Rossman, 2013);
- the world trade regime, which systematically reinforces this power;
- the intellectual property rights regime, which eliminates research carried out in the public interest, undermines state support for sustainable food and agricultural production and forces farmers to generate high returns and use inputs that cause high-level emissions.

'Green jobs' and sustainable development in advanced industrialised countries

It is necessary to focus public policy in the advanced industrialised countries on minimising the disparities between the winners and losers of a transition to a 'greener' economy. In general, it can be expected that 'green' investments will create additional jobs: 'environmentally friendly' activities are often more labour intensive than those in 'brown' industries. Furthermore, the freed resources can be directed away from fossil fuel-based industries. The findings of a number of studies and surveys give the impression that 'green policies' in general and renewable energy (RE) policy in particular can generate considerable extra employment (for an overview Bowen, 2012; Fankhauser et al., 2008; Pollin et al., 2008). According to the International Renewable Energy Agency, the number of jobs created per US dollar of investment or per unit of energy delivered is generally higher in the renewables sector than in the fossil fuel sectors – even though the magnitude and the direction of this effect vary strongly by country and by RE sources (IRENA, 2011).

Nevertheless, it would be naïve to ignore the huge potential for job destruction in 'non-green' industries. Furthermore, the high labour intensity in RE production and the high capital requirements eventually result in lower labour productivity than in conventional energy production. Therefore private-sector investment is less profitable and the cost of lifting economies onto a low-carbon trajectory are quite high. Most importantly, a 'green turnaround' would require that most of the fossil-fuel reserves held as assets by publicly listed companies are not extracted (Carbon Tracker, 2013).

However, the bulk of 'green jobs' will be located in sectors such as agriculture, construction, water and waste management and manufacturing, which do not usually demand higher skills than regular jobs and which are associated with quite bad working conditions, wages and social security protection. Therefore, a 'decent work' agenda, as advocated by the international labour movement, will be just as important for the 'green' industries as it has been for the 'brown' industries.

Despite the fact that there is no clear definition of 'green jobs', it is possible to make some tentative assumptions about their impact (cf. Smith and Bettio, 2008). First, if there is a transition to a 'green economy', the resulting job losses will have a greater impact in male-dominated sectors such as resource extraction, energy production and manufacturing. Second, both good- and bad-quality jobs will be created and it is probable that women will tend to occupy the positions marked by bad conditions. Third, if new demand arises for 'green skills' and they are rewarded adequately, it can be expected that the skill levels will be distributed unevenly among women and men, reinforcing the low valuation of women's work. It may be possible to close the gender gap through the promotion of 'green and decent jobs'; however, this is strongly dependent on public policy and funding.

Obviously, trade unions have a central role to play. They can contribute to putting working conditions higher on the agenda in 'green' policy strategies at the national level, for example by:

- advocating an environmental tax that raises public revenues in order to fund a reduction, for instance, in social security contributions;
- designing policies that align 'green' structural adjustments with local development strategies;
- introducing tax incentives for small and medium enterprises to get involved in the development of 'green skills' as well as in trading sustainably produced products;
- incorporating 'green skills' in existing training and apprenticeship programmes;
- campaigning for public and entrepreneurial awareness of the need for 'green jobs' and 'green skills'.

All in all, environmental concerns should be made a focus of collective bargaining. The challenge for labour movements in industrialised countries is to develop a 'just transition' strategy that avoids 'a very particularistic approach that may well solve local problems by reproducing global inequalities' (Stevis, 2013: 192).

Conclusion

'Green policy' approaches are necessary steps towards a 'just transition', a concept which features prominently on the agenda of global unions. However, social inequality is not the only inequality that threatens people's livelihoods: ecological conflicts are of the utmost concern, both between the North and the Global South, but also within developing countries – and they often have particularly harmful effects on women. Due to the scarcity of water and arable land, these conflicts will intensify in the next few years and even more in the coming decades.

The socio-ecological restructuring of some important sectors of the economy can buy some time for addressing the 'unequal ecological exchange' between the Global North and South and containing activities that disregard 'planetary boundaries' (cf. Röckström et al., 2009). With this in mind, it is obvious that the growth- and debt-based economy of contemporary capitalism is facing an epochal crisis, not just a normal crisis of accumulation (cf. Mahnkopf, 2014, 2015). In this situation, it is doubtful whether there are instruments on offer within capitalism that allow us to escape the crisis. Therefore, we cannot avoid a discussion about the limits of economic growth.

Against this backdrop, the 'greening' of production and consumption has to be framed in terms of triggering profound changes in the relations of forces between the *guardians* of the current energy system (including the fossil fuel industry, its supporters both at the level of government and in the private sector and wealthy consumers), the *prisoners* of the current system (including workers and trade unions in the fossil fuel-based industries) and the billions of *victims* of fossil-fuel capitalism (some of whom are alive already and some have yet to be born). If such changes can be achieved, it may still be possible to alleviate the harsh social conflicts that will be caused by the unavoidable departure from capitalism.

It seems of the utmost importance that we redirect our attention towards a social-ecological system that does not depend on growth the same way that capitalism does. At the same time, we have to respond to the class war from above and to press for an equitable redistribution of wealth, for guaranteed social rights and for rolling out democracy through the extension of participatory elements. While the active engagement of civil society may give rise to hopes, there is also the concern that the transition towards a global socio-ecological system could be marred by violence. It is an open question whether there is a historical opportunity for a 'great transformation' – or whether reactionary forces will benefit once the socio-ecological crisis starts to cause severe political instability. In fact, the likelihood is growing that the crisis, rather than 'galvanizing heroic innovation and international cooperation, [will] simply drive elite publics into even more frenzied attempts to wall themselves off from the rest of humanity' (Davis, 2008). If capitalism is reaching its 'tipping point', local conflicts will intensify to a degree that they threaten stability and peace around the globe.

References

Alexander, N. and Fuhr, L. (2012) *Privatizing the Governance of 'Green Growth'*. Washington, DC: Heinrich Böll Foundation.

Altieri, M.A. and Toledo, V.M. (2011) The Agroecological Revolution in Latin America: Rescuing Nature, Ensuring Food Sovereignty and Empowering Peasants. *The Journal of Peasant Studies* 38(3): 587–612.

Altvater, E. (2002) The Growth Obsession. In Panitch, L. and Leys, C. (eds) *Socialist Register 2002: A World of Contractions*. London: Merlin Press/Fernwood Publishing/Monthly Review Press: 73–92.

Bowen, A. (2012) 'Green Growth', 'Green Jobs' and Labor Market. Policy Research Working Paper No. 5990. Washington, DC: The World Bank.

Carbon Tracker (2013) Unburnable Carbon 2013: Wasted Capital and Stranded Assets. Grantham Research Institute on Climate Change and the Environment. Available at: http://carbontracker.live.kiln.it/Unburnable-Carbon-2-Web-Version.pdf (accessed 13 May 2015).

Chakrabarty, D. (2009) The Climate of History: Four Thesis. *Critical Inquiry* 35: 197–222.

Chikarname, P. (2012) Integrating Waste Pickers into Municipal Solid Waste Management in Pune, India. WIEGO Policy Brief No. 8. Available at: http://wiego.org/sites/wiego.org/files/publications/files/Chikarmane_WIEGO_PB8.pdf (accessed 13 May 2015).

Cline, W.R. (2007) *Global Warming and Agriculture: Impact Estimates by Country*. Washington, DC: Peterson Institute.

CWG/GIZ (2011) The Economics of the Informal Sector in Solid Waste. Available at: www.giz.de/de/downloads/giz2011-cwg-booklet-economicaspects.pdf (accessed 13 May 2015).

Davis, M. (2008) Living on the Ice Shelf: Humanity's Meltdown. TomDispatch.com, 26 June. Available at: www.tomdispatch.com/post/174949 (accessed 13 May 2015).

Dobrusin, B. (2014) Sustainability in Brazil and Argentina: The Trade Unions Within the Commodity Consensus. Global Labour University, Working Paper. Available at: www. global-labour-university.org/fileadmin/GLU_conference_2014/papers/Dobrusin-ArgentinaBrazil.pdf (accessed 13 May 2015).

Dullien, S., Herr, H. and Kellermann, C. (2011) *Decent Capitalism: A Blueprint for Reforming Our Economies.* London: Pluto Press.

ETUC (2012) Towards Rio+20. A Sustainable New Deal for Europe. ETUC-ETUI Conference, Jorlunde/Denmark. Available at: www.etui.org/Events/Towards-Rio-20-A-Sustainable-New-Deal-for-Europe-ETUC-ETUI-Conference (accessed 13 May 2015).

Exner, A., Fleissner, P., Kranzel, L. and Zittel, W. (2013) *Land and Resource Scarcities.* New York: Routledge.

Fankhauser, S. (2013) A Practitioner's Guide to a Low-Carbon Economy: Lessons from the UK. *Climate Policy* 13(3): 345–362. Available at: http://dx.doi.org/10.1080/14693062.2013.749124 (accessed 13 May 2015).

Fankhauser, S., Agrawala, S., Hanrahan, D., Pope, G., Skees, J., Stephens, C. and Yasmine, S. (2008) Economic and Policy Instruments to Promote Adaptation. In Agrawala, S. and Fankhauser, S. (eds) *Economic Aspects of Adaptation to Climate Change: Costs, Benefits and Policy Instruments.* Paris: OECD (Organisation for Economic Co-operation and Development): 85–133.

Georgescu-Roegen, N. (2011 [1972]) Energy and Economic Myths. In Bonaiuti, M. (ed.) *From Bioeconomics to Degrowth: Georgescu-Roegen's 'New Economics' in Eight Essays.* London: Routledge: 58–92.

Gerdes, P. and Gunsillius, E. (2010) *The Waste Experts: Enabling Conditions for Informal Sector Integration in Solid Waste Management: Lessons learned from Brazil, Egypt and India.* Eschbron: Gesellschaft für Internationale Zusammenarbeit (GIZ).

Green European Foundation (2009) *A Green New Deal for Europe.* Brussels: GEF.

Green European Foundation (2011) *Funding the Green New Deal for Europe.* Brussels: GEF.

Green New Deal Group (2008) *A Green New Deal Joined-Up Policies to Solve the Triple Crunch of the Credit Crisis, Climate Change and High Oil Prices.* London: New Economics Foundation.

Green New Deal Group (2013) *A National Plan for the UK: From Austerity to the Age of the Green New Deal.* New Economics Foundation: London.

Gunsilius, E. (2011) *Recovering Resources, Creating Opportunities, Integrating the Informal Sector into Solid Waste Management.* Eschborn: Gesellschaft für Internationale Zusammenarbeit (GIZ).

Gupta, A. (2012) Why India's green growth dream is turning into a nightmare. *Envecologic.* Available at: www.greeneconomycoalition.org/know-how/why-india%E2%80%99s-green-growth-dream-turning-nightmare (accessed 13 May 2015).

Hermann, C. (2014) *Green New Deal, Green Economy and Green Jobs: Consequences for Environmental and Social Justice.* Paper presented at the 9th Global Labour University Conference, Berlin, 15–17 May.

ILO (2012a) *Working Towards Sustainable Development: Opportunities for Decent Work and Social Inclusion in a Green Economy.* Geneva: International Labour Organization (ILO).

ILO (2012b) Are 'Green' Jobs Decent? *International Journal of Labour Research* 4(2). Geneva: International Labour Organization (ILO).

IRENA (2011) Renewable Energy and Jobs: Status, Prospects and Policies. Abu Dhabi. Available at: www.irena.org/rejobs.pdf (accessed 13 May 2015).

ITUC (2012a) Growing Green and Decent Jobs. Available at: /www.ituc-csi.org/IMG/ pdf/ituc_green_jobs_summary_en_final.pdf (accessed 13 May 2015).

ITUC (2012b) Trade Union Resolution on Labour and Environment. Available at: www.ituc-csi.org/IMG/pdf/resolution_-_2nd_trade_union_assembly_on_labour_and_ environment.pdf (accessed 13 May 2015).

Maddison, A. (2001) *The World Economy: A Millennial Perspective*. Paris: OECD Development Centre Studies.

Mahnkopf, B. (2014) ‚Peak Capitalism‘? Wachstumsgrenzen als Grenzen des Kapitalismus. *WSI-Mitteilungen* 67(7): 505–512.

Mahnkopf, B. (2015) Can Green Growth Rescue Capitalism from its Own Contradictions? A Critical Assessment of the 'Green Growth' Approach – with a Special Focus on the European Union. In Dale, G., Mathai, M. and Puppim de Oliveria, J.A. (eds) *Green Growth: Political Ideology, Political Economy and Policy Alternatives*. London: Zed Books (forthcoming).

Martinez-Torres, M.E. and Rosset, P.M. (2014) Dialogo de saberes in la Via Campesina: Food Sovereignty and Agroecology. *The Journal of Peasant Studies* 41(6): 979–997. Available at: http://dx.doi.org/10.1080/03066150.2013.872632 (accessed 13 May 2015).

Mathai, M.V. and Parayil, G. (2013) Towards Equity and Sustainability in the 'Green Economy'. In Puppim de Oliveira, J.A. (ed.) *Green Economy and Good Governance for Sustainable Development: Opportunities, Promises and Concerns*. Tokyo: United Nations University Press: 47–70.

Matthei, L. (2014) The Brazilian Rural Development Model in the Context of Green Economy: Myths and Reality. Paper presented at the 9th Global Labour University Conference, Berlin, 15–17 May.

Perrow, C. (1999) *Normal Accidents: Living with High Risk Technologies.* Princeton, NJ: Princeton University Press.

Piketty, T. (2014) *Capitalism in the Twenty-First Century*. Cambridge, MA: Harvard University Press.

Pollin, R., Garnett-Petier, H., Heintz, J. and Scharber, H. (2008) Green Recovery: A Program to Create Good Jobs and Start Building a Low-Carbon Economy. University of Massachusetts: Political Economy Research Institute and Centre for American Progress.

Pretty, J. (2006) Agro-ecological Approaches to Agricultural Development. Background paper to the World Development report 2008, Available at: http://siteresources.worldbank.org/ INTWDR2008/Resources/2795087-1191427986785/PrettyJ_AgroecologicalApproaches ToAgriDevt%5B1%5D.pdf (accessed 13 May 2015).

Resnick, D., Tarp, F. and Thurlow, J. (2012) The Political Economy of Green Growth: Illustrations from Southern Africa. *Public Administration and Development* 32: 215–228.

Rockström, J. et al. (2009): Planetary Boundaries: Exploring the Safe Operating Space for humanity. In *Ecology and Society* 14(2). Available at: www.ecologyandsociety.org/ vol14/iss2/art32/(accessed 18 May 2015).

Rossman, P. (2013) Food Workers' Rights as a Path to a Low Carbon Agriculture. In Räthzel, N. and Uzzell, D. (eds) *Trade Unions in the Green Economy*. New York: Routledge: 58–63.

Smith, M. and Bettio, F. (2008) *Analysis Note: Green Jobs: A Case for Gender Equality?* Fondazione G. Brodolini, Rome. Available at: http://ec.europa.eu/social/BlobServlet? docId=3971&langId=en (accessed 13 May 2015).

Stevis, D. (2013) Green Jobs? Good Jobs? Just Jobs? US Labor Unions Confront Climate Change. In Räthzel, N. and Uzzell, D. (eds) *Trade Unions in the Green Economy*. New York: Routledge: 179–195.

Svampa, M. (2013) Resource Extractivism and Alternatives: Latin American Perspectives on Development. In Lang, M. and Mokrani, D. (eds) *Beyond Development – Alternative Visions from Latin America*. Ecuador: Fundacion Rosa Luxemburg. Amsterdam: Quito/ Transnational Institute. Available at: www.tni.org/sites/www.tni.org/files/download/ beyonddevelopment_complete.pdf (accessed 13 May 2015).

UNEP (2009) Global Green New Deal. Policy Brief. Nairobi: United Nations Environment Programme (UNEP). Available at: www.unep.org/pdf/A_Global_Green_New_Deal_ Policy_Brief.pdf (accessed 13 May 2015).

Unmüßig, B. (2012) Green Sins – How the Green Economy Became a Subject of Controversy. Berlin: Heinrich Böll Foundation. Available at: www.boell.de/en/ecology/ ecology-society-green-economy-social-perspective-15916.html (accessed 13 May 2015).

UNRISD (2011) Conference – Green Economy and Sustainable Development, Bringing Back the Social Dimension, 10 and 11 October, Geneva. Available at: www.unrisd.org/ 80256B42004CCC77/%28httpInfoFiles%29/C23E19A19F944500C125792C00527A11/ $file/Conference%20booklet%20FINAL.pdf (accessed 13 May 2015).

Wichterich, C. (2012) Die Zukunft, die wir wollen: Eine feministische Perspektive. Berlin: Heinrich Böll Stiftung. Available at: www.boell.de/sites/default/files/Feministische_ Zukunft-i.pdf (accessed 13 May 2015).

Zealand, A. van (2013) Challenges for Sustainability of Social and Solidarity Economy: The Interaction between Popular Economy, Social Movements and Public Policies – Case Studies of the Global Alliance of Waste Pickers. Draft paper prepared for UNRISD Conference Potential and Limits of SSE, May 2013. Available at: www.unrisd.org/ 80256B42004CCC77/%28httpInfoFiles%29/7314038916FCA0CAC1257B720035CEA0/ $file/van%20Zeeland%20draft%20paper.pdf (accessed 13 May 2015).

13 The social investment state and the myth of meritocracy

Heike Solga

Introduction

In economic research, education is regarded as a solution for a wide range of social problems. The Harvard economists Claudia Goldin and Lawrence Katz (2009: 290f.), for instance, argue that 'the lion's share of rising wage inequality can be traced to an increase in educational wage differentials', which is due to an undersupply of skills. The political arena has adopted this view and considers education as the key means of combating poverty and promoting social equality. The European Commission (2009: 5) for instance, states that 'strengthening education is one of the most effective ways of fighting inequality and poverty'. In the same vein, the Organisation for Economic Co-operation and Development (OECD) says:

> The global economic crisis, with high levels of unemployment, in particular among youth, has added urgency to fostering better skills. At the same time, rising income inequality, largely driven by inequality in wages between high- and low-skilled workers, also needs to be addressed. The most promising solution to these challenges is investing effectively in skills throughout the life cycle.
>
> (2012: 3; see also OECD, 2010)

This new orientation of social policy towards 'active' educational investment rather than 'passive' social spending and redistribution is labelled the 'social investment state' approach (Giddens, 1998; Morel, et al., 2012). However, 'increasing educational spending per se may not be a cure-all for economic inequalities [. . .]. If higher education is income dependent, increasing spending may instead solidify existing economic differences – aggravating, not relieving, inequality in OECD states' (Ansell, 2008: 230). Some researchers therefore refer to this social policy approach as 'education only politics' (Brown and Tannock, 2009: 389) or 'educational welfare state' (Brown, 2011: 29). They argue that one of the reasons why this social policy model has gained so much currency is the fact that education is regarded as a means that seems to make everyone a winner (Keep and Mayhew, 2010: 568). A similarly important reason is that

promoting education does not touch on controversial issues of material redistribution such as taxing income, wealth, property rights or inheritances (Keep and
Mayhew, 2010: 566; Mickelson and Smith, 2004: 362).

In so-called meritocratic societies, economic inequalities resulting from unequal
efforts and abilities, given equal educational opportunities, are considered 'just'
(Goldthorpe, 1996: 256; Young, 1958, 1994). This positive conception of equality of educational opportunities is one of the main justifications in political and
public discourses for the social investment state approach (cf. Heath, 2001: 4723;
Meyer, 1994: 730). The focal question of this chapter is why meritocracy can
be used as a legitimation of social inequality in advanced economies and as a
goal for societies that want to be considered 'modern'.

For understanding this belief in education, it is important to distinguish between
inequality of educational opportunities and inequality of educational outcomes.
The former refers to the unequal opportunities of social groups (such as family
background, race or ethnicity) in terms of *access* to education. Higher educational
attainment of children from higher-class backgrounds compared with those from
lower-class backgrounds (or differences between groups defined by other ascriptive characteristics) indicates greater inequality of educational opportunities in a
given society. Inequality in educational outcomes, by contrast, points to the
structure of the educational positions themselves and their overall distribution
– in particular, to the variance in the educational outcomes achieved. That is,
the greater the distance between the highest and the lowest educational outcome
(e.g. in the form of acquired degrees or competencies), the greater is the inequality in educational outcomes in a given society.

This distinction is very important because 'educational opportunities open to
each individual *separately* [equality of opportunity] does not mean 'open to all'
[equality of outcome]' (Hirsch, 1977: 6, insertions by author). Canada and Ireland,
for instance, have low levels of inequality in educational opportunities, but high
degrees of inequality in educational outcomes. On the contrary, the Czech Republic combines high inequalities in educational opportunities with a low level of
inequality in educational outcomes (Solga, 2014: 294). As will be shown below,
the meritocratic justification of social inequality refers not only solely to inequality of educational opportunities, but also to claims that inequality of educational
outcomes and economic inequalities caused by them are functionally necessary
in modern societies.

Based on this differentiation, what are the result of empirical research on the
relationship between educational and economic inequalities that should be positive
in order to support the social investment state approach? In a recent study based
on an international comparison (assessing data from the OECD's *Programme
for the International Assessment of Adult Competencies* (PIAAC 2011/2012)),
Solga (2014) has shown that lower degrees of inequality of educational opportunities are not correlated with the level of economic inequality. In contrast,
reducing inequality of educational outcome – in particular in terms of educational
deprivation (i.e. the proportion of low-literate adults) – is positively associated
with less income inequality. Nonetheless, the degree of social protection is by

far the most important factor for reducing economic inequalities. Social protection is also more important than public educational spending, because it levels the playing field for educational participation by reducing inequalities of disposable income in the parents' generation. Based on her findings, Solga states that 'education should not be overestimated as a means of fighting poverty and reducing inequalities in society' (2014: 289).

Thus, the question remains why, in line with the social investment state approach, meritocracy is still regarded as a justification for social inequality and education as a key factor for combating economic inequalities.[1] To answer the question about the legitimising function of education, I will outline and discuss the five basic characteristics of meritocracy and how they contribute to justifying social inequality. For a better understanding, I will start with a definition of meritocracy.

Definition of meritocracy

Meritocracy is an education-based mode of social stratification that is defined by the following three elements (Goldthorpe, 1996: 255f.):

1 positions of responsibility [. . .] should be allocated on the basis of demonstrated competence [. . .]
2 the matching of education opportunity is bound to natural ability [. . .]
3 achievement is the basis of social inequality in industrial society [. . .].

According to this definition, whereas unequal educational opportunities violate key principles of justice in modern societies, unequal educational outcomes – if solely based on differences in abilities, effort and achievement – are not perceived as a problem (Goldthorpe, 1996: 256; cf. also Young, 1958, 1994). The extent to which meritocratic allocation is achieved in a society is thus determined by the importance of education for obtaining social positions and by the extent to which educational attainment and ultimately access to social positions are independent of social origin (Boudon, 1974: 121ff.). Corresponding to the social investment state idea, the education system is turned into the key organisation for distributing social and occupational positions.

Various studies have shown, however, that learning processes in modern education institutions continue to be designed in such a way that academic success in school and the acquisition of higher-level educational certificates depend on students' proficiency in the language of instruction, their non-school-based education (background), their learning motivation and their study habits – all of which require the collaboration of their parents (Bourdieu, 1984; Lareau, 2000; Pfeffer, 2008). The question is then: Why is it that education, educational careers and educational certificates are seen as legitimising economic inequality in spite of the existing inequalities of educational opportunity (and the violation of the principles of meritocracy) in all advanced societies? There are several reasons for this. All existing studies show a strong link between educational attainment and labour-market outcomes. Corresponding to Goldthorpe's first element, social inequalities in modern societies are thus indeed associated with individual educational attainment.

As the primary motif guiding people's actions and legitimising social positioning, differentiation and inequality, education is thus not only a means of allocating status but also of making sense, of constructing meaning on a daily basis and of motivating individuals to act. In other words, both the interpretation of situations as 'meritocratic' (as a product of solely education-based allocation) and individual action based on this interpretation (or subjective perception) contribute to the incidence and persistence of the legitimising function of meritocracy. Such behaviour is also known as Thomas theorem: 'If men define situations as real, they are real in their consequences' (Thomas and Thomas, 1928: 571f.).

Furthermore, more and more children from disadvantaged social backgrounds have been able to access higher-level education institutions owing to educational expansion. As a consequence, education seems to be universally accessible and to have lost its exclusiveness. The proportion of higher-class children entering universities has, however, increased as well, and thus social inequalities in educational opportunities (that is, the advantage of higher-class children compared to lower-class children) have not changed much (cf. Shavit and Blossfeld, 1993). Moreover, lower-class children in the lower educational groups are left behind (cf. Gesthuizen et al., 2011; Solga and Wagner, 2001). Despite the empirical evidence that educational opportunities are far from being equal, educational expansion is 'publicly understood as a successful example of implementing equal opportunities' (Friedeburg, 1997: 44, own translation; cf. Bourdieu and Passeron, 1977).

The meritocratic ideal of social inequality

In the following, I will discuss why meritocracy is so powerful in terms of legitimising social inequality. My main argument is that the meritocratic ideal of social inequality possesses five essential features that contribute to concealing the true nature of educational and economic inequalities. These five features are: (1) the 'justification' of inequality as a functional necessity for society; (2) the 'natural' foundation of social inequality; (3) the need for organised educational processes; (4) the individual (rather than categorical) definition of inequality; and (5) the de-personification of the definition of achievement.

(1) Functional necessity

Meritocracy is a 'society not of equals, but of the just' (Bell, 1972: 68). The goal of a meritocratic society is thus reduced to changing the processes of allocation ('equality of opportunity') while at the same time maintaining inequalities of outcome. The proponents of meritocracy argue that the latter is necessary in order to create incentives for people to develop their talents. The hierarchical order of occupational positions, that is their unequal social and economic recognition, is therefore considered as a *functional necessity* for the social division of labour (Blau and Duncan, 1967; Davis and Moore, 1945; Parsons, 1959, 1970). The meritocratic ideal determines people's access to education and justifies the need for individually differentiated education participation (and outcomes). In other words, it legitimises the need to maintain unequal educational careers, which, according to the underlying paradigm of talent, supposedly reflect people's individual interests and talents. Differences in educational outcomes (or inequalities in educational outcomes) are hence defined as a necessary condition for producing social order. In other words, equality of outcomes is considered to be dysfunctional.

(2) 'Natural' foundation

Based on the meritocratic ideal, educational differences are defined as differences in talent and effort. Inequality in social status thus is seen as the causal result of biological differences. In other words, social inequalities are ultimately considered to have an ontological basis in 'nature' (see, for example, Herrnstein and Murray, 1994; Scarr, 1996).

Any scientific inquiry into the degree of achieved meritocratic allocation therefore ultimately leads to the question of *nature versus nurture* – that is, the question whether individual differences in achievement are based on biological or social factors (cf. Gou and Stearns, 2002; Rutter, 1997). On the one hand, this assumes (at least analytically) an additive, stepwise connection between biological birth and social environment rather than an interdependent relationship, as has been described by Rousseau (2013 [1755]: 7): 'It is not an easy task to disentangle what is original from what is artificial in man's present nature, and to know well a state that no longer exists and that perhaps never has existed or never will.' Another critical note would be that genetic factors primarily produce within-group differences with regard to 'intelligence' – as has been shown to be the case with regard to height (Tanner, 1994: 1) – whereas between-group (socially defined) differences are primarily caused by environmental factors (cf. Gould, 1995; cf. Tilly, 1998: 4).

Moreover, this nature/nurture dualism disregards the fact that referring to talent and intelligence is a *socially constructed* criterion for defining achievement (cf. Goldthorpe, 1996: 277). Its social construction, however, is disregarded (not to say 'veiled') in the concept of meritocracy. A natural categorisation of differences in talent does not exist. Educational categories are social constructs that need to be defined by society and categorised along social lines in school and other education institutions. By contrast, legitimatised by the meritocratic rhetoric, educational certificates – despite the fact that they represent institutionalised classifications of people – appear as 'natural' differences between individuals (cf. Keep and Mayhew, 2010: 568).

This is the reason why Young (1958) in his highly critical scenario of a meritocratic society and Rawls (1971) in his theory of distributive justic treat talent and social origin as equally arbitrary and as a fortunate coincidence of birth. Neither talent nor social origin represent individual merit, and hence – in terms of justice – do not have to be rewarded in any special way (cf. Bénabou, 2000: 317). Despite all these critical issues, meritocracy can claim legitimacy exactly because educational and social inequalities are constructed as reflecting 'natural differences', suggesting that they are 'unchangeable' (Douglas, 1986: 67, 80).

(3) Organised educational processes

Referring to 'natural inequalities' is, however, not sufficient for justifying education in the sense of a universal mode of allocation in modern societies. For that to happen, educational processes have to be designed in such a way that they provide labour markets with qualification and skills signals for employers, which they can use to allocate individuals to different jobs. What is needed, therefore, are organised and certified educational processes, and not learning as such. One might argue that educational certificates only provide incomplete measures of individual competences, because they do not take (sufficient) account of skills acquired outside of education institutions (cf. Collins, 1979; McIntosh, 2004). But this is precisely what this is *not* about. If competences were everything people needed to succeed at the workplace, today's labour market would be much more competitive, as competences can be acquired in many different ways. But competences have to be acquired in such a way that they provide already validated information about individuals (Weiss, 1995: 145, cf. also Goldthorpe, 1996: 264; Heimer, 1984). In that sense, it is not education and competences per se that matter but documented competences, acquired in institutionalised and certified educational processes.

   The key prerequisite for education to serve as a legitimate link between achievement and position is that individual educational attainment can be observed, measured and compared. That is why it needs to be codified in the form of grade reports, test scores, licences and the like, which are the product of bureaucratic and socially accepted procedures:

> When we hear from all sides the demand for an introduction of regular curricula and special examinations, the reason behind it is, of course, not a suddenly awakened 'thirst for knowledge' but the desire for restricting the supply for those positions and their monopolisation by the owners of educational certificates.
>
> (Weber, 1991 [1921]: 242)

This is the only way to regard individual educational attainment as assured, controlled and hence as *existent* (cf. Heimer, 1984). To argue that participation in these organised educational processes and teachers' assessments of that participation is neutral with regard to origin, as suggested by the meritocratic ideal, means to obscure the meaning and function of educational certificates as 'institutionalized cultural capital', produced through power-dependent certification processes (Bourdieu, 1984, 1986).

(4) Individualisation

In line with the meritocratic ideal, existing educational inequalities are justified by pointing out that these inequalities are based on universal achievement criteria. This presupposes a replacement of inequality defined *categorically* by status/ class (and gender) with inequality defined by *individual* achievement (see above). Thus *individualisation* becomes the primary principle of societal organisation – not, as suggested by Beck (1992), as a process characterised by increasing opportunities and risks for the individual to *choose* from, but *redefined* as an 'individual optimization problem' (Hirsch, 1977: 185). Correspondingly, structural risks become the individual's responsibility (Mayer, 1987, 1991). With its inherent individualised causal attribution, the meritocratic ideal obscures the potential that 'ascriptive forces find ways of expressing themselves as "achievement"' (Halsey, 1977: 184).

In contrast to this meritocratic rhetoric, empirical analyses find limited downward social mobility of children from higher social classes into lower-skilled occupational (class) positions. This suggests that social origin related factors are still at work, protecting higher classes against downward mobility from one generation to the next (Bourdieu, 1984). Moreover, the logic of meritocratic allocation implies a lifetime limitation on educational participation (Riesman, 1997 [1967]: 271), because it is mostly individuals' educational success or failure *prior* to labour market entry that determines their social positioning in later life. As a consequence, the 'early winners' can safely enjoy lifelong returns and social status stability.

These criticisms do not unsettle the meritocratic ideal, because by replacing the categorical explanation of social inequality with an individualising one – accompanied by the belief in 'unrestricted' access to education owing to educational expansion (see above) – the structural causes of unequal educational opportunities and social inequality can be portrayed as being less relevant or supporting meritocratic legitimacy. Owing to the fact that the meritocratic formula refers to individual achievement instead of education and educational degrees as *social constructions*, categorical inequalities disappear and with them the institutional causes of educational and social inequalities.

(5) De-personification

By defining a meritocratic social order as one where 'those who have an earned status or have achieved positions of rational authority' have done so 'by competence' (Bell, 1972: 65), the meritocratic ideal of social inequality ignores the interpretive power of higher-status groups. The definition of merit and achievement is being de-personified. Defining criteria for achievement is the responsibility of education institutions, not education participants (Fischer et al., 1996: 156; Jencks and Riesman, 1968). Moreover, as Coleman (1968: 22) points out, education institutions are not only responsible for defining the criteria for achievement but also for fulfilling them: 'The responsibility to create achievement lies with the educational institution, not the child.' As a consequence, educational institutions as gatekeepers hold a quasi-monopoly in determining life chances (at the level of the individual) and in reproducing or changing social inequalities (at the level of society) (Bell, 1994: 695). The educational success of children and adolescents, therefore, depends not only on their behaviour but crucially also on the opportunities provided to them by schools as organisations (Gomolla and Radtke, 2002: 55).

The meritocratic ideal defines competences – due to their link to 'talent' – as a 'natural' way of assessing achievement. However, these competences, on the one hand, need to be perceived and assessed, for instance by teachers – that is, by socially structured modes of perception. On the other hand, these competences, after being 'discovered', need to be supported and trained. From the point of view of conflict theory, this support and this training do not occur irrespective of social origin, because access to the various education tracks and higher education institutions is based on the *assessment* of prior performance – and this performance is subject to the socially stratified perceptions of teachers and parents discussed (cf. Bourdieu, 1984; Lareau, 2000). The meritocratic ideal, by naturalising and individualising educational inequalities, ignores the importance of social perception when it comes to assessing competence and merit.

Conclusion

Justified by the five essential features of the meritocratic ideal, education in modern societies is presented as an 'opportunity'. Whether or not people make use of this opportunity seems to depend on individual 'talents' and efforts. According to this view, the survival of the 'fittest' is defined and experienced as a fair principle. As a result, 'many believe that competence should be rewarded by success, while incompetence should be punished by failure' (Jencks et al., 1994: 329). This consensus is also shared by the 'unfit' or, in the terminology of the education-based society: those with low skills and no certificates. This is so, following the Thomas theorem, because achievement and educational certificates seem to determine status so *consistently* (Baron and Pfeffer, 1994: 197).

The widespread selection of students and job applicants by achievement thus simultaneously helps maintain and reinforce the meritocratic belief – regardless of the extent to which social origin and educational attainment are disconnected. Education-based inequalities are thus not only accepted by the 'winners' of meritocratic competition, they also guide the actions of those who are the 'losers' (cf. Solga, 2004).

The discussion of the five essential features of the meritocratic ideal of social inequality has shown why individual educational outcomes have to be achieved in formalised, codified and categorising educational processes. This is the only way for them to wield their power as legitimate criteria for allocation. Educational careers in which educational efforts have to be made at an early stage of the life course are part of this codification and categorisation. Assuming a 'natural' foundation and a functional necessity of educational and social inequalities (with the latter 'resulting' from the former), education-based stratification can not only be presented as legitimate but also as efficient (in terms of ensuring that all potential talents in society are discovered and developed, cf. Davis and Moore, 1945). Moreover, the individualisation of educational success and failure serves to obscure this institutional definition of learning opportunities. Intelligence and talent can thus continue to serve as a legitimating myth that attributes existing social inequalities and poverty as a lack of merit (Crocker et al., 1998: 509) – a myth implying that individual talent can be measured accurately. The neo-classical paradigm in economics follows this idea closely by suggesting that individual workers are remunerated according to their (marginal) productivity, which to a large extent depends on educational investment and talent (see Herr and Ruoff in this volume).

Conflict theories have a completely different view of the meritocratic ideal. According to them, the persistence of unequal educational opportunities and the perception of inequality in educational outcomes as being 'natural' and function-ally necessary are caused by social conflicts about the distribution of access and privilege (Collins, 1979; Goldthorpe, 1996; Lenski, 1966; Parkin, 1979, 1982; Weber, 1991 [1921]). In modern societies, where equity is part of the basic democratic consensus and where inequalities can no longer be justified with reference to 'blood' or social origin, there are only two principal criteria that legitimise processes of social inequality aimed at monopolising access to privi-lege: first, property, and second, educational certificates (Parkin, 1982: 178). In a similar vein, Weber stated that 'today, the 'examination' is the universal means of monopolization' (1991 [1921]: 242). Accordingly, conflict theories define educational certificates as a form of social closure supporting the members of the higher social classes in passing on their social status to their children (cf. Sørensen, 2000; Weber, 1994: 126). Nonetheless, all over the world actors and people continue to have an unwavering belief in the meritocratic ideal of social inequality, which in turn serves as a means to maintain educational as well as economic inequalities.

This meritocratic belief underpins the current popularity of the social invest-ment state approach. The meritocratic legitimation of social inequality promotes competition (for higher educational attainment and access to higher positions); however, what is really needed to combat poverty and social inequality is more equality in educational outcomes and social solidarity (cf. Cavanagh, 2002; Green et al., 2008: 138). The latter position suggests that social protection and redis-tribution through the welfare state are necessary in order to reduce economic inequality – as well as education policies that aim at 'providing high levels of education to as many people as possible' and achieving high levels of equality of outcomes (Allmendinger, 2009: 4f., own translation). Yet such education policies are difficult to achieve because they often run 'contrary to the interests of voters', and are likely to 'trigger conflicts over the distribution of wealth' (Allmendinger, 2009: 5; cf. Keep and Mayhew, 2010).

Hence, pursuing an 'education only politics' does not only run the risk that other strategies (such as redistribution, institutional wage-setting, minimum wages above the poverty level and job creation) may fall into oblivion (cf. Bénabou, 2000: 337; Brown et al., 2011: 15ff.; Brown and Tannock, 2009: 389; Della Fave, 1986: 477; Keep and Mayhew, 2010: 565f.; Mickelson and Smith, 2004: 367). It also may 'meritocratise' educational achievement in terms of the five essential features. Achieving a good balance between education – especially reducing inequality in educational outcomes by increasing the overall competence level – *and* social protection against social risks, as realised in the Scandinavian welfare states (of the past), is therefore necessary.

Note

1 Property is the second (widely accepted) legitimation for social inequalities (Parkin, 1982: 178). This pattern of justification, however, is not the topic of this chapter.

References

Allmendinger, J. (2009) Der Sozialstaat des 21: Jahrhunderts braucht zwei Beine. *Aus Politik und Zeitgeschichte* 45: 3–5.

Ansell, B.W. (2008) University Challenges: Expanding Institutional Change in Higher Education. *World Politics* 60: 189–230.

Baron, J.N. and Pfeffer, J. (1994) The Social Psychology of Organizations and Inequality. *Social Psychological Quarterly* 57(3): 190–209.

Beck, U. (1992) *Risk Society*. London: Sage.

Bell, D. (1972) Meritocracy and Equality. *The Public Interest* 29: 29–68.

Bell, D. (1994) The Coming of Post-Industrial Society. In Grusky, D.B. (ed.) *Social Stratification: Class, Race, and Gender in Sociological Perspective*. Boulder, CO: Westview Press: 686–697.

Bénabou, R.J. (2000) Meritocracy, Redistribution, and the Size of the Pie. In Arrow, K, Bowles, S. and Durlauf, S.N. (eds) *Meritocracy and Economic Inequality*. Princeton, NJ: University Press: 317–339.

Blau, P.M. and Duncan, O.D. (1967) *The American Occupational Structure*. New York: John Wiley & Sons.

Boudon, R. (1974) *Education, Opportunity, and Social Inequality*. New York: John Wiley & Sons.

Bourdieu, P. (1984) *Distinction: A Social Critique of the Judgment of Taste*: Cambridge: Harvard University Press.

Bourdieu, P. (1986) The forms of capital. In Richardson, J. (ed.) *Handbook of Theory and Research for the Sociology of Education*. New York: Greenwood: 241–258.

Bourdieu, P. and Passeron, J.P. (1977) *Reproduction in Education, Society and Culture*. London: Sage.

Brown, D.K. (2011) The Social Sources of Educational Credentialism: *Sociology of Education* 74(1): 19–34.

Brown, P., Lauder, H. and Ashton, D. (2011) *The Global Auction. The Broken Promises of Education, Jobs, and Incomes*. Oxford: Oxford University Press.

Brown, P. and Tannock, S. (2009) Education, Meritocracy and the Global War for Talent. *Journal of Education Policy* 24: 377–392.

Cavanagh, M. (2002) *Against Equality of Opportunity*. Oxford: Oxford University Press.

Coleman, J.S. (1968) The Concept of Equality of Educational Opportunity. *Harvard Educational Review* 38(1): 7–22.

Collins, R. (1979) *The Credential Society*. New York: Academic Press.

Crocker, J., Major, B. and Steele, C. (1998) Social Stigma. In Gilbert, D.T., Fiske, S.T. and Lindzey, G. (eds) *The Handbook of Social Psychology*. Boston: McGraw-Hill: 504–553.

Davis, K. and Moore, W.E. (1945) Some Principles of Stratification. *American Sociological Review* 10(2): 242–249.

Della Fave, R. (1986) Towards an Explanation of the Legitimation Process. *Social Forces* 65: 476–500.

Douglas, M. (1986) *How Institutions Think*. Syracuse, NY: Syracuse University Press.

European Commission (2009) Consultation on the Future "EU 2000" Strategy. Commission working document. Brussels.

Fischer, C.S., Hout, M., Jankowski, M.S., Lucas, S.R., Swidler, A. and Voss, K. (1996) *Inequality by Design*. Princeton, NJ: Princeton University Press.

Friedeburg, L. von (1997) Differenz und Integration im Bildungswesen der Moderne. *Zeitschrift für Sozialisationsforschung und Erziehungssoziologie* 17(1): 42–54.

Gesthuizen, M., Solga, H. and Künster, R. (2011) Context Matters: Economic Marginalisation of Low-Educated Workers in Cross-National Perspective. *European Sociological Review* 27(2): 264–280.

Giddens, A. (1998) *The Third Way: The Renewal of Social Democracy*. Cambridge: Polity Press.

Goldin, C. and Katz, L.F. (2009) *The Race between Education and Technology*. Cambridge, MA: Harvard University Press.

Goldthorpe, J.H. (1996) Problems of Meritocracy. In Erikson, R. and Jonsson, J.O. (eds) *Can Education Be Equalized?* Boulder, CO: Westview: 255–287.

Gomolla, M. and Radtke, F.O. (2002) *Institutionelle Diskriminierung*. Opladen: Leske + Budrich.

Gou, G. and Stearns, E. (2002) The Social Influences in the Realization of Genetical Potential for Intellectual Development. *Social Forces* 80(3): 881–910.

Gould, S.J. (1995) Mismeasure by any measure. In Jacoby, R. and Glauberman, N. (eds) *The Bell Curve Debate*. New York: Times Books: 3–13.

Green, A., Preston, J. and Janmaat, J.G. (2008) *Education, Equality and Social Cohesion*. Basingstoke: Palgrave.

Halsey, A.H. (1977) Towards Meritocracy? In Karabel, J. and Halsey, A.H. (eds) *Power and Ideology in Education*. New York: Oxford University Press: 173–186.

Heath, A.F. (2001) Equality of Opportunity. In Smelser, N.J. and Baltes, P.B. (eds) *International Encyclopedia of the Social and Behavioral Sciences*. Oxford: Pergamon: 4722–4724.

Heimer, C.A. (1984) Organizational and Individual Control of Career-Development in Engineering Project Work. *Acta Sociologica* 27(4): 283–310.

Herrnstein, R.J. and Murray, C. (1994) *The Bell Curve: Intelligence and Class Structure in American Life*. New York: The Free Press.

Hirsch, F. (1977) *Social Limits to Growth*. London: Routledge.

Jencks, C. and Riesman, D. (1968) *The American Revolution.* New York: Doubleday.

Jencks, C., Smith, M., Acland, H., Bane, M.J., Cohen, D., Gintis, H., Heyns, B. and Michelson, S. (1994) Inequality: A Reassessment of the Effect of Family and Schooling in America. In Grusky, D.B. (ed.) *Social Stratification: Class, Race, and Gender in Sociological Perspective.* Boulder, CO: Westview: 329–335.

Keep, E. and Mayhew, K. (2010) Moving beyond Skills as a Social and Economic Panacea. *Work, Employment & Society* 24: 565–577.

Lareau, A. (2000) Social Class Differences in Family–School Relationships: The Importance of Cultural Capital. In Arum, R. and Beattie, I.R. (eds) *The Structure of Schooling: Readings in the Sociology of Education.* Mountain View, CA: Mayfield Publishing Company: 288–303.

Lenski, G. (1966) *Power and Privilege.* New York: McGraw-Hill.

Mayer, K.U. (1987) Lebenslaufforschung In Voges, W. (ed.) *Methoden der Biographie- und Lebenslaufforschung.* Opladen: Leske + Budrich: 51–73.

Mayer, K.U. (1991) Soziale Ungleichheit und die Differenzierung von Lebensverläufen. In Zapf, W. (ed.) *Die Modernisierung moderner Gesellschaften.* Frankfurt/Main: Campus: 667–687.

McIntosh, S. (2004) *Skills and Unemployment.* In Gallie, D. (ed.) *Resisting Marginalization – Unemployment Experience and Social Policy in the European Union.* Oxford: Oxford University Press: 140–168.

Meyer, J.W. (1994) The Evolution of Modern Stratification Systems. In Grusky, D.B. (ed.) *Social Stratification: Class, Race, and Gender in Sociological Perspective.* Boulder, CO: Westview: 730–737.

Mickelson, R.A. and Smith, S. (2004) Can Education Eliminate Race, Class, and Gender Inequality? In Anderson, M.L. and Collins, P.H. (eds) *Race, Class, and Gender.* Belmont, CA: Wadsworth Publishing: 361–370.

Morel, N., Palier, B. and Palme, J. (2012) Social Investment: A New Paradigm in Search of a New Economic Model and Political Mobilisation. In Morel, N., Palier, B. and Palme, J. (eds) *Towards a Social Investment Welfare State?* Bristol: Polity Press: 353–376.

OECD (2010) *Learning for Jobs.* Paris: OECD (Organisation for Economic Co-operation and Development).

OECD (2012) *Better Skills, Better Jobs, Better Lives: A Strategic Approach to Skills Policies.* Paris: OECD (Organisation for Economic Co-operation and Development).

Parkin, F. (1979) *Marxism and Class Theory.* London: Tavistock.

Parkin, F. (1982) Social Closure and Class Formation. In Giddens, A. and Held, D. (eds) *Classes, Power, and Conflict.* Basingstoke: Macmillan: 175–184.

Parsons, T. (1959) The School Class as a Social System. *Harvard Educational Review* 29: 297–318.

Parsons, T. (1970) Equality and Inequality in Modern Society, or Social Stratification Revisited. In Laumann, E.O. (ed.) *Social Stratification: Research and Theory for the 1970s.* Indianapolis, IN: Bobbs-Merill: 13–72.

Pfeffer, F.T. (2008) Persistent Inequality in Educational Attainment and its Institutional Context. *European Sociological Review* 24(5): 543–565.

Rawls, J. (1971) *A Theory of Justice.* Cambridge, MA: Harvard University Press.

Riesman, D. (1997 [1967]) Notes on Meritocracy. In Bell, D. and Graubard, S.R. (eds) *Toward the Year 2000.* Cambridge, MA: MIT Press: 265–276.

Rousseau, J.J. (2013 [1755]) *The Essential Writings of Jean-Jacques Rousseau.* London: Vintage.

Rutter, M. (1997) NatureNurture Integration. The Example of Antisocial Behavior: *American Psychologist* 52(4): 390–398.

Scarr, S. (1996) How People Make Their Own Environments. *Psychology, Public Policy, and Law* 2(2): 204–228.

Shavit, Y. and Blossfeld, H.P. (eds) (1993) *Persistent Inequality: Changing Educational Attainment in Thirteen Countries*. Boulder, CO: Westview Press.

Solga, H. (2004) Increasing Risks of Stigmatization. Changes in School-to-Work Transitions of Less-Educated West Germans. *Yale Journal of Sociology* 4: 99–129.

Solga, H. (2014) Education, Economic Inequality, and the Promises of the Social Investment State. *Socio-Economic Review* 12(2): 269–297.

Solga, H. and Wagner, S. (2001) Paradoxie der Bildungsexpansion: Die doppelte Benachteiligung von Hauptschülern. *Zeitschrift für Erziehungswissenschaft* 4(1): 107–127.

Sørensen, A.B. (2000) Symposium on Class Analysis: Toward a Sounder Basis for Class Analysis. *American Journal of Sociology* 105(6): 1523–1558.

Tanner, J.M. (1994) Introduction: Growth in Height as a Mirror of the Standard of Living. In Komlos, J. (ed.) *Stature, Living Standards, and Economic Development*. Chicago: University Press: 1–6.

Thomas, W.I. and Thomas, D.S. (1928) *The Child in America: Behavior Problems and Programs*. New York: Knopf.

Tilly, C. (1998) *Durable Inequality*. Berkeley, CA: University of California Press.

Weber, M. (1991 [1921]) *From Max Weber: Essays in Sociology*. London: Routledge. (First published in German in 1921: *Wirtschaft und Gesellschaft*. Tübingen: Mohr.)

Weber, M. (1994) Open and Closed Relationships. In Grusky, D.B. (ed.) *Social Stratification: Class, Race, and Gender in Sociological Perspective*. Boulder, CO: Westview: 126–129.

Weiss, A. (1995) Human Capital vs. Signalling Explanations of Wages. *Journal of Economic Perspectives* 9(4): 133–154.

Young, M. (1958) *The Rise of the Meritocracy, 1870–2033*. Harmondsworth: Penguin.

Young, M. (1994) Meritocracy Revisited. *Society* 31(6): 87–89.

14 New trends in inequality

The financialisation of social policies

Lena Lavinas[1]

Introduction

According to Michael Burawoy, a third wave of commodification is in progress in the so-called age of neoliberalism (2015: 22). Markets have not only 'come to govern our lives as never before' (Sandel, 2012: 5), but they are also now driven by the rationale of finance. Beyond the increasingly evident fact that everything can be bought or sold, access to financial markets remains indisputably conditional and – unlike rights, which are inherently unconditional-may aggravate exclusion and thus inequalities as well.

Distinct forms of financialisation have become widespread, such as families' growing levels of indebtedness and the privatisation of public goods such as education, health and security. In what follows, I argue that commodification all the way down, as Fraser puts it (2012), has radically and definitively altered non-market dimensions of social life. Worse, this acceleration of commodification has extended a narrow finance-led and market-oriented thinking to production goods, ultimately reframing concepts such as rights. In this way, the notion of rights has been relativised and its universal validity, long posited by principles of citizenship, has been lost.

With this in mind, it comes as no surprise that Robert Shiller, winner of the Nobel Prize in Economics, calls for a reframing of 'the wording of universal rights so that they represent the rights of *all* people to a fair compromise – to financial arrangements that share burdens and benefits effectively'. As financial capitalism moves forward, he adds, 'we ought to see better development of our covenants regarding these "rights," as financial contracts that are more democratic and nuanced, with the rights of mankind refined in more basic terms' (Shiller, 2012: 150). For Shiller, the challenge lies in democratising finance through a system of financial contracts (2012: 235) so as to respond to different purposes and profiles, meeting individual needs and contingencies. To this end, financial education would suffice to narrow knowledge asymmetries and to make finance more user-friendly. Indeed, this logic underpins many anti-poverty programmes in the developing world, whether through micro-credit and micro-finance initiatives or through the provision of conditional cash transfers (CCTs).

In line with this new framework, the social contract loses importance in favour of multiple financial contracts, now seen as a means to meet needs, avoid risks, face uncertainty and enhance well-being through private market provision. Therefore, the idea of the social contract, developed over the course of two and a half centuries in the name of equality and social justice, is subsumed to the logic of finance-led capitalism. As a result, the state excluded from mediating the relationship between market and society, a role that was at the origins of the rationale and the logic of public protection systems, irrespective of their design. Its capacity to regulate financial arrangements that share burdens and benefits effectively (though not always justly and equitably) is in turn obliterated.

My aim in this chapter is to highlight how market incorporation and financial inclusion intertwine as a new model of welfare, particularly salient in the Global South, where social protection systems remain incomplete or even rudimentary. As a consequence, principles of universalism and de-commodified rights, so crucial to promoting equality and enhancing well-being in times of welfare capitalism, have been displaced or denied. Latin America, and Brazil in particular, will serve as examples.

I do this in four sections. After this brief introduction, I propose and revise a definition of financialisation borrowed from Greta Krippner (2012), to then elaborate on this growing trend by contextualising its entanglements with social protection schemes, focusing mostly on Latin America. Here, I argue that the new functionality of social protection schemes in the South is to draw into the market those who have long remained at the margins or even at subsistence levels, a group on the order of tens of millions. Subsequently, I bring in the Brazilian case to illustrate how social policies functioned as critical collateral in fostering the expansion of financial markets among the most vulnerable. Finally, I make some remarks by way of conclusion.

The financialisation of social protection: Latin America as a role model

Financialisation is (by now) a well-recognised historical process. The new domain I will be discussing here, which was largely shielded from finance-led capitalism, but which is now operating within its logic in ever more encompassing terms, is well-being or the provision of social protection.

The 1990s saw a new connection between social protection systems and financial capital. Seeking to boost capital markets, which had remained weak and small scale in the developing world – Latin America included – the financialisation of social policies moved forward on two fronts. On the one hand, pension systems were privatised – a shift from social insurance (pay-as-you-go) and a defined benefit-scheme to a funding system of individual accounts with defined contributions but undefined benefits. On the other hand, in a move that affected those excluded from wage labour and formal job markets, micro-finance and micro-credit mechanisms were broadened alongside the dissemination of targeted cash transfer programmes for poor households, a designation subject to eligibility criteria and conditionalities.

Over the past three decades, Latin America has stood as a privileged stage for many experiments of this sort. A significant number of Latin American countries undertook structural reforms of their pension systems, abandoning a simple pay-as-you-go system in part or altogether (as in the case of Chile) in favour of a funding system (Mesa-Lago, 2007), following the liberal measures recommended by the World Bank (1994). By the 2000s, however, the World Bank itself (2004) recognised that the privatisation of pension systems had not produced the expected results, that is expanded coverage for users, an increase in average benefits and the strengthening of capital markets. Some sort of basic public framework, therefore, had to be reintroduced.

In parallel, new initiatives[2] emerged that aimed at broadening access to small loans (up to $100) among the most vulnerable brackets. With no collateral required (Armendáriz de Aghion and Morduch, 2005; Mosley, 2001), this was meant to serve as a way out of poverty. In keeping with monetarist thinking, it was believed that the poor remained poor because they lacked assets and access to capital.[3] These loans were meant to be set to use in productive activities so as to raise household income and attenuate poverty, as formulated in the World Bank's strategy for social risk management (Holzmann and Jorgensen, 2000). Soares underscores the fact that

> those farther to the left were attracted by the idea of empowering the poorest, women in particular. Conservatives, meanwhile, saw the secondary role of the State and the centrality of the issue of individual entrepreneurship as a positive differential. In the process of promoting this new instrument, and of its consolidation as a crucial development tool, micro-credit was transformed into micro-finance, providing loans, but also a number of insurance and savings programmes, all targeting the poorest sectors of the population.
>
> (2014: 34, own translation)

Finally, a third front cemented a more permanent insertion in the market, now through consumption. This incorporation was made possible through conditional cash transfer programmes, which became indispensable in the fight against extreme poverty and in the valorisation of human capital, such as Progressa-Oportunidades in Mexico, Bolsa Família in Brazil and many others (Lavinas, 2013). Today, such programmes are not only a hallmark of the Latin American continent, but have spread swiftly across the developing world. Myriad systems with similar characteristics and equivalent costs have made it possible for millions of families living under precarious working conditions, or in poverty, to be incorporated into the market. These programmes have reached areas with little integration, where a form of social reproduction still largely characterised by subsistence prevails – in regions and countries marked by indigenous and peasant communities, for instance – and among the several dozens of millions excluded at the urban periphery, whose income deficit generates negative externalities and keeps the market from operating efficiently. Beyond relief, these programmes build on the financialisation of various dimensions of life. Today, almost all Latin American countries adopt conditional cash transfer programmes, with low costs, weak institutional presence, but with impressive visibility (Lavinas, 2013).

Both income security for the elderly and poverty reduction among low-income groups or the worse-off were made to be guaranteed by capital markets – the new providers of welfare – in the form of private insurance, on the one hand, and private loans and micro-finance on the other (Lavinas, 2013: 35). The novelty here is that conditional cash transfer programmes have taken up this push towards commodification: they serve as state-backed collateral for those seeking to obtain consumer credit. CCTs, then, meet two essential needs: they plug the holes of market failures (in terms of access to commodities) and are complementary to incomplete or missing markets. In other words, financial markets that had failed to include loans to the poorest because they lacked collateral became able to incorporate them as borrowers able to keep up with loan payments. CCTs thus not only provide cash, but also help leverage access to credit.[4]

This shift is not trivial. Well-being is no longer tethered to basic rights ensured by the state irrespective of class and status distinctions and of the market value of work or property (Briggs, 1961), but rather, and increasingly, through access to credit and private insurance, which presumes that 'rights' may be subject to collateral or controls. This turning point has already occurred, as selectivity and targeting have arisen at the turn of this century as central mechanisms for regulating entitlements for the poor and the destitute. These coercive practices (reworked in the guise of self-responsibility) undermine the idea of rights existing prior to obligations, and of self-knowledge and fulfilment as a precondition to reward. Indeed, reward, not rights, constitutes the touchstone of this new framework, which, as we shall see, paved the way towards a new model of social regulation in which access is conditional to delivery.

But how to define this pervasive and disruptive process of financialisation, which, as anthropologist Carol Greenhouse writes, 'displaces nonmarket-based regimes of value and the relationships they sustain' (2012: 5)? According to Greta Krippner, 'financialisation is the tendency for profit making in the economy to occur increasingly through financial channels rather than through productive activities. Here "financial" references the provision (or transfer) of capital in expectation of future interest dividends or capital gains' (2012: 4). But as financial channels take up so many dimensions of life as a means to enhance access to both consumer goods and security, as well as paving the way to achieve prosperity, I suggest that the very economy through which this process unfolds is also transformed.

Financialisation extends profit-making opportunities into spheres not yet completely governed by market regimes, as financial techniques and practices re-evaluate public goods or activities related to the sphere of reproduction. Here 'financial' refers to the provision (or transfer) of capital to guarantee access to what used to be non-market services or citizens' rights in expectation of future interest dividends or capital gains.

How was welfare capitalism captured by finance? I suggest that this was made possible in the wake of two distinctive trends in the last quarter of the twentieth century.

First of all, market societies, increasingly under the hegemony of the financial sector, were assigned a distinctive role for welfare capitalism, in which stocks, credit and other financial instruments prevailed over the traditional capital–labour relation. The latter had characterised the golden era of industrial-led capitalism after the Second World War, in which protection through public risk pooling strategies was demanded and managed by the state based on the principle of solidarity. In the current finance-led accumulation regime, labour relations have achieved greater flexibility, as profits are no longer expected to be shared. Redistribution is thus at stake under the rationale that reducing labour costs and inserting capital gains tax exemptions are the present-day mechanisms to foster competitiveness and offset various trade-offs[5] that may undermine the likelihood of success in the global economy. There is no more room for redistribution through wages and earnings, in particular in most developed economies, which is the primary reason for growing inequality in the present time (cf. Hacker and Pierson, 2010; Galbraith, 2012; Stiglitz, 2012; Wilkinson and Pickett, 2010). There is in fact less room for redistribution, since tax cuts lead to a curb on social spending.

Beyond attempts to curb social spending, its structure has changed as well, with cash transfer schemes being privileged over the public provision of a range of social services designed to support a level playing field and ensure social equality. Indeed, the consolidation of financialisation in developed and developing countries is now marked by (1) public pension reforms incentivising voluntary and obligatory membership with securitised retirement and pension funds, (2) public health reforms that privatise specific services and (3) increasing tuition costs in the public education system (to name just a few trends).

Second, the dominant ideology holds that, with the state unreliable and inept when called upon to deliver services with a scope adequate to the evolution of changes and risks, the relevant fields should be addressed on an individual and private basis. The privatisation of public services is meant to address insufficient public provision. This holds particularly true in developing countries where the state, in an attempt to address market failures, has been pushing for minimum income programmes rather than for social investments or the provision of public goods. To better prepare those who are likely to be immediately plagued by economic downturns, banks, private insurance and the financial sector as a whole have emerged as the new 'providers of means' suitable for the task. This shift was supposed to 'empower' those once excluded, forgotten and disqualified. De-individualisation (Rosanvallon, 2011) has thus been replaced by a new relationship between social constraints and the fantasy of open and free life trajectories, breaking with principles of public risk-pooling in favour of self-responsibility and risk-taking.

In the developing world, social infrastructure and access to de-commodified goods and services delivered by the state do not progress at the same pace as the provision of cash, aggravating inequality gaps whose measurement appears increasingly more difficult to gauge. Government failures in delivering basic services and goods foment private spending in realms that used to be public, such as education and health. In turn, the privatisation of basic rights is boosted and universality is jeopardised, a drawback particularly for countries where social heterogeneity and inequality remain the most important challenges ahead.

Boosting consumption and financialisation in the South – the Brazilian case

It is in this context that we observe the emergence of a core issue: the expansion of mass-consumption societies in the Global South, where social and productive heterogeneity remains a resilient structural problem.

As stressed above, what changed in the twenty-first century is the role attributed to social policy, notably in income protection. This dimension has come to play a foundational role in the expansion of mass consumption in the creation of a new cycle of growth. However, contrary to what was hoped for, this new social policy model failed to overcome barriers such as low labour-productivity levels in Latin America (Bielschowsky, 2013; Lavinas and Simões, 2015), which continues to limit development and sustained economic growth.

Social spending has increased between 2002 and 2013 in Latin America, from 15.2 to 19.2 per cent of gross domestic product (GDP) (CEPAL, 2014), but the privileged form of social spending remains monetary income transfers (which amounts to about two-thirds of social spending), to the detriment of spending on health, education, housing and sanitation, which has shown slower progress. Between 1991 and 2011, as contributory and non-contributory monetary transfers registered real growth of about 3.16 per cent, spending on health increased by 1.22 per cent, education by 1.9 per cent and housing by only 0.99 per cent. In 2011, the deficit for health coverage was high, affecting one third of formal workers and 57 per cent of informal workers (CEPAL, 2013). The percentage of workers who do not contribute to social security also remains high (44.6 per cent among employees and 87.6 per cent among freelance workers).

This is further evidence that the provision of de-commodified public services has been overlooked in favour of monetary transfers, with non-negligible implications for individual well-being and for equality of opportunity made available to all. However, the current profile of spending has prioritised addressing market failures rather than the promotion of social homogeneity through policies of equal access to de-commodified services, whose cost would be notably higher.

In addition to securing income, contributory or non-contributory programmes were designed to transfer cash or income to serve as collateral in order to secure access to financial markets, without which mass consumption would fail to consolidate. This is meant to eliminate underdevelopment – that is, the persistent and structural barriers that have blocked the emergence of mass consumption societies in the South, a long-lasting problem faced by latecomers. But these new social policies cannot be effective enough on their own. They must be coupled with financial mechanisms tailored to that end to achieve that purpose.

It is worth mentioning the significant expansion of credit in Latin America as of late. On average, it has risen from 31 per cent of GDP in 2004 to 38 per cent in 2011 (CEPAL, 2014). As Hansen and Sulla (2013) note, credit made to families has expanded more quickly than credit made to corporations, with an emphasis on credit made for consumption.

Brazil is not an exception. Whereas federal social spending on welfare benefits increased in real terms by 300 per cent between 2001 and 2010, over the same period, spending on education doubled and on public health rose by only 60 per cent (Lavinas, 2013: 32f.). These figures uncover the strategic choice that prevailed under the ruling of the Workers' Party, which prioritised cash transfers to individuals and families rather than de-commodified public services.

One should recall that cash and benefits in kind achieve different goals in terms of preserving and enhancing well-being. Though income support varies considerably, either in the form of contributory or non-contributory benefits, they have been tailored for purposes of insurance, smoothing consumption and poverty relief. They tackle primarily income deficits and help in solving problems of market failures. In contrast, benefits in kind address other complex issues referring to equality of opportunity and therefore are intimately related to equity issues (Barr, 2012).

Whereas improvements in adequate sanitation or in the provision of clean water made little progress in the last decade, access to market goods such as cell phones, washing machines and computers soared stunningly (PNAD, 2011): 86.4 per cent of all Brazilian households report having at least one cell phone in 2011, against 31 per cent in 2001. One out of two households now owns a washing machine, but only two in three enjoy adequate sanitation. As for the provision of clean water, no change was reported over the same time period. One should keep in mind that Brazil is home to 62.3 million households. This means that no less than 30 million households – whether poor or not – lack access to clean water. Nothing can justify such a low rate of clean water supply in a high middle-income country such as Brazil.

The standards of public provision remain shamefully low, aggravating the living conditions of low-income households. Poor housing is endemic in metropolitan areas as well as in the countryside, while inappropriate and insufficient sanitation and water supplies are the rule, affecting both lives and the environment. Infant mortality and maternal mortality rates, though in decline, remain higher than the national income would predict. Public transportation falls short on both scale and quality in addressing the needs of a new mass-market society. Judt's prophecy[6] (2010) is self-fulfilling: if public goods are devalued, then privatisation emerges as the alternative to redress deficits of citizenship, 'reinforcing the role of private providers and the trend towards commodification of basic rights' (Lavinas, 2013: 21).

Here, credit and access to capital markets appear as the lever to promote and deepen the integration into this new mass-market society. Credit loans, extremely segmented, private insurances and new financial products become the key elements in fostering growth, signalling that the social mode of regulation has been transformed so as to capture the poor, the indigent, the vulnerable and the low middle class that far outnumber the rich and very rich. Credit and private insurance are meant to bridge the gap to further consumption, ensuring well-being.

This trend spread quickly and by the end of 2014, the level of household indebtedness[7] stood at 48 per cent, as compared with 15 per cent in early 2005[8] (BACEN, 2015). Interest rates in Brazil remain extremely high, especially for short-term consumer credits. There are two modalities of individual loans. Those with lower fees refer to a financial innovation that dates back to Lula's first term and is called 'crédito consignado' – or 'consigned credit'. This form of credit is offered to borrowers with strong collateral – either a public pension or a regular job in the public or private sector. They enjoy interest rates reduced by around 30 per cent per year. By the same token, however, payments are compulsory and automatically deducted from retirement benefits or wages. The higher fees affect borrowers with no collateral, such as vulnerable and precarious workers, and those on welfare. The spread between both groups is striking. Those with no salaried jobs or pensions borrow at a rate ranging from 74 to 94 per cent, following an upswing turn. Those on 'consigned credits' pay half or even two third less. In any case, as the inflation rate has not passed 8 per cent since 2011, it becomes shamefully apparent how high the entrance fee in today's Brazil is for participation in mass consumption and consumerism.

The process of financialisation is being tightened up from both ends. On one hand, consumers are provided with access to credit lines and other financial facilities such as credit cards and other forms of 'bankisation', that is the integration of a large number of low-income groups into the financial sector. Not surprisingly, in 2008–2009, 9.9 per cent of the bottom 20 per cent in the income distribution possessed a credit card, as opposed to 2.2 per cent in 2002–2003 of this same group. In addition, access to private universities,[9] which account for 75 per cent of all college students in Brazil, is also generally made possible through loans. On the other hand, access to private insurance in order to offset the lack of public provision of healthcare is on the rise as well. In this case, one in four Brazilians pays a health insurance premium, as compared with 10.9 per cent in the early 2000s (IBGE, 2012).

A mass-consumption society was thought to prevail over Brazil's underdevelopment; in this vision, it would foment a new path of inward-looking industrialisation boosted by the expansion of the domestic market. The assumption was that innovation would drive increasing productivity and, as a consequence, wages would also rise, lifting Brazil up into the high road of development. In reality, however, China's mass production chains have been supplying the country's demand for cheap manufacturing and consumer goods, fuelled by an overvalued exchange rate (Singer, 2012). Meanwhile, Brazil's industrial productivity rate displayed a negative trend in the 2000s: −1.2 per cent from 2000 to 2009, according to the Department of National Accounts at Instituto Brasileiro de Geografia e Estatística. Brazil has also undergone a process of de-industrialisation, with the manufacturing sector's share of GDP falling 2 percentage points from 2002–2010, and a re-primarisation of the country's exports: in 2014, 48.7 per cent of all Brazilian exports were commodities as compared with 19.4 per cent back in 2002 (SECEX/MDIC, 2015). Structural bottlenecks persist, along with profound inequities inherited from the past.

In my view, social-developmentalism (Carneiro, 2012) as a model of economic growth failed to promote a more genuinely integrated and egalitarian society (see also Manzano et al.'s chapter in this volume). Instead, it strengthened a capital-led market society. It is no accident that banks reported an 11 per cent annual profit rate during Fernando Henrique's (1995–2002) presidential term, soaring to 14 per cent under Lula (2003–2010).[10] In terms of social inclusion and the building of the foundations of a more egalitarian society, the picture is rather bleak. No one can deny that economic growth was essential to diminish poverty rates and that growing earnings have slightly curbed inequality. However, both measures are flawed and imprecise. Poverty rates apply a threshold that remains pretty low, therefore pushing down the level of destitution that determines monetary poverty. Inequality measures do not take into consideration data related to assets, wealth, profits and rents. Neither is it an accurate indicator for representing poverty and inequality. Therefore, current indicators should be referenced with caution.

If Piketty's observations are correct – and this is very likely – then persistent and reinforced inequality is due to the fact that the rate of return on assets has been consistently higher over the long term than the rate of growth (Piketty, 2014: 107). What do we know about this long-term trend in Brazil? Little. Very little. Still, it is well known that two decades of macroeconomic policy based on stratospheric interest rates meant to control inflation (yet again sharply rising) have concentrated wealth in the ranks of the most affluent and powerful. As Nobre puts it,

> in social terms, this had the consequence of determining that any attempt at distributive or compensatory policy would be marginal and incremental; continued high interest rates also guaranteed the survival of an unequal pattern of distribution in which income and the relative position of the richest strata of society would be preserved.
>
> (2013: 81)

By way of illustration, one should recall that in 2013 Brazil spent R$248.8 billion ($113 billion) paying back interest to holders of government bonds, a figure ten times greater than the annual cost of Bolsa Família (R$23 billion or $10.4 billion) that same year (Lavinas, 2014a).

It is also widely known that no democratic government has attempted to reform the tax system in order to make it less regressive. Likewise, they have not tried seriously to address a biased tax system in which indirect taxes on goods and services, affecting the entire population regardless of income level, constitute 49.22 per cent in 2011 (Lavinas, 2014a) of all tax revenues, whereas property and wealth amount only to 3.7 per cent in the same year. In Brazil, no goods or services are completely exempt from consumption taxes, not even those in high demand or even groceries. Moreover, no democratic government has made middle school compulsory or provided day-care as a universal right (only 33 per cent of all children aged three go to a crèche or pre-school, while for the bottom 20 per cent, this share drops to 21.9 per cent, according to PNAD (2012)). Elementary school has achieved full coverage since the late 1990s, but quality is still severely lagging behind, and only a small share of school-children enjoy full-time schooling (mostly in private schools) (INEP, 2012).

Conclusion

We learned from Polanyi (1944) that twentieth-century industrial capitalism was marked by a double and contradictory movement – commodification and de-commodification – in order to accommodate constraints that could otherwise hold up the new accumulation regime. Whereas the market was forcefully pushing for marketisation of all dimensions of life, the capitalist social state lagged behind when it came to offsetting this inexorable trend.

It seems that the role of the state has been reshaped under the hegemony of finance-led capitalism. It continues indispensable in the new march of accumulation, but instead of working against the logic of marketisation, it becomes essential in the incorporation of significant contingents of millions of individuals into the market, people who were previously surviving in non-mercantile or not fully mercantile conditions.

The Brazilian case is a good illustration of this shift. In recent decades – notably under the Workers' Party administrations (2003–2014) – there has emerged a new articulation between policies stimulating economic development and schemes focused on poverty and minimum social standards – regulation of the minimum wage and safety nets. This has financially eased the transition to mass consumption, making the expansion of domestic demand possible where it had been inhibited by neglecting the social element until late in the past century. However, this new link between economic and social policy is not a cure-all for serious equity problems, the resolution of which would imply the promotion of a more homogeneous, egalitarian society. Three-quarters of Brazilian social spending today comes in the form of monetary transfers (contributory or non-contributory), which, given the absence of public provision of a wide range of social services, expands the borders of the market while restricting and wearing down the public sector. Without universal policies that might lead to a true, sweeping de-commodification of the workforce and promote inclusion and equity, social policy understood principally as a means to patch the shortcomings of the market will be subsumed by the market – thus generating inequalities and raising risks. This accelerated process of incorporation into the consumer market partially resolves a standing structural problem: it compensates for the shockingly low productivity of the workforce by unleashing the mass-market economy. This is made possible by a radical and accelerated extension of access to the labour and financial markets for the least fortunate layers of society, via credit – albeit at an extremely high cost.

Brazilian economists celebrate the shift to a consumer society as a striking accomplishment. The scope and scale of the Brazilian market society have indeed grown rapidly, radically and definitively. Is Brazil, as a result, a far more egalitarian society? Probably not. Vulnerability has become exacerbated. The social protection system is being dismantled through mechanisms that divert resources from the social security budget – a specific, exclusive budget running a surplus – into the fiscal budget. Public spheres and common interest are not the driving force behind this new wave of market incorporation.

In a recent piece, Therborn suggests that 'white-collar masses' and other social groups worldwide, critical of contemporary finance-led capitalism, may become the 'rising social forces today that could be functionally equivalent to the organized working classes or the anti-colonial movements of the twentieth century' (2014: 10). If this is the case, a very positive trend for Brazil and Latin America in general would be to have its growing middle class – still modest in size and in features – voicing universal rights and then contributing to consolidating a more homogeneous and inclusive society through the promotion of a new pattern of social inclusion. Time will tell.

The functionality of the welfare state, so effective and essential to capitalist regimes of any sort, supposes that its design is constantly adapting to meet the new challenges created by the accumulation regime and contradictions of capitalism. Under the rule of finance-led capitalism, social protection systems are experiencing a marked shift, particularly in the developing world where they used to be either non-existent or ill-developed. The Keynesian welfare state's greatest virtue was to link macroeconomics and social policies. It ensured that the economy was permanently maintained in conditions of a quasi-boom in order to make it produce at its full potential. This preserved and stimulated full employment – the major source of well-being in market societies. The immediate effect was to contain crises, recessions and depressions, therefore avoiding loss and suffering due to economic volatility. Security had the upper hand. Although occupational welfare offset temporary hazards, it did not suffice in itself to maintain demand in conditions of a 'quasi-boom'. This accounts for the quest of universalising rights beyond entitlements derived from occupational status.

But the new model for articulating social and economic policies is rather different. It is not sufficient to study whether social spending has increased or not. It is important to capture the logic that rules how social spending functions. This new logic does not guarantee security, nor does it cover all risks, as it certainly fails to predict misfortunes derived from unpredictable macroeconomic shocks. Furthermore, this logic also fails to generate sustainable jobs. Levels of indebtedness underlying this dynamic only increase social vulnerabilities. All of this, in turn, suggests that there are new risks as well as further controls and conditionalities attached to benefits. This will certainly produce novel forms of social exclusion resulting from non-compliance with financial contracts.

In the twentieth century, mass-consumption societies and credit expansion have long developed side by side, one backing the other. This was the foundation for a model of development characterised by increasing inclusion, a quest for social homogeneity, as well as gains in productivity and innovation. The result was a distinguished model: social protection was a stabilising factor, while the financial sector diverted resources to consumption and investment, enabling risk-taking.

In the new framework, financial inclusion disregards protection. Indeed, financial inclusion is marketed as protection. Everything is connected to the financial sector: not only access to wage goods and property, but also, and above all else, to insurance (healthcare, student financial aid, pension funds, long-term care, etc.) and new opportunities (via loans).

Without a doubt, we will see a rise in the percentage of families at the risk of poverty, with increasing levels of vulnerability. At the same time, an extremely limited subset of those in poverty, due to the low poverty threshold definition used, will give credence to the believe that poverty is diminishing and that inequality is nothing but a matter of choice.

For this reason, it is misleading to equate the current social policy model of market incorporation in the South to a new Keynesian model, the latter having been a central characteristic of welfare regimes in developed western economies during the last century. For the latter, in addition to a focus on the expansion of consumer markets and a move towards dynamic markets, the provision of a range of de-commodified goods and services contributed to job security, income protection and well-being more generally. It contributed, above all else, to unwinding a vicious cycle of inequality inherent in market societies.

Considering that the current buzzword is 'financial inclusion' as a human right for the next generation, and that the efforts under way in this direction have already taken root in the institutions of social policy, especially in the Global South, it is time to understand how this process is unfolding and to reconfigure the dynamics behind inequalities in peripheral societies.

Notes

1 My deepest thanks go to PhD student Eudes Lopes, with whom I discussed previous drafts of this chapter. His insights have been all-important.
2 The 1970s and 1980s brought pioneering micro-credit experiments across Latin America, driven at the start by Accion International, which was operating in 14 countries in the region by the 1980s.
3 Soares recalls that 'De Soto (1986, 2000), in analysing the Latin American case, declared that capitalism had not developed fully in the region, since the poorest in society, for lack of credit, could not generate capital. This access, meanwhile, was blocked by a lack of well-defined property rights: the poor had assets, but they could not use them as collateral, as they did not legally possess them' (2014: 40).
4 In Brazil, for instance, special consumer credit lines have been set up for Bolsa Família recipients, who can purchase durable and wage goods in instalments. This is also the

case with public pensioners. During Lula's first term, the 'consigned credit line' was launched for those entitled to public pensions. This type of loan was introduced by public banks but was quickly extended to the entire banking system. See the third section of this chapter.

5 One may point out different fiscal and taxes regimes, exchange-rate regimes, minimum wages, as well as larger or minor welfare states.

6 'If public goods – public services, public spaces, public facilities – are devalued, diminished in the eyes of citizens and replaced by private services available against cash, then we lose the sense that common interests and common needs ought to trump private preferences and individual advantage. And once we cease to value the public over the private, surely we shall come in time to have difficulty seeing just why we should value law (the public good par excellence) over force' (Judt 2010: 129).

7 Household income share committed to paying back debts with the financial sector.

8 This figure refers to consumer credit excluding mortgages. If all individual credit loans are considered, then these rates would have been 45.5 and 18.3 per cent respectively.

9 Most private universities rank very low, academically speaking, in Brazil (INEP, 2012).

10 My estimates calculated using data released by the Brazilian Central Bank.

References

Armendáriz de Aghion, B. and Morduch, J. (2005) *The Economics of Microfinance*. Cambridge, MA: MIT Press.

BACEN (2015) Séries Estatísticas. Brasília.

Barr, N. (2012) *The Economics of the Welfare State*. Oxford: Oxford University Press.

Bielschowsky, R. (2013) Padrões regionais e singularidades nacionais do desenvolvimento econômico latino-americano, asiático e russo (1950-fim dos anos 2000). In Bielchowsky, R. (ed.) *Padrões de Desenvolvimento Econômico (1950–2008): América Latina, Ásia e Rússia.* CGEE, Volume 2: 893–910.

Briggs, A. (1961) The Welfare State in Historical Perspectives. *European Journal of Sociology* 2(2): 221–258.

Buraway, M. (2015) Facing an Unequal World. *Current Sociology* 63(1): 5–34.

Carneiro, R. (2012) Velhos e Novos Desenvolvimentismos. *Economia e Sociedade* 21(4): 749–778.

CEPAL (2013) *Panorama Social da América Latina*. Santiago de Chile.

CEPAL (2014) *Pactos para la Igualdad: hacia un future sostenible*. Santiago de Chile.

Fraser, N. (2012) Can Society Be Commodities All the Way Down? Polanyian Reflections on Capitalist Crisis. Working Papers Series, No. 18, Fondation Maison des Sciences de l'Homme & Collège d'Etudes Mondiales.

Galbraith, J. (2012) *Inequality and Instability: A Study of the World Economy Just Before the Great Crisis. New York:* Oxford University Press.

Greenhouse, C. (2012) *Ethnographies of Neoliberalism*. Philadelphia: University of Pennsylvania Press.

Hacker, J.S. and Pierson, P. (2010) *Winner Take-All Politics*. New York: Simon & Schuster.

Hansen, N.J. and Sulla, O. (2013) El crecimiento del credito en America Latina: desarrollo financiero o boom crediticio? *Revista Estudios Economicos* 25(1): 51–80.

Holzmann, R. and Jorgensen, S. (2000) *Manejo Social del Riesgo: un nuevo marco conceptual para la protección social y más allá*. Documento de Trabajo No. 06. Washington, DC: World Bank.

INEP (2012) *Censo Escolar*. Brasil.

Judt, T. (2010) *Ill Fares the Land*. London: Penguin.

Krippner, G. (2012) *Capitalizing on Crisis: The Political Origins of the Rise of Finance.* Cambridge, MA: Harvard University Press.

Lavinas, L. (2013) 21st Century Welfare. *New Left Review* 84: 4–40.

Lavinas, L. (2014a) *Brazil: A New Path to Equality?* International Seminar Brazil: From Dictatorship to Democracy. Providence, RI: Watson Institute for International Studies at Brown University, 11 April.

Lavinas, L. (2014b) A Long Way from Tax Justice: The Brazilian Case. Working Paper No. 22. Berlin: Global Labour University, ILO & GLU.

Lavinas, L. and Simões, A. (2015) Social Policy and Structural Heterogeneity in Latin America: the Turning Point of the 21st Century. In Fritz, B. and Lavinas, L. (eds) *A Moment of Equality of Latin America? Challenges for Redistribution.* Burlington: Ashgate (forthcoming).

Mesa-Lago, C. (2007) *As Reformas de Previdência na América Latina e seus Impactos nos Princípios da Seguridade Social.* Coleção 'Previdência Social', Brasília: Ministério da Previdência Social.

Mosley, P. (2001) Microfinance and Poverty in Bolivia. *The Journal of Development Studies* 37(4): 101–132.

Nobre, M. (2013) *Imobilismo em Movimento*. São Paulo: Companhia das Letras.

Pesquisa Nacional por Amostra de Domicílios (PNAD) (2011).

Pesquisa Nacional por Amostra de Domicílios (PNAD) (2012).

Piketty, T. (2014) Dynamics of Inequality. *New Left Review* 85: 103–116.

Polanyi, K. (1944) *The Great Transformation*. Boston: Beacon Press.

Rosanvallon, P. (2011) *La Société des Egaux*. Paris: Seuil.

Sandel, M.J. (2012) *What Money Can't Buy: The Moral Limits of Markets.* New York: Farrar, Straus and Giroux.

Secex/MDIC (2015) Exportações Brasileiras.

Shiller, R.J. (2012) *Finance and the Good Society*. Princeton, NJ: Princeton University Press.

Singer, A. (2012) *Os Sentidos do Lulismo – Reforma Gradual e Pacto Conservador.* São Paulo: Companhia das Letras.

Soares, C.M.M. (2014) *O Microcrédito como Instrumento de Proteção Social: uma análise comparativa de Brasil e Bolívia.* Master Dissertation, Institute of Economics, Federal University of Rio de Janeiro.

Stiglitz, J. (2012) *The Price of Inequality: How Today's Divided Society Endangers Our Future.* New York: W.W. Norton & Company.

Therborn, G. (2014) New Masses? Social Bases of Resistance. *New Left Review* 85: 7–16.

Wilkinson, R. and Pickett, K. (2010) *The Spirit Level: Why Equality is Better for Everyone.* New York: Penguin Books.

World Bank (1994) *Averting the Old Age Crisis: Policies to Protect the Old and Promote Growth.* Washington, DC: World Bank.

World Bank (2004) *Keeping the Promise of Old Age Income Security in Latin America.* Washington, DC: World Bank.

Part V
Merits and limits of alternative political responses

15 Market regulation, inequality and economic development

Hansjörg Herr[1]

Introduction

The purpose of my chapter is to demonstrate, with the help of heterodox economic theories, that unregulated markets endogenously produce levels of inequality that are unfair and pose a threat to the functioning of the economic system. Only proper institutions and comprehensive regulations can prevent a rise in inequality. Two areas are particularly relevant. The first is the asset market: the wealthier people become, the faster they can increase their wealth. The second is the labour market, which, if left unchecked, tends towards extremely high wage dispersion and a large low-wage sector. The higher the unemployment rate, the greater, in turn, the likelihood of high wage dispersion and inequality. Overall, an unregulated market economy is unstable and is accompanied by stagnation and high unemployment.

The 1970s and 1980s marked the end of the 'golden age' period of capitalism in the developed countries, which had begun after the Second World War. A phase of radical, market-based globalisation started, which was triggered by the deregulation of asset- and labour-markets. In the last decades, all those economic developments predicted at the theoretical level when markets are deregulated can be observed empirically.

In the following section, I will examine the neoclassical paradigm and how it deals with inequality. Against this backdrop, I will analyse the long-term stability of capitalist economies. For this purpose, I will critically discuss the nucleus of neoclassical thinking, the general equilibrium model. The third section is about asset markets and inequality; in the fourth section, I will look at labour markets. The fifth section deals with the instabilities inherent in capitalist economies. In the last section, I will spell out the political implications of my theoretical critique.

Inequality in the general equilibrium model

Adam Smith, one of the first economists analysing capitalism, saw markets as a mechanism capable of co-ordinating the egoistic behaviour of economic agents and, at the same time, producing results beneficial to society as a whole. An economic agent in the market 'intends only his own gain, and he is in this, as in many other cases, led by an invisible hand to promote an end which was no part of his intention. [. . .] By pursuing his own interest he frequently promotes that of the society more effectually than when he really intends to promote it' (Smith, 1904 [1776]: IV 2.9). The outcome of the market process, the argument goes, is the welfare of nations. However, Adam Smith was not advocating ruthless individualism. He also stressed the importance of ethics and charity (Smith, 1759). Overall, the economists of the classical paradigm did not only see the advantages of markets as an allocation mechanism but also understood the dynamic and violent aspects of capitalism.

In contrast, the neoclassical paradigm limited the scope of economic theory. It focused on allocation and static equilibriums. The market became a miraculous institution ensuring optimal allocation, maximising welfare and creating harmony in the economy. Léon Walras, founder of the general equilibrium model that lies at the heart of neoclassical thinking, formulated a clear research agenda:

> man has progressed from a system of guilds, trade regulations, and price fixing to a system of freedom of industry and trade, i.e. to a system of *laisser-faire* [. . .]. The superiority of the latter forms of organisation over the earlier forms lies [. . .] in their closer conformity with material well-being and justice. The proof of such conformity is the only justification for adhering to a policy of *laisser-faire, laisser-passer*. Moreover, socialist forms of organisation should be rejected if it indeed be shown that they are inconsistent with material well-being and justice.
>
> (1993 [1874]: 55)

Walras's model worked the following way. Under conditions of perfect competition, there are a great number of separate households equipped with an exogenously given endowment (hammers, lathes, seeds, labour power, etc.). These households have individual utility functions and want to maximise their utility. A modern example would be a group of people who participate in a reality TV show and thus live in a jungle camp. Everyone in the camp is provided with a parcel. Undoubtedly, the people in the camp can increase their welfare through barter: person (A) does not like chocolate and can exchange it for fried herring, which person (B) hates. An auctioneer calls out relative prices (barter exchange values), which allows all participants in the market to reconcile their individual plans. As soon as the equilibrium set of relative prices is found, the people in the camp exchange their goods.

Vilfredo Pareto (1909) defined this equilibrium condition as a welfare optimum ('Pareto optimum'), in which no market participant can improve their welfare without reducing the welfare of others. Pareto argued that a measure for the utility or satisfaction of groups of people or even a society – a macroeconomic utility function – does not exist. However, this is not a problem because such a utility function is not necessary for the definition of the Pareto optimum. One of the implications of Pareto's argument is the impossibility to claim that expanding the consumption of the poor at the expense of the rich improves the overall welfare in society.

Once production is introduced into the model, complications emerge. As long as all inputs for production are produced and used in the same period as consumption takes place, the world remains simple. Firms are confronted with a set of known technologies, attract inputs and transform them into output in order to maximise their profits. The problems starts when it is assumed that (a) there are several periods of production, (b) capital goods are used for several periods, or (c) people save in order to transfer consumption into the future. There is a long line of economists stressing that under these more complicated conditions, a Pareto optimum only exists when *universal future markets* exist for all products and all future activities are fixed by contracts (Arrow and Debreu 1954; Debreu, 1959). Labour in eight years, for example, is exchanged against a meal in ten years. All future activities of firms have to be fixed today for all future periods. Once the inter-temporal equilibrium is found, the auctioneer announces an inter-temporal system of relative prices. The market never opens again until the end of time. Under certain conditions – especially if there are 'well-behaved' individual utility functions while economies of scale do not exist – a solution for the inter-temporal allocation problem *exists*. Usually, however, there are several equilibriums.[2] The consequence is that there are also several Pareto-optimal solutions and it remains unclear which one is the best. In addition, it cannot be proven that the market *process* is able to find one of the equilibriums. In the model, the auctioneer reveals one of the mathematically determined equilibriums by telling everybody what it is (cf. Arrow and Debreu 1954; Debreu, 1959).

In Arrow–Debreu economies with universal future markets, the future collapses into the present. However, as soon as even one of these future markets does not exist, 'rather terrible things happen to the theory' (Hahn, 1981: 132). After all, it is impossible to fix all transactions today if some of the future markets do not exist. Instead, it has to be assumed that the economic agents act on the grounds of expectations. The problem is that the general equilibrium model does not explain what economic agents expect. In fact, there is simply no economic theory available that can accurately explain expectations. It does not help to assume that agents know the equilibrium conditions in non-existing future markets, as has been argued by the those talking about 'rational expectations' in the tradition of John Muth (1961) and Robert Lucas (1972): 'Just as the classical General Equilibrium Theory has never been able to provide a definite account of how equilibrium prices come to be established, so Rational Expectation Theory has not shown how, starting from relative ignorance, everything that can be learned comes to be learned' (Hahn, 1981: 133). In sum, a Pareto optimum does not exist as soon as universal future markets do not exist.

What can we learn from the general equilibrium model? It shows that a Pareto optimum exists under extreme conditions, but never explains how the market mechanism can establish it. In other words, the conditions under which the invisible hand works are far removed from reality. It seems more plausible to assume that unregulated markets do not have 'welfare maximising' results (cf. Hahn, 1981; 1982). Friedrich von Hayek (1948), who was an economic liberal but closer to the classical paradigm, argues that market competition is a dynamic discovery procedure leading to innovation and economic development. According to him, income distribution is not fair and also not linked to merit. His argument is that many economic agents may search for innovations with the same effort, but it cannot be predicted who will be successful in the market and who will stay poor.

Inequality and asset markets

One of the drivers of inequality is the concentration of wealth and, as a consequence, the concentration of income among a small number of wealthy families. There is a cumulative process leading endogenously to more inequality: the wealthiest households have the highest incomes, which enables them to save more than anyone else and, thus, accumulate wealth faster than anyone else. It does not take much imagination to understand this snowball effect (cf. Kuznets, 1955: 7; Piketty, 2014).

Of course, endogenous wealth concentration is a 'soft' law. In theory, owners of wealth can consume all their income – or their offspring can choose to squander it. Such things happen, but it is unlikely that this contains the trend towards wealth concentration. More importantly, in dynamic societies with high upward mobility, wealth concentration can be slowed down or even reduced if wage incomes become more important for overall incomes. European societies before the First World War showed almost no upward mobility; at the same time, owners of wealth tended not to work and consequently had no wage income. A person not born into the upper class had almost no chance to die as a member of the upper class – except via marriage. After the Second World War, the class of rentiers not working was reduced drastically. Wage income became an important component of income for the top 10 and even the top 1 per cent income earners. At the same time, the income share of top income earners was relatively low during the first few decades after the war. This changed fundamentally in the 1980s. In Anglo-Saxon countries, the income of top managers and, to a certain extent, of sport stars and movie stars, began to represent a large share of top income (Piketty, 2014: 315ff.). And high income transforms itself into wealth. Accordingly, it was both income from wealth and income from very high earnings that led to the concentration of income at the top. In principle, a very high remuneration of managers as well as a high income of dynamic entrepreneurs have the potential to slow wealth concentration down (cf. Kuznets, 1955: 11). However, this potentially countervailing force against wealth concentration was too weak to prevent the increase of inequality. And it became even weaker during the last decades because economic development in the developed countries was less dynamic. In addition, there are the effects of social closure: In the USA, earners of very high wages, to a large extent, come from rich families who send their children to the best schools and have the best professional networks. As a result, the chance of children to move from low- to high-income households during their lifetime has decreased substantially during the last decades (cf. Stiglitz, 2012: 17ff.).

Inequality and labour markets

There are two interlinked sources of inequality located in the labour market – unemployment and wage dispersion. As the unemployed have no wage income, it is obvious that increasing employment reduces inequality within the labour force (at least if the latter is defined as including both the employed and the unemployed). The Organisation for Economic Co-operation and Development (OECD, 2011: 148f.) reports that between the mid-1980s and the mid-2000s, increasing employment in the OECD countries decreased the inequality of market income among the working-age population by 0.18 points annually. During the same period, rising wage dispersion drove up inequality in the working-age population by 0.106 points per year. Thus, overall inequality within the working-age population only decreased slightly. When the unemployed are only able to get low-paid jobs, the income inequality reducing effect of increasing employment is small.

Unemployment in deregulated labour markets leads to falling nominal wages as the unemployed undercut existing wage levels. In the neoclassical paradigm, a process of falling nominal wages leads to falling real wages and an increase of labour demand. The Keynesian paradigm voices three objections to this line of argument.

First of all, there is a close link between changes in nominal unit-labour costs, which depend on productivity, nominal wage development and the price level – both at the theoretical and the empirical level (Herr, 2009; Keynes, 1930). If unemployment leads to a decreasing nominal wage *level*, the price level will fall and deflation will grip the economy. In fact, cumulative processes of deflation can lead to economic collapse. They increase the real debt burden in domestic currency and undermine the financial system, which, as a result, stops to supply loans. In addition, product demand suffers: if firms and households expect prices to decrease, they will postpone spending (Fisher, 1933). John Maynard Keynes (1936: 14) was right to criticise the neoclassical paradigm (which he called the classical school) by stating that 'workers, though unconsciously, are instinctively more reasonable economists than the classical school, inasmuch as they resist reductions of money wages'. Importantly, deflation is not a ghost of the past. Japan, after the end of its real estate and stock-market bubble in the early 1990s, suffered from falling unit-labour costs and deflation for more than two decades (Herr and Kazandziska, 2011). Currently, the eurozone is in danger of falling into deflation.

Second, unemployment leads to an exploding low-wage sector. The main point is that the least-skilled workers (including workers discriminated against by employers on the grounds of their race, ethnicity, gender, age, etc.) have the most limited opportunities in competitive labour markets. If there are not sufficient jobs, the better-skilled workers (or those perceived to be better skilled by the employers) crowd out less-skilled workers. In unregulated labour markets, it may happen that the least-skilled workers earn less than a living wage. Recent examples are the very low wages and the very poor working conditions in the informal sector – which is an entirely market-driven sector – in Brazil and South Africa (Leubolt, 2014a, 2014b). Even in Germany, which until early 2015 had no statutory minimum wage, a low-wage sector developed that forced some full-time employees to top up wages with benefits in order to make ends meet (Bosch and Weinkopf, 2008). In spite of the emergence of a sector with precarious working conditions and low wages (as a result of the so-called Hartz reforms between 2003 and 2005), the total number of hours worked in Germany did not increase (2015) (Statistisches Bundesamt, 2015). These examples show that very low and falling wages do not increase employment. In a labour market without proper institutions and protection – in particular under conditions of surplus labour – there may not be full employment even if workers may earn less than the living wage.

Third, wages for certain groups of employees can increase to a very high level in an unregulated wage bargaining system. Companies with high profits, for example in the mining industry, may be willing to pay more than other companies. Occupational groups with significant bargaining power can push for above-average wages. Certain people, such as managers in the financial sector, can follow rent-seeking strategies in order to push up their salaries and bonuses. Professional athletes and other 'stars' can also exploit their positions to bargain for very high wages.

The conclusion is that unregulated labour markets are likely to lead to high and even extreme inequality and unstable economies. In particular in situations of high unemployment, there is a power asymmetry between employers and individual workers, which can lead to rapidly declining wages of certain groups of workers and falling wages overall that are not compensated for by the creation of additional jobs. Trade unions are organisations addressing the power asymmetry in labour markets to some degree and make sure that wage negotiations take place on a more equal footing. In contrast to neoclassical thinking, unions are not alien to a capitalist economy. On the contrary, they are a precondition for an inclusive and democratic type of capitalism and help to stabilise economic development. Comprehensive empirical work shows that there is a strong correlation between increasing union density and low wage dispersion (cf. Autor et al., 2005; Bound and Johnson, 1992; Burniaux et al., 2006; Card et al., 2004; Freeman, 1980; Koeniger et al., 2007).

In the OECD countries taken as an aggregate, wage dispersion increased during the last decades. Usually, the theoretical explanations offered for this development refer to skills-based technological development, globalisation, or a lack of investment in education. However, none of these explanations are convincing. The OECD countries show highly diverging trends in wage dispersion in spite of the fact that they are exposed to the same technological developments and forces of globalisation. Similarly, education systems cannot explain the different developments. For example, whereas there is a strong polarisation of the wage structure in the USA, in France and some other countries wage dispersion was reduced. Additionally, there are huge variations in gender wage gaps across different countries.[3]

Apart from that, there are some other theoretical shortcomings. Marginal productivities, which are behind all the mainstream explanations of wage dispersion, cannot be calculated in any meaningful way. What is the marginal productivity of an engineer working as part of a research team and what the marginal productivity of an accountant or a teacher? Do the salaries of investment bankers or top managers really reflect their superior marginal productivity compared with Nobel Prize winners in physics or chemistry? It is more plausible to assume that wage dispersion can be explained with reference to labour-market institutions such as statutory minimum wages, wage bargaining systems, legal extension mechanisms of collective bargaining agreements, opportunities for rent-seeking possibilities, and so on (see Herr and Ruoff's chapter in this volume).

Macroeconomic instability

It seems to be clear, at the empirical level, that the more unequal income distribution is, the lower is gross domestic product (GDP) growth (cf. Berg and Ostry, 2011; Cingano, 2014; Hein, 2014). Neoclassical economists (cf. Berg and Ostry, 2011; Cingano, 2014) explain this phenomenon with supply-side effects. They argue, for example, that high levels of inequality may

- prevent poor income groups, under conditions of imperfect credit markets, from investing sufficiently in human capital (education, health);
- lead, in democratic societies, to tax reforms that are harmful to the incentive system underpinning market economies;
- create political instability and unrest.

The authors in this camp add that targeted pro-poor policies can reduce state expenditure and free funds for investments in the public infrastructure.

In supply-side economics, increasing top income shares are considered economically less dangerous than very low incomes (Cingano, 2014: 6). Undoubtedly, a low-income sector can have negative supply-side effects, for example malnutrition, the exclusion from education or a lack of finance for entrepreneurship. These effects have to be contained through political interventions. But a one-sided approach is not adequate and it is also not convincing that the rich pulling away from the rest does not harm growth. In the Keynesian paradigm, output depends on demand. Of course, supply-side conditions, for example productivity and innovations of all kinds, are also important for economic development and rising living standards. But productivity increases without sufficient demand produce negative employment effects and, if working time is not reduced, unemployment. In addition, Verdoorn's law states that higher growth in manufacturing (we could add the high-quality service sector) leads to higher productivity increases, which spill over to the entire economy (Thirlwall, 2013: 43ff.). These dynamic effects of high growth are based on traditional economics of scale, but even more on positive learning effects, advantages of economic clusters and the accumulation of knowledge.

With employment (*L*), real gross domestic product (*GDP*), and labour productivity $\left(\pi = \dfrac{GDP}{L} \right)$, it follows that $L = \dfrac{GDP}{\pi}$. This implies that the change in employment ($\dot{L}$) is by definition identical with the change of real output ($\dot{GDP}$) minus the change of labour productivity ($\dot{\pi}$). The formula $\dot{L} = \dot{GDP} - \dot{\pi}$ shows that insufficient GDP growth in relation to productivity developments leads to no or low additional employment. Real GDP depends on different demand elements, namely (gross) investment demand (*I*), consumption demand (*C*), government demand (*G*) and exports minus imports (*Ex* – *Im*).

Investment demand is the most unstable demand element. It depends on 'animal spirits' (Keynes, 1936) or 'entrepreneurship' (Schumpeter, 1983 [1934]) *and* on sufficient, cheap long-term finance. 'Animal spirits' and 'entrepreneurship' are sociological categories stressing that private investment is not based on objective calculations but on impulses to exploit opportunities, innovative ideas, trust in the future, the social and political situation, the preparedness to take risks and mass psychology. It is possible that investment demand is highly volatile, but also that it stagnates for long times.

In almost all countries, consumption demand is by far the biggest element of demand. It depends on current income and other factors like the availability of consumer credit, expectations about future income and the degree of uncertainty felt by households. Income distribution is a major factor determining the level of consumption demand. The main explanation is that the propensity to consume out of income depends on income distribution. As the rich, and especially the super-rich, have a lower propensity to consume than poorer households, a more unequal income distribution reduces consumption demand. In the United States in the period of 1986–2012, for example, the saving rate of the top 1 per cent income earners was above 25 per cent, of the top 10 per cent over 15 per cent and of the remaining 90 per cent around 1 per cent (Saez and Zuckmann, 2014).

Anti-cyclical fiscal policy is imperative to limit cyclical ups and downs and high government demand over a cycle – caused, among other things, by the provision of public goods – can contribute to stabilising long-term aggregate demand. Importantly, long-term government expenditure should be funded with the help of a working tax system. This way, the government can avoid increasing public debt. There is no clearly determinable debt-to-GDP ratio that makes public debt dangerous. But it should be kept in mind that public debt can have negative distributional effects – notably if the poor have to put up with a high tax burden and the rich are able to pocket the interest paid to service public debt. Furthermore, public debt makes the economy more vulnerable to shocks, which can be caused, for example, by a hike in interest rates.

Whereas trade deficits reduce aggregate demand, surpluses increase it. It is obvious that not all countries in the world can have trade surpluses and countries with high and persistent external surpluses do not only export goods and services but also unemployment. High current account deficits lead in most cases to high foreign debt (the only exception is when current account deficits are financed via foreign direct investment and the equity portfolio). This debt is usually in foreign currency and exposes deficit countries to currency crises with potentially long periods of stagnation. Only the United States and a small number of other countries issuing internationally used currencies can become indebted in their own currency and thus are immune to over-indebtedness in a foreign currency. Overall, high imbalances in current accounts tend to destabilise the world economy (Herr, 2013).

The equation $L = \dfrac{GDP}{\pi}$ with $GDP = I + C + G + (Ex - Im)$ shows that many things can go wrong in a capitalist economy and that full employment is not guaranteed. First of all, aggregate demand can be highly unstable and result in unstable development of GDP and employment. Unemployment rates may fluctuate over the short term and destabilise both wage development and the entire economy. For such fluctuations, unstable investment is the main explanation, but shocks at the level of the world market can also quickly change aggregate demand.

Second, given unused capacities and the level of productivity, aggregate demand can be insufficient to create high employment. One of the key explanations for insufficient demand is an income distribution unequal to a degree that consumption demand is depressed. Independently of this, investment demand can be very weak when the expectations of firms, banks and private wealth-owners are low for a long period of time. In such a constellation of economic forces, high consumption as well as government- and export-demand can lead to full capacity utilisation without full employment being realised. Especially in developing countries such a situation can occur.

Third, it is not only the volume of aggregate demand that is important, but also its structure. Investment demand is the only demand element that increases production capacities. In the medium and long run, production capacities must develop in such a way that increasing excess capacities and a lack of production capacities are avoided. For example, it makes no sense to increase production capacities if the other demand elements are insufficient. This again shows the importance of high consumption demand for a prosperous economic development. Roy Harrod (1939) and Evsey Domar (1946) worked out the conditions for GDP growth, under which consumption demand (for reasons of simplification, government demand and international trade are not considered) and investment demand develop in such a way that full capacity utilisation (full employment of capital) is realised. This is the so-called warranted growth rate ($\dot{GDP}w$). It follows that

$\dot{GDP}w = \dfrac{s}{k}$, where ($s$) is the saving rate of a country (gross savings to GDP)

and (k) is the incremental capital–output ratio (that is, the extra capital needed to produce an additional unit of GDP), which reflects technology, among other things. This suggests that given the saving ratio, which is relatively stable, investment demand must develop in such a way that the (k) in the above formula is realised. Not only is the full employment of capital desirable, but also the full employment of labour. Given (Lp) as population growth and ($\dot{\pi}$) as productivity growth, the so called natural growth rate ($\dot{GDP}n$), which guarantees full employment of labour, must be $\dot{GDP}n = Lp + \dot{\pi}$. To guarantee full employment of capital *and* full employment of labour, the following conditions must be met: $GDP = GDPw = GDPn$. The likelihood for this to happen is slim because the key variables (the saving rate, the marginal capital coefficient, population growth and productivity growth) are determined exogenously. Joan Robinson (1956) called a world in which the actual growth rate equals the warranted and the natural growth rate the 'golden age', emphasising its mystical nature (cf. Thirlwall, 2013: 15ff.). History has made it clear that the market mechanism alone will not be able to move us closer to such a socio-economic configuration. Put differently, an unregulated market economy does not lead to acceptable economic or acceptable social results, namely an acceptable level of income inequality and low unemployment.

Conclusion

Full employment, as well as decent working conditions and wages supporting growth in freedom for all (Sen, 1999), are the precondition for inclusive development and an efficient use of resources in society. Full employment ensures that there is a power balance between capital and labour and it contributes to creating a fair and economically advantageous income distribution. A 'golden age' economy does not emerge under conditions of unregulated markets; it requires comprehensive political interventions. In what follows, I will briefly discuss what kind of interventions are needed (cf. Dullien et al., 2011; Herr and Kazandziska, 2011).

For full employment and stable economic development, a comprehensive strategy of macro-economic demand management is needed. Part of it is to guarantee that investment demand and other demand elements have the right proportions. What matters is not just the volume of investment but also its structure and quality. In particular, developing countries need high investment, because the introduction of new technologies may allow them to catch up with developed countries.

Keynes assumed that it would not work to use fiscal policy as the main instrument to manage the volume and the structure of demand. Instead, he proposed the socialisation of investment:

> a somewhat comprehensive socialisation of investment will prove the only means of securing an approximation of full employment; though this need not exclude all manner of compromises and of devices by which public authority will co-operate with private initiative. But beyond this no obvious case is made for a system of State Socialism.
>
> (1936: 378)

What matters in the process is the existence of institutions and mechanisms of democratic decision-making that bring together employers' associations, unions, government, representatives of civil society and experts, who can then share information and determine technological development (Rodrik, 2009). There are several dimension of the socialisation of investment:

- Governments can use private companies in order to realise long-term infrastructure projects.
- Natural monopolies like energy production and the water supply as well as public goods like public transport, education and healthcare should be provided by the public sector.
- Non-profit enterprises can get involved, to a stronger degree, in investment. Building societies, for instance, have an important role to play in the stabilisation of the real estate sector.
- State-owned companies are not per se less efficient than private companies. However, it seems to be vital for their economic success that they are managed in a transparent fashion and are exposed to competition.
- Collectively or locally owned financial institutions together with strong development banks can influence the level and structure of investment.
- For ecological reasons, governments will have to intervene in the allocation of resources and development of new technologies. Investment under a green new deal could become an important step towards ecologically sustainable development (see Mahnkopf's chapter in this volume).
- Reducing the size of the private, 'for-profit' sector may also have positive redistribution effects.

Furthermore, consumption demand should in principle be funded by current income. To guarantee demand that is sufficient, inequality has to be checked with the help of a whole range of policies, for example:

- co-ordinated wage bargaining plus extension mechanisms;
- sufficient minimum wages;
- a competition policy aimed at reducing rent-seeking;
- the strict regulation of the financial system – including the abolition of the shareholder value corporate governance system – to reduce profit mark-ups;
- progressive taxation;
- tight social safety nets;
- the provision of public goods.

Moreover, fiscal policy should have a strong anti-cyclical orientation, stimulating the economy in crisis phases and slowing it down during booms. External imbalances should be kept to a minimum. A globally regulated system of trade, currency exchange and finance seems to be the best option to achieve this. A stable financial system, which at the same time finances investment and innovation, is also of key importance for economic development. All speculative aspects of the financial system including shadow banking should be regulated (see Evans's chapter in this volume). The change of the nominal wage level in a country should be guided by trends in productivity development plus a moderate inflation target. In this scenario, the development of wages becomes the anchor of the development of prices (Herr and Horn, 2012).

Kuznets (1955: 9) expected an increasing pressure of legal and political decisions to reduce inequality when countries achieved higher levels of per capita income. For him, this was the key argument why inequality starts to decrease after a certain level of development. Here, he was obviously wrong. From the 1970s onwards, most countries in the world have been pursuing policies that have been increasing inequality. What we can learn from Kuznets is that inequality cannot be reduced without pressure for change and political mobilisation.

Globalisation, especially unregulated international capital flows, demands global solutions wherever and whenever possible. However, there is also space for political interventions at the national level. Wage dispersion, for example, can be contained. If governments co-ordinate the nominal wage level and the exchange rate and pursue a successful industrial policy, even a combination of a strong compression of wage dispersion and a balanced current account can be achieved. The same argument can be made for improving working conditions and establishing a social safety net as well as ecological standards. Also, to give another example, public banks acting on a local level or development banks can play an important role for a positive economic and social development. There is also no global restriction to administering natural monopolies with the help of state-owned companies. The tax system can be restructured in a way that tax evasion becomes much more difficult. Of course, such fundamental changes can only be achieved over a period of several years or even a decade.

It is obvious that unions have an important role to play in transforming society. In some areas, for example wage dispersion and wage co-ordination, unions are key drivers of change; in other areas, they have to restrict themselves to intervening in public debates and searching for allies.

Notes

1 I would like to thank Alexander Gallas and Frank Hoffer for valuable debates.
2 This means that the system of equations has several mathematical solutions.
3 For an empirical overview, cf. OECD (2011: Chapters 1 and 2); for a review of the theoretical debate, cf. Kierzenkowski and Koske (2012).

References

Arrow, K.F. and Debreu, G. (1954) Existence of an Equilibrium for a Competitive Economy. *Economica* 22: 265–290.

Autor, D.H., Katz, L.F. and Kearny, M.S. (2005) *Trends in U.S. Wage Inequality: Re-Assessing the Revisionists*. NBER Working Paper No. 11627.

Berg, A. and Ostry, J.D. (2011) *Inequality and Unsustainable Growth: Two Sides of the Same Coin*. IMF Staff Discussion Note 11/08. Washington, DC: International Monetary Fund (IMF).

Bosch, G. and Weinkopf, C. (eds) (2008) *Low-Wage Work in Germany*. New York: Russell Sage Foundation.

Bound, J. and Johnson, G. (1992) Changes in the Structure of Wages in the 1980s: An Evaluation of Alternative Explanations. *The American Economic Review* 82(3): 371–392.

Burniaux, J.M., Padrini, F. and Brandt, N. (2006) *Labour Market Performance, Income Inequality and Poverty in OECD Countries*. OECD Economic Department Working Papers, No. 500. Paris: Organisation for Economic Co-operation and Development (OECD).

Card, D., Lemieux, T. and Riddell, C.W. (2004) Unionization and Wage Inequality: A Comparative Study of the U.S., the U.K., and Canada. *Journal of Labour Research* 25: 519–559.

Cingano, F. (2014) *Trends in Income Inequality and its Impact on Economic Growth*. OECD Social, Employment and Migration Working Papers No. 163. Paris: Organisation for Economic Co-operation and Development (OECD).

Debreu, G. (1959) *Theory of Value*. New York: Wiley.

Domar, E. (1946) Capital Expansion, Rate of Growth, and Employment. *Econometrica* 14(2): 137–147.

Dullien, S., Herr, H. and Kellermann, C. (2011) *Decent Capitalism: A Blueprint for Reforming our Economies*. London: Pluto Press.

Fisher, I. (1933) The Debt Deflation Theory of Great Depressions. *Econometrica* 1(4): 337–57.

Freeman, R.B. (1980) Unionism and the Dispersion of Wages. *Industrial and Labour Relations Review* 34(1): 3–23.

Hahn, F. (1981) General Equilibrium Theory. In Bell, D. and Kristol, I (eds) *The Crisis in Economic Theory*. New York: Basic Books.

Hahn, F. (1982) Reflections on the Invisible Hand. *Lloyd's Bank Review* 144: 1–21.

Harrod, R. (1939) An Essay in Dynamic Theory. *Economic Journal* 49(139): 14–33.

Hayek, F. von (1948) *Individualism and Economic Order*. Chicago: Chicago University Press.

Hein, E. (2014) *Distribution and Growth After Keynes*. Cheltenham: Edward Elgar.

Herr, H. (2009) The Labour Market in a Keynesian Economic Regime: Theoretical Debate and Empirical Findings. *Cambridge Journal of Economics* 33(5): 949–965.

Herr, H. (2013) Financial Liberalisation, Deregulated Labour Markets and New Asset Market-Driven Capitalism. In Bhowmik, S.K. (ed.) *The State of Labour: The Global Financial Crisis and Its Impact*. New Delhi: Routledge: 55–82.

Herr, H. and Horn, G. (2012) Wage Policy Today. Global University Working Paper No. 16.

Herr, H. and Kazandziska, M. (2011) *Macroeconomic Policy Regimes in Western Industrial Countries*. London: Routledge.

Keynes, J.M. (1930) *Treatise on Money*. Cambridge: Cambridge University Press.

Keynes, J.M. (1936) *The General Theory of Employment, Interest and Money*. Cambridge: Cambridge University Press.

Kierzenkowski, R. and Koske, I. (2012) Less Income Inequality and More Growth – Are They Compatible? Part 8. The Drivers of Labour Income Inequality – A Literature Review. OECD Economic Department Working Papers No. 931. Paris: Organisation for Economic Co-operation and Development (OECD).

Koeniger, W., Leonardi, M. and Nunziata, L. (2007) Labor Market Institutions and Wage Inequality. *ILR Review* 60(3): 340–356.

Kuznets, S. (1955) Economic Growth and Income Inequality. *The American Economic Review* 45(1): 1–28.

Leubolt, L. (2014a) Social Policies and Redistribution in South Africa. Global Labour University Working Paper No. 25.

Leubolt, L. (2014b) Social policies and Redistribution in Brazil. Global Labour University Working Paper No. 26.

Lucas, R. (1972) Expectations and the Neutrality of Money. *Journal of Economic Theory* 4: 103–124.

Muth, J.F. (1961) Rational Expectations and the Theory of Price Movements. *Econometrica* 29(3): 315–335.

OECD (2011) *Divided We Stand. Why Inequality Keeps Rising.* Paris: Organisation for Economic Co-operation and Development (OECD).

Pareto, V. (1909) *Manuel d'Èconomique Politique.* Paris: Giard & Brière.

Piketty, T. (2014) *Capital in the Twenty-First Century.* Cambridge, MA: Harvard University Press.

Robinson, J. (1956) *The Accumulation of Capital.* London: Macmillan.

Rodrik, D. (2009) Industrial Policy: Don't Ask Why, Ask How. *Middle East Development Journal* 1(1): 1–29.

Saez, E. and Zucman, G. (2014) *The Distribution of US Wealth, Capital Income and Returns since 1913.* Available at: https://thenextrecession.files.wordpress.com/2014/10/saezzucman2014slides.pdf (accessed 16 May 2015).

Schumpeter, J. (1983 [1934]) *The Theory of Economic Development.* New Brunswick, NJ: Transaction Books.

Sen, A. (1999) *Development as Freedom.* New York: Oxford University Press.

Smith, A. (1904 [1776]) *The Wealth of Nations*, 5th edition. London: Methuen.

Smith, A. (1759) *Theory of Moral Sentiments*, 6th edition. Available at: www.econlib.org/library/Smith/smMS.html (accessed 16 May 2015).

Statistisches Bundesamt (2015) *Volkswirtschaftliche Gesamtrechnung* Tabelle 81000-0015.

Stiglitz, J.E. (2012) *The Price of Inequality.* New York: W.W. Norton & Company.

Thirlwall, A.P. (2013) *Economic Growth in an Open Developing Economy.* Cheltenham: Edward Elgar.

Walras, L. (1993 [1874]) *Elements of Pure Economics.* London: Routledge.

16 The role of the public sector in combating inequality

Christoph Hermann

Introduction

In recent decades, the public sector, including public infrastructures and services, has mostly been discussed with respect to its efficiency. The general assumption has been that public providers of goods and services tend to underperform compared with private-sector companies and therefore present a drag on economies aiming to make the best out of scarce resources. Economists in the developed and developing world have advised governments to privatise not only state enterprises but also public infrastructures in order to boost productivity and economic growth. In cases where privatisation is not possible, they have suggested using public–private partnerships and subcontracting to emulate private-sector business strategies.

While privatisation is supposed to improve public-sector productivity, little attention has been paid to the redistributive effects of public services. Even though redistribution is not the prime objective of public service provision, low-income earners differ from high-income earners in how they are affected by equal access to essential services such as healthcare, education, transport and energy. My chapter attempts to fill this gap and discusses the effects of public services for income distribution and, consequently, the role of the public sector for combating inequality. At the same time, it also explores the consequences for social equality and social justice of privatisation, marketisation and public sector cuts.

The chapter starts with a theoretical and historical account of the public sector and its role in a predominantly private and market-based economy. The next part presents the rationale and the political underpinnings of the shift towards privatisation and marketisation. The following two sections deal with the redistributive effects of public services and of privatisation and marketisation. The chapter ends with some concluding thoughts.

The evolution of the public sector

The public sector is a contested concept and as such open to different interpretations. What seems to be clear is that the public sector deals with government provision and that it is more than government administration. It includes a variety of economic activities that are carried out by public establishments rather than private companies. According to orthodox economic theory, the public provision of goods and services is acceptable when they have certain qualities that prevent markets from functioning properly (Altvater, 2004). For the provision of public services two conditions are particularly important:

1   The existence of positive externalities, which impact on third parties that are not directly involved in the market transaction. The classical case is healthcare: if the spread of infectious diseases is curtailed by providing treatment to ill people, not only those being treated benefit, but also society at large (Altvater, 2004: 52f.).
2   The existence of so-called natural monopolies, which makes it impossible or undesirable to have more than one provider for a particular service (Baumol, 1977). The classical case are the network industries such as electricity, as well as gas and water supplies. Up to the 1980s, it was widely believed that in these cases, it is preferable that governments or non-profit organisations should provide these services rather than private-sector companies (Clifton et al., 2003: 23).

In the real world, the scope of the public sector was not so much the result of theoretical considerations but of social conflicts, political pressures and pragmatic solutions to pressing problems. The expansion of public utilities (water, gas, electricity) in the rapidly growing European cities in the late nineteenth century was, for example, driven by the need to provide services to poor households and to prevent the spread of contagious diseases. Private water suppliers had previously focused on connecting factories and wealthy neighbourhoods to these networks. The consumers were able to afford fees high enough that granted a decent return on investment for private providers (Millward, 2005: 44). As the prospect of returns on investment was considerably worse in the case of poor neighbourhoods, it was often the local authorities that had to step in and build the communal infrastructures needed to provide the poor with acceptable living conditions. In Britain, this was part of what has been described as municipal socialism (Sheldrake, 1989). As such, it was also a correction or an alternative to the prevailing market economy. Gerold Ambrosius (2008: 528) has argued that European governments opted for public provision rather than imposing public regulation on private monopolies because they assumed that ownership would be more effective in terms of controlling output.

After the Second World War and after the traumatic experience of the Great Depression, the pressure to tame markets and provide equal access to essential services became even greater (Millward, 2005: 172). As a result, governments took over network industries such as gas and electricity. In some countries, they also nationalised key companies in the mining, petroleum, production and banking sectors. In the UK, nationalisation also included the creation of the National Health Service (NHS), integrating hundreds of public and voluntary hospitals and providing free healthcare for all citizens across the country. By providing comparably cheap inputs for the rest of the economy, the public sector proved to be highly functional for the Fordist mass production and consumption model of the post-war years. In the developing world, public ownership became an important element in post-colonial nation-building and subsequent import-substitution strategies. However, often, nationalisation was simply a pragmatic response to private-sector failures and the protection of insolvent companies and associated workplaces (including the nationalisation of failing banks in the recent financial crisis).

During the post-war decades, economists have interpreted the growth of the public sector as a result of economic progress. Because of increasingly saturated markets for mass produced goods, the public sector and especially public services such as education were expected to become key investment areas in the new, affluent societies. Fred Hirsch (1977: 4), for example, noted that '[a]s demands for purely private goods are increasingly satisfied, demands for goods and facilities with a public (social) character become increasingly active'. William Baumol (2012) went even further and argued that because many public services are highly labour-intensive, meaning that workers can only very gradually be replaced by labour-saving technologies, the public sector must necessarily expand at the expense of the private economy. However, because of burgeoning private-sector productivity gains, Baumol argued that advanced economies can afford to have large public sectors (2012: 62f.).

In Europe, the growth of the public sector and especially of public services went hand in hand with the expansion of the welfare state. The British sociologist T.H. Marshall (1950) argued that in modern democracies, citizens have not only civil and political but also social rights, such as the right to basic economic welfare and education. In this conception, access to public services became an essential feature of what has been described as 'social citizenship' (Mahnkopf, 2008: 72f.). In France and parts of Southern Europe, the provision of public services was not so much perceived as an individual right of citizens, but as a collective responsibility of the state (Ambrosius, 2008: 529). As Birgit Mahnkopf (2008: 72f.) notes,

> [u]ntil the 1980s, there remained a vital cross-party and even cross-country consensus in the European Union that certain goods and services ought to be excluded from the functioning of the market [. . .]. Public services were perceived as essential for creating and strengthening social cohesion and thus were strongly related to social justice, even if their economic efficiency proved to be lower than under market conditions.

Theorists of the welfare state such as Gøsta Esping-Andersen (1991) emphasised the de-commodifying effects of modern welfare states, reducing inequality caused by a purely market-based distribution of social wealth. However, Esping-Andersen also showed that different welfare-state conceptions have different consequences for equality. While conservative welfare states tend to reproduce inequality by linking benefits to previous contributions, and liberal social policies based on means-testing are limited to alleviating the situation of the poor, the social democratic welfare regime is 'committed to equalize living conditions across the citizenry' (Esping-Andersen and Myles, 2011: 646). It does so by combining the payment of universal cash benefits that cover more than minimum needs with the public provision of social services, which in other systems are provided by unpaid female family members or by fees-charging private agencies. As a result, the social democratic welfare states of Northern Europe are not only leading in terms public service expenditure and public employment, but also display very low levels of inequality.

Privatisation and marketisation

The perception of the public sector changed in the 1970s. During this period, the discourse of market failure was gradually replaced by the discourse of state failure (Megginson and Netter, 2001). This shift took place against the backdrop of a major economic crisis that had ended more than two decades of economic growth in Western Europe and North America. In the wake of the economic slow-down, public-sector expenditure tended to increase faster than gross domestic product (GDP) growth, adding to the fiscal crisis of the state (O'Connor, 1979). Given the increasingly scarce resources, which were caused not only by slow growth, but also by tax breaks granted by newly elected conservative governments, an increasing number of economists found that the public sector was inherently inefficient and that this was a major social and economic problem. In a nutshell, critics argue that governments pursue a number of different and perhaps contradicting goals with public companies, which distracts them from the main objective, namely improving efficiency (Megginson and Netter, 2001: 330). This is not the place to discuss the validity of such claims.[1] However, from the 1980s onwards, the improvement of efficiency has become the main goal of public-sector reform, while other objectives such as the promotion of equality and social justice were increasingly marginalised.

To some extent, the abolition of public monopolies was the result of the invention of new information and communication technology that reduced the need to maintain extensive and costly material networks and created the possibility that various competing providers can use the same infrastructure. However, more than anything the 'shift to privatization was something of a leap of faith' (Nellis, 2006: 6). As Malcolm Sawyer (2009: 70) notes:

> The big push towards privatisation can be dated as starting in the early 1980s, and gathering pace from the late 1980s. [. . .] This push [. . .] has clearly gone on alongside the rise and dominance of neoliberalism at the national and international levels. Privatization epitomizes neoliberalism in terms of the further expansion of markets and competition in economic life, the entry of capital into new areas and the greater importance of the financial sector and of profits and the pursuit of profits at the expense of all other considerations.

Privatisation typically started with the divestment of public enterprises in dominantly private sectors such as manufacturing, banking and mining. However, it was not for long that the same policies were applied to traditional public sectors such as telecommunications, energy, water, and parts of transport. In Europe, the Conservative Thatcher government in Britain, which came into power in 1979, was among the first to embark on a systematic privatisation programme (Florio, 2004; Leys, 2001). From the mid-1990s onwards, Britain was followed by governments across Europe with various political backgrounds, partly spurred by European legislation and the alleged creation of European public service markets (Frangakis and Huffschmid, 2009).

In the developing world, privatisation was widely promoted as part of the Washington Consensus and through the International Monetary Fund (IMF) and World Bank support programmes that were increasingly linked to the implementation of privatisation policies. About 70 per cent of all structural adjustment loans made by the World Bank during the 1980s contained a privatisation component (Cramer, 1999: 2). Privatisation became part of a new development agenda that promised economic growth based on the liberalisation of markets and the rollback of the state in all conceivable economic areas. As in the developed world, the main claim was that privatisation will increase efficiency (Cramer 1999: 3). The World Bank continued to push for privatisation and expanded the scope of state divestment to include not only state enterprises but also public infrastructures such as water and electricity networks – in spite of at best ambiguous results and growing resistance by the affected populations (Fine and Bayliss, 2007).

More recently, the privatisation of public services such as telecommunications, transport and energy has been complemented by a marketisation of service areas that are more difficult to sell for political and economic reasons. This includes the marketisation of healthcare and education through the creation of internal markets, outsourcing, the formation of public–private partnerships (including private financing initiatives) and the promotion of New Public Management techniques. The common idea behind the different processes of marketisation is that service providers are subjected to similar economic pressures as private companies in the hope that they will adopt similar efficiency-enhancing strategies (Hermann, 2011a). The same rationale has been applied to third-sector organisations which, as a result, increasingly look like private profit-seeking enterprises. Marketisation processes were often coupled with public-sector cuts. The lack of funding led to a deterioration of service quality that spurred the development of a parallel layer of private providers providing the same services at a significantly higher quality. As described below, the emergence of two-tier healthcare and education systems are particularly corrosive for social equality.

The public sector and equality

While there is a large amount of literature on public service efficiency, there are only a few studies on the effects of the public sector on equality. Part of the problem is that it is difficult to determine the value of freely accessible or subsidised services. However, the Organisation for Economic Co-operation Development (OECD) has calculated the cash value of social services such as healthcare, education, social housing, childcare and elderly care. The value of these services increases disposable household income on average by 29 per cent. For comparison, the share of cash benefits amounts to 23 per cent of disposable income. There are only a few OECD countries where the value of cash transfers as proportion of disposable income is higher than that of services (Verbist et al., 2012: 32).[2]

Access to public services not only increases household income; it also tends to reduce inequality. Across the OECD, healthcare, education, social housing, childcare and elderly care reduce inequality by a fifth; that is, the Gini coefficient is 20 per cent lower when the income effect of these services is taken into account (on average the Gini coefficient falls from 0.30 to 0.24). The effect varies between a 16 per cent decline in Greece and a 24 per cent reduction in the UK (Verbist et al., 2012: 35f.). For other inequality measures, the effect is even larger: The ratio of income that goes to the top and bottom 10 per cent of the income scale drops by one fourth if social services are taken into account; and that between the top 20 and bottom 20 of the income scale falls by almost one third. Again there is a considerable variation of the effect among OECD countries, reaching from 46 (Mexico) to 17 per cent (Slovenia) in the first case; and from 49 (Mexico) to 19 per cent (Slovenia) in the second (Verbist et al., 2012: 35f.).

The equality-enhancing effect of public services is not limited to developed countries. Nora Lustig et al. (2013: 10) have found in a study covering six Latin American countries that access to public services such as healthcare and education reduces inequality more than taxes and cash benefits.[3] In fact 'governments in Latin America redistribute mostly through public spending on education and health' (Lustig, 2012: 3f.). Even in Brazil, whose benefits programme includes Bolsa família,[4] healthcare and education have a greater impact on equality than the combined effect of taxes and social spending (Lustig 2012: 3f.).

The main reason for the equality-enhancing effect of public services is that the (cash) value of public services accounts for a significantly larger proportion of the income of poor households than of rich households (in absolute terms the contribution of public services to household income in the OECD is quite similar across different income segments). On average the use of healthcare, education and other services accounts for 76 per cent of the income of the poorest quintile of the income scale in the OECD countries, as opposed to 14 per cent for the richest income quintile (Verbist et al., 2012: 34).

Because the lowest income group benefits most from public services, the promotion of public services also reduces poverty. Poverty rates (measured as 50 per cent of median disposable income) fall by 50 per cent if the value of healthcare, education and other services are taken into account. On average, poverty rates decrease from 10 to 5 per cent. In this area, there is also considerable variation among OECD countries: In Belgium, Ireland and the UK, the poverty rate declines by close to 60 per cent; in Estonia and in Sweden by about

27 per cent. Without the income-enhancing effect of social services, poverty levels range from 6 to 18 per cent; with social services from 3 to 10 per cent (Verbist et al., 2012: 37).

The OECD study only covers social services such as healthcare and education. If other public services such as transport, water and energy are taken into account, the equality-enhancing effects of public services is even greater. Even though these services are not freely accessible, they are subsidised in many countries – at least until they are subjected to privatisation and liberalisation. As with the (cash) value of freely accessible services, these subsidies make up for a larger part of the budget of low-income than of high-income earners and thus have a redistributive effect. Among the rare studies exploring the distributional effects of subsidised services, Neil Fearnley (2006: 31) has found that in Britain bus subsidies predominantly benefit lower-income households, women and those aged below 24 or above 60.

However, the equality-enhancing effect of services differs between sectors. In a study of 13 European countries, Maria Vaalavuo has shown that while primary and secondary education clearly reduces inequality, tertiary education can even increase the gap between the rich and the poor. Yet much depends on the choice of indicators and the calculation of data. Vaalavuo states that while 'The very poorest do not benefit from higher education [. . .] the hypothesis of higher education as pro-rich is only partially accurate' (2011: 118ff.).

In addition to altering income distribution, public services also promote equality by providing comparably decent jobs, especially for low-skilled workers and for marginalised groups such as women, people of colour and migrant workers (Hermann and Atzmüller, 2008). Public employment accounts for 15 per cent of total employment in the OECD and for more than 25 per cent in Sweden, Norway and Denmark.[5] In a comparison between public- and private-sector wage systems in Italy, France and the UK, Paolo Ghinetti and Claudio Lucifora (2008: 246) have found that average wages in the public sector are higher and wage dispersion is lower than in the private sector. The authors also note that low-skilled workers (blue-collar and service staff) in particular tend to be better off in the public sector because in this segment the gap between public- and private-sector wages is highest (Ghinetti and Lucifora, 2008: 248). Other studies have compared the gender wage-gap and have found that the difference between male and female wages tend to be smaller in the public than in the private sector (Meurs and Ponthieux, 2008).

Privatisation and inequality

Privatisation has eroded the equality-enhancing effects of public services in several ways. In the European Union (EU), the liberalisation of public-service markets went hand in hand with a ban on public subsidies and a shift towards market-oriented prices. There is some evidence that prices have increased after liberalisation, while other evidence shows a decline. The difficulty is to determine how much of the change in prices was the result of privatisation, and how much was the result of other developments – such as increases in oil prices or technological innovations. What seems to be clear is that the expectation of falling prices was in many cases overly optimistic. Even supporters of privatisation such as John Nellis (2006: 17) have cautioned that 'under state ownership many governments set utility prices at less than cost-covering levels'.

However, even without subsidies public providers tend to be cheaper than their private competitors. Massimo Florio has compared the development of gas and electricity prices in various EU member states and has found that one of the most prevalent factors explaining price differences is public ownership. Publicly owned gas and electricity providers tend to offer lower prices than their private counterpart (Florio, 2013: 176, 217).[6] Price increases have a negative effect on equality because they affect the poor more than the rich. The related expenses make up for a significantly larger part of the budget of low-income households. Energy prices are a particular sensible issue. According to the British Department of Energy, households that spend more than 10 per cent of their income on energy bills are considered to be suffering from fuel poverty. After falling in the second half of the 1990s, the number of households affected by fuel poverty in the UK increased from two million in 2003 to 4.5 million in 2011 (Department of Energy and Climate Change, 2013: 18).

Profit-orientation and cost-recovery have also meant that households who cannot pay their bills are more frequently disconnected. Christoph Hermann and Richard Pond (2012: 49) report from a case study on the liberalised European electricity market that while previously staff would have worked out a solution with households struggling to pay their bills, social concerns no longer play a role in the new corporate thinking. David Macdonald reports that up to 9.6 million people were affected by electricity cut-offs in South Africa between 1994 and 2002 following increasing corporatisation and a move towards cost-recovery (2009: 26).

However, the analysis of average prices may be misleading. Liberalisation and privatisation have typically led to a differentiation in prices. Christoph Hermann and Jörg Flecker (2012: 194f.) report from a series of case studies in liberalised European public-service markets that one of the first things management did to respond to the new market environment was to introduce variable prices for different groups of users. For a profit-oriented provider, it is quite rational to offer different tariff schemes with a discount for large users (Florio, 2013: 337). As Steve Thomas (2002: 8) reports from the British experience:

> The introduction of retail competition for large consumers allowed them to negotiate better prices, but it seems that much if not all of the price reduction was paid for by small consumers. The extension of retail competition to small consumers seems to have made the problem worse and has also given electricity companies an incentive to discriminate against poor consumers that did not exist while retail supply was a monopoly business.

In the British case, price changes particularly affected households with prepayment meters as opposed to customers who are debit payers. Prices for the latter group have declined much faster than for the former (Waddams Price and Young, 2003: 112). Households on prepaid schemes are generally poor households. Yet even among debit payers, there are considerable differences in electricity prices depending on the volume of consumption. In 2007, standard high-usage consumers in the UK only paid half of what standard bottom consumption households pay per kilowatt hour of electricity. Again low-volume users are often low-income households (Florio, 2013: 292f., 337).

Price discrimination is often linked with problems to access information (Florio, 2013: 297). Some of the elderly citizens, for example, may not be familiar with the internet and hence have problems to find the cheapest offer. As low-volume users, they are not exactly in the focus of the advertising activities of profit-oriented service providers. In addition, transaction costs caused by surveying changing prices and switching suppliers can eat up possible savings from a new contract. Many users in the now fully liberalised European electricity markets are not even contemplating a move to a new electricity provider (Van Gyes and Vandekerckhove, 2012: 187). Furthermore, there may simply not be a 'best deal' for low-volume consumers such as citizens who only need a standard landline, or who can only afford a prepaid cell phone. Unsurprisingly, Judith Clifton et al. (2011: 506) found in a study on consumer satisfaction in the telecommunications sector in Britain and Spain that 'those not working, the elderly and the lower-educated were indeed more dissatisfied with prices'.

In social services such as healthcare, the consequences of discrimination are particularly dramatic. The threat is not so much privatisation but the underfunding of public providers and the introduction of fees and co-payments. As Mohan Rao (2010: 268) states with respect to the Indian healthcare system, the increasing weakness of the public system encourages those who can afford it to search for help in the burgeoning private healthcare industry, even though they have to pay a lot of money for treatment. Hence while 50 per cent of the poorest income quintile in India uses public as opposed to private hospitals, only 20 per cent of the highest income quintile relies on the public system (Chakraborty et al., 2013: 14). As Lustig (2012: 3) notes with respect to public healthcare and education in Latin America, '[t]he main problem [. . .] is not access but the low quality of these services'.

However, profit-oriented public service providers not only focus on large or well-off customers; they also focus on geographic areas where they can achieve high enough revenues. In the liberalised European postal markets, for example, providers focus on urban areas where they can exploit economies of scale, while closing down post offices and terminating related services in the sparsely populated countryside (Hermann, 2011b: 259f.). Mildred Warner (2006: 618) shows in a study on the delivery of municipal services in the USA that rural communities rely more often on public provision than suburban or metropolitan areas because they are not interesting for private contractors. Rural municipalities had been experimenting with the outsourcing of services to private companies until the mid-1990s, but many had returned to public provision by 2002. 'This return to public delivery [. . .] provides additional indication of problems with access to alternative market forms of service delivery – especially for rural communities' (Warner, 2006: 618).

In sum, poor users are highly unattractive for providers in liberalised and privatised public service markets: They struggle to pay bills, are often low-volume users and many of them are based in rural areas or areas that are not easily accessible, which also means that it is more costly to connect them to the network (Estache et al., 2002: 16). Not surprisingly, connection rates of low-income households are much lower in the developing world than of wealthy citizens. Only 10 per cent of the poorest income quintile has access to electricity in low-income countries, but almost 80 per cent of the richest quintile (Estache, 2006: 6).

Privatisation not only affects services users; it also has a profound impact on those who deliver the services in their daily work (Hermann and Flecker, 2012; Schmelzer-Roldán, 2014). The search for greater public sector efficiency often takes the form of work intensification, precarisation and fragmentation of public-sector employment relations. The result is increasing wage differentials between managerial staff and non-managerial employees, between skilled and unskilled workers, as well as between core and peripheral workers (Hermann and Flecker, 2012: 196ff.).

A widespread effect of privatisation is an upward adjustment of manager salaries to private-sector standards. Top managers are therefore among the main beneficiaries of public divestment, especially if they are offered stock options of the newly privatised firms. However, while managers see their incomes increasing, many non-managerial workers are confronted with wage cuts, especially newly hired workers (Hermann and Flecker, 2012: 200).

Conclusion

The public sector, no doubt, plays a critical role in combating inequality. As I have shown, low-income earners benefit more from access to public services than high-income earners because the value of these services make up for a disproportionally larger share of their income. In addition to the quantitative gains for poor households, there is also a qualitative dimension. As Mahnkopf (2008: 81f.) notes, 'There will only be pressure for higher standards and optimal supply if access to public services is enabled as a social right and is available for all people through their status as citizens, including the well-to-do middle classes'.

If services are only provided for the poor, there is a high risk that their quality diminishes – as is shown by the deteriorating public healthcare systems in Eastern Europe, India and other parts of the world. In spite of the positive effect of public services for the promotion of social equality, much of the debate on public-sector reforms in the last decades has been mostly about questions of efficiency. Since the 1970s, the general wisdom of (orthodox) economics is that the private sector can provide the same services more efficiently. Hence governments around the world have introduced far-reaching privatisation and marketisation programmes, partly enforced by the World Bank and the EU. Little attention has been paid to the social impact of resulting changes even though privatisation and marketisation tend to reverse the equality-enhancing effect of public services and benefit high-income earners more than low-income households. Public sector cuts, as widely introduced in the current crisis, also hurt the poor more than the rich. The mentioned OECD study has not only shown that public services reduce inequality. It has also revealed a 'strong link between changes in the relative size of health, education and housing services [. . .] and changes in the effectiveness of these services to reduce inequality across countries' (Verbist et al., 2012: 59). Comparing data from 2000 and 2007, the authors show that countries that have increased spending on social services during this period have reduced inequality, while countries that have reduced spending recorded a rise in inequality (Verbist et al., 2012: 59).

Notes

1 See Tatahi (2006), among others, for a refutation of these claims.
2 Including Austria, Germany and Poland.
3 Argentina, Bolivia, Brazil, Mexico, Peru and Uruguay.
4 See Manzano et al.'s chapter in this book.
5 Employment in general government and public corporations; 2008 figures from the OECD (2011).
6 Public ownership made no difference in the liberalised European telecommunication sector.

References

Altvater, E. (2004) What Happens When Public Goods Are Privatized. *Studies in Political Economy* 74: 45–77.

Ambrosius, G. (2008) Konzeption öffentlicher Dienstleistungen in Europa. *WSI Mitteilungen* 10: 527–535.

Baumol, W.J. (1977) On the Proper Cost Tests for Natural Monopoly in a Multi Product Industry. *American Economic Review* 67(5): 809–822.

Baumol, W.J. (2012) *The Cost Disease: Why Computers Get Cheaper and Health Care Doesn't.* New Haven, CT: Yale University Press.

Chakraborty, L., Singh, Y. and Jacob, J.F. (2013) Analyzing Public Expenditure Benefit Incidence in Health Care: Evidence from India. Working Paper No. 748, Levy Economics Institute.

Clifton, J., Comín, F. and Díaz Fuentes, D. (2003) *Privatization in the European Union: Public Enterprises and Integration.* Dordrecht: Kluwer Academic Publishers.

Clifton, J. et al. (2011) Is Market-Oriented Reform Producing a 'Two-Track' Europe? Evidence from Electricity and Telecommunications. *Annals of Public and Cooperative Economics* 82(4): 495–513.

Cramer, C. (1999) *Privatization and the Post-Washington Consensus: Between the Lab and the Real World?* Centre for Development Policy & Research Discussion Paper No. 0799, School of Oriental and African Studies, University of London.

Department of Energy and Climate Change (2013) *Annual Report on Fuel Poverty Statistics 2013.* UK Government.

Esping-Andersen, G. (1991) *The Three Worlds of Welfare Capitalism.* Cambridge: Polity Press.

Esping-Andersen, G. and Myles, J. (2011) Economic Inequality and the Welfare State. In Salverda, W., Nolan, B. and Smeeding, T. (eds) *The Oxford Handbook of Economic Inequality.* Oxford: Oxford University Press: 639–644.

Estache, A. (2006) *Infrastructure: A Survey of Recent and Upcoming Issues.* Washington, DC: World Bank.

Estache, A., Foster, V. and Wodon, Q. (2002) *Accounting for Poverty in Infrastructure Reform. Learning from Latin America's Experience.* Washington, DC: World Bank.

Fearnley, N. (2006) Public Transport Subsidies in the UK: Evidence of Distributional Effects. *World Transport Policy and Practice* 12(1): 30–40.

Fine, B. and Bayliss, K. (2007) Rethinking the Rethink: The World Bank and Privatization. In Bayliss, K. and Fine, B. (eds) *Privatization and Alternative Public Sector Reform in Sub-Saharan Africa Delivering on Electricity and Water.* Basingstoke: Palgrave Macmillan: 55–87.

Florio, M. (2004) *The Great Divesture: Evaluating the Welfare Impact of the British Privatizations 1979–1997.* Cambridge, MA: MIT Press.

Florio, M. (2013) *Network Industries and Social Welfare: The Experiment that Reshuffled European Utilities.* Oxford: Oxford University Press.

Frangakis, M. and Huffschmid, J. (2009) Privatization in Western Europe. In Frangakis M. et al. (eds) *Privatization against the European Social Model: A Critique of European Policies and Proposals for Alternatives.* Basingstoke: Palgrave Macmillan: 9–29.

Ghinetti, P. and Lucifora, C. (2008) Public Sector Pay Gap and Skill Levels: A Cross-Country Comparison. In Jeune, M., Leschke, K. and Watt, A. (eds): *Privatisation and Liberalisation of Public Services in Europe: An Analysis of Economic and Labour Market Impacts.* Brussels: ETUI: 233–260.

Hermann, C. (2011a) Commodification, Consequences and Alternatives: Lessons from the Privatization of Public Services in Europe. Paper presented at the International Initiative for Promoting Political Economy (IIPPE), 20–22 May.

Hermann, C. (2011b) The Liberalization of European Postal Markets: The Response of Firms and Impacts on Employment and Services. *Competition & Change* 15(4): 253–273.

Hermann, C. and Atzmüller, R. (2008) Liberalisatoin and Privatization of Public Services and the Impact on Employment, Working Conditions and Labour Relations. In Jeune, M., Leschke, J. and Watt, A. (eds) *Privatisation and Liberalisation of Public Services in Europe: An Analysis of Economic and Labour Market Impacts.* Brussels: ETUI: 175–193.

Hermann, C. and Pond, R. (2012) Concentration and Disintegration: Company Responses in the Electricity Sector and Consequences for Employment. In Hermann, C. and Flecker, J. (eds) *Privatization of Public Services: Impacts for Employment, Working Conditions and Service Quality in Europe.* New York: Routledge: 33–54.

Hermann, C. and Flecker, J. (2012) Conclusion: Impacts of Public Service Liberalization and Privatization. In Hermann, C. and Flecker, J. (eds) *Privatization of Public Services: Impacts for Employment, Working Conditions and Service Quality in Europe.* New York: Routledge: 192–205.

Hirsch, F. (1977) *Social Limits to Growth.* London: Routledge & Kegan Paul.

Leys, C. (2001) *Market-Driven Politics: Neoliberal Democracy and the Public Interest.* London: Verso.

Lustig, N. (2012) Taxes, Transfers, and Income Redistribution in Latin America. *Inequaltiy in Focus* 1(2): 1–5.

Lustig, N., Pessino, C. and Scott, J. (2013) The Impact of Taxes and Social Spending on Inequality and Poverty in Argentina, Bolivia, Brazil, Mexico, Peru and Uruguay: An Overview. CEQ Working Paper No. 13.

Macdonald, D. (2009) Electrical Capitalism: Conceptualizing Electricity and Capital Accumulation in (South) Africa. In Macdonald, D. (ed.) *Electrical Capitalism: Recolonising Africa on the Power Grid*. Cape Town: HSRC Press: 1–50.

Mahnkopf, B. (2008) Privatization of Public Services in the EU: An Attack on Social Cohesion and Democracy. *Work, Organisation, Labour & Globalisation* 2(2): 72–84.

Marshall, T.H. (1950) *Citizenship and Social Class and Other Essays*. Cambridge: Cambridge University Press.

Megisson, W. and Netter, J. (2001) From State to Market: A Survey of Empirical Studies on Privatization. *Journal of Economic Literature* 39(2): 321–389.

Meurs, D. and Ponthieux, S. (2008) Public and Private Employment and the Gender Wage Gap in Eight European Countries. In Jeune, M., Leschke, J. and Watt, A. (eds) *Privatisation and Liberalisation of Public Services in Europe: An Analysis of Economic and Labour Market Impacts*. Brussels: ETUI: 261–284.

Millward, R. (2005) *Private and Public Enterprise in Europe: Energy, Telecommunications and Transport 1830–1990*. Cambridge: Cambridge University Press.

Nellis, J. (2006) Privatization – a Summary Assessment. Working Paper No. 87. Washington, DC: Center for Global Development.

O'Connor, J. (1979) *The Fiscal Crisis of the State*. New York: St. Martin's Press.

Rao, M. (2010) 'Health for All' and Neoliberal Globalization: The Indian Rope Trick. In Panitch, L. and Leys , C. (eds) *Socialist Register 2010*. London: Merlin Press: 262–278.

Sawyer, M. (2009) Theoretical Approaches to Explaining and Understanding Privatization. In Frangakis, M. et al. (eds) *Privatization against the European Social Model: A Critique of European Policies and Proposals for Alternatives*. Basingstoke: Palgrave Macmillan: 61–76.

Schmelzer-Roldán, S.E. (2014) *The Impact of Electricity Sector Privatization on Employees in Argentina and Brazil*. Munich: Rainer Hampp Verlag.

Sheldrake, J. (1989) *Municipal socialism*. Farnham: Gower Publishing.

Tatahi, M. (2006) *Privatization Performance in Major European Countries since 1980*. Basingstoke: Palgrave Macmillan.

Thomas, S. (2002) The Impact of Privatisation on Electricity Prices in Britain. Presentation to the IDEC National Seminar on Public Utilities, São Paulo, 6–8 August.

Vaalavuo, M. (2011) Towards an Improved Measure of Income Inequality: The Impact of Public Services on Income Distribution – An International Comparison. PhD thesis. Florence: European University Institute.

Van Gyes, G. and Vanderkerckhove, S. (2012) The Citizen-User Perspective: Results from a Cross-Country Survey. In Hermann, C. and Flecker, J. (eds) *Privatization of Public Services: Impacts for Employment, Working Conditions and Service Quality in Europe*. New York: Routledge: 169–191.

Verbist, G., Förster, M. and Vaalavuo, M. (2012) *The Impact of Publicly Provided Services on the Distribution of Resources: Review of New Results and Methods*. OECD Social, Employment and Migration Working Papers No. 130. Paris: Organisation for Economic Co-operation and Development (OECD).

Waddams Price, C. and Young, A. (2003) UK Utility Reform: Distributional Implications and Government Response. In Ugaz, C. and Waddams Price, C. (eds) *Utility Privatization and Regulation: A Fair Deal for Consumers?* Cheltenham: Edward Elgar: 101–124.

Warner, M. (2006) Market-Based Governance and the Challenge for Rural Governments: US Trends. *Social Policy & Administration* 40(6): 612–631.

17 Progressive tax reform in the OECD countries

Opportunities and obstacles

Sarah Godar, Christoph Paetz and Achim Truger[1]

Introduction

The substantial increases in disparities of wealth and income distribution over the last decades, in combination with the need for tax increases due to the budgetary stress experienced since the Great Recession, have led to calls for progressive tax reforms in many Organisation for Economic Co-operation and Development (OECD) countries. The dominant economic argument against such reforms is that they are detrimental to growth and employment and lead to increased tax avoidance. In this chapter, we provide a critical assessment of the standard arguments and complement them with a macroeconomic perspective. In our view, there is more room for manoeuvre for national governments to increase the progressivity of the tax system and to raise additional revenue than is often suggested. We start with an overview of the regressive taxation trends since the 1980s and show that despite some changes there are no signs of a comprehensive trend reversal, precisely because of the allegedly strong efficiency/equity trade-off that supposedly does not allow for such changes. We then give a critical assessment of the standard wisdom regarding the negative economic effects of progressive tax reform. Finally, we introduce a macroeconomic perspective into our analysis and draw some conclusions concerning future tax policies on the national and international level.

Traditional standards of tax justice under pressure

Traditionally, the aims of taxation in the industrialised countries in the area of distribution were (a) to avoid tax privileges for specific sources of income (comprehensive income approach) and (b) to achieve a high degree of progressivity. However, these goals have come under increasing pressure since the 1980s. According to the OECD (2011: 267), market incomes have become more unequal in most OECD countries since the mid-1980s. Additionally, redistribution by the state has on average become less effective, especially since the mid-1990s. Strong drops in the top marginal income tax rates and in the corporate income tax rates, as well as an increasing dualisation of the income tax (that is, increasing privileges for capital income) demonstrate that the traditional standards of tax justice have come under severe pressure in recent decades.

On average, taxes on personal income used to be the most important source of revenue for OECD countries. They accounted for about 30 per cent of total tax revenues in the 1980s. Since then, their relative importance has declined to about 24 per cent while the weight of social security contributions has increased (OECD, 2012a: 23). Top statutory tax rates can be used as an indicator for broad international trends and a proxy for the intended redistributive effects of income-tax systems. Since the 1970s, the top income-tax rates have declined in nearly all OECD countries. In 1981, the top statutory personal income tax (PIT) rate in the OECD countries was on average 65.7 per cent. If we only consider the countries already included in the dataset from 1981, the average rate declined to 50.7 per cent in 1990, to 48.9 per cent in 2000, and to 45.8 per cent in 2010 (OECD, 2012b: 33). In the meantime, other countries have joined the OECD; if we include them, the average tax rate in 2010 was 41.7 per cent.

Recently, many European governments deliberately broke with the comprehensive income approach by subjecting the capital income of individuals to a separate tax schedule with a single tax rate while retaining progressive taxation in the area of labour income. In many OECD countries (for example Sweden, Finland, Austria, Germany, Spain, Ireland and Japan), certain types of capital income of individuals (such as interests, dividends and capital gains) are excluded from progressive income taxation (Deloitte, 2013; OECD, 2013a). As Schratzenstaller (2004: 23) points out, this trend of dualisation has affected many West European countries. Capital gains are most frequently taxed at a rate lower than the individual marginal income-tax rate. Additionally, there are manifold tax reliefs, which apply to different types of capital gains (Deloitte, 2013). Since 1981, the maximum overall tax burden on dividends has declined significantly (OECD, 2013a).

The taxation of corporate income has been characterised for nearly three decades by an international race to the bottom in terms of nominal tax rates. If we examine the countries for which OECD data are available since 1981, the (unweighted) average corporate income-tax rates declined by more than 20 percentage points – from 47.5 in 1981 to only 27.2 in 2012. Virtually all countries in the sample cut these tax rates significantly.

However, one should note that the falling tax rates are at first sight not reflected in the revenues generated: until 2007, corporate taxes as a percentage of GDP increased significantly in most OECD countries as compared with the levels of the 1970s and 1980s (see Figure 17.1). Despite declining considerably in 2008–2009, the average level in 2010 was still higher than in the 1970s and 1980s. Part of the explanation of this puzzle may be that declining nominal rates were to some extent accompanied by measures to broaden the tax base. Another explanation may be that 'stimulated by the steep fall in corporate tax rates, which in some countries are now well below the top PIT [personal income tax] rate, growing incorporatisation has been boosting CIT [capital income tax] revenues at the expense of the personal income tax' (EC, 2010: 23). However, the most likely cause of this strong development of corporate tax revenues lies in the rising share of corporate profits in gross domestic product (GDP) (Devereux et al.,

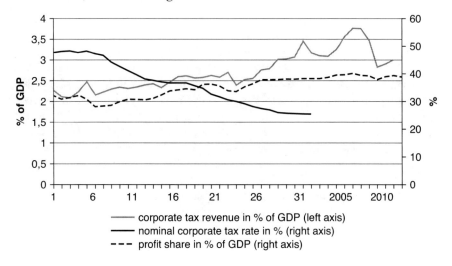

Figure 17.1 Corporate taxation, OECD averages 1970–2012
Source: OECD (2014a); EC (2014a).

2004: 26). In fact, the average OECD adjusted profit share has increased quite substantially over the last decades (see Figure 17.1): since reaching its trough in 1975, it went up from about 28 to almost 39 per cent of GDP in 2012, that is, by almost 39 per cent (EC, 2014a).

Compared with the 1970s, the revenues from property taxes as a percentage of GDP have on average remained fairly stable in the OECD countries. This points to a considerable fall in the effective taxation of private wealth because, as shown by Piketty and Zucman (2013), the ratio of private wealth to national income has risen considerably since 1970 in many rich countries.

Current trends and policy proposals

In the face of rising inequality and strong budgetary pressures in many OECD countries since the Great Recession, there are some signs that the downward trend in redistributive taxation may have come to a halt recently. In the majority of the OECD countries, top statutory income-tax rates were increased after the financial crisis (IMF, 2013: 26). Since then, a number of countries have also increased their maximum tax rates on the capital income of individuals. Remarkably, since the economic crisis the average level of corporate-tax rates seems to have stabilised (OECD, 2013a) and some countries saw a broadening of the corporate-tax base. Belgium, Greece, Ireland, Portugal, Spain and the UK increased their taxes on immovable property (EC, 2012: 29; IMF, 2013: 26).

While the developments mentioned are steps in the direction of greater tax justice, there are also some steps in the opposite direction: since 2009, many governments have raised their value-added tax rates in order to generate additional revenues (EC, 2013: 31; IMF, 2013: 26). In addition, there were numerous increases in excise taxes. As pointed out by the European Commission (EC, 2013a: 30), the revenue generating measures since 2009 have heavily focused on consumption taxes, which are regressive in nature.

In the last years, many important international institutions have presented proposals on how to respond to the need for fiscal consolidation in terms of socially acceptable tax reforms.[2] While there seems to be a widely shared belief that combating tax evasion, limiting tax avoidance and introducing a financial transaction tax should be priorities, opinions differ when it comes to the need for truly progressive tax reforms. Whereas the trade unions, the International Labour Organization (ILO), the United Nations Conference on Trade and Development (UNCTAD) and some non-governmental organisations (NGOs) make such demands, dominant mainstream institutions like the European Commission, International Monetary Fund (IMF) and OECD are very hesitant, if not openly opposed to such reforms.

The conventional wisdom of the IMF (2013) with regard to consolidation on the revenue side focuses on broadening the base of the value-added tax as well as of the personal and corporate income taxes, on increasing recurrent taxes on residential property and on extending environmental taxation. Their aim is to raise additional revenues without affecting low-income households too much – a view that is shared by the OECD (2012c). Both institutions suggest introducing additional transfers in order to mitigate the regressive impact of the proposed changes. One of the most repeated OECD proposals is to close tax loopholes and to reduce 'tax expenditures which mostly benefit the well-off' (OECD, 2012c: 3) in order to promote growth and reduce inequality. According to the OECD, the least distortive taxes, such as taxes on immovable property and consumption, are supposed to be the least detrimental in economic terms but could lead to higher inequality. Similarly, the

> European Council invites Member States, where appropriate, to review their tax systems with the aim of making them more effective and efficient, removing unjustified exemptions, broadening the tax base, shifting taxes away from labour, improving the efficiency of tax collection and tackling tax evasion.
>
> (European Council, 2012: 3)

Although some of the proposed measures at least show a concern for negative distributional effects of taxation and may lead to a reduction in income inequality, more fundamental reforms are not considered, namely increasing the personal and corporate taxation as well as the general taxation of wealth.[3] Obviously, the main reason for the reluctance to propose fundamental changes consists in the perceived trade-off between equity and efficiency. As the OECD (2012d: 39) puts it: 'Simply raising marginal personal income tax rates on high earners will not necessarily bring in much additional revenue, because of effects on work intensity, career decisions, tax avoidance and other behavioural responses.'

Standard arguments against progressive taxation

The standard arguments against progressive taxation rely on claiming that it creates negative incentives for private households and firms and reinforces tax avoidance.[4] However, it can be argued, on the basis of mainstream arguments (e.g. Rosen and Gayer, 2008; Salanié, 2011) and other literature, that these effects need not be large. This suggests that the equity/efficiency trade-off is probably rather small. Furthermore, government spending financed with the additional revenue may offset or even overcompensate for the negative effects of taxation on output and employment.

Taxing private households

Turning first to the private household sector, the most important negative incentive effects discussed in the literature refer to labour supply, savings and – more recently – to tax avoidance. The typical argument raised against progressive income taxation is that taxes reduce the compensation for work, thus lowering the opportunity cost of leisure and reducing labour supply. Theoretically, however, the overall effect on labour supply is indeterminate (Salanié, 2011: 18). Since high-income earners are often assumed to be high-productivity workers, Salanié argues that discouraging them from supplying their labour may cause a greater welfare loss than discouraging the labour supply of the low-productivity worker (Salanié, 2011: 88). However, as Giacomo Corneo (2005: 17) puts it, the substitution effect is only relevant as long as a person's working potential is not exhausted. In general, considering the need to earn a living in combination with social norms, the notion that individuals decide about their labour-market participation with respect to the income-tax rate is not very convincing.

Therefore, it hardly comes as a surprise that empirically, labour supply seems rather inelastic with respect to wages, which also means that it does not respond strongly to drops in the real wage. In a meta-study, Evers et al. (2008: 32) review empirical estimates of the wage elasticity of labour supply, namely the percentage reaction of labour supply to a change of 1 per cent in the wage rate. The mean of the empirical distribution of the estimated elasticities for the labour supply of men is 0.07 and the median is 0.08. The respective values for women are 0.43 and 0.27 or 0.34 and 0.26 excluding outliers. This implies that on average, a percentage change in the net hourly wage rate, holding other things equal, leads to a 0.07 percentage change in hours worked by men and 0.43 (0.34) by women. The evidence that the female labour supply is more sensitive to wages can partially be explained by the fact that on average women still undertake a much higher load of unpaid work in the private household than men (OECD, 2012e: 73).

In addition, Alvaredo et al. (2013: 9) suggest that the model of pay determination used in much of the optimal tax literature may be oversimplified. They consider the possibility that the growing bargaining power of top income earners helps them to increase their compensation at the expense of other income groups.[5]

From this perspective, lower top marginal tax rates provide an incentive to increase bargaining efforts which have nothing to do with productivity-enhancing work efforts. Higher top incomes may thus be the result of redistribution between income groups rather than of additional economic activity. If we include the effect of top marginal tax rates on bargaining efforts, there may be room for a higher marginal tax rate because discouraging bargaining efforts can have positive effects on economic efficiency.

Although it is often argued that taxes on capital income discourage savings and therefore investment and growth, economic theory does not provide clear results supporting this view. This is not astonishing since even in a very simple model of consumption, the effect of taxation on saving is indeterminate (Salanié, 2011: 289). Banks and Diamond (2010: 6) review different versions of models, commonly applied in optimal tax theory. In their view, the literature has little to say about the optimal tax rate for capital income.

Instead of actually changing behaviour in real terms, wealthy households may simply avoid a tax – for example by formally becoming a resident of a tax haven or by opening a bank account in a tax haven protected by complicated legal structures that conceal its true ownership. Henry (2012: 36) estimates that the value of offshore financial assets today ranges between \$21 and \$32 trillion. Hollingshead (2010: 3) suggests that 'current total deposits by non-residents in offshore and secrecy jurisdictions are just under US\$10 trillion'. Finally, Zucman (2014: 54) arrives at a lower bound estimate of €5.8 trillion.

Even if one believes only the lowest estimate to be realistic, obviously, tax planning and tax evasion might represent a threat to the governments' ability to effectively redistribute income and wealth. However, Piketty et al. (2011) estimate an average long-run elasticity of top incomes with respect to the net-of-tax rate of about 0.3 to 0.4. In order to compute the optimal top marginal tax rate, they develop a model integrating three different components of this overall elasticity: a supply side effect (real behavioural adjustments), a tax-avoidance effect and a compensatory bargaining effect. For the USA, they estimate that the top marginal tax rate is well below its revenue maximising point. Diamond and Saez (2011: 171) also suggest that the US top tax rate of 42.5 per cent would only be optimal if the elasticity of the tax base were 0.9. This is much higher than the 'mid-range estimate' of 0.25 that they have made on the grounds of the empirical literature. With a similar approach, the IMF (2013: 34–37) calculates a range of revenue-maximising top PIT rates for 16 OECD countries. In 12 countries, the actual top rate is below or in the lower half of that range, indicating substantial leeway for increased tax rates.

Taxing corporations

According to mainstream economic reasoning, the tax that is seen as most detrimental to economic growth is the CIT. It discourages 'the activities of firms that are most important for growth: investment in capital and productivity improvements' (OECD, 2010: 20). Furthermore, high CIT rates are supposed to induce firms to move their production abroad and thus decrease domestic employment. The theoretical mechanism behind these effects lies in the effect of the CIT on the cost of capital: the basic neoclassical idea is that

> firms accumulate capital as long as the return to investment exceeds the cost of finance and depreciation. Due to decreasing returns to scale, there is a marginal project that just breaks even, i.e. which earns a return that precisely matches the costs (pre-tax rate of return on the marginal investment project is defined as the cost of capital).
>
> (de Mooij and Ederveen, 2008: 684)

It follows that increasing CIT will make marginal projects unprofitable. However, this standard approach relies on very narrow theoretical assumptions. The fact that firms invest as long as the return to investment is *higher* than the cost of capital does not offer any answer to the question of *how much* higher the return on investment in a given pre-tax situation might be. The neoclassical break-even point is only reached under perfect competition and it implies that firms do not realise profits on their marginal investment project. However, under conditions of an imperfectly competitive market, firms realise more than zero profit on the marginal investment project. This suggests that there will still be an incentive to invest as long as the corporate tax does not completely deplete this economic profit. What is more, Musgrave and Musgrave (1989: 306) point out that the effects of corporate taxes on investment depend on the specification of the investment function, that is, on the underlying theory of investment. Investment may depend, ceteris paribus, inversely on the interest rate and therefore on taxation through its effect on the cost of capital. But we should include many other variables in the investment function, relaxing the ceteris paribus assumption, for example past sales, the business climate and unit labour cost. In addition, the potentially positive long-run effects of public funding of R&D expenditure and human capital accumulation should be considered – as well as the potentially positive agglomeration effects that may compensate for the negative effects of taxation (Brühlhart et al., 2012).

The empirical evidence suggests that investment behaviour is affected by CIT, but it is hard to get reliable estimates of the magnitude and thus the relevance of this effect. There is not much empirical evidence of tax effects on aggregate real investment. Evidence from micro-level studies hints at negative effects of taxes on investment ranging from rather inelastic (−0.25) to more elastic (−1) responses of investment, but it is difficult to transfer these results to aggregate investment at the macroeconomic level (Hanlon and Heitzman, 2010: 148). A meta-study by de Mooij and Ederveen (2008: 689) on the impact of taxation on foreign direct investment shows effects that vary considerably: on average 'a 1-percentage point increase in a tax measure in a certain location reduces foreign capital by 3.3 per cent'. However, the standard deviation of 4.4 is very high, and foreign direct investment cannot be used as a proxy for aggregate real investment as it also includes financial investment. Two recent studies trying to assess investment effects of corporate tax cuts in Germany (Reinhard and Li, 2011) and the UK (Maffini, 2013) come to the sobering result that there is no convincing evidence that the goal of encouraging investment was reached. Reinhard and Li even conclude that 'market opportunities and competitive pressures appear to be more important for investment decisions than domestic tax changes' (2011: 735).

It is sometimes suggested that tax cuts pay for themselves because the lower tax rates will substantially increase investment and corporate income. This implies that the economy is situated on the downward sloping part of the Laffer curve where tax hikes trigger such a strong decrease in the tax base as to overcompensate for the positive effect of the tax rate increase on revenues. Recent empirical estimates, however, show that this is improbable. After reviewing the literature and estimating the effects of CIT rate reductions for 17 OECD countries from 1982 to 2005, Riedl and Rocha-Akis (2012: 665) conclude that

> on average, the tax base is inelastic with respect to the domestic statutory rate. In other words, on average, the statutory CIT rates are in the upward sloping region of the Laffer curve, indicating that a unilateral rise in the statutory CIT rate would result in a less-than-proportional decrease in that country's CIT base and, therefore, a higher level of CIT revenues.

It is also remarkable that although they find substantial effects of the CIT rate on the country's aggregate CIT base, income per capita and real unit labour costs are found to have substantially stronger effects (Riedl and Rocha-Akis, 2012: 656).

Besides the real behavioural reactions to taxation, a much-debated issue today are the avoidance strategies of firms, which manipulate the tax base in a country without actually changing the level of economic activity. According to an OECD report (2013b), multiple opportunities exist for corporations to shift income among entities and thus to countries where lower tax rates or special exemptions apply. Examples for such opportunities are using licences for brands, patents or other financial services provided by a foreign subsidiary in a low tax jurisdiction as well as the manipulation of transfer pricing. Although there are no reliable numbers about how much profit-shifting actually occurs (OECD, 2013b: 15), the existence of profit-shifting activities is largely unquestioned. Heckemeyer and Overesch (2013: 8) review the empirical literature on the profit-shifting behaviour of multinational firms. On average, the 25 studies estimate a semi-elasticity of reported profit or earnings before interest and taxes with respect to the international tax differential between a country and other subsidiary locations of 1.55 with a relatively high standard deviation of 2.23. Although at first sight the number seems substantial, it implies that on average a country with an overall tax rate on corporate profits of 20 per cent may increase its rate by 5 percentage points or one quarter at a cost of losing only 7.75 per cent of its tax base. Hence due to tax avoidance, it would not receive the full revenue benefits of the tax increase but after all more than two-thirds of it.

All in all, the case against progressive taxation turns out to be substantially weaker than claimed by mainstream approaches. Both from a theoretical and an empirical point of view, the negative effects on growth and employment and the erosion of the tax base may not be large. What is more, factors other than taxation (the cyclical condition of the economy, infrastructure investment, research and development expenditures, the educational system as a provider of a qualified workforce) may be much more important for real private investment. If these factors can be enhanced through government expenditure, financed through progressive taxation, then the overall economic effect of the latter may well be positive. These days, even authors from the IMF (Ostry et al., 2014) conclude that there is no negative correlation between redistribution and growth.

Macroeconomic arguments for progressive taxation

From a macroeconomic perspective, it is possible to strengthen the case for redistributive taxation even further. If the economy is constrained by insufficient demand, and if inequality is detrimental to private consumption, redistributive taxation may strengthen growth and employment via the resulting increase in private consumption.

Recent multiplier estimates tend to strengthen the traditional Keynesian proposition that fiscal policy is effective, especially under the current conditions in the euro area with monetary policy at the lower bound and fixed exchange rates within the currency union (Auerbach and Gorodnichenko, 2012; Batini et al., 2012). As suggested by the standard Keynesian textbook models and the Haavelmo Theorem, the expenditure multiplier tends to be larger than the revenue side multiplier (Gechert and Rannenberg, 2014) suggesting that increasing (progressive) taxation in order to finance government spending may actually be conducive to growth and employment.

In addition, there is also a macroeconomic rationale for revenue-neutral redistributive tax reform. Keynes (1937: 219ff.) placed particular emphasis on the importance of investment demand because he was convinced that its high volatility in combination with the multiplier process was the most important cause for fluctuations of overall economic activity. Investment demand depends on the fluctuating subjective expectations of firms with regard to profitability of real investment and the monetary rate of interest, which in turn is influenced by the fluctuating liquidity preference of economic agents. However, private consumption also plays a central role, particularly the fact that it is assumed to be dependent on current disposable income. Keynes contends that private consumption is positively related to overall disposable income in the economy, with the marginal propensity to consume indicating how large the share of the income is that goes into additional consumption and the residual going into savings. If overall income rises because of an increase in investment activity, this will lead to an additional increase in private consumption, which in turn will generate an additional increase in income, and so on. The higher the marginal propensity to consume, the stronger the induced multiplier process.

Based on these theoretical assumptions, it is possible to derive a negative relationship between the disparity in the income distribution and private consumption: if lower income households have a higher propensity to consume than higher income ones, redistribution in favour of low-income households will increase the overall propensity to consume and therefore private consumption. In this case, redistributive taxation would strengthen private consumption demand and hence increase growth and employment.

However, the underlying hypotheses regarding private consumption behaviour are certainly not without controversy (cf. van Treeck and Sturn, 2012: 13ff.). The Keynesian consumption function assumes that private consumption depends on current real disposable income. In addition, it is presupposed that the marginal propensity to consume or to save in different income classes remains unchanged if there is a change in income distribution. However, other theories of consumption may lead to different results, at least for some extended time periods. The result to be expected, a weakening of consumer demand, could at least be mitigated or in the extreme even be overcompensated. Overall, the response of private consumption to increasing income inequality seems to depend on country-specific factors, mainly on the access of lower- and middle-income groups to credit (van Treeck and Sturn, 2012: 13ff.).

Therefore, one can expect an increase in consumer spending via a fiscally induced reduction in income inequality. This raises the question under which conditions such an increase in demand will actually be transformed into higher overall economic activity. Obviously the answer depends very much on the underlying macroeconomic paradigm. According to New Consensus Macroeconomics (NCM) (Clarida et al., 1999), the dominant paradigm, higher overall economic activity will most likely only be a short-term result. In the long run, the so-called NAIRU (non-accelerating inflation rate of unemployment) and the associated output and employment equilibrium will prevail and erase the short-term impacts on employment. However, as shown by Marc Lavoie (2009), the NCM model can easily be transformed into post-Keynesian macroeconomic approaches with some stepwise modifications that are closer to the traditional Keynesian analysis, namely assigning an important role to aggregate demand, both in the short and the long term (cf. Hein, 2008: Chapter 6). These approaches have certainly gained plausibility because of the considerable shock of the Great Recession. According to them, redistribution through the tax system can systematically lead to higher growth and employment. Thus, from a macroeconomic point of view, the trade-off between equity and efficiency might well disappear even in the long run.

Conclusions

The opportunities for a truly progressive reform of the tax system – reversing the long-term international trend of increasing disparities in income and wealth distribution, while at the same time raising urgently needed revenues for government budgets – have developed in a rather favourable way over the last few years. There are some signs that the downward trend in redistributive taxation may have come to a halt recently. At the same time, a number of international institutions have commented in a more or less progressive way on how to respond to the need for fiscal consolidation in terms of socially acceptable tax reforms. Against this background, the conclusions to be drawn from this chapter for tax policy are at least twofold.

First, there is a widespread consensus on the international level that tax evasion and avoidance should be combated and a financial transaction tax should be introduced. This should be used to implement reforms in the most ambitious way possible. The EU commission's revision of the Savings Directive making 'financial products that have similar characteristics to debt claims' and income from investment funds subject to an automatic exchange of information among member states (EC, 2014b) as well as the new global standard of automatic information exchange as suggested by the OECD and the G20 (OECD, 2014: 3) are important steps against tax evasion by individuals. In the area of corporate taxation, the same applies to the OECD Action Plan in Base Erosion and Profit Shifting (OECD, 2013c).

However, much more could be achieved, for example by the more comprehensive approach of unitary taxation which would make multinational companies submit their worldwide consolidated accounts (covering all parts of the company engaged in a unitary business) to local tax authorities so that their internal transfers would no longer be of interest (Picciotto, 2012). This should be complemented with minimum tax rates to prevent harmful tax competition. In general, the harmonisation of tax rates, especially with respect to capital income, would be extremely helpful in reducing the pressure for national tax policies. A global wealth tax as proposed by Piketty (2014: Chapter 15) could be the ultimate goal for the international taxation of extremely rich private households. A Financial Transaction Tax covering both spot and derivative assets could help reduce the size and volatility of financial markets while at the same time generating substantial revenue (Schulmeister et al., 2008). However, as has become clear especially with the financial transaction tax (Schulmeister, 2014), for all of these proposals there is the serious danger that they will be delayed, watered down or not be implemented at all due to political pressure by states or partisan interests.

Second, quite independently of the success of the measures on the international level, national tax policies should seek to achieve a substantially higher level of redistributive taxation even without international coordination. The scope for redistributive tax policies on the national level has been shown to be considerably larger than claimed by the dominant mainstream view and institutions. Therefore, there is no need for national tax policies to restrict their efforts to the rather faint-hearted measures proposed by many influential international institutions like broadening the tax base and increasing taxation of residential property. Instead, for many national governments, there seems to be substantial leeway to increase top PIT and CIT rates as well as the taxation of capital in general. This leeway can substantially be increased by determined efforts at increasing tax compliance. National governments should use this leeway, as it would increase revenues for essential public uses, decrease inequality and encourage progressive reforms at the international level.

Notes

1 We are very grateful to Alexander Gallas, Hansjörg Herr, Christoph Scherrer and Till van Treeck for helpful critical comments and suggestions. The usual disclaimer applies.
2 See EC (2012, 2013c); ETUC (2010); European Attac Network (2013); European Council (2012); ILO (2011); IMF (2013); ITUC (2010); OECD (2012c, 2012d, 2013b); Tax Justice Network (2013); UNCTAD (2012).
3 In fairness, the IMF does at least discuss the possibility of an increase in personal income taxation (IMF, 2013: 33).
4 It should be stressed, however, that a decrease in labour supply or in savings can only be classified as clearly detrimental if one follows a narrow neoclassical logic and assumes that the economy is in an equilibrium over the long run (cf. Atkinson, 1993). Otherwise, a decrease in labour supply can also lead to a decrease in involuntary unemployment and a decrease in savings will lead to an increase in private consumption and in turn to higher growth.
5 See also Herr and Ruoff's chapter in this volume. They argue that the wage structure is not determined by marginal productivities – which are very hard to define in many cases – but by institutions and conventions.

References

Alvaredo, F., Atkinson, A., Piketty, T. and Saez, E. (2013) The Top 1 Percent in International and Historical Perspective. *Journal of Economic Perspectives* 27(3): 3–20.

Atkinson, A.B. (1993) Introduction. In Atkinson, A.B. and Mogensen, G.V. (eds) *Welfare and Work Incentives: A North European Perspective*. Oxford: Oxford University Press: 1–19.

Auerbach, A.J. and Gorodnichenko, Y. (2012) Fiscal Multipliers in Recession and Expansion. In Alesina, A. and Giavazzi, F. (eds) *Fiscal Policy after the Financial Crisis*. Chicago: Chicago University Press.

Banks, J. and Diamond, P. (2010) The Base for Direct Taxation: Prepared for the Report of a Commission on Reforming the Tax System for the 21st Century. Institute for Fiscal Studies. Available at www.ifs.org.uk/mirrleesreview (accessed 22 May 2015).

Batini, N., Callegari, G. and Melina, G. (2012) Successful Austerity in the United States, Europe and Japan. IMF Working Paper. Washington, DC: International Monetary Fund (IMF).

Brühlhart, M., Jametti, M. and Schmidheiny, K. (2012) Do Agglomeration Economies Reduce the Sensitivity of Firm Location to Tax Differentials? *The Economic Journal* 122 (563): 1069–1093.

Clarida, R., Gali, J. and Gertler, M. (1999) The Science of Monetary Policy: A New Keynesian Perspective. *Journal of Economic Literature* 37(4): 1661–1707.

Corneo, G. (2005) Steuern die Steuern Unternehmensentscheidungen? In Truger, A. (ed.) *Können wir uns Steuergerechtigkeit nicht mehr leisten?* Marburg: Metropolis: 15–38.

De Mooij, R. and Ederveen, S. (2008) Corporate Tax Elasticities: A Reader's Guide to Empirical Findings. *Oxford Review of Economic Policy* 24(4): 680–697.

Deloitte (2013) International Tax Guides and Highlights, for different countries. Available at: https://dits.deloitte.com/#TaxGuides (accessed 22 May 2015).

Devereux, M., Griffith, R. and Klemm, A. (2004) Why Has the UK Corporation Tax Raised So Much Revenue? The Institute for Fiscal Studies WP04/04.

Diamond, P. and Saez, E. (2011) The Case for a Progressive Tax: From Basic Research to Policy Recommendations. *The Journal of Economic Perspectives* 25(4): 165–190.

European Attac Network (2013) For a Europe-Wide Coordinated Levy on Wealth. Available at: www.attac.org/sites/default/files/EAN-Wealth-Levy-Concept.pdf (accessed 22 May 2015).

EC (European Commission) (2010) Taxation Trends in the European Union. Eurostat Statistical Books. Available at: http://ec.europa.eu/taxation_customs/resources/documents/taxation/gen_info/economic_analysis/tax_structures/2010/2010_main_results_en.pdf (accessed 22 May 2015).

EC (European Commission) (2012) Taxation Trends in the European Union. Data for EU Member States, Iceland and Norway. Eurostat Statistical Books. Available at: http://ec.europa.eu/taxation_customs/resources/documents/taxation/gen_info/economic_analysis/tax_structures/2010/2010_full_text_en.pdf (accessed 22 May 2015).

EC (European Commission) (2013) Taxation Trends in the European Union. Eurostat Statistical Books. Available at: http://ec.europa.eu/taxation_customs/resources/documents/taxation/gen_info/economic_analysis/tax_structures/2013/report.pdf (accessed 22 May 2015).

EC (European Commission) (2014a) Annual Macroeconomic Database.

EC (European Commission) (2014b) COUNCIL DIRECTIVE 2014/48/EU of 24 March 2014 amending Directive 2003/48/EC on taxation of savings income in the form of interest payments. *Official Journal of the European Union*: 50–78. Available at: http://ec.europa.eu/taxation_customs/taxation/personal_tax/savings_tax/revised_directive/index_en.htm (accessed 22 May 2015).

European Council (2012) European Council conclusions. 1–2 March, Brussels. Available at: http://register.consilium.europa.eu/pdf/en/12/st00/st00004-re01.en12.pdf (accessed 22 May 2015).

ETUC (2010) ETUC Resolution on the Economic Crisis: New Sources of Finance. Available at: www.etuc.org/documents/economic-crisis-new-sources-finance#.VV9qu0Yvsrk (accessed 22 May 2015).

Evers, M. et al. (2008) The Wage Elasticity of Labour Supply: A Synthesis of Empirical Estimates. *The Economist* 156(1): 25–43.

Gechert, S. and Rannenberg, A. (2014) Are Fiscal Multipliers Regime-Dependent? A Meta Regression Analysis. IMK Working Paper No. 139. Düsseldorf: Macroeconomic Policy Institute (IMK) at Hans Boeckler Foundation:

Hanlon, M. and Heitzman, S. (2010) A Review of Tax Research. *Journal of Accounting and Economics* 50: 127–178.

Heckemeyer, J. and Overesch, M. (2013) Multinationals' Profit Response to Tax Differentials: Effect Size and Shifting Channels. ZEW Discussion Paper No. 13-045. Available at http://ftp.zew.de/pub/zew-docs/dp/dp13045.pdf (accessed 22 May 2015).

Hein, E. (2008) *Money, Distribution Conflict and Capital Accumulation. Contributions to 'Monetary Analysis'*. Basingstoke: Palgrave Macmillan.

Henry, J. (2012) The Price of Offshore Revisited. New Estimates for 'Missing' Global Private Wealth, Income, Inequality, and Lost Taxes. Tax Justice Network. Available at: http://www.taxjustice.net/cms/upload/pdf/Price_of_Offshore_Revisited_120722.pdf (accessed 22 May 2015).

Hollingshead, A. (2010) Privately Held, Non-Resident Deposits in Secrecy Jurisdictions. Global Financial Integrity. Available at: www.gfintegrity.org/storage/gfip/documents/reports/gfi_privatelyheld_web.pdf (accessed 22 May 2015).

IMF (2013) *Fiscal Monitor 2013*: *Taxing Times*. Washington, DC: International Monetary Fund (IMF).

ILO (2011) World of Work Report 2011. Making Markets Work for Jobs. Geneva: International Labour Organization (ILO). Available at: http://www.ilo.org/wcmsp5/groups/public/@dgreports/@dcomm/@publ/documents/publication/wcms_166021.pdf (accessed 22 May 2015).

ITUC (2010) Global Unions Statement to the G20. Available at: www.ituc-csi.org/IMG/pdf/01-tuacG8G20-Seoul_English.pdf (accessed 22 May 2015).

Keynes, J.M. (1937) The General Theory of Employment. *Quarterly Journal of Economics* 51(2): 209–223.

Lavoie, M. (2009) Taming the New Consensus: Hysteresis and Some Other Post-Keynesian Amendments. In Fontana, G. and Setterfield, M. (eds) *Macroeconomics and Macro-economic Pedagogy*. Basingstoke: Palgrave Macmillan: 191–213.

Maffini, G. (2013) Corporate Tax Policy under the Labour Government, 1997–2010. *Oxford Review of Economic Policy* 29(1): 142–164.

Musgrave, R. and Musgrave, P. (1989) *Public Finance in Theory and Practice*. 5th edition. New York: McGraw-Hill.

OECD (2010) Tax Policy Reform and Economic Growth. Paris: Organisation for Economic Co-operation and Development (OECD). Available at: http://dx.doi.org/10.1787/9789264091085-en (accessed 22 May 2015).

OECD (2011) Divided We Stand: Why Inequality Keeps Rising. Paris: Organisation for Economic Co-operation and Development (OECD). Available at: http://dx.doi.org/10.1787/9789264119536-en (accessed 22 May 2015).

OECD (2012a) Revenue Statistics 2012. Paris: Organisation for Economic Co-operation and Development (OECD). Available at: www.oecd-ilibrary.org/taxation/revenue-statistics-2012_rev_stats-2012-en-fr (accessed 22 May 2015).

OECD (2012b) Taxing Wages 2011. Paris: Organisation for Economic Cooperation and Development (OECD). Available at: www.oecd-ilibrary.org/taxation/taxing-wages-2011_tax_wages-2011-en (accessed 22 May 2015).

OECD (2012c) Income Inequality and Growth: The Role of Taxes and Transfers. OECD Economics Department Policy Notes No. 9. Paris: Organisation for Economic Co-operation and Development (OECD).

OECD (2012d) OECD's Current Tax Agenda 2012. Paris: Organisation for Economic Co-operation and Development (OECD). Available at: www.oecd.org/tax/OECD CurrentTaxAgenda2012.pdf (accessed 22 May 2015).

OECD (2012e) Gender Equality in Education, Employment and Entrepreneurship: Final Report to the MCM 2012. Paris: Organisation for Economic Co-operation and Development (OECD). Available at www.oecd.org/employment/50423364.pdf (accessed 22 May 2015).

OECD (2013a) Tax Database: Overall Statutory Tax Rates on Dividend Income/Top Income Rates. Paris: Organisation for Economic Co-operation and Development (OECD).

OECD (2013b) Addressing Base Erosion and Profit Shifting. Paris: Organisation for Economic Co-operation and Development (OECD). Available at: http://dx.doi.org/10.1787/9789264192744-en (accessed 22 May 2015).

OECD (2013c) Action Plan on Base Erosion and Profit Shifting. Paris: Organisation for Economic Co-operation and Development (OECD). Available at: http://dx.doi.org/10.1787/9789264202719-en (accessed 22 May 2015).

OECD (2014) Automatic Exchange of Financial Account Information. Background Information Brief. Available at: www.oecd.org/ctp/exchange-of-tax-information/Automatic-Exchange-Financial-Account-Information-Brief.pdf (accessed 22 May 2015).

Ostry, J., Berg, A. and Tsangarides, C. (2014) Redistribution, Inequality and Growth. IMF Staff Discussion Note 14/02. Washington, DC: International Monetary Fund (IMF).

Picciotto, S. (2012) Towards Unitary Taxation of Transnational Corporations. Tax Justice Network. Available at: http://www.taxjustice.net/cms/upload/pdf/Towards_Unitary_ Taxation_1-1.pdf (accessed 22 May 2015).

Piketty, T. (2014) *Capital in the Twenty-First Century.* Cambridge, MA: Harvard University Press.

Piketty, T. and Zucman, G. (2013) Capital Is Back: Wealth–Income Ratios in Rich Countries 1700–2010. Available at: http://piketty.pse.ens.fr/files/PikettyZucman2013WP.pdf (accessed 22 May 2015).

Piketty, T., Saez, E. and Stantcheva, S. (2011) Optimal Taxation of Top Labor Incomes: A Tale of Three Elasticities. NBER Working Paper No. 17616. Available at: http:// www.nber.org/papers/w17616 (accessed 22 May 2015).

Reinhard, L. and Li, S. (2011) The Influence of Taxes on Corporate Financing and Investment Decisions against the Background of the German Tax Reforms. *The European Journal of Finance* 17(7–8): 717–737.

Riedl, A. and Rocha-Akis, S (2012) How Elastic Are National Corporate Income Tax Bases in OECD Countries? The Role of Domestic and Foreign Tax Rates. *Canadian Journal of Economics* 45(2): 632–671.

Rosen, H. and Gayer, T. (2008) *Public Finance.* New York: McGraw-Hill.

Salanié, B. (2011) *The Economics of Taxation.* 2nd edition. Cambridge, MA: MIT Press.

Schratzenstaller, M. (2004) Towards Dual Income Taxes – A Country Comparative Perspective. CESifo DICE Report, ifo Institut für Wirtschaftsforschung 3: 23–30.

Schulmeister, S. (2014) *The Struggle over the Financial Transactions Tax: A Politico-Economic Farce.* WIFO Working Papers No. 474. Vienna: Austrian Institute of Economic Research.

Schulmeister, S., Schratzenstaller, M. and Picek, O. (2008) *A General Financial Transaction Tax. Motives, Revenues, Feasibility and Effects.* Research Study by the Austrian Institute of Economic Research. Available at: www.wifo.ac.at/jart/prj3/wifo/resources/ person_dokument/person_dokument.jart?publikationsid=31819&mime_type=application/ pdf (accessed 22 May 2015).

Tax Justice Network (2013) World Forum Declaration on Tax Justice. Available at: http:// taxjustice.blogspot.de/2013/04/world-forum-declaration-on-tax-justice.html (accessed 22 May 2015).

UNCTAD (2012) *Trade and Development Report, 2012: Policies for Inclusive and Balanced Growth.* Geneva: UNCTAD. Available at http://unctad.org/en/PublicationsLibrary/ tdr2012_en.pdf (accessed 22 May 2015).

van Treeck, T. and Sturn, S. (2012) Income inequality as a cause of the Great Recession? A Survey of Current Debates. For the International Labour Organization (ILO) project 'New Perspectives on Wages and Economic Growth'. Available at: www.boeckler.de/ pdf/p_treeck_sturn_2012.pdf (accessed 22 May 2015).

Zucman, G. (2014) *Steueroasen: Wo der Wohlstand der Nationen versteckt wird.* Berlin: Suhrkamp.

Part VI
Tools for counter-strategies

18 Contextualising strategies for more equality

Christoph Scherrer

Introduction

Inequality is on the increase in most countries. Combating this trend requires not only an understanding of its causes but also the development of effective counter-strategies. Some successful campaigns are analysed in the next chapter. A number of campaigns to rein in inequality, however, have proven rather unsuccessful in recent times. The German campaign 'umFAIRteilen' and the Swiss campaign to cap high salaries come to mind. Even in the showcase country for reducing inequality, Brazil under the Lula and Dilma presidencies, the improvements resulted from the redistribution of income within the working class and not from higher taxes on the rich (Lavinas, 2014).

I address the issue of strategic interventions from the perspective of trade unions. My objective is to develop a set of questions for trade unions that will help them to develop a context-sensitive set of strategies for combating inequality. I am not laying out a single strategy because countries not only differ in terms of their levels of inequality, but also with respect to their labour-relations cultures, the dominant attitudes towards economic divides and their political systems. My approach is informed by social movement theory.

Before I discuss items to be considered for counter-strategies, I highlight the opportunities for trade unions to mitigate inequality through collective bargaining and political advocacy. I argue that failure to address inequality will in the long run undermine the very existence of trade unions. In this struggle, trade unions can draw on various power resources, which depend on their members' position in the labour market, their organisational strength, their institutional embeddedness and their ability to frame concerns in such a way that these resonate both with potential allies and bystanders. Nevertheless, unions should not take for granted the support of their members and officials for an egalitarian agenda because it could be that they have acquiesced to hierarchies in the workplace or in society as a whole.

Through collective bargaining and organising, trade unions can contribute in a major way to diminishing inequalities among workers. Given the extensive literature on the topic of how to organise the unorganised, I focus on political advocacy with regard to the issue of inequality. Advocacy work requires the exploration of political opportunity structures; that is, identifying access points and allies in the political process. While for most unions access to economic policymaking is limited, windows of opportunity do occasionally open and can even be created sometimes.

Since some campaigns against inequality have misjudged the public's attitude towards inequality, a major section of my contribution is dedicated to highlighting the general ambivalence of the public concerning the issue. This is done mainly with reference to public opinion in Germany. Despite the fact that the German case is not representative for other countries, some of its ambivalences will certainly also be visible elsewhere. While devising a strategy, the likely response of privileged groups should also be considered. Therefore, I discuss briefly some of the likely reactions from this side. My contribution ends with some considerations for customising a strategy aimed at combating inequality.

Trade unions and inequality

Trade unions' collective bargaining and social policy advocacy have been singled out as being among the most important factors for successfully countering economic inequality in industrial societies (Brady et al., 2013; Huber and Stephens, 2001). While one would expect, in a representative democracy, that governments will respond to the majority of voters who are not benefiting from rising inequality, they have at times contributed to reinforcing it, have failed to respond, or have reacted in a timid fashion only. Hacker and Pierson (2010: 173) provide a convincing explanation for this paradox: 'The art for policymakers is not to respond to the median voter; it is to minimize the trade-offs when the desires of powerful groups and the desires of voters collide.' Organised interests predominate in processes of agenda-setting. Correspondingly, unions play an important role in reducing inequality, but the flipside of the coin is that the decline in union density has been identified as a major cause for rising inequality in post-industrial democracies (Huber and Stephens, 2014).

Trade unions have also contributed to narrowing gender wage gaps (Blau and Kahn, 2003). However, at times, they have chosen to protect insiders and have thus reinforced labour-market segmentation – not only, but also at the expense of women (Hill, 1968). Therefore, combating inequality remains, for some trade unions, a challenge within their own ranks.[1]

Failure to address inequality may have no immediate effect on trade unions as organisations. However, their position in the labour market as well as in the realm of politics will suffer in the long term. The difficulties attached to limiting labour supply may represent the structural reason why unions, despite professions to the contrary, practise exclusion. Once a labour movement has embraced the principle of exclusion, in each new decision-making situation labour leaders are likely to perceive the costs and risks of becoming more inclusive as being higher than the maintenance of exclusionary policies. This holds especially true if the decisions taken are the result of bureaucratic procedures and calculations. With an eye to union coffers, organising poorly paid workers in precarious low-wage sectors surely appears less worthwhile than organising workers with relatively secure public-sector jobs (Voos, 1987).

In the long term, however, such short-term cost-avoidance strategies will not pay off. The membership will shrink in numbers for three reasons. First, growing wage differentials between unionised and unorganised sectors will increase the incentive for management to avoid union representation of their workforce. In hiring for new plant locations or in introducing new production methods, management will invariably try to hire workers from groups who were previously excluded from the labour market. It would be also a mistake to believe that the skill premium the current members receive is guaranteed for life, especially given the opportunities for cross-border outsourcing, which nowadays even exist in the case of medical services. Second, these new groups will remember their earlier experiences as victims of discrimination and will be less open to organising efforts by established unions. Third, unions that traditionally practised exclusion will find hardly any people in their ranks who would be capable of approaching and organising new workers.

The history of the US labour movement offers a good example of the long-term consequences of exclusionary practices. The craft unions in the American Federation of Labor (AFL) lost their strong position in the labour market in the wake of Taylorism and Fordism. As a consequence of their inability to form alliances, it became possible to isolate them politically (Montgomery, 1987). As the Congress of Industrial Organizations (CIO) overcame exclusionary practices, it succeeded in organising industrial workers. But in the early 1950s, the CIO unions abandoned this agenda again. The aborted attack on the bastions of racist exclusion in the South left a bitter legacy. Powerful Southern politicians doggedly chipped away at the political influence of unions within the Democratic Party (Davis, 1986: 92). Despite the more welcoming attitude towards blacks and later also immigrant workers, the US trade-union movement was not able to overcome its relative isolation. In the wake of the financial crisis of 2008, the last major bastion of US trade unionism, the public sector, has come under attack by right-wing governors (Paul, 2015). The exorbitant increase in wealth concentration of the last decades and the use of this wealth by conservative billionaires has provided the right-wing with substantial financial resources and media access.

In sum, if unions address inequality through collective bargaining, organising and policy campaigns, this will diminish their funds and absorb human energies. The failure to do so, however, threatens the very existence of trade unions in the long run.

The strategic repertoire of trade unions

What do trade unions have to consider if they want to challenge inequality successfully? In the following sections, I argue that they have to be aware of their power resources, identities and political opportunities.

Four sources of workers' power can be identified: structural, associational, institutional and discursive power (cf. McGuire, 2013: 37). Structural power (that is, market or logistical power) is determined by the demand for labour, which is usually higher for skilled labour. As a result, skilled labour commands more market power. Because of these differences in power, the use of market power usually leads to inequality within the working-class – unless the more powerful groups of workers practise solidarity with the less powerful ones. Associational power is what trade unions are about: they are associations of workers that try to overcome the weak position of individual workers vis-à-vis the concentrated power of capital. If workers relied solely on market and associational power, the fate of a majority of them would be left to the vagaries of the business cycle. On the basis of institutional power, they can defend their right to collective bargaining even during times of crisis. Their institutional power rests on their past organisational and political successes. In the political sphere, the institutional power of trade unions varies a lot across countries. However, most trade unions lack access to economic policy-making in the fields of monetary, financial and foreign economic policy. Access to these fields is limited even when traditionally labour-friendly parties are in government (Hachmann and Scherrer, 2012).

Finally, workers' organisations can make use of discursive power. Discursive power can be defined as the ability to convince others of one's own arguments. It depends on the ability to frame one's concerns in such a way that it resonates with other people's understanding of the world. The messages have to be 'framed' according to chosen target groups. But words are usually not enough. The best propaganda for trade unions is usually victories for their members. A subgroup of discursive power is symbolic power, that is appeals to prevalent morals. This power can be employed effectively by groups of workers with little market and institutional power if their treatment by management or state violates common morality (Chun, 2009).

Although these power resources are not set in stone, trade unions cannot employ them at will. They are the product of history and specific contexts. History is embodied in a trade unions' identity. From Richard Hyman we learn that trade unions can be categorised according to whether they perceive themselves as class, society, or market actors (Hyman, 2007). A 'business union' cannot easily transform itself into a 'social movement union' and vice versa. Thus, each organisation has to reflect on its strengths and weaknesses, as well as assessing whether it can 'stretch' its identity somewhat in order to make a contribution to the struggle against inequality.

For effective campaigning, unions need to be aware of the fact that attitudes among its members, its activists and its officials may diverge. While officials can be ordered to organise a campaign, it will usually only be successful if they subscribe to the aims pursued. There are reasons to suspect that not all officials support strategies aimed at combating inequality. It is not unheard of that some trade-union officials have career expectations beyond moving up in the trade-union bureaucracy. In quite a number of countries, officials belong to the middle class and employ informal workers in their households. In other words, a strategy aimed at combating inequality should not take for granted the spontaneous support of officials.

Trade-union activists contribute to campaigns because of their idealism and willingness to sacrifice time and to forgo material benefits. Therefore, activists should be listened to carefully. Some of them might overshoot and push demands that do not resonate with other union members or the general public. But since their over-commitment is very valuable for any campaign facing adversity, a place has to be found for them.

As membership-based organisations, union leaderships have to make sure that the rank-and-file supports their strategy. On the one hand, a campaign should be based on issues that interest the members. On the other hand, campaigners might want to push the other members somewhat in order to ensure that general standards of justice are met or the survival of the organisation is ensured. After all, the workplace is usually organised in a hierarchical way, and some members might be comfortable with their position and thus not overly interested in addressing inequality.

Given different organisational histories and the specificity of contexts, it cannot be ruled out that the strategies of trade unions and their allies lead to conflicts with other unions. For example, one trade union may choose an insider-lobby strategy, another street mobilisation, in which case the insiders might feel disturbed by the outsiders. Or one trade union goes for collective bargaining, keeping the state out, while another litigates in court. For the labour movement to be successful and not to be divided, the different strategies should be accepted and seen as complementing one another (cf. Deakin et al., 2015).

Political opportunities

Before strategies are devised, the political opportunities for pursuing them should be assessed. Scholars in social movements studies have come up with the concept of the 'political opportunity structure' (POS). A POS refers to the openness of a political system to the demands of social forces such as trade unions (Meyer, 2004). It includes 'the stability or instability of that broad set of elite alignments that typically undergird a polity; the presence or absence of elite allies and the state's capacity and propensity for state repression' (McAdam et al., 1996: 27). A POS analysis encompasses first of all an assessment of the political processes in the targeted field. Who are the actors; where are the access points for trade unions in the government, the parliament and the policy network? From Bob Jessop (1990), we have learned about the selectivity of the state: certain demands find support in the state apparatuses, others not. As most of today's states have been internationalised along the lines of neoliberal principles, demands raised in this volume tend to belong to the latter category. Therefore, it is a prerequisite for success to carefully identify potential allies and potential for support in the media, among different social groups and among the electorate. Of course, it is important to also assess political opportunities in the light of one's own resources, identity and so on.

While a particular POS might seem quite closed, openings do occur. A window of opportunity can be an electoral campaign or an event which, in our case, highlights especially egregious aspects of inequality. As the emergence of windows of opportunity cannot be easily predicted, a certain strategic flexibility is necessary. Likewise, a POS should also not be seen as being set in stone. A carefully laid out long-term strategy might be able to change the POS structure, for example by preparing the intellectual ground, building trust through small-scale activities with allies and so on. In some cases, it might even be possible to trigger events that open up windows of opportunity.

The ambivalences of public opinion

There are promising signs concerning the public's attitude towards inequality. For example, a 2012 survey conducted in a number of countries revealed that most people would prefer significantly lower salaries for chief executive officers (CEOs). However, as some of the failed campaigns for higher taxes for the rich or caps on executive pay suggest (Kampagnenleitung der 1:12-Initiative, 2014), a closer analysis of public sentiment is necessary. The same survey on the adequate remuneration for CEOs also revealed that the public is not aware of the prevalent levels of inequality. The respondents from the USA estimated that the ratio of executive pay to unskilled worker pay is 30 to 1. In fact, it was 350 to 1 (Kiatpongsan and Norton, 2015). Thus any campaign for diminishing inequality will have to raise the public's awareness of the issue.

But even if members of the middle and working classes are aware and critical about rising inequality, it does not automatically follow that they will support redistribution. For example, surveys among US citizens show that despite rising inequality, the share of respondents saying that upper-income earners pay too little tax declined from 77 per cent in 1992 to 61 per cent in 2013. And these days, more Americans are critical of the tax share paid by the poor (8 per cent in 1992, 19 per cent in 2013; Rampell, 2013).

While the desire to see the rich pay more is a majoritarian position even in the USA, it needs to be added that the people responding to such surveys in advanced industrial countries find overall tax levels are too high. On the one hand, these findings are an encouragement for those demanding more progressive taxation. On the other hand, they caution against changing tax rates because this will quickly run into opposition. A closer look at the surveys reveals that the degree of support for progressive taxation and overall tax levels depends to a significant degree on the respondents' economic standing (Barnes, 2015). In addition, tax acceptance varies across nations and groups. The level of trust in government explains some of the differences. If the level is low, then taxation is viewed critically because people suspect that they will not benefit from tax-funded government programmes (Barnes, 2015: 57).

Inequality in Germany: perceptions and positions

A large study on the attitudes of Germans on inequality (Engel, 2014a) reveals an ambivalent stance of the respondents. Most were likely to consider their own standard of living as unjust if it was much below what they expected on the grounds of their qualifications and efforts. Those whose income was much above of what they could expect were much less likely to find their income level unjust (Engel, 2014b: 84). Importantly, the group of 'overachievers' was much smaller (6.7 per cent) than the 'underachievers' (45 per cent). Therefore, one could expect a larger audience for the issue of unjust income distribution. Nevertheless, for most respondents the deviation between their expectations and their achieved standard of living was rather small, which also meant that only a few considered their own standard of living to be unjust (Engel, 2014b: 86).

Whether income distribution is considered to be just or unjust is also very much informed by people's attitudes towards work. Overwhelmingly, the respondents believed that hard work deserves a higher income. Only 6 per cent did not agree, while 4 per cent were neutral. However, a substantial but smaller majority felt that not just the results of hard work but also hard work in itself should be rewarded with a higher income. The downside of this sentiment is that it is accompanied with the rejection of the idea that everyone should have a similar level of funds at their disposal (72 per cent of respondents) (Burmeister and Engel, 2014: 173).

Another obstacle for the combat against inequality are positive attitudes towards competition. Competition was seen as making people work hard and come up with new ideas by 76 per cent of the respondents. This was accompanied by the conviction that income differences between human beings are acceptable because they reveal the degree to which individuals have made good on their life chances (59 per cent in favour; Burmeister and Engel, 2014: 176). Nevertheless, redistribution also received support. 63 per cent were in favour of taxing more the people who are economically successful. 50 per cent agreed to the statement that it is the responsibility of the government to make sure that everyone has a sufficient income (Burmeister and Engel, 2014: 176).

The support or rejection of the position that the government is responsible for securing a decent living standard for all was influenced, to a degree, by people's incomes and qualifications (Burmeister and Engel, 2014: 179, 180). This finding was confirmed by another large survey conducted recently (INSA-Meinungstrend, 2014) and seems to hold across many countries (Barnes, 2015: 57). It also depends on the peer-group effect. In communities consisting mostly of rich people, poorer people are more likely to consider their own position unjust. In communities with a more even income distribution, income differences are considered to be 'normal' (Engel, 2014b: 89). For activists, these findings call for adjusting national strategies to the specificities of local contexts.

As a comparative study of US and German attitudes towards inheritance tax revealed a few years ago, inherited wealth is seen as legitimate to a significantly stronger degree by Germans than by Americans (Beckert, 2007). This is confirmed by the survey discussed above. The notion of passing on wealth so that one's children have better life chances was popular even among the lowest income group (Burmeister and Engel, 2014: 185, 190). From the perspective of economic liberalism, this position is in conflict with meritocracy. However, if the merit criterion is not applied to individuals but to families, which many Germans seem to do (but also some Americans; cf. Mankiw, 2014), the support for competition as well as for passing on wealth is less contradictory. The legitimacy of inherited wealth is deep-rooted; the right of the next generation to take over from their parents emerged before modern property rights emerged (Penner, 2014).

However, under certain circumstances, support for inherited wealth may erode. When asked whether it was just that high-income families send their offspring to private schools, the answers of the respondents in Germany, a country with a small private-education sector, were evenly distributed between 'agree' and 'disagree'. Households with children were less supportive of this statement because they may have seen the existence of private schools as an unjust discrimination of their own children (Burmeister and Engel, 2014: 190).

Culture and inter-subjective meaning-making

The differences between countries in terms of the level of trust in government and of attitudes towards inherited wealth points to the importance of inter-subjective meaning-making, that is of culture. Michéle Lamont et al. (2014) discuss cultural processes that contribute to inequality through the routinised and taken-for-granted activities of both the rich and the poor. In particular, they explore how identification processes such as racialisation and stigmatisation, as well as rationalisation processes such as standardisation and evaluation produce (and reproduce) inequality. In Gramscian terms, inequality has become 'common sense'; its existence and practices are seen as natural. As 'common sense' is not an instance of 'false consciousness' but a pattern of inter-subjective meaning-making based on inherited ideas and concrete practices, it does not suffice to lift up 'common sense' to the level of 'good sense' through education and other interventions appealing to individuals. In addition, practices have to be changed and this includes routines and lifestyles,

An example from the world of finance can be used to illustrate this challenge. Capital-based pension systems contribute to financialisation processes, which in turn aggravate inequality.[2] Once such a system is established, its existence feeds on itself because not only the financial industry, the pension-fund trustees (sometimes even trade unions) and the fund's employees become dependent on it, but also the current and prospective beneficiaries. For example, the California Public Employees Retirement System (CalPERS), known for its shareholder activism, decided to pursue riskier strategies in order to make up for the losses accrued during the crisis (Walsh, 2010). It appears that a return to a public system is only possible once a private system can no longer be economically sustained (Riesco, 2009).

Responses of the rich

As already pointed out, wealthy people and powerful business lobbies have successfully exerted influence over politics in order to secure their share of national income and wealth. An extensive empirical study, covering five consecutive US Congresses, found that representatives are significantly more likely to respond to the preferences of rich citizens than of citizens with less income (Hayes, 2012). The economic preferences of citizens with low income do not even make it into the campaign appeals at the level of US states. The lowest level of responsiveness was found for Democratic parties in states with comparatively greater income inequality (Rigby and Wright, 2013). One reason why the concerns of the poor are neglected is their lack of political participation. Rising inequality reinforces political abstention: The more inequality and, in particular, the less labour protection and social support, the fewer low-educated citizens are participating in politics (Schneider and Makszin, 2014).

Studies in the tradition of Gramsci have gone beyond pointing out the lobbying power of capital. They have shown how representatives of capital have been able to universalise their particular interests in such a way that they could count on the passive consensus of a major part of society and did not have to rely on coercion so much (Scherrer, 2011). This insight raises the bar for counterstrategies. It is not sufficient to scandalise the undue influence of the rich and the negative consequences of rising inequality for ordinary citizens. One also has to study more closely why so many people acquiesce to policies that increase inequality.

However, if challenged, the rich can mobilise their resources for their defence. In the aftermath of the financial crisis, billionaires' money bankrolled the Tea Party in the USA, which started in protest against using taxpayers' money for bailing out financial institutions to eventually support the agenda of finance against reform-minded Democrats (MacGillis, 2014). In the German federal state of Hamburg, where a conservative–green coalition government tried to abolish grammar schools (traditionally the preserve, in the stratified German school system, of middle- and upper-middle-class children), well-to-do parents mounted a successful campaign that stopped the reform (Mannitz and Schneider, 2014). In Brazil, the middle classes were strongly supported by the tycoon-controlled media when they took to the streets and vented their dissatisfaction over more expensive domestic and personal services, which resulted from the PT government's social and minimum-wage policies (Saad-Filho, 2015).

Besides enjoying privileged access to the media (to different degrees from country to country), the rich base their defence on access to expert knowledge. The overwhelming majority of think tanks support the causes of the rich and of business (Plehwe, 2012). Most economists warn against the introduction or the raising of minimum wages, unfazed by the existence of counterevidence.[3] In international organisations, there are plenty of experts counselling more government austerity, the deregulation of labour markets and the weakening of trade unions – despite the existence of dialogue with global union federations (Rückert, 2015) and the odd acknowledgement that rising inequality is a problem (OECD, 2011). The latest manifestation is their treatment of Southern European countries, especially of Greece.

In the past, if challenged by a government with a popular mandate for more radical redistribution, the rich in some countries supported military coups in defence of their privileges, for example, in 1964 against João Goulart in Brazil (Skidmore, 1988), in 1973 against Salvador Allende in Chile, and recently against Yingluck Shinawatra and her supporters from the poorer segments of society in Thailand (Camroux, 2014). The Goulart experience may explain to some degree why the PT government is cautious in its treatment of Brazil's elites (Leite, 2014). Of course, a military coup does not linger in the background in all countries.

Contextualising strategies

Trade unions have made an important contribution to combating inequality. Globalisation, technology, neoliberal policies and the new composition of work-forces have weakened trade unions in most countries. The result has been rising economic inequality, which was also caused because in numerous cases trade unions have not tried forcefully enough to organise precarious workers and have given limited support to struggles for more equality in the policy arena. Both these strategic flaws have reinforced their weakness. For the sake of their own organisational survival and, of course, for the working class, trade unions should become more aware of the issue of inequality and should devote more resources and energy to developing counter-strategies.

At the initial stage of any intervention aimed at combating inequality, trade unionists should assess their own organisation's role in sustaining or even foster-ing inequality in the workplace. Recognising behaviours that sustain inequality would be a first step towards achieving a change of course. The next step would be to analyse the degree to which the identified behavioural patterns have become part of the identity of members, officials and the entire organisation. It would be naïve to think that behaviour can be changed quickly. Therefore, specific strategies have to be devised that tackle the attitudes of the organisation's stake-holders. For the purposes of policy advocacy, these attitudes also have to be taken into account. If positions defending the status quo prevail, activists with an egalitarian agenda have to develop argumentative strategies and incentive structures with the purpose of changing these attitudes.

Since any strategy will fail if power resources are not mobilised, the resources of the responsible organisation and its members have to be assessed before a strategy is launched. Underutilised resources, for example discursive power, should receive more attention. It should be explored to which extent these resources can be mobilised 'in-house' or with the help of allies in academia, among non-governmental organisations (NGOs), or even in government.

Successful policy advocacy requires a good understanding of the POS and the possibilities for changing it in order to improve access. The POS also depends on the resources that can be mobilised. Since the opportunities for trade unions in the economic field are usually limited, the identification and possible creation of windows of opportunities is of special importance. As standards of economic justice vary among countries, regions and income strata, attitudes of the various publics need to be studied carefully. The common sense of neoliberalism should not be underestimated – and neither should the likely counter-mobilisation of the privileged be disregarded. Given the commonality of sentiments concerning the just nature of inequality and the right to pass on wealth, two approaches are needed: the recognition of existing sentiments in short- and medium-term strategies and a longer-term strategy for changing them. In sum, the challenge is to develop strategies that are both differentiated enough to mobilise different groups and can nevertheless bring these groups together in a large coalition for change.

Notes

1 See Britwum's chapter in this volume.
2 See Evans's and Lavinas's chapters in this volume.
3 See Herr and Ruoff in this volume.

References

Barnes, L. (2015) The Size and Shape of Government: Preferences over Redistributive Tax Policy. *Socio-Economic Review* 13(1): 55–78.

Beckert, J. (2007) *Inherited Wealth*. Princeton, NJ: Princeton University Press.

Blau, F.D. and Kahn, L.M. (2003) Understanding international differences in the gender pay gap. *Journal of Labor Economics* 21(1): 106–144.

Brady, D., Baker, R.S. and Finnigan, R. (2013) When Unionization Disappears: State-Level Unionization and Working Poverty in the United States. *American Sociological Review* 78(5): 872–896.

Burmeister, L. and Engel, U. (2014) Glück, Zufriedenheit und Zuversicht – Soziale Lagen in Deutschland. In Engel, U. (ed.) *Gerechtigkeit ist gut, wenn sie mir nützt: Was den Deutschen wichtig ist – Eine Umfrage*. Frankfurt: Campus: 193–214.

Camroux, D. (2014) Putsch Nummer 12: Thailands Eliten verspielen die Zukunft des Landes. *Le Monde diplomatique*, 10 July.

Chun, J.J. (2009) *Organizing at the Margins – The Symbolic Politics of Labor in South Korea and the United States*. Ithaca, NY: Cornell University Press.

Davis, M. (1986) *Prisoners of the American Dream: Politics and Economy in the History of the American Working Class*. London: Verso.

Deakin, S., Fraser Butlin, S., McLaughlin, C. and Polanska, A. (2015) Are Litigation and Collective Bargaining Complements or Substitutes for Achieving Gender Equality? A Study of the British Equal Pay Act. *Cambridge Journal of Economics* 39(2): 381–403.

Engel, U. (ed.) (2014a) *Gerechtigkeit ist gut, wenn sie mir nützt: Was den Deutschen wichtig ist – Eine Umfrage*. Frankfurt: Campus.

Engel, U. (2014b) Lebensverhältnisse der Deutschen. In Engel, U. (ed.) *Gerechtigkeit ist gut, wenn sie mir nützt: Was den Deutschen wichtig ist – Eine Umfrage*. Frankfurt: Campus: 57–96.

Hachmann, L. and Scherrer, C. (2012) Can a Labor-Friendly Government Be Friendly Towards Labor? A Hegemonic Analysis of Brazilian, German and South African experiences. In Mosoetsa, S. and Williams, M. (eds) *Labor in the Global South, Challenges and Alternatives for Workers*. Geneva: International Labour Organization (ILO): 141–158.

Hacker, J.S. and Pierson, P. (2010) Winner-Take-All Politics: Public Policy, Political Organization, and the Precipitous Rise of Top Incomes in the United States. *Politics & Society* 38(2): 152–204.

Hayes, T.J. (2012) The Representational Sources of Political Inequality. Unpublished UC Riverside PhD thesis. Available at: http://escholarship.org/uc/item/4sd105b3 (accessed 1 June 2015).

Hill, H. (1968) The Racial Practices of Organized Labor: The Contemporary Record. In Jacobson, J. (ed.) *The Negro and the American Labor Movement*. Garden City, NY: Anchor.

Huber, E. and Stephens, J.D. (2001) *Development and Crisis of the Welfare State: Partisan Politics Global Markets*. Chicago: Chicago University Press.

Huber, E. and Stephens, J.D. (2014) Income Inequality and Redistribution in Post-Industrial Democracies: Demographic, Economic and Political Determinants. *Socio-Economic Review* 12(2): 245–267.

Hyman, R. (2007) How Can Trade Unions Act Strategically? *Transfer* 13(2): 193–210.

INSA-Meinungstrend (2014) *Was sind für Sie gegenwärtig die drei wichtigsten politischen Themen?* INSA-Consulere, 23–27 Kalenderwoche 2014.

Jessop, B. (1990) *State Theory: Putting Capitalist States in Their Place*. Cambridge: Polity.

Kampagnenleitung der 1:12-Initiative (2014) Rückschau auf die 1:12-Initiative. In Bischel, I., Knobloch, U., Ringger, B. and Schatz, H. (eds) *Denknetz-Jahrbuch 2014: Kritik des kritischen Denkens*. Zurich: 224–228.

Kiatpongsan, S. and Norton, M.I. (2015) How Much (More) Should CEOs Make? A Universal Desire for More Equal Pay. *Perspectives on Psychological Science* (forthcoming). Available at: http://nrs.harvard.edu/urn-3:HUL.InstRepos:13348081 (accessed 1 June 2015).

Lamont, M., Beljean, S. and Clair, M. (2014) What is Missing? Cultural Processes and Causal Pathways to Inequality. *Socio-Economic Review* 12: 573–608.

Lavinas, L. (2014) A Long Way from Tax Justice: The Brazilian Case. Global Labour University Working Paper No. 22. Geneva: International Labour Organization (ILO).

Leite, P.M. (2014) *Dilma tenta evitar armadilha de Jango*. 23 November. Available at: http://paulomoreiraleite.com/2014/11/23/com-levy-os-outros-dilma-foge-de-armadilha-de-jango/ (accessed 2 June 2015).

MacGillis, A. (2014) Tea Party Populism Is Dead. The GOP Is Back in Bed with Wall Street. *New Republic*, 30 October.

Mankiw, N.G. (2014) How Inherited Wealth Helps the Economy. *New York Times*, 21 June. Available at: www.nytimes.com/2014/06/22/upshot/how-inherited-wealth-helps-the-economy.html (accessed 1 June 2015).

Mannitz, S. and Schneider, J. (2014) Vom „Ausländer" zum „Migrationshintergrund": Die Modernisierung des deutschen Integrationsdiskurses und seine neuen Verwerfungen. In Nieswand, B. and Drotbohm, H. (eds) *Kultur, Gesellschaft, Migration: Die reflexive Wende in der Migrationsforschung*. Wiesbaden: Springer VS: 69–96.

McAdam, D., McCarthy, J. and Zald, M. (eds) (1996) *Comparative Perspectives on Social Movements*. Cambridge: Cambridge University Press.

McGuire, D. (2013) *Reframing Trade – Union Mobilisation against the General Agreement on Trade in Services (GATS)*. Munich: Reiner Hampp Verlag.

Meyer, D. (2004) Protest and Political Opportunities. *Annual Review of Sociology* 30: 125–145.

Montgomery, D. (1987) *The Fall of the House of Labor: The Work Place, the State, and American Labor Activism, 1865–1925*. Cambridge: Cambridge University Press.

OECD (2011) Divided We Stand: Why Inequality Keeps Rising, Paris: Organisation for Economic Co-operation and Development (OECD). Available at: http://dx.doi.org/10.1787/9789264119536-en (accessed 1 June 2015).

Paul, A. (2015) The Right's Attack on US Government Unions. *Equal Times*, 12 March.

Penner, J.E. (2014) Intergenerational Justice and the 'Hereditary Principle'. *The Law & Ethics of Human Rights* 8(2): 195–217.

Plehwe, D. (2012) Attack and Roll Back: The Constructive and Destructive Potential of Think Tank Networks. *Global Responsibility – Newsletter of the International Network of Engineers and Scientists for Global Responsibility* 64: 10–12.

Rampell, C. (2013) On Whether the Rich Pay Too Little in Taxes. *New York Times*, 18 April. Available at: http://economix.blogs.nytimes.com/2013/04/18/on-whether-the-rich-pay-too-little-in-taxes/ (accessed 2 June 2015).

Riesco, M. (2009) The End of Privatized Pensions in Latin America. *Global Social Policy* 9(2): 273–280.

Rigby, E. and Wright, G.C. (2013) Political Parties and Representation of the Poor in the American States. *American Journal of Political Science* 57(3): 552–565.

Rückert, Y. (2015) The Global Unions in the System of Global Governance: The Embedding of Trade Union Political Demands in the Bretton Woods Organizations. Unpublished dissertation University of Kassel and University of Oviedo.

Saad-Filho, A. (2015) Brazil: The Debacle of the PT. *Monthly Review*, 30 March. Available at: http://mrzine.monthlyreview.org/2015/sf300315.html (accessed 2 June 2015).

Scherrer, C. (2011) Reproducing Hegemony: US Finance Capital and the 2008 Crisis. *Critical Policy Studies* 5(3): 219–247.

Schneider, C.Q. and Makszin, K. (2014) Inequality Ramifications for Democracy: Forms of Welfare Capitalism and Education-Based Participatory Inequality. *Socio-Economic Review* 12(2): 437–462.

Skidmore, T. (1988) *The Politics of Military Rule in Brazil, 1964–1985*. Oxford: Oxford University Press.

Voos, P.B. (1987) Union Organizing Expenditures: Determinants and Their Implications for Union Growth. *Journal of Labor Research* 8(1): 19–30.

Walsh, M.W. (2010) Public Pension Funds Are Adding Risk to Raise Returns. *New York Times*, 8 March. Available at: www.nytimes.com/2010/03/09/business/09pension.html?ref%20=%20marywilliamswalsh (accessed 2 June 2015).

19 (Un)typical labour struggles

Creative campaigns to challenge inequality

Michelle Williams

Introduction

In recent decades, neoliberal globalisation has mutated capitalism in new and unfamiliar ways. It has intensified and accelerated inequality by dismantling welfare systems, industrial and labour-market regulations and state capacity to regulate financial systems, while simultaneously opening economies to fiercely aggressive market actors. Ever more aspects of life, including nature, have become commodified. We are witnesses to continuing crises, weaker states, ineffective labour movements and the increased power of capital. This is accompanied by an increase in the number of people who are living precarious lives.

There are two primary categories of responses to these developments: responses from above (led by the state and capital) and responses from below (led by movements and civil society). The responses from above either foreground the state's role through a renewal of Keynesian attempts to fix the global economy or look to the market through more neoliberalism in the form of austerity programmes and, in the USA, through the war economy. There have also been responses from below, from civil society including labour movements that invoke people's power and garner the support of ordinary citizens. These range from the 'end of growth' school, which argues for the end of a fossil-fuel addicted mode of production, to the alternative economies movement that sees local communities exchanging in alternative local currencies. The solidarity economy movement, in which alternative forms of production, consumption and finance are based on collective ownership and democratic decision-making, is another response emerging in various places in the world such as Brazil, Argentina, Germany, Italy, Spain and the USA. We have also seen a response that argues for de-globalisation, largely associated with Walden Bello (2013) in the Philippines.

What has been labour's response to these changes in late capitalism? Drawing on ten case studies that formed part of the Global Labour University's research project on 'the causes and consequences of inequality', in this chapter I look at various campaigns that challenge inequality and the role that labour has played in these campaigns.[1] The cases are conventional and unconventional campaigns in which unions play some kind of role and that either directly or indirectly address issues of inequality. The campaigns demonstrate that workers are involved in fights against the pernicious effects of late capitalism, especially the resulting inequality, forcing states to act on behalf of their citizens. What has been labour's role in these struggles?

Responses from labour

For much of the twentieth century, labour movements were at the forefront of most social, political and economic struggles for social transformation (Choi, 1993; Collier and Mahoney, 1997; Scipes, 1996; Seidman, 1994; Valenzuela, 1989; von Holdt, 2002). Workers' organisations also secured vital reforms in 'workplace organization, labour law frameworks and trade union structures, promoting the voice and visibility of working-class actors in key institutional arenas' (Chun and Williams, 2013: 2; cf. Suh, 2009; Webster, 1985). The specific ways in which workers and their organisations have intervened in social struggles has varied across time and place, but they have clearly played an instrumental role in shaping the contours of societies for much of the twentieth century.

However, we must be careful in drawing simplistic path-dependent conclusions about their continued role today. Indeed, with the neoliberal mutations in capitalism, labour movements have been systematically weakened and often see themselves on the sidelines of social struggles as they defensively try to hold on to their past gains (Baccaro, 2010; Urban, 2012). For example, the myriad 'service delivery' protests in South Africa over the past 15 years have seen little support from organised labour, while the worker-led factory takeovers in Argentina enjoyed little assistance from unions. Similarly, the US labour movement was unable (or uninterested) in tapping into the enormous energy created by the Occupy movement in the aftermath of the 2008 financial crisis. Yet, workers and their collective movements still have a vital role to play and there are examples where they are engaging in local struggles as well as opportunities for forging 'new labour internationalism' (Kay, 2011; Stevis and Boswell, 2008; Webster, et al., 2008: 210).

The question for us, then, is what has been labour's response to increasing inequality? Workers and their organisations are responding to the changes in capitalism and the causes and consequences of inequality in varying ways, some of which pose challenges to capitalism and others which help ameliorate the pernicious effects of inequality. While there are continuities with past practices, it is not simply a return to the repertoires of twentieth-century political unionism or social movement unionism that we are seeing. Rather, in certain instances a transformative unionism that maintains a degree of autonomy from party-political structures while forming issue-based alliances with social movements, civic organisations and political parties and engaging the state and corporations is emerging. By transformative unionism, I mean a politics in which a tradition of struggle is kept alive (or rebuilt) and one that inspires workers to believe that another world is possible and worth fighting for. Unions have often become 'vehicles for lowering the expectations as well as disciplining recalcitrant workers' (Gindin, 2012: 33), which forecloses the possibility for radical alternatives in society. Transformative unionism, thus, challenges this pervasive tradition of unionism that has emerged with the growing power of capital by injecting a utopian moment. This transformative unionism attempts to challenge both commodification and exploitation that are simultaneously the key features of late capitalism. Not all the cases discussed here, however, demonstrate moments of transformative unionism, but have been included as they are union-led campaigns that are trying to become more effective in their reform programmes which have potentially radicalising effects. For example, a campaign for a universal minimum wage can affect accumulation and also raise public awareness about inequality, fair wages, societal interests and a just society. In the remaining parts of the chapter, I look at ten different campaigns that show labour's involvement in fighting the causes or consequences of inequality, some of which are also pursuing transformative unionism.

Campaigns to overcome inequality

Drawing on ten creative campaigns to challenge inequality, we see varying degrees of involvement by labour movements. The campaigns include the Brazilian labour movement's struggle for gender equality and its minimum wage campaign; Argentina's mass campaign for income redistribution; the South African Treatment Action Campaign (TAC) for access to HIV–AIDS drugs; the National Union of Metal Workers of South Africa's (NUMSA) initiative for climate justice and socially owned renewable energy; the Namibian Basic Income Grant campaign; the New Trade Union Initiative's (NTUI) efforts to organise informal workers in India; the Indian movement for access to forest land; Germany's minimum wage and Emmely campaigns; and the European Financial Transaction Tax campaign.

In looking at labour movements' responses to inequality, it is useful to see that they operate along two axes, lying on a spectrum from (1) highly involved to marginally involved and (2) typical to untypical. When we look at the campaigns along these two axes, it is clear that unions are fighting back, but the degrees to which and the issues around which they fight are rooted in local conditions, particular histories of class formations and their respective political contexts.

Labour-movement involvement

What is especially interesting is that labour's role varies across the campaigns from highly involved to marginally involved. The campaigns on the one side of the spectrum of high-level union involvement include those that directly and indirectly address issues of inequality – such as the Climate Justice campaign in South Africa; the Minimum Wage campaigns in Germany and Brazil; the struggles of shack dwellers for basic services in India; the struggle for redistribution in Argentina; and the struggle for gender equality in Brazil. While unions are leading all of these campaigns, they are doing so by building links with a broader base of support and drawing out common issues that affect communities.

One of the most innovative and challenging campaigns led by a trade union is NUMSA's campaign for climate justice. Vishwas Satgar (2015) shows how the metalworkers shifted their understandings of development to a radical climate justice perspective that includes economic and energy democracy, energy equality and protection of the natural world. Steeped in the manufacturing sector, it is quite extraordinary that NUMSA has taken the initiative to pursue a campaign that moves beyond fossil-fuel, environmentally destructive manufacturing in favour of such things as a 'socially owned renewable energy' sector. The way in which the union has used the issue of energy and climate justice to energise debate about issues beyond the shop-floor through worker-led forums, workshops and study circles suggests a new politics is being pursued within NUMSA.

The minimum wage campaigns in Brazil and Germany also demonstrate high-level union involvement in the campaigns. Fred de Melo (2015) and Jörg Nowak (2015) show that in both cases the campaign was led by the main labour federations – Central Única dos Trabalhadores (Unified Workers' Central) and Deutscher Gewerkschaftsbund (Confederation of German Trade Unions). Both federations fought to not only pass legislation ensuring a minimum wage but also to raise the floor of the minimum. In both places, the public awareness and ensuing debates included issues of a just society, unacceptably high levels of inequality and the need for more state intervention in the economy to regulate banks and corporations. While the minimum wage is not necessarily a transformative issue, the fact that two major union federations were pursuing offensive struggles that affected the working class as a whole harks back to earlier visions of the role of unions in pursuing social transformation.

Shifting from the traditional labour federations to a new initiative that focuses on the precariat, the New Trade Union Initiative (NTUI) in India brought together informal workers into a non-politically aligned federation of over 300 trade unions and social movements at its founding conference in 2006 (Vyas, 2014). The NTUI's efforts to organise shack-dwellers and informal sector workers place it on the spectrum of highly involved unions that are trying to combine worker issues with broader community issues. The importance of NTUI's initiative is that it is creating solidarity among informal workers who are usually characterised by fragmented and marginal positions within the economy and society.

Moving from the new union initiative of informal sector workers, the Argentine movement for income redistribution is an innovative campaign that brought the issue of inequality into the homes of the general public. Luis Campos (2015) shows how the National Front Against Poverty (Frenapo) was a creative, non-partisan and broad movement pushing the government to adopt progressive measures that would eliminate poverty and was a first of its kind in Argentina. The struggle to eradicate poverty came in the context of growing unemployment and increased insecurity for large numbers of Argentines. The campaign was led by a broad coalition of forces, including the Argentinian Workers' Union (CTA), unemployed movements, peasants, indigenous groups and human rights groups. The CTA's role in the campaign was instrumental as the largest partner in the coalition, but it did not control or lead the process. As an autonomous and independent union, CTA has a history of taking up issues beyond the shop-floor such as public services and housing and has been organising the informal sector workers for over a decade. The campaign shifted the public debate about income redistribution and placed moral pressure on the state to ensure wider redistribution across society.

Another struggle that takes up inequality is the Brazilian struggle for gender equality led by the National Secretary of the Women Workers of CUT (SNMT/ CUT), which ran an innovative campaign for 'equality of opportunities in life, in work and in the labour movement' (da Costa, 2015). The SNMT has been vital in mainstreaming gender within CUT and has influenced a number of its positions, such as quotas, through its original campaign in 1988. In 2008, CUT decided to re-launch the current campaign as women's positions in society, work and the home continue to be characterised by extreme forms of inequality, marginalisation and discrimination. The campaign calls for equality in life, in the workplace and in the labour movement and has a series of initiatives in each category. It uses methods such as information sharing, policy interventions, seminars and educational workshops. By focusing on women's issues, the campaign indirectly addresses inequality in society as women bear the greatest social burden of social reproduction and are most affected by poverty and inequality.

All of these campaigns have seen labour movements play a central role in pioneering creative campaigns that challenge inequality. In the following cases – access to HIV–AIDS drugs in South Africa, the Basic Income Grant in Nambia and the Emmely campaign in Germany – I move down the spectrum to campaigns in which labour has been involved, but has not led the struggles.

Mark Heywood (2015) takes us down the journey of accessing anti-retroviral drugs in South Africa. Looking at the TAC's struggle for universal access to anti-retroviral drugs reveals that the campaign was fundamentally about issues of inequality and part of its success was gaining the support of the main labour federation, the Congress of South African Trade Unions (COSATU). The class basis of HIV–AIDs in South Africa mirrors apartheid cleavages – the overwhelming majority of those infected and affected are the working class and poor, and especially women. The struggle, therefore, importantly affected those who could not afford the expensive drug cocktail. Thus, the TAC's struggle was not only about access to life-saving drugs, but also a struggle to overcome class-based inequalities in accessing these drugs. The alliance forged with COSATU was crucial to the TAC's success as COSATU was able to directly mobilise over two million people and register pressure on the Presidency. The TAC's struggle demonstrates how citizens (many of whom were members of unions) became actively engaged in creative struggles against both the state and transnational pharmaceutical corporations and in the process challenged the unequal access to life-saving drugs and deepened democratic activism.

Moving from the world of health as a universal right, Herbert Jauch (2015) shows us how the Namibian Basic Income Grant (BIG) initiative was an attempt to pioneer a universal grant system that would help alleviate dire conditions of the poor. Facing heavy resistance from international bodies such as the International Monetary Fund (IMF), the initiative ran a pilot project to demonstrate that the BIG could be administered and that it would have positive developmental impacts and reduce inequality. The developmental impacts of the pilot surpassed the expectations of those involved in the project as it not only alleviated dire conditions of poverty, but it also had other unintended consequences of reducing domestic violence, empowering women and increasing the school attendance rate of children. There were a number of crucial organisations that supported the BIG such as churches, trade unions (the main Namibian federation was actively involved), NGOs, AIDS organisations, legal aid, labour research units and, surprisingly, the business community and some international agencies. While the initiative was not expanded to the national level due to complex internal political wrangling, the initiative nevertheless demonstrated the positive correlation between providing universal basic income, decreasing poverty and inequality, and revitalising democracy. Labour's support for the campaign was vital and also demonstrates its willingness to forge links with a range of organisations, explore new types of programmes that do not directly affect its members and engage in pilot projects. On all these fronts, the Namibian federation was charting new paths of labour activism that addressed issues of commodification.

Going from universal income to a particular case of a woman unjustly fired from her job, Jörg Nowak (2015) explains that the Emmely campaign in Germany also directly attempted to challenge the differential treatment of workers and managers, thus combating inequality, but only received marginal union support. It was a bottom-up campaign in defence of a shop clerk who lost her job for ostensibly stealing a €2 coupon. Two things that are noteworthy in this campaign is that the struggle was largely waged outside of formal union structures and primarily invoked symbolic protests, which centred around the unjust world in which bankers get away with 'stealing' billions of euros while a shop clerk is fired after 32 years of service for two euros. Interestingly, in Germany we have cases – minimum wage and Emmely – of an institutionalised trade union movement and grassroots movements engaging in struggles to directly challenge inequality, but with varying union support. The impact and scope of the two campaigns also varies as the minimum wage campaign was a long-term campaign aimed at restructuring the entire labour market and was therefore attempting to address structural causes of inequality, while the Emmely campaign focused on an individual case invoking moral public support and setting a precedent in case law for workers' rights. While it did not address structural causes of inequality, the debate it sparked broadened public awareness and further highlighted the unacceptable levels of inequality in society.

While labour movements were not at the helm of these struggles, their support and involvement was vital to the campaigns and, conversely, helped push the unions out of their traditional comfort zones to pursue untypical campaigns. There are two campaigns – the struggles for access to land in India and the European Financial Transaction Tax – that directly and indirectly challenge inequality in which labour's role is low on the spectrum of labour-movement involvement.

C.R. Bijoy (2014) brings us back to India by focusing on the issue of access to land, which is one of the biggest causes of rural poverty. Bijoy argues that the forest movement led by Adivasis[2] demonstrates how labour movements are largely absent in one of the most crucial struggles in India. Nearly 25 per cent of the population (approximately 200 to 250 million people) depend on forests for their livelihoods and lives and yet the forests have been an ever-increasing site of expropriation and commodification. The struggles have received widespread support from a range of organisations, including at times agricultural labour movements, but have been led by local, indigenous communities. The movement has developed its own forms of power to contest the political terrain, which range from legal cases to forcibly occupying land. What is most noteworthy in this case is the relative absence of labour on an issue that affects vast numbers of the population.

Moving to Europe, Peter Wahl (2015) argues that the European Financial Transaction Tax (FTT) campaign also represents a campaign that directly challenges inequality on a very macro level and which became the flagship demand of the 'global justice movement'. While finance and taxation is one of the leading causes of inequality, very few labour movements (for example the AFL–CIO) supported the campaign but were not integrally involved. For the past 15 years, civil society organisations in different European countries (most notably France and Germany) have pushed for the FTT and have slowly influenced some government leaders in a 'coalition of the willing'. The 2008 economic crisis shifted the balance of power in favour of supporters of the tax with public opinion shifting strongly in support. With public pressure mounting, the EU Commission's draft directive aligns with proposals emanating from civil society and went beyond expectations, especially in terms of tax evasion. While civil society has been bolstered in recent years, the finance industry remains strongly opposed and continues to have substantial influence over policy-makers and political leaders. A notable feature is the low level of labour-movement involvement in the campaign, despite its central role in challenging big finance capital.

As these campaigns demonstrate, labour has only been marginally supportive of the struggles for land in India and the financial transaction tax in Europe, but both Bijoy (2014) and Wahl (2015) insist that labour has a vital role to play. Taken together, this wide range of experiences shows that workers and their collective organisations are to varying degrees engaging in creative and innovative campaigns that challenge inequality in society and in the process are developing new legacies of struggle.

(Un)typical issues and practices

The second axis on which I analyse the campaigns is the type of issues and practices invoked. In all of these initiatives, labour has played a role, often diverging significantly from its traditional activities. Indeed, the campaigns covered show that labour has been forced to diverge significantly from traditional issues of the shop-floor that have preoccupied labour for the greater part of the twentieth century to broaden its range of issues and repertoires of activities. While we have witnessed an increase in general strikes against austerity in Western Europe (Nowak and Gallas, 2014), many other struggles today look to new and creative tactics that transcend the strike – such as creative pilot projects of alternatives, global campaigns that link different nodes in the production cycle, symbolic struggles aimed at winning public support and broad alliances with a wide range of civil society organisations. The campaigns also demonstrate enormous creativity in both the goals and tactics used as well as the importance of framing issues in a manner that speaks to larger issues and social transformation as well as creating solidarity across labour and communities. The various campaigns teach us the importance of linking the various local struggles with global networks in order to scale up the efforts.

Satgar (2015) shows that NUMSA's climate justice campaign not only demonstrates a union willing to pursue a very creative and untypical issue, but that it also works on different fronts: 'It seeks to ensure the needs of workers and communities are met while attempting to address the challenges of climate change.' The approach is eclectic and includes 'contesting electricity price increases, seeking to influence the procurement and rollout of solar water heaters and advancing an agenda to achieve socially owned renewable energy options' (Satgar, 2015). To get the members up to speed with the heady and complex world of climate justice, the union has had a three-year programme of education, research and development groups, workshops, study tours, international visitors and conferences. Out of these myriad activities, at its national congress 2012 NUMSA adopted two important resolutions, 'Climate Change and Class Struggle' and 'Building a Socially Owned Renewable Energy Sector in South Africa', which have also helped guide the union as it develops and engages the policy arena. Vital for NUMSA's campaign has been the (re)education of workers and an intensive programme of internal capacity-building around cutting-edge green ideas. The NUMSA climate justice campaign introduced radical alternatives into the national energy debate and provided concrete suggestions such as its socially owned renewable energy proposal.

The more traditional issue of a minimum wage was at the heart of crucial campaigns led by labour in Brazil and Germany. Fred de Melo (2015) and Jörg Nowak (2015) show the Brazilian and German campaigns for a minimum wage directly address issues of inequality by forcing the state to pass minimum wage legislation that protect workers at the bottom of the wage hierarchy. The Brazilian case, however, is not entirely typical. Melo shows how the minimum wage in Brazil not only sets the wages for workers at the bottom – it also 'determines the floor for pension, welfare, and unemployment insurance benefits' (2015). Thus it has a central role in policy-making within Brazil and – together with other programmes such as Bolsa Família – the minimum wage campaign directly challenges inequality as over 30 million people receive an income corresponding to the minimum wage as of 2012. In both countries, the campaigns were waged through mass demonstrations and marches, public awareness raising and engagement with policy-makers and political parties. In both places, the campaigns garnered widespread support from the public (in Germany, this support had to be built step-by-step because the public was initially against it). As a result, the Brazilian real minimum wage value has risen by 68 per cent since the first march in 2004 and is set to incrementally increase through 2023. In Germany, the minimum wage legislation was only passed by the German Parliament in July 2014 and has a much more modest goal in terms of incremental increases, but secured universal coverage that began in January 2015.

What is particularly noteworthy about the German minimum wage campaign is that it demonstrates trade unions' capacity to shape public discourse in order to win support for the idea of a minimum wage, even for those who are not members of unions. In Brazil the battle was assisted by the progressive political environment created by the Workers' Party coming to power, the moral mandate from the public and constitutional provision that ensures people have a basic existence. In Germany on the other hand the dynamics of electoral competition opened up space for the DGB to forge alliances with left political parties to push through the minimum wage. The range of activities used is also noteworthy as information campaigns, protests, research, lobbying and collective bargaining were enlisted in the campaign. Thus, the minimum wage campaigns in both Brazil and Germany demonstrate the efficacy of creative union organising that invokes widespread public support to pressurise left political parties.

Focusing on one of the NTUI affiliates, the solid waste transportation workers' union – Kachra Vahatuk Shramaik Sangh (KVSS) – Mouleshri Vyas (2014) highlights the innovative organising strategies that evolved as KVSS worked in the informal sector, which is the largest source of employment in India. With the growing numbers of workers in informal and contract work, the KVSS pioneered strategies to reach out to workers and articulate their common interests across spatial and cultural divides. Thus, NTUI unions organise at the neighbourhood level and are pioneering democratic internal practices that deepen member participation. They also focus on small issues that are relatively easily won in order to build confidence and organising skills. This long-term process also deepens workers understanding of and trust in the union. Moreover, building incrementally also brings concrete changes to the lives of workers. One of the most crucial lessons is the importance of universal struggles that are rooted in local actions. Vyas explains that workers face many of the same issues even if they are spatially separated and building on this commonality through local actions strengthens the movement as a whole. Thus, by focusing on the informal sector and contract workers, the NTUI initiative is directly challenging the 'precarisation of labour' and exploring very local practices that combine through universal framing of the issues.

The CTA's experience in Argentina also demonstrates untypical practices for the union (Campos, 2015). While the CTA was the main driver of the campaign, it was framed as a human rights issue, not a labour issue, which helped it gain widespread support. Over three million people supported the campaign and its climax was to present the government with the results of a referendum in support of it. One of the most creative aspects of the campaign was framing the issue of eradicating poverty in terms of citizenship and rights, which resonated with the general public. In the process, it was creating symbolic power by winning public support for its demands. The Frenapo experience demonstrates the synergistic relations that unions can forge with a broad range of organisations in civil society for a common purpose. The events of history overtook the campaign (Argentina had five presidents between 20 December 2001 and 5 January 2002), but the campaign managed to penetrate public opinion and the centre-left government that has been in power since 2003 has taken up a number of the issues of the campaign and has pursued various social policies that fall within the guidelines of the campaign (Campos, 2015).

Perhaps one of the most untypical and innovative campaigns I look at is the TAC in South Africa (Heywood, 2015). The innovative strategies and tactics that the campaign used introduced new forms of struggle into South African protest politics, which tend to rely heavily on a confrontational approach. The TAC used symbolic protests in which moral and legal (and constitutional) legitimacy were the underpinning sources of power. The innovative way in which the TAC reclassified struggles for access to anti-retroviral drugs centred on human rights and enlisted support from both national and international actors. The reframing of the issues transformed the struggle from a special-interest struggle into a struggle for basic rights. The methods used included high visibility, the use of public media to deepen public awareness and understanding, provocative T-shirt slogans (for example, 'HIV POSITIVE'), court cases using the progressive legal framework and charging public leaders of culpable homicide. The rights framework helped frame the struggle as 'just' and the existing pro-poor laws meant that litigation became a powerful tool to build power from below.

The European Financial Transaction Tax campaign also demonstrates enormous creativity. One of its most notable features is that the campaign successfully tapped into the zeitgeist voicing a general frustration with neoliberal economic policies. This, together with the fact that the campaign was able to galvanise civil society, meant that 'some parts of the elites were ready to take concrete steps' (Wahl, 2014: 6). The cases demonstrate the importance of building on the old forms of power (for example strikes, collective bargaining, negotiations and internal capacities) with new forms of power (for example symbolic power, public support and pilot projects) in the creative struggles to challenge inequality. In the next section, I highlight some preliminary lessons for transformative unionism that I can draw from these cases.

Gestural lessons

With the mutations in capitalism since the 1970s, workers' power in the labour market and their share in the social surplus have diminished (Bieler et al., 2008). While scholars see two possible responses in terms of labour organising (Pillay, 2013) – a return to social movement unionism (Clawson, 2008) as well as increasing defensive struggles and political incorporation (Fairbrother and Webster,

2008; Schiavone, 2007) – we also see an interesting shift in social movements that are looking to draw labour into popular struggles outside the workplace in order to strengthen their appeal to symbolic power. Here it is not the traditional union leverage at the point of production that is being looked to. Rather, in trying to frame a struggle in terms of moral and legal rights, unions are seen as a vital source of power as their participation in struggles increases the legitimacy of such claims (Chun, 2009). For example, COSATU's support for the TAC legitimated the claims for medication as a right affecting everyone and not simply a medical issue for a relatively small group. Similarly, the union federation's support for the BIG in Namibia increased the legitimacy of the campaign in the public sphere. Interestingly, the cases demonstrate the importance of not only pursuing typical labour campaigns, but also campaigns on untypical issues such as health, universal basic income, taxation, land and climate change. In fact, some of the most creative campaigns are on untypical issues and force labour to pursue broader alliances and new tactics.

One of the most significant lessons from the cases speaks directly to the nature and character of trade-union alliances with political parties and the state. The political unionism of the twentieth century saw trade unions emerge as arms of political parties, often subordinated to the political mandates of the party, which contrasts with the social movement unionism of the 1980s, in which unions looked to society and popular struggles for their alliances (Pillay, 2013). While these distinctions are still relevant to understanding the character and orientation of many unions, a number of the cases drawn on here are pursuing a transformative unionism that draws on elements of both political and social movement unionism. Unions are often in a stronger position by keeping autonomy from political parties, but maintaining open relations to support progressive policies championed by parties as well as maintaining the capacity to contest regressive and anti-social state policies. It is clear that governments have a vital role to play in championing social transformation, but that they often lack political will to play this transformative role. Thus, they are often unwilling to implement people-friendly (and worker-friendly) laws and policies, regulate capital and steer the economy in redistributive directions. It is therefore crucial for labour movements to have the capacity to challenge the state. This is most vividly demonstrated in minimum wage campaigns in Brazil and Germany, where the unions were able to forge alliances with left political parties in order to push the state and fight for new legislation. What is important to note is that unions are political, but not aligned (or subordinated) to a single party.

While the cases suggest caution when it comes to forming alliances with political parties and state institutions, they also highlight the importance of forging broad alliances with a range of organisations in civil society in order to keep pressure on the state. For example, the Financial Transaction Tax campaign has sought broad alliances in civil society – including organised labour – and with political parties and individual members of parliament. Similarly, the struggles for land and the new union initiative in India, the basic income grant in Namibia and the labour struggles in Germany demonstrate the efficacy and importance of broad social alliances. The benefits from such alliances include sharing of resources, ideas and the increase in public support that is crucial for policy change. The alliances, however, are not without their drawbacks as many organisations in civil society are often weak and have limited organisational capacity, limited finances and loosely committed members. It is often through these collective struggles that the unions share some of their organisational capacities with their alliance partners.

Another important lesson from the campaigns is the need to work at various scales – local, national, regional and global – and the ways in which they can link up in creative and interesting ways (McBride and Smith, 2013; McCallum, 2013). For example, the Financial Transaction Tax joined national struggles into a cross-border regional campaign, while the local struggle of Emmely in Germany was scaled up into a national campaign raising the issue of inequality and an outdated anti-labour legal framework. Similarly, the Adivasi struggle for land in India constantly moved from local struggles to the national level, making claims on government at both levels.

The issue of existing institutional, legal, and policy spaces are often ignored or under-acknowledged as areas of struggle, but are increasingly recognised as important avenues of struggle. The TAC in South Africa and the minimum wage campaign in Brazil teach us that there are often important spaces within the existing legislative and constitutional framework within a country. It behoves movements to explore these avenues in order to exploit latent opportunities within the existing institutional, legal and policy apparatuses. In addition to finding openings in the current legal framework, the campaigns also highlight the importance of maintaining mobilisation as the legal arena cannot replace it.

Linked to challenging the legal system is the importance of alternative expertise and knowledge production in the form of reports and documents that contests the 'truth' espoused by corporations and 'experts'. The importance of this is demonstrated in the two South African campaigns, the financial transaction tax campaign and the income redistribution campaign in Argentina. The campaigns put alternative information in the public realm, challenging the dominant views on the issues they put on the agenda. This is a vital part of the struggle to win public support and symbolic leverage. Focusing on pilot projects and alternatives also shifts practices from only protesting against something (which often means maintaining the highly iniquitous status quo) to envisioning transformative alternatives in practice. NUMSA's energy workshops and socially owned renewable energy programme, for example, provide alternative scenarios around which labour can mobilise. Thus, in creating alternative understandings, the struggles also propose alternative scenarios for the ways things can be done.

In conclusion, the campaigns range from typical to untypical issues, direct and indirect ways of overcoming inequality, with some led by trade unions and others led by social movements with trade unions as one of several partners in the process. The range of campaign issues and the varied trade union involvement have much to teach us about the role of labour in combating inequality today.

Notes

1 For a fuller discussion of the campaigns, see the articles in a special issue of the *Global Labour Journal* (2015) which I guest-edited.
2 Adivasis are tribal and ethnic populations in India. They are the aboriginal inhabitants of the Indian subcontinent.

References

Baccaro, L. (2010) Does the Global Financial Crisis Mark a Turning Point for Labour. *Socio-Economic Review* 8(2): 341–348.
Bello, W. (2013) *Capitalism's Last Stand? Deglobalization in the Age of Austerity.* London: Zed Books.
Bieler, A., Lindberg, I. and Pillay, D. (eds) (2008) *Labour and the Challenges of Globalisation: What Prospects for Transnational Solidarity?* London: Pluto Press.
Bijoy, C.R. (2014) *The Forest Movement in India: Undoing Historical Injustice.* Paper written for the Global Labour University Inequality Project, working package 6.
Campos, L.E. (2015) The National Front Against Poverty: The Struggle for Income Redistribution. *Global Labour Journal* 6(3): forthcoming.
Choi, J.J. (1993) Political Cleavages in South Korea. In Koo, H. (ed.) *State and Society in Contemporary Korea.* Ithaca, NY: Cornell University Press: 13–50.
Chun, J.J. (2009) *Organizing at the Margins: The Symbolic Politics of Labour in South Korea and the United States.* Ithaca, NY: ILR Press.
Chun, J.J. and Williams, M. (2013) Labour as a Democratizing Force?: Lessons from South Africa and Beyond. *Rethinking Development and Inequality* 2: 1–9.
Clawson, D. (2008) Neo-Liberalism Guarantees Social Movement Unionism. *Employee Responsibilities and Rights Journal* 20: 207–212.
Collier, R.B. and Mahoney, J. (1997) Adding Collective Actors to Collective Outcomes: Labor and Recent Democratization in South America and Southern Europe. *Comparative Politics* 29(3): 285–303.
da Costa, M.L. (2015) CUT's Struggle for Gender Equality: The Campaign for 'Equality of Opportunities in Life, in Work and in Labor Movement'. *Global Labour Journal* 6(3): forthcoming.
de Melo, F.L.B. (2015) The Minimum Wage Campaign in Brazil and the Fight Against Inequality. *Global Labour Journal* 6(3): forthcoming.
Fairbrother, P. and Webster, E. (2008) Social Movement Unionism: Questions and Possibilities. *Employee Responsibilities and Rights Journal* 20: 309–313.
Gindin, S. (2012) Rethinking Unions, Registering Socialism. In Panitch, L., Albo, G. and Chibber, V. (eds) *The Question of Strategy: Socialist Register 49.* Wales: The Merlin Press.
Heywood, M. (2015) The Treatment Action Campaign (TAC) in South Africa: Lessons for and Learning from the Labour Movement. *Global Labour Journal* 6(3): forthcoming.
Jauch, H. (2015) The Rise and Fall of the Basic Income Grant (BIG) Campaign: Lessons from Namibia. *Global Labour Journal* 6(3): forthcoming.
Kay, T. (2011) *NAFTA and the Politics of Labor Transnationalism.* New York: Cambridge University Press.
McBride, S. and Smith, S. (2013) In the Shadow of Crisis: Economic Orthodoxy and the Response of Global Labour. *Global Labour Journal* 4(3): 206–229.

McCallum, J. (2013) *Global Unions, Local Power: the New Spirit of Transnational Labour Organizing*. Ithaca, NY: ILR Press.

Nowak, J. (2015) Union Campaigns in Germany Directed against Inequality: The Minimum Wage Campaign and the Emmely Campaign. *Global Labour Journal* 6(3): forthcoming.

Nowak, J. and Gallas, A. (2014) Mass Strikes against Austerity in Western Europe: A Strategic Assessment. *Global Labour Journal* 5(3): 306–321.

Pillay, D. (2013) Between Social Movement and Political Unionism: Cosatu and Democratic Politics in South Africa. *Rethinking Development and Inequality* 2: 10–27.

Satgar, V. (2015) A Trade Union Approach to Climate Justice: The Campaign Strategy of the National Union of Metal Workers of South Africa. *Global Labour Journal* 6(3): forthcoming.

Schiavone, M. (2007) Moody's Account of Social Movement Unionism: An Analysis. *Critical Sociology* 33(1–2): 279–309.

Scipes, K. (1996) *KMU: Building Genuine Trade Unionism in the Philippines, 1980–1994*. Quezon City: New Day Publishers.

Seidman, G. (1994) *Manufacturing Militance: Workers' Movements in Brazil and South Africa, 1970–1985*. Berkeley, CA: University of California Press.

Stevis, D. and Boswell, T. (2008) *Globalization and Labor: Democratizing Global Governance*. Lanham, MD: Rowman & Littlefield.

Suh, D. (2009) *Political Protest and Labor Solidarity in Korea: White-Collar Labor Movements After Democratization (1987–1995)*. London: Routledge.

Urban, H.J. (2012) Crisis Corporatism and Trade Union Revitalization in Europe. In Lehndorff, S. (ed.) *A Triumph of Failed Ideas: European Models of Capitalism in Crisis*. Brussels: European Trade Union Institute: 219–242.

Valenzuela, S. (1989) Labor Movements in Transitions to Democracy: A Framework for Analysis. *Comparative Politics* 21(4): 445–472.

von Holdt, K. (2002) Social Movement Unionism: The Case of South Africa. *Work, Employment and Society* 16(2): 283–304.

Vyas, M. (2014) Unionising Contract Labour: Challenges and Strategies. Paper written for the Global Labour University Inequality Project, working package 6.

Wahl, P. (2014) The European Civil Society Campaign on the Financial Transaction Tax. Global Labour University Working Paper No. 20. Geneva: International Labour Organization (ILO).

Wahl, P. (2015) More than Just Another Tax: The Thrilling Battle over the Financial Transaction Tax, Background, Progress and Challenges. *Global Labour Journal* 6(3): forthcoming.

Webster, E. (1985) *Cast in a Racial Mould: Labour Process and Trade Unions in the Foundaries*. Johannesburg: Ravan Press.

Webster, E., Lambert, R. and Bezuidenhout, A. (2008) *Grounding Globalization: Labour in the Age of Insecurity*. Malden, MA: Blackwell Publishing.

20 Countermeasures against inequality

Christoph Scherrer and Timm B. Schützhofer

Introduction

Various contributions to this book have discussed drivers of economic inequality and have proposed policies that may reduce inequality. The proposed measures cover numerous policy fields and represent everything from proposals for small-scale, limited change to calls for the fundamental restructuring of our societies. The chapters covering global imbalances and the causes of the current financial and economic crisis remind us that the fight against inequality is not only an end in itself, but also a means to reduce the instability inherent in the global economic system.

On the one hand, the breadth of the policy recommendations contained in this volume opens up space – not just for trade unionists, but for people with a variety of backgrounds and positions in society – to join the struggle against inequality. On the other hand, the broad spectrum of proposals runs the risk of spreading the resources available for this struggle too thinly over too many fields so that there is a risk of interventions evaporating without effect. In our contribution, we want to systematise some of the recommendations according to content, space and time. We believe that this will allow for a more focused debate on the opportunities and constraints that campaigns for specific proposals are faced with. Successful campaigning requires detailed knowledge of the political context to be addressed[1] and a careful staging of demands that reflects this context. For this purpose, it is imperative to assess whether proposals are likely to resonate in existing political spaces or not and which types of interventions are needed to create such spaces. Furthermore, it is crucial to acknowledge that campaigning has a temporal dimension, which requires an understanding of how different demands build on one another; that is, how one demand can open up space for another, more far-reaching one.

In light of this, we will distinguish recommendations according to policy field, time horizon, governance level, level of welfare-state development, as well as potential partners for alliances. The time horizon gauges the political challenges attached to implementing specific proposals: Will the proposals require only policy adjustments, more far-reaching institutional changes, a fundamental regime shift, or even a systemic transformation? Proposals for policy adjustments fall into the category 'short-term'; proposals that require major institutional change or are faced with determined, powerful opposition are placed in the category 'long-term'. The levels of governance start with the shop-floor and end with the global level. Some proposals are context-specific; others are adequate responses to inequality in many countries. The former fall under the category 'particular proposal'; the latter under the category 'universal proposal'. This systematisation will hopefully lay the ground for further strategic discussions both inside and outside the labour movement.

We will start with looking at so-called win–win proposals that are popular in the public debate about inequality, namely the idea of a 'green new deal', the belief that providing more educational opportunities is a way of 'lifting up' disadvantaged groups and the call for the 'financial inclusion' of the poor. Based on the critical assessment of these proposals by Mahnkopf (Chaper 12), Solga (Chapter 13) and Lavinas (Chapter 14), we point out their limits and move on to categorising proposals from the other chapters according to their time horizons. Next, we discuss the strategic implications of the existence of different levels of economic development and governance. Finally, we examine taxation and labour-market policies in order to show how a strategy could combine the different levels on the grounds of a sequenced action plan.

The limits of mainstream proposals

The proponents of a 'green new deal' claim that it will produce a 'win–win' situation resulting in job creation, secure living conditions for vulnerable groups, inclusive growth and, of course, the protection of the global ecosystem. As Mahnkopf points out, the project of a green new deal stays committed to the growth paradigm. However, within the logic of capitalism as we know it, growth and a protected ecosystem do not go together. Efficiency gains in the use of energy and materials will not reduce their overall consumption and a growing economy will be accompanied by increasing pollution.

According to institutions such as the World Bank, the Organisation for Economic Co-operation and Development (OECD) and the European Commission, opening up education opportunities represents a similar 'win–win' solution to the inequality problem, benefiting not only the poor, but society overall. However, as Solga points out, they ignore the difference between educational opportunities and educational outcomes. Meritocratic reasoning justifies different income levels, if only they are based on different levels of achievement, ignoring that the poor have rather limited chances to compete even if equal access to education is guaranteed. Therefore, Solga rightly rejects 'education-only' politics.

Similarly, even critics of the behaviour of financial actors in the current crisis such as Robert Shiller (2012) keep arguing that if poor people are provided better access to finance, they will be able to invest in their human capital and take up business opportunity that will lift them out of poverty. However, as Lavinas shows, the widening of access to small loans for those without collaterals may increase the vulnerability of low-income people exposing them to macroeconomic and political shocks.

In the light of the shortcomings of mainstream approaches to addressing rising inequality, we believe that it is crucial to move towards more fundamental reforms. For instance, the expansion of formal finance should be accompanied by strengthening co-operatives and community-based financial institutions.[2] Considering that '[e]ven the weakest communities generally have enough grocery stores, farmers, street sellers, basket-makers, bakeries, shoe repairers, personal transport suppliers, and so on' (Bateman, 2014: 8), the problematic tendency of microfinance towards individualisation makes it unlikely that 'financial inclusion' will reduce poverty on a broad scale (ibid.). This should not be taken to imply that poor people should not have access to loans, but that it is necessary to strengthen public banks, financial co-operatives and community-based finance. This way, credit could be geared towards projects based on democratically agreed investment strategies that actually enhance collective capabilities and improve living conditions.[3]

Levels and contexts

Trade unions can start taking action against inequality already at the level of their organisation. They can open up leadership positions for women and other groups of workers who tend to be excluded from top-level decision-making, for example for reasons of ethnicity or qualification (Britwum and Ledwith, 2014). In processes of collective bargaining, union officials can make use of the structural power of strong groups among their membership to help weaker groups. In organising drives, they can choose to address workers whose market power and wages are rather low – despite the fact that these workers are often more difficult to organise and that their contribution to union funds are rather limited. Britwum reminds us (Chapter 3) that inequalities based on gender, caste and ethnicity are not rendered a thing of the past by globalising capitalism. Rather, groups with a comparably weaker position in the labour market are taken advantage of in order to depress wages (Gordon et al., 1982). Therefore, it is in the self-interest of trade unions to fight for the rights of these groups, among them women's rights, and to make sure that they are enforced. Trade unions whose reach does not go beyond male-only industries run the risk of becoming isolated, both within the labour movement and society more broadly.[4]

Importantly, the success of such 'internal' interventions also depends on their context. The move towards more equal representation within the union leadership will not have much of an effect if the surrounding community is not supportive (cf. Jess, 2014). Compressing the wage structure through collective bargaining may require legal limits on outsourcing and on the precarisation of labour. The success of organising drives is even more dependent on the prevailing regime in labour law and the balance of social forces. In other words, 'internal' interventions need to be accompanied by strategies addressing external conditions, which are set at other levels, some of them even at the international level. For example, the force behind a threat of relocation does not only depend on skill and capital requirements, but also on international treaties concerning trade and investment.

Once these treaties have reduced tariffs and have removed capital controls, changes become much harder to achieve: treaties of this type have a lock-in effect (Scherrer, 2005).

People developing strategies also have to keep in mind differences between nations concerning the level of welfare-state development and the size of the agricultural sector. In nations with a developed welfare state, given the undermining forces of globalisation, strategies will in many cases have to aim at the preservation of existing entitlements. In countries with less developed welfare states and a growing economy, it may be possible to go on the offensive in order to increase the benefits available for workers. In countries with a large rural population such as India and South Africa, support mechanisms may have to differ from those used for urban, industrial populations (Fakier and Ehmke, 2014).

Obviously, further differentiations have to be made, for example with reference to the different legacies of colonialism in the Global South (Nunn, 2012). In countries like Uruguay, where settler colonies exterminated or expelled the indigenous population, inequalities are usually not as pronounced as in other colonised countries – unless slave labour has played an important historical role like in Brazil. In contrast, in countries where the indigenous population stayed in the majority, for example, in South Africa, deeply entrenched cleavages have to be overcome (Leuboldt, 2015).

At the international level, trade unions not only have to struggle for access to the main forums of global economic governance but also have to overcome conflicts within their own ranks, which are partly rooted in the international division of labour. A campaign for the inclusion of core labour rights in international trade agreements, for instance, may seem like a natural objective of all trade unions around the world. However, if this happens at the expense of liberalising economies that have not yet reached sufficient competitiveness to withstand foreign competition, then such a clause might not be viewed very favourably by trade unions in these countries (cf. Khor, 1995).

In this context, the links between struggles across different levels have to be kept in mind. Struggles at different levels can reinforce each other; successful struggles at the lower level may constitute stepping stones for making inroads at the higher level and struggles at the higher level may have supportive effects on struggles at the lower level while also needing the latter in order to gain traction. How different governance levels interact and can be addressed in struggles for a more equal distribution of gains along global value chains is discussed by Anner and Hossain, who examine labour struggles in export processing zones (EPZs) in Honduras and Bangladesh (Chapter 7). Improvements in safety standards must be combined with legally binding agreements and a strengthening of trade unions on the shop-floor in order to make sure that agreements are enforced.[5] Trade-union participation in bipartite safety committees can be an important tool for trade-union organising on the shop-floor (Schützhofer, 2014).

Pushing for public procurement policies that take working conditions along the value chain into account can support struggles located at the initial stages of a transnational production processes (Bovis, 2006). Public procurement policies and preferential public investment credits can also be used to strengthen small- and medium-sized enterprises and co-operatives in local contexts. This way, governments can use their purchasing power in order to secure fair remuneration and working conditions beyond the public sector.[6] These local initiatives, however, can only flourish if public procurement liberalisations through free trade and investment agreements at the international level can be resisted.

The temporal dimension

The contributors to this volume have put forward a variety of policy recommendations. Some can be achieved within the current economic and political structures and institutions, while others require a major break with these structures and institutions and thus may be only achievable over the long term. The challenge is how to connect short-term with long-term strategies. If a movement against inequality is to be sustained, there have to be prospects of change in the nearer future; if it wants to address the root causes of inequality, it has to go beyond the status quo, which requires tenacity and a longer view.

On all governance levels and in all policy fields, there are measures within reach over a rather short period of time. Conditional cash transfer and work schemes help to alleviate the effects of social inequality; better safety regulation in EPZs may address working conditions that pose a health risk; and better access to the formal financial sector may help people who only have access to money lenders operating in the informal sector. While these measures may not address the root causes of inequality, they can contribute to improving the working and living conditions of working people. Some short-term improvements, especially charitable assistance to the poor, however, carry the risk of pacification, which ultimately stabilises exploitative structures. Improvements have to be linked to empowerment – such as the right to organise and to strike.[7]

In the aftermath of the global financial crisis, new regulations have been introduced. However, these are superficial modifications that may serve to re-legitimise the speculative behaviour of finance (Scherrer, 2015). Therefore, Trevor Evans (Chaper 6) calls both for more comprehensive re-regulation that addresses the too-big-to-fail problem and for a standardisation of financial instruments, under which finance has to provide proof that new instruments about to be introduced are beneficial to non-financial sectors. He also proposes prohibiting the use of borrowed money for speculative activities. These reforms require substantial institutional changes.

In order to address some of the root causes of financialisation such as the global current account imbalances, a Keynesian New Deal in the core capitalist economies would be required. Such a regime shift would end the German mercantilist growth model as well as debt-based growth in other core countries.[8] It would also entail a new approach based on a democratically agreed investment and development strategy culminating in the socialisation of investment, which would be operating on the grounds of the control of credit expansion plus a stakeholder model of corporate governance. The strengthening of public development banks could be an important initial and achievable step for more socially and environmentally desirable investment.[9]

Likewise, the transition to a 'green economy' amounts to a fundamental restructuring of our societies, at least if the growth paradigm is abandoned in the process. Nevertheless, some first steps are possible that could lead to increase ecological sustainability and social equality and are thus necessary preconditions for a 'just transition'. Among the interventions proposed by Mahnkopf are the 'greening' of agriculture and forestry as well as improved solid waste management in the Global South and the creation of 'green jobs' in the Global North. In the energy sector, the switch to renewables could be combined with a move towards co-operatives and community-based ownership.[10]

A major challenge for strategies aiming at institutional change (not to speak of regime change) is that trade-union members may not see how these strategies are linked to their present-day struggles. Therefore, campaigns for policy changes at the national and the international level need to address this issue. A feeling of detachment may be most pronounced in the case of financial sector reform. It is, therefore, paramount to highlight the effects of shareholder-value strategies on employment or of financial speculation on pensions.

Against this backdrop, we will now turn to the implications of our considerations for two specific policy fields: taxation and labour-market policies. While the latter can be regarded as belonging to the core competences of trade unions, the former's strategic significance has rarely been recognised by the labour movement. We will present the recommendations in the field of labour policy in the form of a matrix based on the exemplary case of Germany (see Table 20.2). In the case of taxation policy, we have chosen to refrain from doing so because a more detailed analysis would be needed in order to provide a similarly neat categorisation.

Taxation policies

Various contributors to this volume have called for moving towards progressive tax systems, either in the form of a general proposal or in the context of specific countries.[11] We also learn from them that both taxes and spending must be considered when the redistributive impact of fiscal policies is assessed. Along these lines, there are calls for including domestic revenue mobilisation based on fair and progressive taxation systems in the post-2015 development agenda (Haldenwang and Schiller, 2015). Since Godar et al. have dealt with opportunities and obstacles for progressive tax reform in OECD countries, we will focus in this chapter on the Global South. In particular, we will look at Latin America, which represents an unequal world region, but also the only region where inequality has been reduced significantly since the turn of the millennium: the Gini coefficient dropped from 0.542 in 2002 to 0.486 in 2013 (ECLAC, 2015).

As Nicola Liebert (2011) points out, the mobility of capital and the competition for foreign direct investment have limited the ability of individual countries to impose taxes on transnational corporations and investors. This highlights the need to co-ordinate tax policies. On the international level, an important part of the struggle to gain tax sovereignty over footloose capital could be a push for closing down tax-havens.[12] Such a campaign could build on the progress made in closing tax havens for individuals in recent years and on the public's preference for a fair distribution of the tax burden.[13] Since many tax havens are part of OECD countries, social movements and trade unions in the North can put pressure on policy-makers in the respective countries. Of course, as success depends on international co-operation, change will be hard to come by in this area and is achievable only in the medium term.

The ability to tax is often severely restricted in developing countries. While progressive taxation in OECD countries can be seen as a matter of political will and of strengthening existing institutions, in some states of the Global South institutional change is required for establishing an effective tax authority, with high levels of tax evasion and informality causing severe obstacles to establishing a taxation system capable of generating sufficient income and contributing to less inequality (Goméz-Sabaini and Morán, 2014). Even in Latin America, where income levels are comparatively high, the fiscal monopoly of the state remains fragile: taxation is characterised by relatively low levels of collection, high levels of evasion and a regressive structure (Goméz-Sabaini and Jiménez, 2012). Limited taxing capacities are usually related to an outward economic orientation based on resource extraction and primary exports resulting in low levels of domestic integration and diversification (Burchardt, 2012). It can be assumed that the infrastructure and reproductive work provided by the public sector is hence of minor importance to the often intertwined economic and political elites.

Despite progress in recent years, the level of tax evasion remains alarmingly high in Latin America (Boeckh, 2011). This impairs massively the possibility to diminish inequality by providing high quality public education, universal healthcare and a high level of social protection.[14] For a variety of reasons, neither foreign aid nor income from natural resources can fully compensate for lacking tax revenue. These revenues are often volatile and limit the responsiveness of governments to its own citizens (Jansen Hagen, 2015; Moore, 2004).

Encouragement for campaigns to expand the welfare state and to fight for progressive taxes comes not only from surveys in Latin America (Castelletti, 2008: 2) but also from concrete actions of citizens for better public provisions for transportation, health and education. In Chile, a student movement is contesting the neoliberal education system (Cabalin, 2012). In Brazil, access to the transport infrastructure, health and education had traditionally been the privilege of the middle classes. Recently, the working class has also gained access to these areas, but investment did not keep up with this development, which caused a wave of protests (Stolte, 2014).

Tax specialist Tasha Fairfield (2013) has identified two possible strategies for taxing the wealthy, which can be used by governments interested in raising more revenue (see Table 20.1). The proposed strategies combine the aims of securing revenue and a progressive taxation system, the strategic focus depends on the conditions and circumstances in each specific case.

Table 20.1 Strategies for taxing the wealthy

	Tempering elite antagonism circumvents elites' political and/or investment power	*Mobilising public support counterbalances elites' political power*
Fiscal Policy Domain Tax-Side	Attenuating impact Obfuscating incidence Legitimating appeals (Horizontal equity)	Legitimating appeals (Vertical equity)
Benefit-Side	Compensation Emphasising stabilisation	Linking to popular benefits

Source: Fairfield, 2013: 44

Fairfield is contrasting a strategy of tempering elite antagonism with a strategy that tries to mobilise public support. Most governments do not want to antagonise the economic elites and resort, therefore, to legitimating appeals and horizontal equity, which provides little room for vertical redistribution. They may also try to appease the wealthy by spending tax revenue on projects that benefit the wealthy. This way, efforts to tax the rich turn into a zero-sum game in line with the fiscal contract argument – the people who pay for the government receive the bulk of the benefits and strengthen their hold on fiscal policy decisions (cf. Timmons, 2005).[15]

Alternatively, a progressive government can try to mobilise public support. The concept of vertical equity provides progressive taxes with legitimacy and if it is tied to public spending that benefits ordinary citizens, it could have a mobilising effect (Fairfield, 2013). However, assuming that social movements and trade unions exercise little influence over government action, they can hardly make credible promises that increasing taxes on the wealthy will actually benefit their members and supporters. There is evidence that the perception of public services and the willingness to pay taxes is interrelated (Daude and Melguizo, 2010; Daude et al., 2012). Furthermore, a strong and unified labour movement is needed to gain leverage in fiscal policy debates. As Deppe (2015) points out for the German case, the orientation of trade unions towards the shop-floor and the tendency to defend sectoral interests may reduce the attention they pay to wider political issues such as taxation.

The difficulties in changing the tax system call for a medium-term strategy. In this context, the left-wing government in Ecuador is an interesting case. Against the backdrop of a strengthened tax administration and high levels of support from popular sectors, it has not only increased fiscal revenue from 15.5 per cent in 2006 to 20.5 per cent in 2013 (SRI, 2015), but has also reduced the share of regressive taxes on consumption (SRI, 2007; SRI, 2014).

The probably most symbolic individual case was against Alvaro Noboa, a (now) five-times presidential candidate believed to be the country's richest citizen. The tax authority demanded that he pays his taxes. After he refused, it decided to expropriate 'La Clementina', the country's largest banana plantation.

Subsequently more than 1,600 plantation workers bought the plantation with a credit from the National Financial Corporation (CFN) (Redacción Económica, 2014).

Apart from this high-profile case, the changes have mainly focused on improving the collection of taxes from corporations and high-income individuals. Meanwhile, accumulated wealth has remained largely untouched. At the moment of writing, there are first signs that this might change. The executive branch has passed a progressive inheritance tax reform to the National Assembly, which also attempts to tax money in international trusts. Such reforms help to slow down or even reverse the trend towards the concentration of wealth, but they are not hugely effective in terms of raising public revenue. Hence, it is more difficult to link this tax to popular benefits. Nevertheless, the Ecuadorian government is trying to do so by introducing a clause that there is one way to avoid paying the tax, namely to pass on the equivalent amount of shares to employees.

Ultimately, the issue of taxation becomes associated with the ideological conflict between capital and labour: Do we believe the capitalist narrative that wealth is generated by the few who own capital, or do we understand that it is the result of the labour of the many?

Labour-market policies

The labour market has been a major driver of inequality in many countries. As Herr and Ruoff show (Chapter 5), changes in functional income distribution made personal income distribution more unequal. They reflect the increasing profit share as well as the concentration of wealth. Both these developments are driven by the decline of the public sector, higher profit claims of holders of financial assets and the weakening bargaining power of trade unions.[16]

Of even greater importance is the increasing wage dispersion in the OECD countries. At the top, management is reaping the benefits of large-scale operations, shareholder value incentive systems, increased inter-company cross-border mobility and greater political clout. At the lower end, technological changes, trade with labour-abundant economies, migration and new labour-market practices such as outsourcing and precarisation have reduced the labour-income share. These processes have also weakened trade unions, which have had to moderate their demands due to threats of the relocation and the deregulation of labour laws (Hacker and Pierson, 2010).

In India, a combination of low productivity in agriculture, a growth dynamic in the manufacturing sector insufficient for absorbing the rural labour surplus and a rigidly layered segmentation of the labour market on the basis of caste and the discrimination of women has contributed to rising inequality.[17] The case of Brazil also underlines the impact of labour-market dynamics on economic inequality, albeit in reverse. Under the Lula and Rousseff presidencies, a number of labour-market policies were enacted, among them significant increases of the minimum wage and of social assistance, the expansion of public-sector employment and the creation of additional labour courts. In a favourable international business climate, these measures have contributed significantly to job creation, more formal employment, wage increases, increases in the wage share, decreasing gender disparities and an overall lowering of economic inequality.[18]

The positive example of Brazil leads the way for strategising about labour-market policies that reduce economic inequality. As Herr and Ruoff argue, the existence of a minimum wage seems to be of key importance in this context. Increasing the minimum wage and expanding its coverage is a matter of policy adjustment in those countries where there is a wage floor by law. In some contexts, it could also imply that institutional change is needed, for example in Germany, where the recent implementation of the minimum wage was the result of an eight-year campaign led by the labour movement.[19] If the increases are supposed to be steady and insulated from changes of government, a specific body responsible for setting the minimum wage has to be established. Besides, the expansion of its coverage may meet with resistance of employer groups that are politically powerful (for example in agriculture). In countries with a large informal sector, the challenges of implementation are immense. Prospects are probably best for workers with workplaces where other labour relations are formalised, for example, workers employed by subcontractors in manufacturing (Webster et al., 2008).

Importantly, as Herr and Ruoff point out, wage dispersion cannot be addressed solely with a minimum wage. It also requires co-ordinated bargaining, which can be achieved by pattern-bargaining or sectoral bargaining. The latter may also require institutional change, for instance the establishment of strong employers' associations acting as a counterpart for labour in sector-wide negotiations. Sectoral bargaining may reinforce wage dispersion if the sectors with weaker bargaining power are not supported by workers in stronger sectors in their pursuit of wage increases. Addressing this issue may also require institutional change, for instance the formation of strong union federations.

Herr and Ruoff are also calling for labour-market regulation that prevents precarious work. As mentioned, trade unions can tackle this issue through collective bargaining, but without being able to build on supportive legal provisions they will face a constant uphill battle. Changes of labour law are a matter of policy adjustments; however, their enforcement tends to require institutional changes in the form of the effective monitoring of compliance and the establishment of effective sanctioning mechanisms. In countries with a significant surplus of workers, such as India, a range of policies including agricultural policies in favour of smallholders are necessary to balance demand and supply for labour. In other words, a regime shift is required in this context.

For increasing the wage share, that is making functional income distribution more equal, trade-union density has to be raised and collective bargaining power strengthened.[20] Given that the forces that have undermined trade union power have the upper hand, a reversal of this development requires institutional changes – if not a wholesale regime shift. Shop-floor struggles and organising have to be complemented by political strategies that, on the one hand, change labour laws in favour of trade unions and, on the other hand, limit competition among employers.

Table 20.2 Recommendations for labour market policies in Germany

Recommendations		Timeframe		Governance Level	Potential Partners for Alliances
	Short-term	Medium-term	Long-term		
Reducing wage dispersion	Minimum wage	Closing loopholes Awareness campaign Hiring additional customs officers tasked with monitoring compliance	Securing constant raises of the minimum wage	Returning to collective bargaining agreements covering all workers	National: Reregulation of temporary and part-time work EU labour mobility: measures to prevent competition via wages occurring between countries and through migration Co-ordinated minimum wages in the EU (fixed percentage of national median wages)	Critical academics Labour NGOs representing migrant workers Anti-poverty NGOs, churches, charities, and social services Political parties Employers who want protection from competition via wages
	Co-ordinated bargaining	Overcoming trade union fragmentation through mergers Harmonising expiration of collective agreements	Sectoral bargaining Extension Mechanisms Compulsory membership for employers in employers' associations	Co-ordinating sectoral bargaining (including horizontal co-ordination) EMU-wide sectoral bargaining	National: Defending autonomy of collective bargaining but also establishing mechanisms for monitoring wage development and making recommendations EMU: Creation of extension mechanisms at the European level	Primarily requires trade union solidarity Employers wanting to protect themselves against employee poaching

Increasing wage share	Preventing precarious employment	Attaching stricter conditions to fixed-term contracts	Limiting successive fixed-term contracts Awarding tenders in public sector only if subcontractors employ permanent workers covered by social security Limiting labour brokering		National: Minimum Wages Reregulation of temporary and part-time work EU labour mobility: see above	Labour NGOs representing migrant workers Critical Academics Anti-poverty NGOs, churches, charities, and social services providers Political parties
	Increasing union density Strengthening collective bargaining	See trade union revitalisation literature				
Global Keynesian New Deal	International macroeconomic co-ordination	Active anti-cyclical fiscal policy in the EU Symmetric adjustment mechanisms to reduce current account imbalances	Deepening EMU integration (fiscal union, EMU labour market regulation, EMU taxes, etc.) Reregulating financial system (reducing profit mark-ups and stimulating long-term investment) Replacing shareholder-value corporate governance with stakeholder approach Rolling out economic democracy	New, global 'Bretton Woods'-style monetary system with fixed and adjustable exchange rates Certain controls of international capital flows to make a global monetary system work, creation of space for national economic policy International anti-trust court for regulation of MNCs	International agreements International institutions tasked with co-ordination	Critical academics Certain industrial groups including smaller companies Progressive governments NGOs, social movements

This challenge is covered by the literature on trade-union revitalisation[21] and will, therefore, not be explored further.

Labour markets are also highly dependent on macroeconomic developments. In the United States, the financial crisis has caused unemployment and has depressed wages, which has worsened income inequality.[22] Macroeconomic volatility has had similar effects in Brazil and India.[23] For this reason, the authors of the country case studies in this volume (Chapters 8–11) call for a shift away from neoliberal macroeconomic policy towards what Hein and Detzer call a 'Global Keynesian New Deal' (Chapter 9). Such a New Deal encompasses the re-regulation of the financial sector as well as the re-orientation of macroeconomic policies towards stabilising domestic demand and international macroeconomic policy co-ordination. In other words, it amounts to a regime shift. While pursuing demand-oriented macroeconomic policies can build on previous policy regimes, financialisation and globalisation will undercut interventions of this type. Therefore, curbing financialisation and co-ordinating macroeconomic policies among nations are necessary preconditions for change. However, financialisation is embedded in the accumulation regime of the United States, is politically reinforced through the hegemony of finance capital and is institutionalised at the global level through international treaties and international organisations (Scherrer, 2015). Macroeconomic co-ordination requires the cooperation of the major economic powers, which is only possible if there are similar political constellations of forces within the national boundaries of each of the countries in question – a precondition that is hard to meet.

Conclusion

As the Brazilian Labour Party (PT) has demonstrated, it is possible to reverse the trend towards increasing inequality.[24] However, given the current, less favourable economic environment for Brazil, setbacks cannot be ruled out. Both the Brazilian example and the chapters of this book highlight that there are multi-dimensional drivers of inequality. Addressing these drivers requires profound changes in the current form of capitalism. Only long-term strategies based on strong working-class solidarity and support from allies in politics and civil society will bring about these changes. However, some policy adjustments and institutional changes are more easily achievable and their attainment may provide the basis for institutional and structural changes. And yet, it is not possible to lay out a definite strategy in this chapter. After all, strategies have to be context-sensitive and have to be based on a careful conjunctural analysis of the political opportunities and resources for change.[25]

In light of this, we would like to conclude the book with a list of points labour activists and trade unionists may want to consider when they discuss strategies against economic inequality:

- In order to keep everyone involved motivated, an intervention of a trade union should start with raising awareness among its members of the effects of inequality, both on the organisation and on its members as workers. Against this backdrop, it becomes possible to assess what kind of inequalities concern the members and may undermine power of the union in the long run.
- After having identified key issues, the appropriate level for a strategy should be discussed: what can be done within the trade union; through collective bargaining; through organising; and through political action at the local, regional, national and international level? In what ways are the different levels connected? Which levels should be prioritised for interventions and which ones should be left to allies to work on? In which policy fields is the trade union regarded as an important actor? Where is its expertise acknowledged and where should it focus on capacity-building for future struggles?
- For any policy initiative, an assessment of the political opportunity structure is required. This involves asking the following questions: Who are the primary actors and where are points of access? As the political opportunity structure is not set in stone, possibilities for changing it should be explored, in particular by identifying windows of opportunity. Since windows of opportunity tend to open and close again, it is not only important to choose the right entry point, but also get the timing right: It can be necessary to react quickly – or to build momentum instead of intervening right away.
- Opportunities for political action need to be checked against the resources at hand in terms of membership mobilisation, finance and expertise. Are these resources well used, or could they be used more efficiently? What other opportunities are lost?
- Potential allies need to be identified: what are their interests in the campaign, what might motivate them to co-operate and what kind of reciprocity is required to maintain the alliance? As sentiments towards inequality and particular policies differ hugely between different groups, the right frames for the issues at stake have to be developed – with the aim of reaching staff, members, workers from other unions and non-unionised workers, potential allies and the general public.
- The likely counter-strategies of the privileged should also be taken into account.

As powerful trends drive up inequality, the struggle against it requires strategic thinking over a long time horizon. It can start with small steps aimed at mobilisation, but it also needs to take into account the existence of structural constraints working against interventions for more equality. We hope that our systematisation of the reforms proposed in this book will contribute to this kind of strategising.

Notes

1 See also Scherrer's chapter in this volume.
2 See also Gross et al.'s and Evans's chapters in this volume.
3 See also Evans's chapter in this volume.
4 See also Scherrer's chapter in this volume.
5 See also Webster and Morris's chapter in this volume.
6 See also Gross et al.'s chapter in this volume.
7 See Gross et al.'s chapter in this volume.
8 See also Palley's and Hein and Detzer's chapters in this volume.
9 See also Evans's and Herr's chapters in this volume.
10 See also Webster and Morris's chapter in this volume.
11 See also Gross et al.'s, Lavinas's, and Godar et al.'s chapters in this volume.
12 See also Webster and Morris's chapter in this volume.
13 See also Scherrer's chapter in this volume.
14 See also Lavinas's chapter in this volume.
15 For a critique, see Fairfield (2013).
16 See also Hein and Detzer's chapter in this volume.
17 See also Ghosh's chapter in this volume.
18 See also Manzano et al.'s chapter in this volume.
19 See also Williams's chapter in this volume.
20 See also Herr and Ruoff's chapter in this volume.
21 See also Williams's chapter in this volume.
22 See also Palley's chapter in this volume.
23 See also Manzano et al.'s and Ghosh's chapters in this volume.
24 See also Manzano et al.'s chapter in this volume.
25 See also Scherrer's chapter in this volume.

References

Bateman, M. (2014) The Rise and Fall of Muhammad Yunus and the Microcredit Model. Saint Mary's University, International Development Studies. Working Paper Series No. 1. Available at: www.smu.ca/webfiles/BATEMANIDSWP.pdf (accessed 6 June 2015).

Boeckh, A. (2011) Staatsfinanzierung und soziale Gerechtigkeit in Lateinamerika. In Wehr, I. and Burchardt, H.J. (eds) *Soziale Ungleichheiten in Lateinamerika: Neue Perspektiven auf Wirtschaft, Politik und Umwelt.* 1st edition. Baden-Baden: Nomos: 71–90.

Bovis, C.H. (2006) Public Procurement in the European Union: Lessons from the Past and Insights to the Future. *Columbia Journal of European Law* 12.

Britwum, A.O. and Ledwith, S. (eds) (2014) *Visibility and Voice for Union Women: Country Case Studies from Global Labour University Researchers.* Munich: Rainer Hampp Verlag.

Burchardt, H.J. (2012) Von der vernünftigen Suche nach Leidenschaft: Ein Vorschlag Gesellschaftsanalyse und Sozialpolitik-Forschung zu dezentrieren. In Burchardt, H.J., Tittor, A. and Weinmann, N. (eds) *Sozialpolitik in globaler Perspektive: Asien, Afrika und Lateinamerika.* Frankfurt: Campus-Verlag: 69–92.

Cabalin, C. (2012) Neoliberal Education and Student Movements in Chile: Inequalities and Malaise. *Policy Futures in Education* 10(2): 219–228.

Castelletti, B. (2008) Taxes in Latin America: Do Wealth and Inequality Matter? OECD Development Centre, Policy Insights No. 79. Paris: Organisation for Economic Co-operation and Development (OECD).

Daude, C. and Melguizo, Á. (2010) Taxation and More Representation? On Fiscal Policy, Social Mobility and Democracy in Latin America. OECD Development Centre, Working Paper No. 294. Paris: Organisation for Economic Co-operation and Development (OECD). Available at: www.oecd-ilibrary.org/docserver/download/5km5zrrs9bbt.pdf? expires=1433507325&id=id&accname=guest&checksum=5DC3DFB5A0CE7B183B 798EBFE304F1A2 (accessed 6 June 2015).

Daude, C., Gutiérrez, H. and Melguizo, Á. (2012) What Drives Tax Morale? OECD Development Centre, Working Paper No. 315. Paris: Organisation for Economic Co-operation and Development (OECD). Available at: www.oecd-ilibrary.org/docserver/ download/5k8zk8m61kzq.pdf?expires=1433508381&id=id&accname=guest&checksum =25825C37C814223A80DDD014A989D941 (accessed 6 June 2015).

Deppe, F. (2015) *Einheit oder Spaltung? Überlegungen zur Debatte um die Einheitsgewerkschaft.* Berlin: Rosa Luxemburg Stiftung (Analysen). Available at: www.rosalux. de/fileadmin/rls_uploads/pdfs/Analysen/Analysen19_Gesell_Einheitsgewerkschaft_web. pdf (accessed 6 June 2015).

ECLAC, Economic Commission for Latin America and the Caribbean (2015) *Social Panorama of Latin America 2014.* Available at: http://repositorio.cepal.org/bitstream/ handle/11362/37627/S1420728_en.pdf?sequence=4 (accessed 4 June 2015).

Fairfield, T. (2013) Going Where the Money Is: Strategies for Taxing Economic Elites in Unequal Democracies. *World Development* 47: 42–57.

Fakier, K. and Ehmke, E. (eds) (2014) *Socio-Economic Insecurity in Emerging Economies: Building New Spaces.* London: Routledge.

Gómez-Sabaini, J.C. and Jiménez, J.P. (2012) Tax Structure and Tax Evasion in Latin America. Naciones Unidas, CEPAL. Available at: www.eclac.cl/publicaciones/xml/5/ 45935/SERIE_MD_118.pdf (accessed 3 June 2015).

Gómez Sabaini, J.C. and Morán, D. (2014) Tax policy in Latin America. Assessment and Guidelines for a Second Generation of Reforms. Macroeconomics of Development Series. Available at: www.daghammarskjold.se/wp-content/uploads/2014/12/2014-Tax-policy-in-Latin-America_CEPAL.pdf (accessed 6 June 2015).

Gordon, D.M., Edwards, R. and Reich, M. (1982) *Segmented Work – Divided Workers.* Cambridge: Cambridge University Press.

Hacker, J.S. and Pierson, P. (2010) Winner-Take-All Politics: Public Policy, Political Organization, and the Precipitous Rise of Top Incomes in the United States. *Politics & Society* 38(2): 152–204.

Haldenwang, C. von and Schiller Calle, A. von (2015) *Greater Mobilisation of Domestic Revenue in Developing Countries – A Key Issue for the Post-2015 Agenda.* German Development Institute. Available at: www.die-gdi.de/uploads/media/German_Development_ Institute_vonHaldenwang_vonSchiller_02.02.2015.pdf (accessed 10 June 2015).

Jansen Hagen, R. (2015) Rents and the Political Economy of Development Aid. In Congleton, R.D. and Hillman, A.L. (eds) *Companion to the Political Economy of Rent Seeking.* Cheltenham: Edward Elgar: 248–275.

Jess, C. (2014) New Zealand Women, Work and Unions. In Britwum, A.O. and Ledwith, S. (eds) *Visibility and Voice for Union Women: Country Case Studies from Global Labour University Researchers.* Munich: Rainer Hampp Verlag: 138–157.

Khor, M. (1995) Trade and Worker Rights, Discussion with Pharis Harvey. In Cavanagh, J. (ed.) *South–North Citizen Strategies to Transform a Divided World.* Discussion Draft. San Francisco: International Forum on Globalization: 28–35.

Leuboldt, B. (2015) *Transformation von Ungleichheitsregimes: Gleichheitsorientierte Politik in Brasilien und Südafrika.* Wiesbaden: Springer.

Liebert, N. (2011) *Steuergerechtigkeit in der Globalisierung: Wie die steuerpolitische Umverteilung von unten nach oben gestoppt werden kann.* 1st edition. Münster: Westfälisches Dampfboot.

Moore, M. (2004) Revenues, State Formation, and the Quality of Governance in Developing Countries. *International Political Science Revue* 25(3): 297–319.

Nunn, N. (2012) Culture and the Historical Process. *Economic History of Developing Regions* 27(S1): 108–126.

Redacción Económica (2014) De jornaleros a dueños de La Clementina. *El Telégrafo*, 6 February. Available at: www.telegrafo.com.ec/economia/item/de-jornaleros-a-duenos-de-la-clementina.html (accessed 28 May 2015).

Scherrer, C. (2005) GATS: Long-term Strategy for the Commodification of Education. *Review of International Political Economy* 12(3): 484–510.

Scherrer, C. (2015) Das US-Finanzkapital: Durch mehr Regulierung weiter hegemonial? *PROKLA: Zeitschrift für kritische Sozialwissenschaft* 45(2).

Schützhofer, T.B. (2014) Can Decent Work and Export Oriented Growth Strategies Go Together? Lessons from Nicaragua's Export Processing Zones. ICDD Working Papers No. 11. Available at: www.uni-kassel.de/upress/online/OpenAccess/978-3-86219-810-8. OpenAccess.pdf (accessed 7 June 2015).

Shiller, R.J. (2012) *Finance and the Good Society.* Princeton, NJ: Princeton University Press.

SRI, Servicio de Rentas Internas (2007) *Cumplimiento de la Recaudación de Impuestos.* Quito, Ecuador: Servivio de Rentas Internas.

SRI, Servicio de Rentas Internas (2014) *Informe Mensual de Recaudación.* Quito, Ecuador: Servivio de Rentas Internas.

SRI, Servicio de Rentas Internas (2015) *Comperativa Presión Fiscal América Latina Europa.* Base de Datos.

Stolte, C. (2014) *Protest statt Begeisterung – Brasilien vor der Weltmeisterschaft.* Hamburg: German Institute of Global and Area Studies (GIGA). Available at: www. giga-hamburg.de/de/system/files/publications/gf_lateinamerika_1404.pdf (accessed 6 June 2015).

Timmons, J.F. (2005) The Fiscal Contract: States, Taxes, and Public Services. *World Politics* 57(4): 530–567.

Webster, E., Benya, A., Dilata, X., Joynt, K., Ngoepe, K. and Tsoeu, M. (2008) *Making Visible the Invisible: South Africa's Decent Work Deficit.* SWOP, University of the Witwatersrand.

Index